Contents

LIFE PROCESSES AND LIVING THINGS

Topic		Page	National Curriculum coverage
1	Life processes	8	AT2.1a,c
2	Cells working together: moving particles	10	AT2.1b,d
3	Cell division	12	AT2.1f
4	Human diet and nutrition	14	AT2.2a,b
5	Food and digestion	16	AT2.2a,b
6	The circulation of blood	18	AT2.2c
7	Blood	20	AT2.2c
8	The breathing system	22	AT2.2d/e,f,g
9	Responding to our surroundings	24	AT2.2h/i
10	Sense organs	26	AT2.2j
11	Hormones: the chemical messengers of the body	28	AT2.2k
12	Homeostasis	30	AT2.2m,n,o,p
13	Infectious diseases	32	AT2.2q
14	Drugs	34	AT2.2r
15	Plants: roots, stems and leaves	36	AT2.3f
16	Photosynthesis: how plants make food	38	AT2.3a,b,c,d
17	Plant transport systems	40	AT2.3f,g,h
18	Plant hormones	42	AT2.3e
19	Adaptation	44	AT2.5a
20	Food chains	46	AT2.5c,d,e
21	Populations and competition	48	AT2.5b
22	Human impact on the environment	50	AT2.5b
23	Pollution on a global scale	52	AT2.5b
24	Variation	54	AT2.4a
25	Genes and chromosomes	56	AT2.4a,c,d,e,f,g, AT2.1e
26	Asexual and sexual reproduction	58	AT2.4b
27	Human reproduction	60	AT2.4
28	Controlling reproduction	62	AT2.4l
29	Evolution	64	AT2.4i,j
30	Artificial and natural selection	66	AT2.4h
	Practice questions – Life processes/living things	68	
	Answers to practice questions	70	

Contents

MATERIALS AND THEIR PROPERTIES

Topic		Page	National Curriculum coverage
1	Everyday materials	72	AT3.1
2	Solids, liquids and gases	74	AT3.1a
3	What is matter made up of?	76	AT3.1a
4	Speeding up and slowing down	78	AT3.1a
5	Simple substances	80	AT3.1g
6	Mixing things together	82	AT3.1g
7	Metals and non-metals	84	AT3.1g
8	What are elements made of?	86	AT3.1b,c,d
9	Arranging electrons	88	AT3.1e,d
10	Arranging elements – looking for patterns	90	AT3a
11	Arranging elements – an introduction to the Periodic Table	92	AT3.b,c
12	Joining atoms together – the ionic bond	94	AT3.1f,h,i,j
13	More about ionic compounds	96	AT3.1i,j
14	Joining atoms together – the covalent bond	98	AT3.1k,l
15	Structures	100	AT3.1l,m
16	Solutions	102	AT3.2
17	Separating mixtures of solids	104	AT3.2
18	Separating mixtures of liquids	106	AT3.2b
19	Purifying liquids	108	AT3.2b,c
20	Physical and chemical changes	110	AT3.3
21	Chemical reactions and equations	112	AT3.2r,s
22	How much?	114	AT3.2t
23	Fossil fuel	116	AT3.2a,b,d
24	Crude oil and its uses	118	AT3.2f,g,h,i,l
25	The air	120	AT3.2p
26	More about combustion	122	AT3.2d
27	Nitrogen and its uses	124	AT3.2p,q,r
28	Acids and alkalis	126	AT3.2
29	More about salts	128	AT3.2
30	Limestone – a useful rock	130	AT3.2o
31	Metals from ores	132	AT3.2j,k
32	Iron and its uses	134	AT3.2m
33	Aluminium and its uses	136	AT3.2l
34	Copper and its uses	138	AT3.2n
35	Reactivity of metals	140	AT3.2k
36	Different types of rocks	142	AT3.2x
37	Sedimentary and metamorphic rocks	144	AT3.2x,y
38	The Earth and its structure	146	AT3.2z
39	Movements in the Earth	148	AT3.2z
40	Patterns in the Periodic Table, Group 1 and Group 0	150	AT3.3c,d,e,f
41	Patterns in the Periodic Table, Group 7 and the transition metals	152	AT3.3h,j,k,l
42	Compounds of halogens and their uses	154	AT3.3g,i
43	Rates of reaction	156	AT3.3l
44	Changing rates of reactions	158	AT3.3m,n
45	Energy changes and catalysts	160	AT3.3n,o,u,v
46	Biological catalysts	162	AT3.3p,q
	Practice questions – Materials	164	
	Answers to practice questions	166	

Contents

PHYSICAL PROCESSES

Topic		Page	National Curriculum coverage
1	The solar system	168	AT4.4a
2	Gravity and satellites	170	AT4.4b
3	Stars	172	AT4.4c
4	Observing the universe	174	AT4.4d
5	Forces in action	176	AT4.2e,g
6	Speed	178	AT4.2a
7	Velocity and acceleration	180	AT4.2c,d
8	Forces on solids stretching	182	AT4.2j
9	Friction	184	AT4.2b
10	Frictional forces	186	AT4.2h,i
11	Pressure	188	AT4.2k
12	Waves	190	AT4.3a,c,d,e,g
13	Reflection and refraction	192	AT4.3d
14	Prisms	194	AT4.3,h
15	Using electromagnetic radiation	196	AT4.3i,j,k
16	Sound	198	AT4.3i
17	Ultrasound	200	AT4.3i
18	Seeing sound	202	AT4.3
19	Static electricity	204	AT4.1n,q
20	Dangers and uses of static electricity	206	AT4.1o
21	Simple electric circuits	208	AT4.1e,b
22	Resistance	210	AT4.1c,d,f,g
23	Series and parallel	212	AT4.1a
24	Using electricity	214	AT4.1i,l
25	Electricity in the home	216	AT4.1k,l
26	Paying for electricity	218	AT4.1m
27	Magnets and electromagnets	220	AT4.1r,s
28	Using electromagnets	222	AT4.1s
29	Electric motors and generators	224	AT4.1x,s,1u
30	Power around the country	226	AT4.1w
31	Where does energy come from?	228	AT4.5a
32	How hot is it?	230	AT4.5a,b
33	Convection and radiation	232	AT4.5b,c
34	Saving energy and being efficient	234	AT4.5e
35	Energy sources and power stations	236	AT4.5d,e
36	Power from renewable energy sources	238	AT4.5e
37	Radioactivity	240	AT4.6a,b,c,
38	Radioactive isotopes	242	AT4.6e,f,g
	Practice questions – Physical processes	244	
	Answers to practice questions	246	
	Glossary	247	

Introduction

Essential Science for GCSE covers the basic content of the Science Course at Foundation level (F/H). It is suitable for examinations in Double or Single Award GCSE Science. The book can be used in a variety of ways:

- for classwork
- for homework
- as a revision guide
- as a reference source
- for reading before a lesson, and as a summary after the lesson
- for the lesson itself
- to provide the scientific knowledge needed for investigations.

Each topic is set out as a double-page spread.

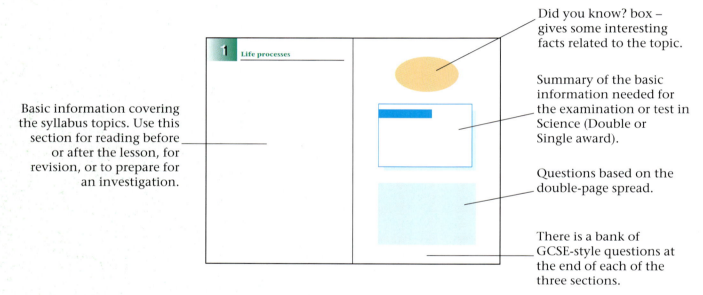

Basic information covering the syllabus topics. Use this section for reading before or after the lesson, for revision, or to prepare for an investigation.

Did you know? box – gives some interesting facts related to the topic.

Summary of the basic information needed for the examination or test in Science (Double or Single award).

Questions based on the double-page spread.

There is a bank of GCSE-style questions at the end of each of the three sections.

You will find the material in the book in three sections:
Life Processes and Living Things (Biology)
Materials and their Properties (Chemistry)
Physical Processes (Physics)

The glossary at the end of the book explains the scientific words that are highlighted in the text.

Life processes and living things

1 Life processes

LIFE PROCESSES ARE COMMON TO ANIMALS AND PLANTS

As animals and plants develop, they grow bigger and heavier.

To grow, plants and animals feed. Plants use light energy to turn carbon dioxide and water into food. Animals get food by eating plants or other animals.

Living things need to move and grow. The energy for this comes from food. Living things transfer the energy from food and use it to move and grow. The transfer is called **respiration**. Usually oxygen is used and carbon dioxide is produced by respiration.

Reproduction means producing young ones. For most living things it involves a sperm and egg joining together.

Being sensitive means that animals and plants react to their surroundings.

Living things make waste chemicals as they break substances down and build up new ones. Some of the wastes are poisonous. Getting rid of wastes is called **excretion**.

ALL ANIMALS AND PLANTS ARE MADE OF CELLS

Animals and plant cells have three important parts in common. A thin **membrane** which controls the movement of substances in and out of the cell. **Cytoplasm** where the chemical reactions happen, and a **nucleus** which contains the information to control the cell.

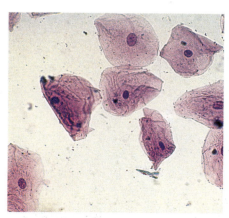

Cells of a human cheek

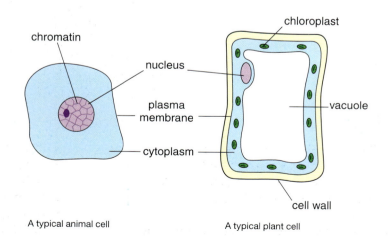

A typical animal cell   A typical plant cell

Cells working together: tissues

Cells usually have special jobs to do. We say they are specialised. They work together to do each job. Groups of specialised cells are called **tissues**. For example, in animals, muscle tissue has the function of moving parts of the body. In plants, photosynthetic tissue has the function of feeding the plant by photosynthesis.

Single muscle cell inside the tissue

Single photosynthetic cell inside the tissue

Organs are made of tissue

Inside animals and plants, tissues work together to make organs. **Organs** have a particular job (or function). In the human body, examples of organs are the heart which pumps the blood, the stomach, where digestion of food begins, and the kidneys, which control water and excrete waste. In the human body, jobs are shared by organs working together – an organ system. An example of this is the digestion and absorption of food. This job is done by the digestive system, which is made up of the gut, the liver and the pancreas.

The main organ system of the human body

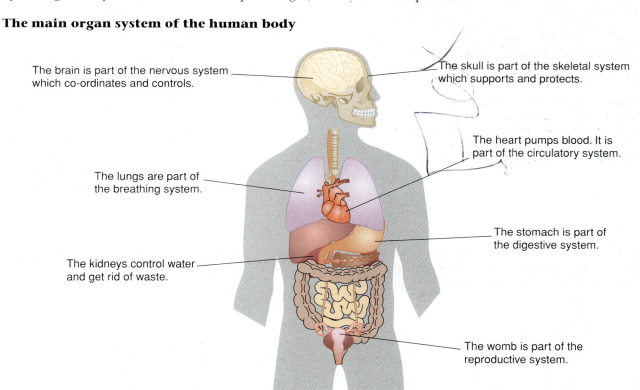

- The brain is part of the nervous system which co-ordinates and controls.
- The skull is part of the skeletal system which supports and protects.
- The lungs are part of the breathing system.
- The heart pumps blood. It is part of the circulatory system.
- The kidneys control water and get rid of waste.
- The stomach is part of the digestive system.
- The womb is part of the reproductive system.

Summary

1. All animals and plants feed, grow, reproduce, respire, excrete, move and are sensitive.
2. Cells have a nucleus, membrane, and cytoplasm.
3. Plant cells also have a cell wall, vacuole and chloroplasts.
4. Tissues are groups of cells with similar functions.
5. Organs are made of tissues. Organs combine to form organ systems.

Questions

1. List seven life processes.
2. State three differences between animal and plant cells.
3. What is the function of photosynthetic tissue?
4. How are the cells in photosynthetic tissue suited to their function?
5. Give two examples of human organ systems.

2 Cells working together: moving particles

Living things need to be supplied with substances such as food and oxygen. They also need to excrete waste substances such as carbon dioxide. The substances that cells need are all particles (**molecules**). Molecules in a gas or liquid are moving in all directions all the time. When particles move from place to place we call this **diffusion**. Molecules move across cell membranes by **diffusion**. In diffusion the particles of gases or liquids *spread from an area of higher concentration to an area of lower concentration*.

Micro-organisms get oxygen from their surroundings; this is an example of diffusion in action.

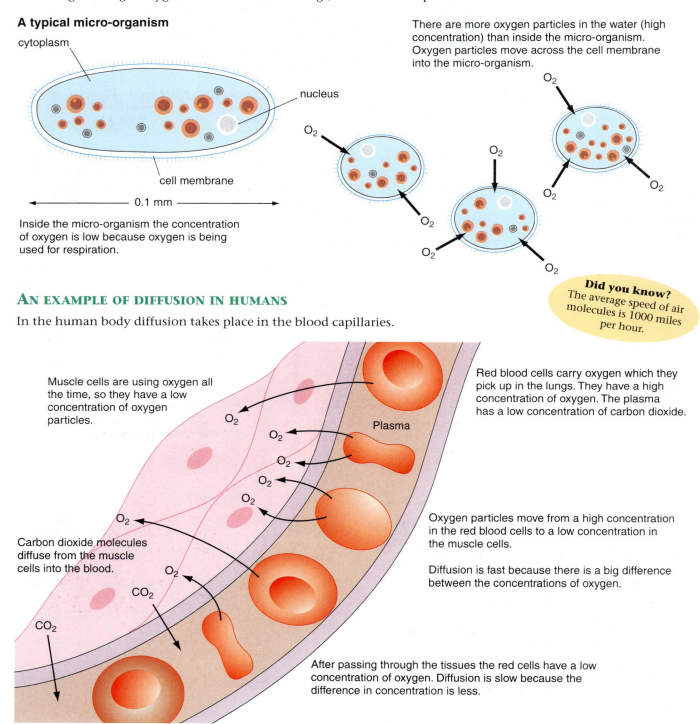

A typical micro-organism

cytoplasm

nucleus

cell membrane

0.1 mm

Inside the micro-organism the concentration of oxygen is low because oxygen is being used for respiration.

There are more oxygen particles in the water (high concentration) than inside the micro-organism. Oxygen particles move across the cell membrane into the micro-organism.

Did you know? The average speed of air molecules is 1000 miles per hour.

AN EXAMPLE OF DIFFUSION IN HUMANS

In the human body diffusion takes place in the blood capillaries.

Muscle cells are using oxygen all the time, so they have a low concentration of oxygen particles.

Carbon dioxide molecules diffuse from the muscle cells into the blood.

Red blood cells carry oxygen which they pick up in the lungs. They have a high concentration of oxygen. The plasma has a low concentration of carbon dioxide.

Oxygen particles move from a high concentration in the red blood cells to a low concentration in the muscle cells.

Diffusion is fast because there is a big difference between the concentrations of oxygen.

After passing through the tissues the red cells have a low concentration of oxygen. Diffusion is slow because the difference in concentration is less.

An example of diffusion in plants

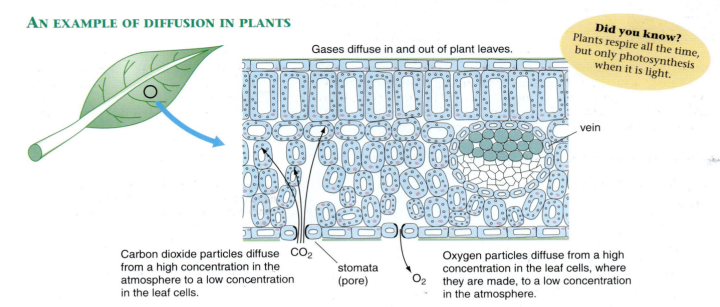

Did you know? Plants respire all the time, but only photosynthesis when it is light.

Gases diffuse in and out of plant leaves.

Carbon dioxide particles diffuse from a high concentration in the atmosphere to a low concentration in the leaf cells.

stomata (pore)

Oxygen particles diffuse from a high concentration in the leaf cells, where they are made, to a low concentration in the atmosphere.

Osmosis is a special type of diffusion. It only happens through a special membrane like the cell membrane. Water molecules are small enough to move through the membrane during osmosis. Bigger molecules such as sugars and salts cannot move through the membrane. If there are more water molecules (a higher concentration) on one side of the membrane, the molecules will move to the side with the lower concentration. Osmosis happens until the concentration of water molecules is almost the same on both sides.

A demonstration of osmosis

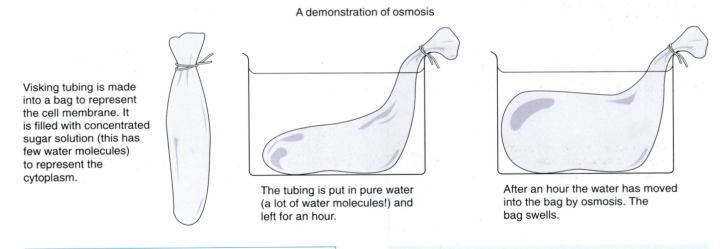

Visking tubing is made into a bag to represent the cell membrane. It is filled with concentrated sugar solution (this has few water molecules) to represent the cytoplasm.

The tubing is put in pure water (a lot of water molecules!) and left for an hour.

After an hour the water has moved into the bag by osmosis. The bag swells.

Summary

1. Diffusion is the spreading of a liquid or gas from a higher to a lower concentration.
2. Oxygen, needed for respiration, diffuses into cells through the cell membrane. Carbon dioxide diffuses out of cells.
3. Carbon dioxide, needed for photosynthesis, diffuses into the leaf.
4. The greater the difference in concentration the faster the rate of diffusion.
5. Osmosis is the diffusion of water across a cell membrane which only lets water through. The water moves from a dilute to a more concentrated solution.

Questions

1. Explain how a micro-organism living in fresh water gets oxygen and gets rid of carbon dioxide
2. Explain how oxygen moves from a red blood cell to muscle tissue.
3. Carbon dioxide diffuses into plant leaves through stomata. Explain why it is important that the carbon dioxide is continually used up in the leaf.

3 Cell division

When living things grow their cells divide. When a human egg is fertilised by a sperm it becomes a single cell which contains all the information needed to make a person. Within a day or so it begins to divide, first into two cells then four, then eight and so on. After seven days it has grown into a ball of cells by cell division. The ball of cells sticks in the lining of the womb and grows into a foetus. The foetus carries on growing by cell division. Eventually the baby will be born and grow into an adult.

A ball of eight cells

Chromosomes

The information that controls the characteristics of a living thing is carried in the nucleus of each of its cells. When cells divide we see that the information inside the nucleus is carried on **chromosomes**. Chromosomes are made of a chemical called **DNA**. We can only see chromosomes when cells divide.

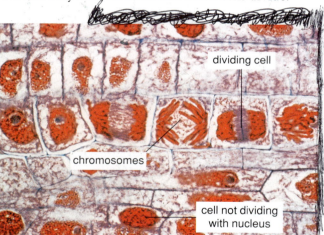

Cells of an onion root tip can be seen under the microscope. As the root tip grows, the cells divide. In dividing cells we can see chromosomes.

Animal and plants do not have the same number of chromosomes.

Cell division for growth and replacement

When animals and plants grow or cells are replaced, the new cells are exactly like the originals. In humans, each new cell has 46 chromosomes. This kind of cell division is called **mitosis**. In mitosis each chromosome makes a copy of itself by doubling its DNA.

During mitosis the chromosome and its copy separate and the new cells each have the original number of chromosomes. Each chromosome has made a copy, so the new cells are identical.

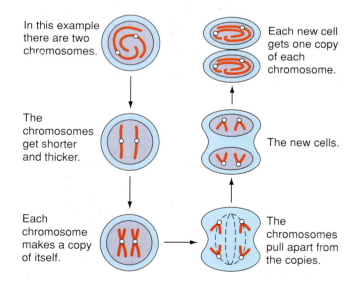

In the human body mitosis is happening wherever tissues are growing, for example, bone and skin.

12

The Human Genome Project

The Human Genome Project is mapping every gene on our chromosomes. There are over 100 scientists working on the project. So far 30 000 genes have been found. Each human chromosome carries thousands of genes. A **gene** is a small part of a chromosome. Each gene controls a characteristic, for example hair colour. There can be different versions of each gene, for example, black hair, brown hair and fair hair. The different versions are called **alleles**. In most body cells the chromosomes are in pairs. One half of the pair comes from the mother and one half from the father.

You can see more of the project on the Internet at http://www.ncbi.nlm.nih.gov/SCIENCE96

Reproduced with permission from the National Center for Biotechnology Information

Meiosis

Cells which make eggs and sperm divide in a special way called **meiosis**. First copies of the chromosomes are made; then the cell divides twice to make four cells. Each has a single set of chromosomes.

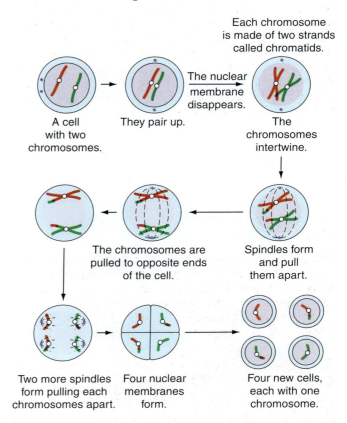

These special cells made by meiosis are called **gametes**. They only have half the normal chromosome number. Examples are sperm cells, egg cells, pollen and ovules. When two gametes join in fertilisation the chromosome number is complete.

Did you know?
This is part of an Internet page describing the Human Genome Project. It shows chromosome number and the genes which have been mapped.

Questions

1. How many chromosomes does a human body cell have?
2. What does a gene do?
3. Give three examples of genes mapped by the Human Genome Project.
4. Describe three things that happen to chromosomes during mitosis.

Summary

1. The nucleus of a cell contains chromosomes. Chromosomes are made of DNA. The chromosomes control the characteristics of living things.
2. Cell division called mitosis happens when tissues grow or when cells are replaced.
3. In body cells the chromosomes are normally in pairs.
4. Genes are found on chromosomes. Genes have different forms called alleles.
5. Sex cells (gametes) are made by meiosis. They have half the chromosome number of body cells. When a sperm fertilises an egg the number is complete.

4 Human diet and nutrition

A balanced diet

To stay fit and healthy we need a **balanced diet**.

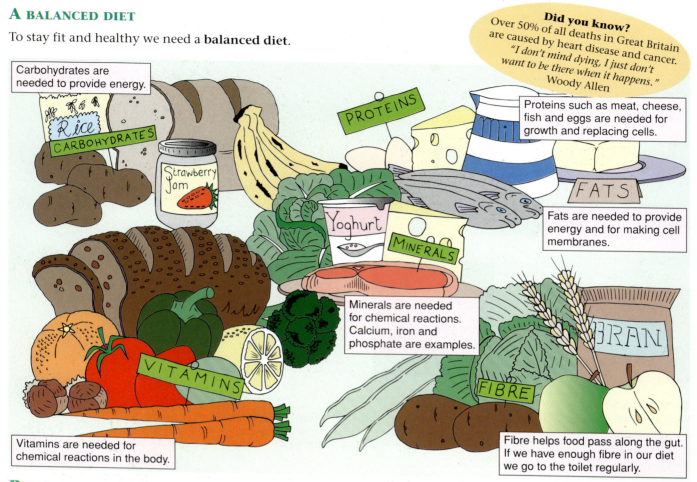

Did you know?
Over 50% of all deaths in Great Britain are caused by heart disease and cancer.
"I don't mind dying, I just don't want to be there when it happens."
Woody Allen

Carbohydrates are needed to provide energy.

Proteins such as meat, cheese, fish and eggs are needed for growth and replacing cells.

Fats are needed to provide energy and for making cell membranes.

Minerals are needed for chemical reactions. Calcium, iron and phosphate are examples.

Vitamins are needed for chemical reactions in the body.

Fibre helps food pass along the gut. If we have enough fibre in our diet we go to the toilet regularly.

Planning for healthy eating

A balanced diet contains all the components above. We should try to eat something from each category every day. What we eat depends on our lifestyle, culture, family and friends, but we do have a choice.

Choosing a healthy diet

- **Eat less fat**
  Many of the foods we eat contain too much fat. Pizza, chips, biscuits, crisps, chocolate and other snacks contain so much that we should not eat them every day
- **Eat less sugar**
  Sugar contains a lot of energy. If we don't exercise enough, eating lots of sweets, biscuits, cakes and puddings will cause us to become overweight
- **Eat a varied diet**
  Choose low fat, high fibre foods. Choose examples from each group of foods each day
- **Eat plenty of fruit and vegetables.**
  They contain fibre and may protect us against cancer.

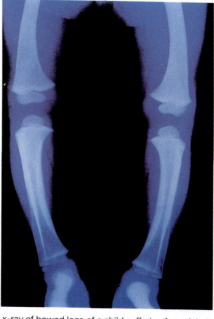

A diet lacking in vitamin C results in scurvy. People who have a diet lacking vitamin D may suffer from rickets.

x-ray of bowed legs of a child suffering from rickets

14

Reg Vernon retired early from work at the age of fifty. Two years later he died of a heart attack. He had shown signs of heart disease before, but not working meant that he could spend more of his time lying on the sofa, smoking, drinking beer and eating takeaway meals. His weight increased until he was more than 140 kg when he died.

What was wrong about Reg's lifestyle? It is possible that he had a high fat diet throughout his life. Too much fat, especially animal fat, can lead to heart attacks and strokes. Heart attacks and strokes are caused by fat sticking to the inside walls of blood vessels. The vessels become thin inside. Blood clots can easily stick inside the vessel and stop the blood flowing. When the blood flow to the heart stops the heart tissues dies. This is a heart attack. A stroke is a similar thing happening in the brain.

Too much sugar and alcohol meant that he easily put on weight. He had little exercise and so did not use up his energy. Unused energy turns to fat.

Reg would have been more likely to reach an old age if he had not smoked, taken regular exercise and eaten a more balanced diet containing less fat and more vitamins.

Energy in food

The food we eat contains energy. We measure energy in kilojoules. You can work out how much energy people need in a day by their age and their lifestyle.

A teenage girl, for example needs approximately 9600 kilojoules (2285 kilocalories) per day: a pregnant woman needs 12 000 (2857 kilocalories) kilojoules.

This table of food values tells us the energy content in kilojoules of 100 g of common foods. A small piece of pizza or small serving of chips has a mass of 100 g.

Food	kJ	Food	kJ	Food	kJ
Apple	196	Dahl	380	Pizza	982
Bacon (fried)	1975	Digestive biscuits	1981	Pork pie	1564
Baked beans	270	Fish fingers	975	Porridge	188
Banana	337	Fried cod	834	Potato (boiled)	343
Beefburger	1099	Lettuce	51	Potato (fried)	1065
Boiled cabbage	35	Mars Bar	1885	Raw carrot	117
Bread (white)	948	Meat curry	668	Rice (white)	522
Bread (brown)	991	Milk chocolate	2214	Roast chicken	902
Butter	3041	Milk (skimmed)	142	Roast peanuts	2364
Chapati	860	Milk (whole)	272	Sardines in oil	906
Cheese	1682	Moussaka	810	Shepherd's pie	497
Cornflakes	1567	Orange	113	Spaghetti	499
Crisps	2224	Peas	223	Tomato	60

SUMMARY

1. A human diet contains carbohydrates, proteins and fats. Minerals, vitamins and fibre are also needed to keep us healthy. These components should be in the right proportions.

QUESTIONS

1. What are the components of a balanced diet? Give a reason for each component.
2. Explain why it is unhealthy to eat pizza and chips every day of the week.

5 Food and digestion

What digestion means

When we eat food it has to be digested before our body can use it. Most of the food chemicals are **insoluble**. This means they will not dissolve in water. Particles that will not dissolve in water cannot diffuse into our body cells. The process of **digestion** is when large food molecules are broken down into smaller particles. These smaller particles can diffuse into our body cells. The large insoluble molecules are broken down into smaller soluble molecules.

Parts of the digestive system produce **enzymes** which speed up the digestion of food. When the food has been digested it is absorbed through the wall of the intestine. The small soluble molecules pass through the wall into the blood vessels surrounding the intestine. The blood vessels around the intestine are the starting point of a journey for the food molecules. From there they are carried around the whole body to wherever they are needed.

Enzymes and Digestion

The breakdown of the large food molecules is speeded up by enzymes. Speeding up chemical reactions is called **catalysis**. Enzymes are made by special tissues along the length of the gut. As the food passes along the gut, the enzymes pour onto the food.

There are three kinds of enzymes:

Carbohydrases catalyse the breakdown of starch into sugars. Carbohydrases are made in the salivary glands, pancreas and small intestine.

Proteases catalyse the breakdown of proteins into amino acids. Proteases are made in the stomach, pancreas and small intestine.

Lipases catalyse the breakdown of fats into fatty acids and glycerol. Lipases are made by the pancreas and small intestine.

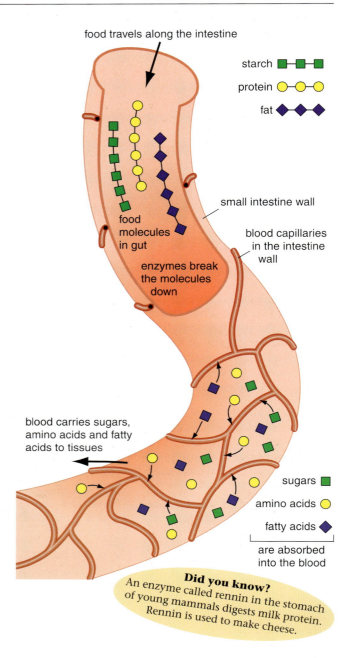

Did you know? An enzyme called rennin in the stomach of young mammals digests milk protein. Rennin is used to make cheese.

THE HUMAN DIGESTIVE SYSTEM

The digestive system is one of the organs systems of the body. Its function is to break food down and absorb it into the body. The digestive system includes the gullet, stomach, liver, pancreas, small intestine and large intestine. The intestines are also known as the gut.

oesophagus
Food is pushed through the gut by waves of contraction of the muscle in the gut wall. This process is called peristalsis and it is this which pushes food down the oesophagus.

liver
The liver produces an alkaline substance called bile which neutralises the stomach acid. The bile helps to break down large drops of fat into smaller droplets. This process is callled emulsification. Emulsification increases the surfacre area of the fats allowing the lipase enzymes to work on them more easily.

gall bladder
Stores bile from the liver.

small intestine
The wall of the small intestine secretes a juice which contains protease, carbohydrase and lipase enzymes which finish the breakdown of protein to amino acids, carbohydrates to sugars and fats to fatty acids and glycerol. The digested food is now absorbed through the wall of the intestine into the blood. The surface area of the wall is enormously increased by finger like folds called villi.

mouth
Salivary glands produce saliva which contains the enzyme salivary amylase. The enzyme is a carbohydrase which begins the breakdown of starch to sugar. The saliva also helps to lubricate the food.
pH6.7

stomach
The stomach produces gastric Juice which contains a protease enzyme called pepsin and an acid called hydrochloric acid. Pepsin breaks long chains of proteins into smaller chains called peptides. The acid helps to kill bacteria and break up meat fibres.
pH2

pancreas
The pancreas produces pancreatic juice which contains lipase which breaks down fats, amylase which breaks down starch and a protease which continues the breakdown of proteins.
pH8

large intestine
In the large intestine bacteria secrete an enzyme called cellulase which breaks down cellulose to sugars. Cellulose is the substance found in plant cell walls. Water and vitamins are absorbed through the wall of the large intestine. Waste material called faeces are removed from the rectum via the opening called the anus.

SUMMARY

1. The digestive system breaks food down so that we can absorb it.
   - Proteins are broken down into amino acids
   - Fats are broken down into fatty acids and glycerol
   - Carbohydrates are broken down into sugars. These smaller molecules are soluble and can be absorbed into the body.
2. The breakdown of large molecules into smaller ones is speeded up (catalysed) by enzymes.

QUESTIONS

1. What are the two main functions of the digestive system?
2. Make a list of the organs which are part of the digestive system.
3. Describe how each of the following is involved in digesting the food:
   a. the stomach
   b. the liver
   c. the pancreas
   d. the small intestines.
4. How are food molecules transported from the intestines to the cells of the body?

6 The circulation of blood

Our blood system transports food and oxygen to all the cells in the body and transports waste away from cells.

How the circulation of blood was discovered

Until the 17th century people in Europe thought that blood flowed out of the heart into the body, and then back to the heart. William Harvey (1578–1657) cut open living animals to look at working hearts. He thought that blood must travel from the heart in arteries and then back to the heart in the veins. He convinced people that this happened by showing that a vein, if blocked, refills with blood on the side of the blockage farthest from the heart. This proved that blood flowed back to the heart in the veins.

Harvey's experiment on circulation

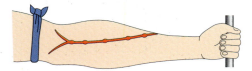
Tie ligature around the upper arm. Small swellings show up in the vein

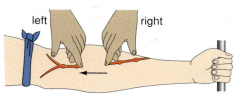
The vein is blocked with the right finger whilst the left finger pushes the blood towards the swelling

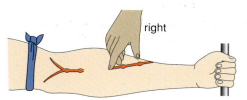
Remove the left finger

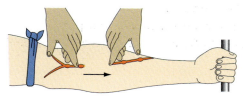
Push blood back with the left finger

Harvey also predicted that vessels called capillaries link arteries to veins. After Harvey had died, capillaries were discovered. The capillaries are where substances are exchanged between the blood and the cells by diffusion.

Arteries and veins

Blood flows from the heart through **arteries** and returns through **veins**. **Capillaries** join arteries to veins. Arteries have thick, elastic walls. As blood flows through they stretch a little, then spring back to help push the blood along.

Veins have thinner walls than arteries. The walls cannot stretch. When the blood reaches the veins the pumping effect of the heart is lost. The muscles around veins help blood flow through by squeezing. Valves in the veins stop the blood leaking back, so it flows towards the heart.

Capillary walls are only one cell thick. Capillaries spread through tissues so that substances such as food, oxygen and waste can easily diffuse to and from the blood.

The circulatory system

The system is a *double* system. For every complete circuit of the body, the blood passes through the heart twice. Blood flows from the heart to the tissues taking food and oxygen. Blood returns to the heart in the veins, now low in oxygen. It is then pumped from the heart to the lungs where it gets more oxygen. It returns to the heart. It is pumped out of the heart around the body a second time.

Did you know? Your heart beats about 100 000 times every day.

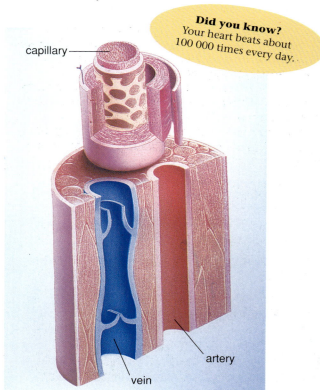

The human heart is like two pumps working together. The left side of the heart pumps blood around the body, the right side pumps blood to the lungs.

There are two chambers on each side of the heart. The top chamber (**atrium**) collects blood from the veins and pumps it into the bottom chamber (**ventricle**). Each atrium fills up as blood returns through the veins. The atria squeeze inwards (contract) together forcing the blood through valves into the ventricles. The ventricles squeeze (contract) next, forcing the blood out of the heart through valves. The valves only allow blood to move one way, so it can only flow out of the heart. The blood from the right ventricle goes to the lungs. The blood from the left ventricle goes into the aorta and then around the whole body.

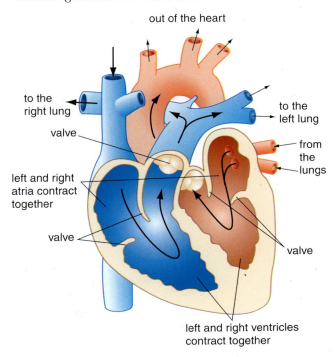

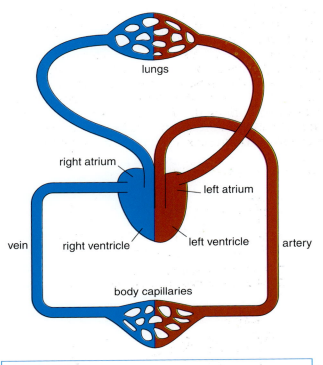

HEART ATTACK

The wall of the heart is made from muscle fibres. Heart muscle fibres are special. They can contract and relax throughout our lives without getting tired. Heart muscle is supplied with oxygen and food through the coronary artery. A heart attack happens when the coronary artery gets blocked. The heart muscle dies when blood cannot reach it.

Heart muscle is damaged when the coronary artery is partly blocked. Eventually it is so damaged that a heart transplant is needed.

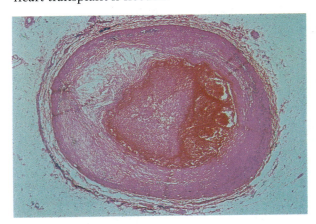

Artery blocked with fatty deposits

SUMMARY

1 The circulatory system transports food, oxygen and waste around the body.
2 The heart is a double pump.
3 Blood flows from the heart to the organs in arteries and returns through veins.

QUESTIONS

1 Make a table to show the differences between arteries and veins.
2 Why is the heart called a double pump?
3 What is the function of the valves in the heart?

7 Blood

What is blood?

The human circulatory system contains about five litres of blood. Blood has the following jobs:

- to absorb oxygen in the lungs and transport the oxygen around the body
- to transport carbon dioxide from the body tissue cells to the lungs
- to transport the products of digestion from the intestines to the body tissue cells
- to help fight off infection
- to transport waste from body tissue cells to the liver and kidney
- to transport hormones from glands to target organs.

Plasma is the liquid part of the blood. Its job is to transport

- carbon dioxide from the body tissues and organs to the lungs
- the products of digestion from the intestines to the body organs
- waste from the liver to the kidneys.

What is blood composed of?

If we look at a drop of blood under the microscope we see that it is composed of a liquid part called *plasma*. In the plasma there are two kinds of cells; red cells and *white cells*, and small fragments of cells called *platelets*.

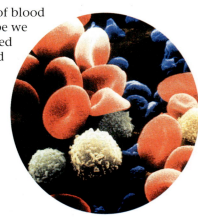

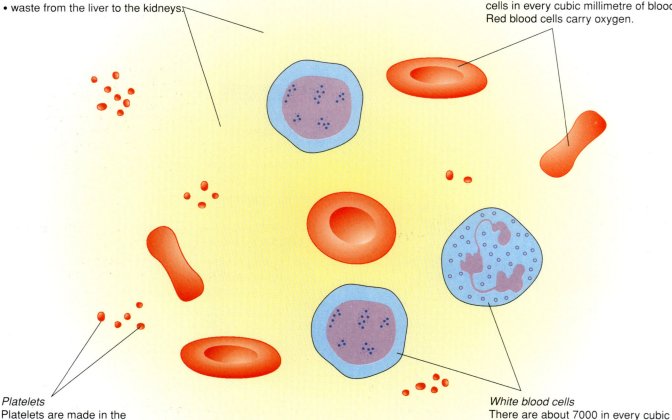

Red blood cells
There are about 5 million red blood cells in every cubic millimetre of blood. Red blood cells carry oxygen.

Platelets
Platelets are made in the red bone marrow. They help the blood to clot.

White blood cells
There are about 7000 in every cubic millimetre of blood. They are part of the body's defence system against microbes.

Red blood cells

Red blood cells have two important features.
- Their biconcave shape gives a cell membrane with a large surface area. This large surface means that more oxygen can diffuse in and out of the cell.
- They do not have a nucleus. This makes more space inside the cell for a chemical called haemoglobin, which has a red colour (pigment).

The function of haemoglobin

Haemoglobin reacts with oxygen in a very special way. As the red blood cells pass through the lungs, oxygen diffuses into the cells and joins onto the haemoglobin. A new chemical called **oxyhaemoglobin** is formed. The red cells carry the oxyhaemoglobin around the body to the cells in the organs and tissues. When the red cells reach tissue and organ cells which have little oxygen, oxyhaemoglobin splits into oxygen and haemoglobin. The oxygen is used by the organ and tissue cells.

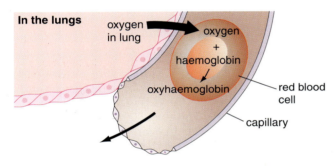

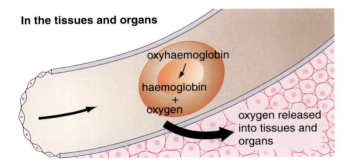

White blood cells

The white blood cells are part of the body's immune system.

White blood cells can:
- make antibodies
- kill microbes by engulfing them
- make you immune by 'remembering' infections you have had before.

The HIV virus and AIDS

People who are infected with the HIV virus can develop AIDS (Acquired Immune Deficiency Syndrome). The HIV virus attacks the white blood cells. The immune system stops working properly and the body loses its defence against disease. There is no cure for HIV infection.

HIV virus can be passed from one person to another in three ways:

1. blood to blood contact, for example by drugs users sharing needles
2. by a mother infecting her unborn child
3. by having sex with an infected person.

> **Did you know?**
> Carbon monoxide is a dangerous gas produced by car exhausts, cigarette smoke and badly ventilated gas heaters. If we breathe in carbon monoxide, it joins onto haemoglobin more readily than oxygen. The haemoglobin turns into carboxyhaemoglobin, which cannot carry any oxygen. Our cells become starved of oxygen and die.

Summary

1. Blood consists of fluid plasma in which there are red cells, white cells and platelets.
2. Red cells have no nucleus and contain haemoglobin, which transports oxygen.
3. White blood cells form the body's defence system.
4. Platelets help blood to clot.

Questions

1. Make a table to summarise the components of blood. Include their functions.
2. Red blood cells carry oxygen. How is a red blood cell adapted to this job?

8 The breathing system

The breathing system is in the chest, or thorax. It is separated from the lower part of the body, the abdomen, by a large sheet of muscle called the **diaphragm**. The breathing system includes the lungs, trachea, bronchi, bronchioles and alveoli, ribs and diaphragm.

The air we breathe in contains 21% oxygen. There is less oxygen when we breathe out. Only 16% of breathed-out air is oxygen.

Only a small part of breathed-in air is carbon dioxide (0.03%). When we breathe out 4% of the air is carbon dioxide.

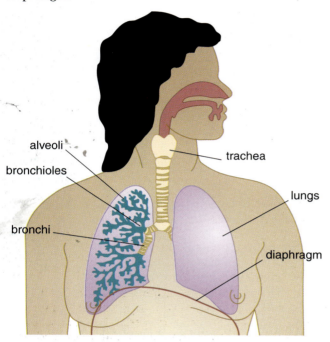

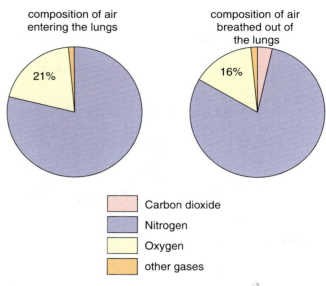

composition of air entering the lungs

composition of air breathed out of the lungs

- Carbon dioxide
- Nitrogen
- Oxygen
- other gases

The breathing system takes air into and out of the body. In the lungs oxygen gets into the blood by diffusion. Carbon dioxide gets out of the blood by diffusing into the lung air spaces.

Most of the inside of the lungs is made of millions of air sacs called **alveoli**. The alveoli are surrounded by blood capillaries. Oxygen and carbon dioxide diffuse across the thin membrane of the alveolus. The inside of each alveolus is wet, so oxygen dissolves in the moisture and can easily diffuse into the blood.

Did you know?
The surface area of the alveoli in a typical person is the same as a tennis court.

Breathing in

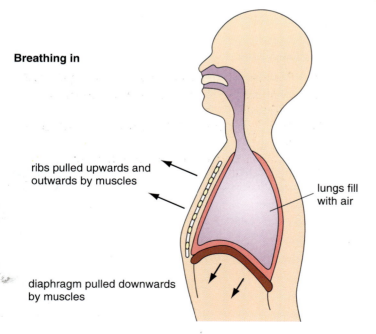

Breathing out

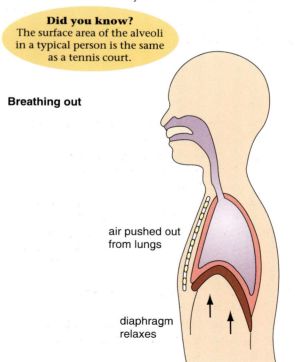

22

RESPIRATION

All cells **respire**. Cells need oxygen for respiration. Oxygen is taken to cells in the blood. During respiration oxygen reacts with sugars. The energy is released from the sugars, and carbon dioxide and water are waste products. Respiration using oxygen is called **aerobic respiration**. When people exercise they respire aerobically. Their body sugars are used to make energy and they breathe quickly and deeply to get enough oxygen.

glucose sugar + oxygen → water + carbon dioxide + energy

When people exercise hard, their heart and lungs may not be able to supply enough oxygen to the muscles. Their muscles can still release energy but this time by **anaerobic respiration**. Oxygen is not used. The sugar is not turned into carbon dioxide, instead lactic acid is made. Lactic acid causes the muscles to ache. Cramp is a sign of lactic acid formation. Eventually the blood takes the lactic acid away to be dealt with in the liver. Oxygen is needed to get rid of the lactic acid, so people exercising continue to breathe hard even when they have finished.

glucose sugar → lactic acid + energy

USES FOR ENERGY

Plants and animals respire. Plants use some of the energy to build up new molecules. For example, glucose is made into starch, fats or oils for storage. It can also be made into protein which the plant uses to build new cells.

Animals transfer the energy from respiration to move muscles and to make new molecules for growth and reproduction. Warm blooded animals use energy to keep a steady body temperature.

USING ANAEROBIC RESPIRATION

The baking and brewing industries use yeast. Yeast is a micro-organism that respires anaerobically. Bakers add yeast to their bread. The yeast makes carbon dioxide as it respires the sugars in the flour. The bread dough fills up with carbon dioxide gas and gets bigger. We say the bread *rises*.

We call respiration by yeast **fermentation**. Yeast makes alcohol as well as carbon dioxide when it respires. Fruit and starchy foods can be made into alcoholic drinks by fermentation. The yeast is added to barley, hops and malt to make lagers and beer. Wine is made by fermenting grapes.

Glucose → alcohol + carbon dioxide

SUMMARY

1. All living things respire. There are two kinds of respiration
   a. aerobic – which uses oxygen. Glucose sugar is broken down into water, carbon dioxide and energy.
   b. anaerobic – no oxygen is used. The glucose is turned into lactic acid or alcohol.
2. Energy produced by respiration is used to build new molecules, enable muscles to contract and is used by some animals to keep a steady body temperature.
3. The breathing system includes the lungs, ribs, diaphragm, bronchi and alveolus.
4. The alveoli have a moist, thin surface with a large surface area to help diffusion of gases.

QUESTIONS

1. Which gases are exchanged in aerobic respiration?
2. How much oxygen is removed from the air we breathe in?
3. Why do your heart and lungs work faster when you run?
4. Marathon runners often suffer from cramp. Explain why.

9 Responding to our surroundings

> **Did you know?**
> Your tongue can only taste sweet, sour, salt and bitter. The other part of taste is the smell of food. This explains why if your nose is bunged up you can't taste your food.

Special nerve cells in our body inform our brain about changes in our surroundings. The cells are called **receptors**. They respond to the changes in our surroundings; these changes are called **stimuli**. Receptors change a stimulus into nerve impulses. The impulses are carried to the brain by nerve cells.

Skin receptors are sensitive to changes in temperature and pressure.

Nerve cells

Nerve cells carry messages called impulses. Each nerve cell is called a **neurone**. Neurones are long and thin so they can take messages from one part of the body to another. Nerves are bundles of neurones.

The skin

The skin is covered with receptor cells. Skin receptor cells are in the dermis. Above the dermis are the dead cells of the **epidermis**. If this layer is thick, the skin is less sensitive. If the layer is thin the skin is more sensitive. Each type of receptor cell senses a different stimulus, such as touch, pressure, pain or temperature. Each sends a message to the brain if it senses that stimulus.

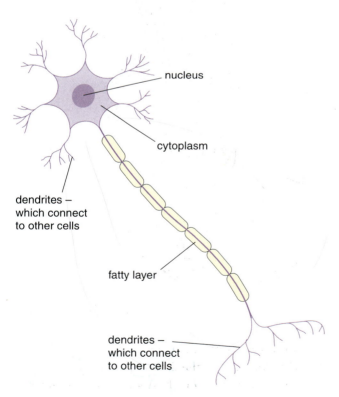

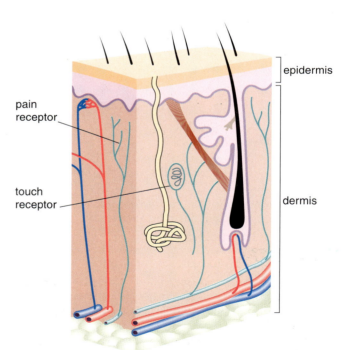

24

Quick reactions

We react to stimuli around us. The pain receptors in our skin sense if we burn ourselves. They send a message to the spinal cord along sensory nerves. Nerve cells in the spinal cord take the message to the brain. The brain then sends a message to our muscles to move, and we pull our hand back. The same thing happens with other receptors. The brain receives messages about our surroundings and sends messages to muscles so we can respond.

Some of our responses are automatic (just as the footballer's responses are automatic). They are called **reflex actions**.

How the brain co-ordinates our movements

The brain, spinal cord and nerve cells work together to co-ordinate our movements. Think of the many movements a football player makes every second. His arms, body and legs are all co-ordinated by the brain. They are changing position all the time to react to changes around him. The movement of the ball is the stimulus for action. The eye senses light from the ball and a message is sent to the brain along a sensory nerve. The brain works out what to do. Messages are sent down the spinal cord to muscles. The muscles react by moving.

- The *stimulus* is light from the ball
- The *receptors* are the eyes, which sense the light
- The brain works out what to do. It is the *co-ordinator*
- The muscles move the leg to kick the ball. This is the *response*.

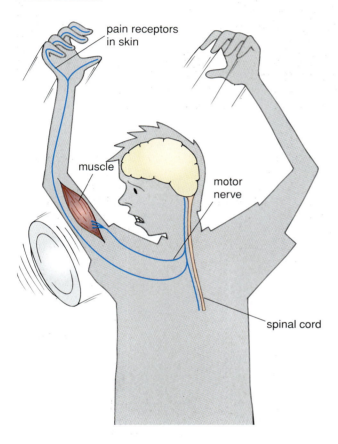

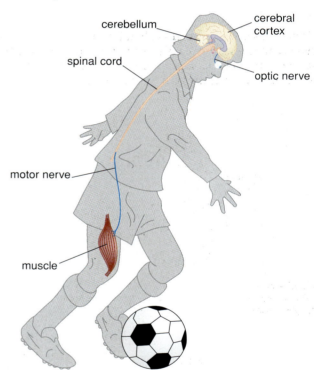

Did you know? A nerve impulse can travel at over 100 metres per second.

Summary

1. Cells called receptors sense stimuli such as light, sound, movement, chemicals, temperature and pressure. Receptors are in the skin, nose, tongue, ear and eye.
2. Messages from receptors pass along nerves to the brain. The brain co-ordinates the response.
3. Some of our responses are automatic. They are called reflex actions.

Questions

1. How is a nerve cell suited to its job?
2. What stimuli does the skin sense?
3. What receptors are involved when you taste your food?
4. We usually jump when we are startled by a loud noise. Explain how this response comes about. Refer to the spinal cord and sense organs in your answer.

10 Sense organs

THE EYE

We see because receptor cells in the back of our eyes sense the stimulus of light. The light rays enter the eye through the cornea. How much light gets into the eye is controlled by the iris. The iris is a coloured ring of muscle which controls the size of the pupil. As light rays enter the eye they are bent by the cornea and then the lens. The bending makes them focus on the retina at the back of the eye. The retina is made of receptor cells. The light stimulus is sensed by receptor cells. The receptor cells send a message to the brain. Nerve cells in the optic nerve take the message. The brain co-ordinates the message to make a picture.

Did you know? Special cells in our eyes allow us to see colour. Only a few animals such as birds and apes have these cells, so most animals probably only see things in black and white.

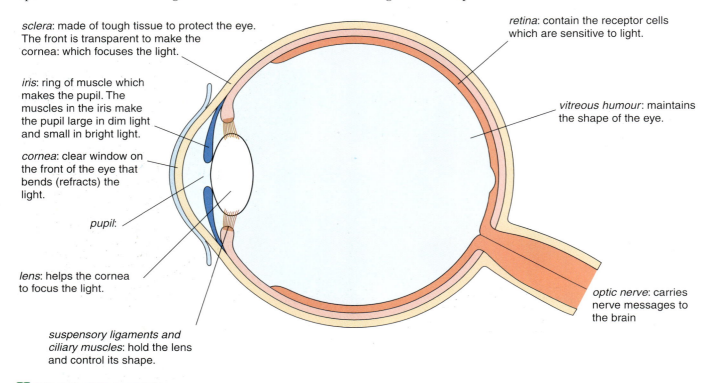

sclera: made of tough tissue to protect the eye. The front is transparent to make the cornea: which focuses the light.

iris: ring of muscle which makes the pupil. The muscles in the iris make the pupil large in dim light and small in bright light.

cornea: clear window on the front of the eye that bends (refracts) the light.

pupil:

lens: helps the cornea to focus the light.

suspensory ligaments and ciliary muscles: hold the lens and control its shape.

retina: contain the receptor cells which are sensitive to light.

vitreous humour: maintains the shape of the eye.

optic nerve: carries nerve messages to the brain.

HOW WE SEE THINGS

The light entering the eye comes from all parts of the tree. Each ray of light is bent by the cornea and an upside down image of the tree forms on the retina. The lens focuses light coming from an object which is either close to the eye or far away. The receptor cells send a pattern of nerve messages to the brain. The brain changes the messages into what you see.

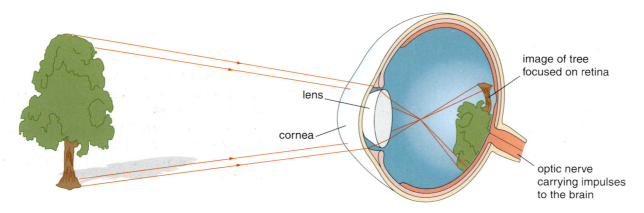

The human ear

The ear senses two stimuli:
sound and *changes in our position*.

Sound vibrations go into the ear and make the ear drum vibrate. The vibrations are carried by the middle ear bones (ossicles). The vibrations pass into fluid in the **cochlea**. Receptor cells in the cochlea sense the vibrations and turn them into nerve messages. The messages move along nerve cells to the brain.

Fluid inside the balance organs (semi circular canals) moves when our position changes. The movement affects the receptors cells. They sense the movement and turn it into nerve messages. The messages move along nerves to the brain. The brain co-ordinates our response, so we keep our balance.

When the fluid in our balance organs moves too much we get travel sick.

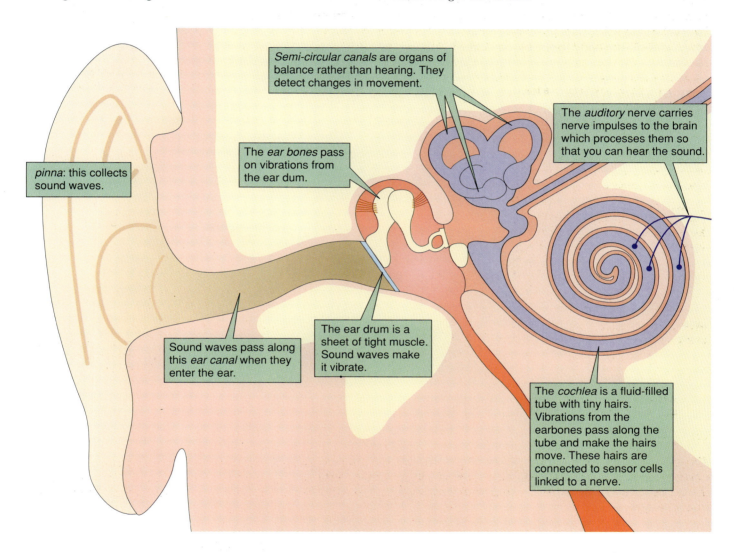

Summary

1. The eye contains receptors which detect light. These are at the back of the eye in the retina.
2. Messages travel from the retina of the eye to the brain along the optic nerve.
3. The ear contains two sets of receptor cells. The cells in the cochlea detect sound. The cells in the balance organ detect changes in position.

Questions

1. What is the job of the iris in the eye?
2. Explain how the cornea and lens form an image on the retina of the eye.
3. Which cells in the eye are receptor cells?
4. What stimuli does the ear sense?
5. Explain how sound travels through the ear into the cochlea.

11 Hormones: the chemical messengers of the body

Have you ever been worried and experienced sweating, butterflies in your stomach and a dry mouth? These effects are caused by the hormone **adrenaline**, which is made in your **adrenal glands**. Like all hormones adrenaline is transported in your blood and affects certain parts of your body. **Hormones** are made by glands and are carried in the blood. They have an effect on certain target organs. Adrenaline works very quickly. Other hormones work more slowly. They control growth, reproduction and blood sugar levels.

Hormones work in a different way from nerves

Hormones are made in glands, which have a good blood supply. The hormones get straight into the blood and travel around the body in the blood. Some hormones take a long time to have an effect. Nerves work more quickly. An example is when you pull your hand away from a hot object. Often nerves and hormones work together.

The glands which produce hormones

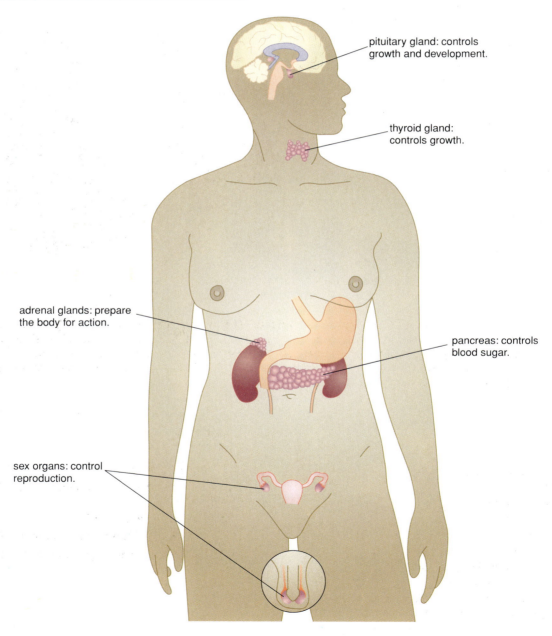

pituitary gland: controls growth and development.

thyroid gland: controls growth.

adrenal glands: prepare the body for action.

pancreas: controls blood sugar.

sex organs: control reproduction.

Controlling blood sugar

The amount of glucose sugar in the blood has to be just right. Too much sugar and our kidneys get rid of it in urine. Too little and we become unconscious. The pancreas makes hormones which control glucose sugar. If the pancreas senses that there is too much glucose in the blood it makes a hormone called **insulin**. Insulin travels in the blood. When it reaches the liver it helps the liver cells to take glucose from the blood and store it.

The pancreas also senses when the glucose level of the blood is too low. It produces the hormone **glucagon**. This hormone has the opposite affect to insulin. It helps the liver to release glucose into the blood. The amount of glucose in the blood increases.

The pancreas works all the time controlling the level of glucose in the body. All body cells need glucose for energy. Glucose levels in the blood are very high after eating and low after exercise or when we have not eaten for a while.

Diabetes

We need the right amount of blood sugar – too much can be fatal. If a person's pancreas does not produce enough insulin, their blood sugar level rises. This is called **diabetes**. High blood sugar can affect the brain causing a coma and even death. People suffering from diabetes can easily control their illness by injecting insulin into their blood.

Some people produce insulin, but their liver cells do not react to it. They control their illness by eating only small amounts of sugar and exercising properly.

Summary

1. Many body processes are controlled by hormones.
2. Hormones are produced by glands and released directly into the bloodstream.
3. Hormones travel in the blood until they reach the organ they work on.
4. Blood sugar is controlled by insulin and glucagon which are produced by the pancreas.
5. Diabetes can be treated by injecting insulin or controlling the diet and exercise.

Questions

1. What is a hormone?
2. What happens if we have too much or too little glucose?
3. What gland makes insulin?
4. What effect does insulin have on the body?
5. What hormone has the opposite effect to insulin?

12 Homeostasis

The cells inside our body will die if conditions change too much. They need the right amount of water and just enough of the right mineral salts such as calcium, sodium and iron. Cells also need to be at the correct temperature for enzymes to work. This is 37 °C. Keeping things the same inside the tissues of the body is called **homeostasis**.

Homeostasis means controlling the internal environment of a person so that it remains fairly constant. An important part of homeostasis is getting rid of wastes. The following organs are all involved in this process:
- the *blood* transports wastes
- the *lungs* get rid of carbon dioxide
- the *liver* turns protein waste into urea
- the *kidney* gets rid of urea and controls water and minerals.

Homeostasis in a warm place

The skin is trying to lose heat quickly:
- sweat is produced which cools the skin as it evaporates
- blood moves into the vessels in the surface of the skin so that heat in it can escape from the body easily (it makes him look red!)
- he has to drink to replace the water lost in sweat. He will only make a little urine.

Homeostasis in a cold place

The skin is trying to stop heat from escaping:
- no sweat is produced
- hairs stand on end to trap air and increase insulation
- the blood is diverted from the skin so that it keeps warm (it makes him look pale!)
- he does not get thirsty and any spare water in his body will go into urine.

How the skin helps keep a constant body temperature

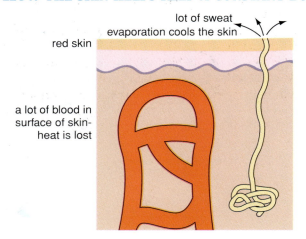
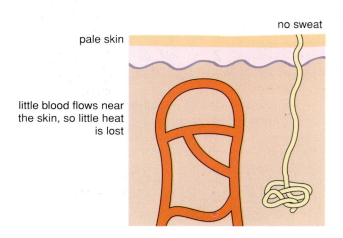

Removing wastes

Getting rid of harmful waste chemicals from the body is called **excretion**. Wastes are made by all cells, so they are carried away from the cells in the blood until they reach the excretory organs. **Carbon dioxide** is carried to the lungs, **mineral salts** to the skin and **urea** (made from waste proteins) from the liver to the kidneys.

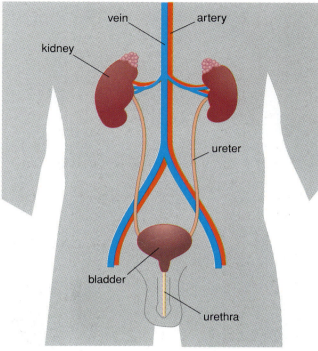

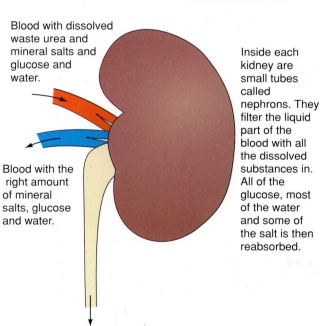

Blood with dissolved waste urea and mineral salts and glucose and water.

Blood with the right amount of mineral salts, glucose and water.

Inside each kidney are small tubes called nephrons. They filter the liquid part of the blood with all the dissolved substances in. All of the glucose, most of the water and some of the salt is then reabsorbed.

The urea, waste water and mineral salts goes to the bladder. It is called urine.

The kidneys and homeostasis

The kidneys control the amount of water in the body by linking up with the brain. The brain senses when you have drunk a lot of water because your blood contains a lot of water. It sends a chemical message through your blood to your kidneys to let more water pass out in the **urine**. Your urine will be dilute and a pale yellow colour. If you have not been drinking enough, or have been sweating a lot, your brain sends a message for the kidney to absorb more water. There will be less urine and it will be a deep yellow colour.

Kidney dialysis and transplants

Of all the kidney's jobs, removing waste urea is one of the most important. When someone's kidneys do not work properly, the urea can build up in their blood and poison them. There are two solutions to this problem. The person can be put on a dialysis machine or be given a transplant.

In **dialysis** the blood is filtered until all the urea is removed. This takes several hours. The person has to return quite soon for more dialysis.

A diseased or faulty kidney can be replaced with a healthy kidney from a donor.

Summary

1. The waste products urea and carbon dioxide have to be removed from the blood.
2. CO_2 is removed by the lungs. Urea is removed by the kidneys.
3. Homeostasis means keeping constant internal conditions for the cells of the body.
4. The internal conditions controlled in homeostasis are water content of the body, mineral salt content and temperature.

Questions

1. Give two ways in which the body is cooled in hot weather.
2. People in very hot conditions may need to eat salty food. Explain why.
3. What three useful substances can be reabsorbed by the kidneys?
4. Explain how the kidneys and brain work together.

13 Infectious diseases

Our world is full of **micro-organisms** such as **bacteria** and **viruses**. They are so small that we can only see them with a powerful microscope. Most micro-organisms, like the bacteria in the mouth, do no harm. Some bacteria and viruses can get inside our body and cause disease. This happens when we have been infected by contact with other people or if we eat food that has been kept in unhygienic conditions.

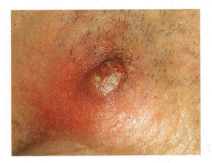

A bacterium called Staphylococcus lives on our skin. If it gets inside sweat glands it causes boils or spots.

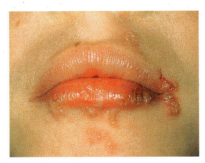

Cold sores caused by a virus called Herpes. The virus infects our saliva glands.

Smallpox was a virus disease easily passed from one person to another. There is no danger from smallpox now; the virus was killed in a programme of vaccinations.

Viruses

Viruses are small particles, much smaller than bacteria. They infect cells and can only reproduce inside a cell.

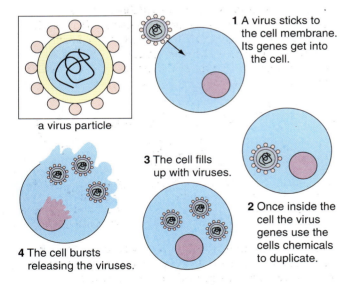

1. A virus sticks to the cell membrane. Its genes get into the cell.
2. Once inside the cell the virus genes use the cells chemicals to duplicate.
3. The cell fills up with viruses.
4. The cell bursts releasing the viruses.

The virus sticks to a cell when it makes contact. Its genes get into the cell, but its protein coat stays outside. Its genes control the genes of the cell, instructing them to make more viruses. The new viruses eventually burst out of the cell. The cell dies, and the viruses can now infect new cells. The viruses make us feel ill because of the wastes they make. An example of this happening is when you have 'flu'. The influenza virus is to blame. It is reproducing inside the cells of your throat, windpipe and lungs. Other examples are the cold viruses, of which there are at least 100 types.

Bacteria

There are many types of bacteria. They are different from viruses. They have a structure more like a cell, with a cell wall and a membrane.

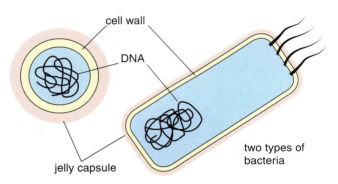

two types of bacteria

In the right conditions, bacteria can reproduce very quickly by cell division. In 24 hours one bacterium can produce millions. An example of this is the bacteria in the sweat under your arms. After a few hours there are so many you can smell the waste they make. The best way to control them is to wash them off!

Infectious bacteria cause disease by getting inside tissues, either through a body opening or a cut. An example is *Clostridium* which lives in soil. It gets inside the body through a cut, reproduces, and its wastes cause the symptoms of **tetanus**, which are muscle stiffness and the general feeling of being unwell. Tetanus can cause death if not treated.

LIVING CONDITIONS AND LIFESTYLE AFFECT THE SPREAD OF DISEASE

E.coli bacteria

E. coli. bacteria live in the intestines of animals and people. The bacterium is also in raw meat. When we cook meat the bacterium dies. It can be transferred from raw meat to cooked meat when someone handles both without being careful. The micro-organism reproduces in the cooked meat. Cooked meat can also be infected by the bacteria from raw meat if the two also are stored together. When someone eats the cooked meat, they get infected.

AIDS

At the end of the year 2000, 36 million people were estimated to be infected with the HIV virus. They were suffering from AIDS. In some countries many people are being infected because they cannot afford contraceptives. In countries with poor AIDS education programmes infection rates are also high. In parts of the UK there are high infection rates because drug addicts use the same needles and pass the virus to each other.

HIV is transferred from one person to the other by sexual intercourse or by sharing used hypodermic needles.

HOW THE BODY DEFENDS ITSELF AGAINST MICRO-ORGANISMS

The skin stops bacteria and viruses getting into the body. When we cut ourselves the blood quickly clots on exposure to the air. This happens because soluble blood protein turns into solid fibres. The fibres make a mesh which traps red blood cells. The platelets in our blood help this happen. The mesh is called a *scab*. Soon new skin grows to replace the scab.

White blood cells protect us from germs in two ways. Some white blood cells destroy micro-organisms by engulfing them.

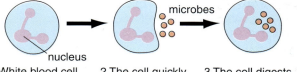

1 White blood cell.
2 The cell quickly surrounds the microbes.
3 The cell digests the microbes. They are destroyed.

Other white blood cells make **antibodies**. The antibodies surround and destroy germs. White cells make a different antibody for each type of germ. White cells can remember germs, so if a person is infected again the right antibodies are produced and the germ is destroyed.

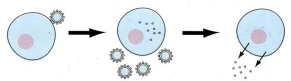

1 The white cell recognises the microrganism.
2 The cell makes antibodies.
3 The antibodies are released. They stick to the microrganisms and destroy them.

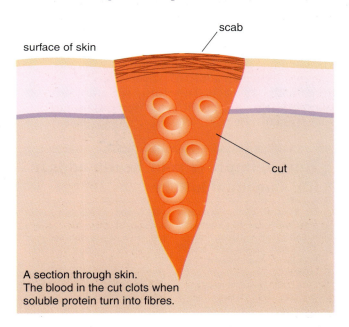

A section through skin. The blood in the cut clots when soluble protein turn into fibres.

Making antibodies is called the **immune response**. Some antibodies work by making the waste from the micro-organisms harmless. These are called *antitoxins*.

SUMMARY

1. Bacteria and viruses cause infectious diseases when large numbers enter the body.
2. As a result of contact with people who have a disease or unhygienic conditions micro-organisms can infect the body.
3. The body has a number of defences including the skin and the immune response.

QUESTIONS

1. Describe the differences between viruses and bacteria.
2. How do infectious bacteria cause disease?
3. Explain why raw meat and cooked meat should not be stored next to each other in a butcher's shop.
4. Why don't people usually suffer from the same infectious disease twice?

14 Drugs

Drugs are substances which affect the way the body works. Some drugs are medicines used to treat pain or illnesses. Examples are paracetamol used to treat pain, and antibiotics used to treat infection. We usually take small amounts of drugs. Using too much of a useful drug can have serious consequences. Taking a large amount of paracetamol is an overdose. The paracetamol harms body cells and can damage the liver or cause death.

Other drugs are not medicines. They are substances that change how we feel or our mood. They are usually harmful chemicals which make the user feel good but which can harm the body at the same time. Everyday examples are the caffeine in our coffee, tea and coke which stimulate our bodies and keep us awake. Alcohol makes people feel happy, but it affects the nervous system by slowing down reactions and can cause lack of self control and unconsciousness. People who drink large quantities can suffer from liver and brain damage.

Drug abuse

Some commonly abused drugs and the problems with them

Opiates are drugs which come from the opium poppy. In medicine they are given as painkillers. Heroin is the most common. It is either injected or sniffed by people who are using it, producing a relaxed feeling. After using heroin for a few weeks the person begins to rely on the drug so much that they are very ill without it. It is an expensive drug and users often have to spend so much money they get into financial difficulties.

Ecstasy is a stimulant which produces a rise in heart rate, increased sweating, and there can be a loss of body co-ordination. For some people it makes them calm. Others enjoy their surroundings and music more. After using a lot of the drug, users may become depressed.

Solvent abuse

Solvents are chemicals which dissolve other chemicals. They easily turn into a gas by evaporation. Glue is often dissolved in a solvent. People sniff the solvent. The solvent is absorbed into their blood through the skin inside their nose and mouth. It is transported to the brain and affects it. Some people feel drunk and out of control when they sniff glue. The solvent can damage the lungs, liver, kidneys and brain as it travels in the blood. People have died by inhaling their own sick after sniffing glue solvent.

Gas canisters are also used for sniffing. The solvent quickly gets into the blood stream and affects the brain. The gas is so cold it can freeze the person's windpipe, causing death.

Young people using solvents are often influenced by their friends. They do not want to feel left out.

How dangerous are drugs?

There have been some tragic deaths when people have used drugs for fun.

When certain drugs such as heroin are used frequently the human body starts to depend on the drug. This continues until the user cannot live properly without the drug. The person is addicted. The chemical processes inside their body have changed. When an addicted person stops taking the drug their body reacts. They suffer withdrawal symptoms and are very ill. Addiction can be cured with specialist help.

How to improve your health odds in life's unequal lottery

Mr Lard died of a suspected heart attack less than hours after winning the national lottery. The wealth should have bought happiness but instead only disaster.

Mr Lard, 56, a former graphic designer was warned of a potential heart attack in June 2000. By the time he died he weighed more than 21 stone, mainly due to his weakness for consuming large quantities of German larger and eating dodgy takeaways.

He is said to have disregarded medical advice to lose weight and join a fitness club, and give up smoking 40 cigarettes a day.

Mr Lard's comparatively early end may in part have been determined by his weight at birth. The poorer the parent's background, the likelier that a baby will be of low birth weight, and the greater the chance that when he or she reaches middle age, cardiovascular disease will occur.

Tobacco

Cigarette smoke is a mixture of nicotine, tar droplets, carbon monoxide and other gases. The drug in tobacco is **nicotine**. It is quickly absorbed into the blood vessels of the lungs and travels around the body in the blood. Nicotine affects the brain and nerves. It stimulates the users and makes them feel better. Smokers use tobacco to reduce stress and worry.

Smoking affects health

Tobacco contributes to 100 000 premature deaths every year in the UK. Smokers often suffer from some of the following: heart disease, heart attacks, lung infections, bad circulation, throat ulcers, cancer of the mouth, lung cancer, blood clots, emphysema and bronchitis.

healthy lung

lung of a smoker

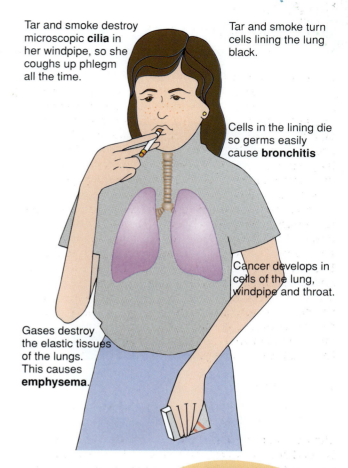

Tar and smoke destroy microscopic **cilia** in her windpipe, so she coughs up phlegm all the time.

Tar and smoke turn cells lining the lung black.

Cells in the lining die so germs easily cause **bronchitis**

Cancer develops in cells of the lung, windpipe and throat.

Gases destroy the elastic tissues of the lungs. This causes **emphysema**.

Did you know? Every five minutes someone in the UK dies from a disease connected with smoking tobacco.

Summary

1. Solvents, alcohol and nicotine are three drugs which may harm the body. Other drugs such as heroin and ecstasy can also be abused.
2. Solvents affect how we behave and damage the heart, liver and lungs.
3. Smoking tobacco causes lung cancer, and lung diseases such as bronchitis and emphysema. It is an important cause of heart disease.
4. Too much alcohol causes liver and brain damage.

Questions

1. What are solvents and how do people abuse them?
2. Explain the meaning of the word 'addiction'.
3. Make a list to summarise the harmful effects of smoking tobacco.

15 Plants: roots, stems and leaves

Most plants have three main parts. A *stem* to hold the plant up straight. Usually the stem also transports water, food and minerals around the plant. The stem holds the *leaves* so they get as much sunlight as they can. The job of leaves is to make food. *Roots* hold the plant firmly in the soil and soak up water and minerals.

Stems hold leaves near the sunlight.

Roots absorb water and minerals, so they have a large surface area.

Leaves have a large surface to use sunlight energy.

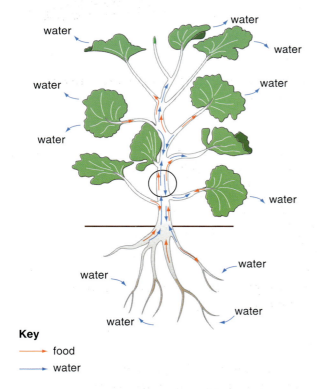

Key
→ food
→ water

Food, water and minerals are transported in the stem. They move to and from the leaves and roots.

Roots hold the plant firmly in the ground.

Looking inside a plant

We can see inside a plant by cutting thin sections – a thousandth of a millimetre thick – through stems, roots and leaves. The tissues can clearly be seen.

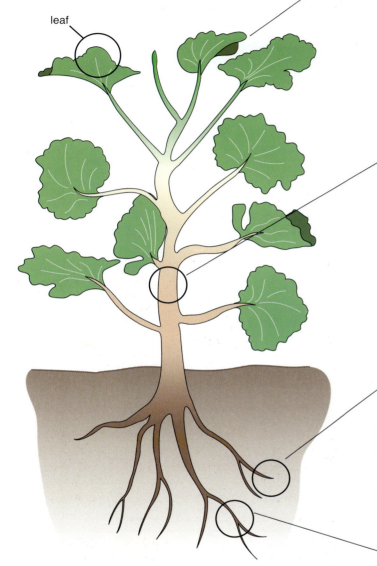

Leaf
Thin leaf blade so gases can easily diffuse in and out. Contains **photosynthetic tissue**.
  Vein containing transporting tissue. Waxy surface to stop water loss. **Stomata** on lower surface to control water loss.

Stem
Vascular tissue which supports the stem and transports food, water and minerals.

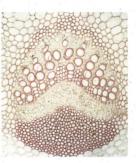

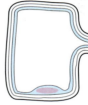

A **root hair bold** has a large surface area through which water is absorbed.

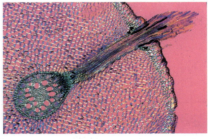

Root
Anchors the plant and transports water, food and minerals.

Summary

Plants have:
- roots which hold them firmly in the ground and absorb water and minerals.
- stems to hold them up straight and transport substances between the roots and leaves.
- leaves to use sunlight for making food and controlling water loss.

Questions

1. What are the two main jobs of roots?
2. What three things do stems transport?
3. Why does a leaf have
   a stomata
   b a waxy surface
   c a thin blade?
4. Some plants do not have vascular tissue. What do you think they look like?

16 Photosynthesis: how plants make food

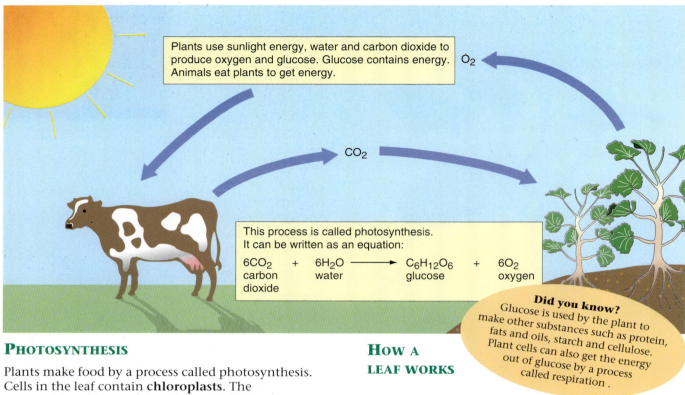

Plants use sunlight energy, water and carbon dioxide to produce oxygen and glucose. Glucose contains energy. Animals eat plants to get energy.

This process is called photosynthesis. It can be written as an equation:

$$6CO_2 + 6H_2O \longrightarrow C_6H_{12}O_6 + 6O_2$$
carbon dioxide + water → glucose + oxygen

Did you know? Glucose is used by the plant to make other substances such as protein, fats and oils, starch and cellulose. Plant cells can also get the energy out of glucose by a process called respiration.

Photosynthesis

Plants make food by a process called photosynthesis. Cells in the leaf contain **chloroplasts**. The chloroplasts are full of a green substance called chlorophyll. When sunlight shines on the cell the chlorophyll absorbs the sunlight energy. The energy is used to change carbon dioxide and water into a sugar called **glucose**. Glucose contains the energy from the sunlight. Oxygen is produced as a waste product.

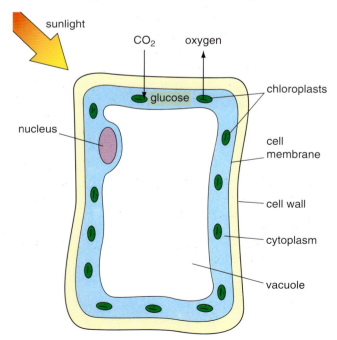

How a leaf works

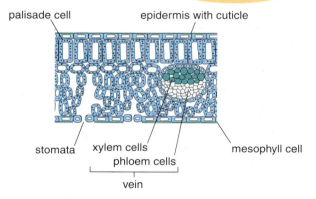

A closer look at the inside of a leaf shows how well suited it is to its job of photosynthesising.

The **xylem** cells in the vein bring water from the roots. When glucose has been produced it is transported to other parts of the plant in the **phloem** cells of the vein.

The leaf is thin so that light reaches all the cells.

The **palisade cells** near the surface, contain lots of chloroplasts so that sunlight energy can be absorbed.

Although the leaf has a waxy surface, there are holes called stomata to allow carbon dioxide and oxygen to get in and out by diffusion. Air spaces around the **mesophyll cells** let the gases circulate inside the leaf.

INVESTIGATING PHOTOSYNTHESIS

If a plant is photosynthesising it will make glucose sugar. Most plants quickly turn the sugar into insoluble starch in their leaves. If you find starch in a plant leaf, it is evidence that photosynthesis has happened. You can test a leaf for starch using the following method.

A test for starch

1. Take the leaf off the plant and put it in boiling water. This stops any chemical reactions in the leaf. Remove it from the water.
2. Set up this apparatus.

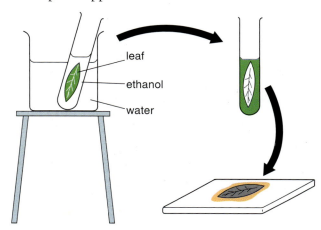

3. Heat the water in the beaker until it is boiling. Turn the Bunsen burner off. This is for safety reasons. Ethanol easily catches fire when near a flame.
4. As soon as you have turned off the Bunsen burner, put the leaf in a boiling tube. Pour ethanol over the leaf in the tube. Put the tube in the beaker of boiling water. Leave the leaf until the chlorophyll dissolves in the ethanol. The ethanol should be green and the leaf white.
5. Take the leaf out with tweezers and put it on a white tile. Carefully pour iodine solution over the leaf to test for starch. A blue-black colour indicates starch.

WHY ARE PLANTS GREEN?

The chlorophyll in plants absorbs all the colours of light except green. Green light is reflected to your eye, so plants look green. This is because plants use the energy in red, yellow, orange, blue, indigo and violet to photosynthesise.

TAKING IT FURTHER: LIMITING FACTORS

How could you measure the *rate of photosynthesis* of a plant? One way with a plant such as pond weed would be to measure how much oxygen it produces in a certain time. But what factors affect the rate? The answer is light, carbon dioxide, and temperature. Sarah and Laura used an oxygen sensor to measure oxygen production for pond weed at different light intensities. Look at the graph they got.

Increasing the light intensity does increase the rate of photosynthesis (see curve A–B), so the low light intensity is limiting the rate. After point B even high light intensity does not increase the rate any more. Low temperature and carbon dioxide can also limit the rate of photosynthesis.

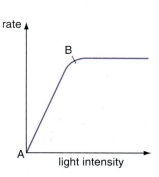

Did you know?
One square metre of ground in Great Britain receives 1 million kJ of light energy in a year.

SUMMARY

1. Green plants photosynthesise to make food.
2. During photosynthesis light energy is absorbed by chlorophyll, which is a green substance inside chloroplasts.
3. The energy absorbed is transferred to convert carbon dioxide and water into glucose sugar and oxygen.
4. Oxygen is released as a by-product.
5. Glucose can be stored as starch.
6. Leaves are suited to the job of photosynthesising.
7. The rate of photosynthesis can be limited by low light, carbon dioxide and temperature.

QUESTIONS

1. What is the job of chlorophyll in the process of photosynthesis?
2. Write a word equation to summarise photosynthesis.
3. Give four ways in which a leaf is suited to its job of photosynthesising.

17 Plant transport systems

For a plant, transporting means moving food and water around. Water is absorbed by the root hair cells which provide a large surface area to absorb all the water a plant needs. Dissolved in the water are mineral salts. The water moves in the plant through tissue called *xylem*. The food made in the leaves is moved around the plant in the *phloem* tissues.

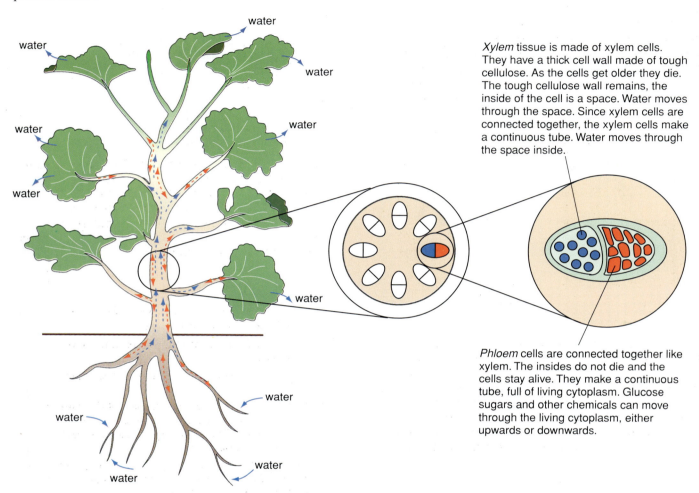

Xylem tissue is made of xylem cells. They have a thick cell wall made of tough cellulose. As the cells get older they die. The tough cellulose wall remains, the inside of the cell is a space. Water moves through the space. Since xylem cells are connected together, the xylem cells make a continuous tube. Water moves through the space inside.

Phloem cells are connected together like xylem. The insides do not die and the cells stay alive. They make a continuous tube, full of living cytoplasm. Glucose sugars and other chemicals can move through the living cytoplasm, either upwards or downwards.

HOW A PLANT IS SUPPORTED

Plants do not have a skeleton. Young plants rely on water for support. When cells are full of water, they bulge outwards, like a blown up balloon. A young plant is supported by these bulging cells full of water. As plants grow and get older, the xylem cell walls get thicker and stronger. The xylem is arranged as a system of tubes and the strong, thick xylem walls support the plant. In some plants the xylem cells make a thick layer called *wood*.

Wood is xylem tissue.

Transpiration

Plants lose water vapour through their leaves. This loss of water is called **transpiration**. Transpiration happens when water evaporates from the cells inside the leaf. The water passes out of the leaf through tiny holes, or pores, called **stomata**.

Plants also need stomata to get carbon dioxide gas for photosynthesis. The carbon dioxide in the atmosphere diffuses into the leaf through the stomata. The stomatal pore is surrounded by two guard cells. The cells swell up when they are full of water and the pore opens. When a plant is losing too much water, the guard cells lose water and the pore closes. When the pore closes less water is lost by evaporation.

open stomata   closed stomata

Counting stomata

To count stomata you can strip the epidermis from a leaf and look at it under the low power of a microscope. An easier way is to paint a small strip of nail varnish on the surface of a leaf. After 10 minutes peel the strip off and mount it onto a microscope slide. By using this method you can compare the number of stomata on the top and bottom surfaces of different leaves. Stomata on the surface of a leaf are shown above.

What factors affect transpiration?

Transpiration is more rapid in hot, dry and windy conditions. This is because transpiration is evaporation of water. Hot conditions increase the energy of the water particles. So they evaporate quickly. If the air is dry around the plant, water diffuses more quickly from the inside of the leaf, where there are lots of water particles, to the surrounding air where there are few. Wind blows more particles away from the surface of the leaf.

How do plants survive in hot, dry and windy places?

Many plants have a thick layer of wax on the surface which stops them losing too much water.

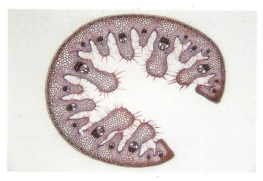

transverse section (TS) of a Marram grass leaf

Other plants have special features which help them to survive in dry and windy environments.

Marram grass has leaves which can fold in dry conditions. The stomata are sunk into furrows on the inner side. Interlocking hairs help to hold in water vapour and reduce water loss. The outer epidermis has a thick cuticle and no stomata.

Summary

1. Water enters a plant through root hair cells which have a large surface area.
2. Mineral salts are dissolved in the water that a plant absorbs.
3. Water moves through the plant in the xylem tissue.
4. Plants lose water from the surface of their leaves by evaporation. This loss of water is called transpiration. Transpiration is quicker in hot, dry, windy conditions.
5. Most of the water lost by plants is through tiny holes called stomata. The size of stomata is controlled by guard cells.
6. The two main methods of support for plants are the bulging cells when they are full of water and the strong xylem tissue.
7. Nutrients such as sugar are transported around the plant in the phloem tissue.

Questions

1. How does a plant get the mineral salts it needs?
2. Describe how water travels around a plant after it has been absorbed by the roots.
3. What does the word transpiration mean?
4. Why do plants need stomata?
5. How are some plants adapted to life in dry or windy places?

18 Plant hormones

Plant responses

Although we can't usually see them moving, plants do respond to their surroundings. They respond to light, gravity and water, but each part of the plant responds in a different way.

Light
Plant shoots grow towards the light. This is called positive phototropism. Growing towards the light helps the plant to be in the best position to **photosynthesise**.

Gravity
When a plant is put on its side, the shoot will grow away from gravity. This is called **negative geotropism**. The roots will still grow down towards gravity. This is called **positive geotropism**. It is an advantage for shoots to grow away from gravity. The leaves and stems are lifted above the ground. Roots need to grow downwards to get into the soil.

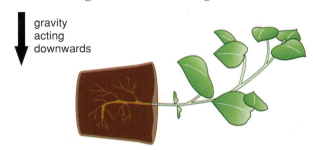

Water
Plant roots grow towards water. This is an advantage when soil moisture is low.

Phototropism explained

In 1881 Charles Darwin found that shoot tips were sensitive to light. He thought that something in the shoot caused it to move towards light. He reasoned that a substance moved from the tip to the growing part of a shoot.

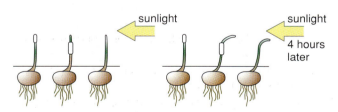

To test his idea he used three seedlings. He covered the tip of one with a paper cap, the shoot of one with paper and left one uncovered. He arranged them so that the sunlight shone from one side.

His results showed that the tip was sensitive to light.

We know now that plants make chemicals which regulate growth. They are called **plant hormones**. One type of plant hormone is **auxin**. When light shines on one side of a shoot, the shoot bends towards the light. This happens because the auxin moves to the side of the shoot opposite the light. The auxin causes the cells in the side away from the light to grow more quickly, so the shoot bends.

Explaining geotropism

We still have a lot to learn about geotropism. Like all scientific mysteries, we have to look at what clues there are before we can try to explain how it works.

It is the tip of the root which responds to gravity.

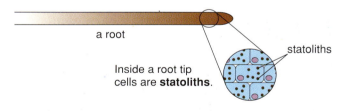

Inside a root tip cells are **statoliths**.

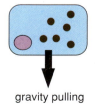

Gravity seems to pull the statoliths to the side of the cell on which gravity is acting.

Root cells on the side where the statoliths have collected grow more slowly.

The root grows towards gravity.

How plant hormones are used

Weedkillers

Auxins are used as **weedkillers** because they stimulate growth. A small amount sprayed onto a plant makes it grow so quickly that it dies. An example is 2-4 D. This is a synthetic auxin which is spread on lawns. Broad-leaved plants such as dandelions absorb it more quickly than grass. They grow so fast they die, leaving the grass behind. Used in this way the synthetic auxin is a selective **weedkiller**.

A lawn treated with selective weedkiller

Seedless fruit

Plant hormones are used to treat flowers that have not been pollinated. A good crop is produced and the fruit is seedless.

Producing new plant by cuttings

Hormone rooting powder contains auxin. Cuttings are taken from plant stems or leaves and dipped in the powder. The auxin stimulates rapid growth of root cells.

Controlling the ripening of fruit

Fruit is often picked long before it is ripe. Unripe fruit such as tomatoes and bananas are easier to transport. They are less likely to be damaged if they are knocked. Before the fruit is sent to the shops it has to ripen. The green tomatoes and bananas will only sell if they are red or yellow. The unripe fruit is kept in an atmosphere of ethene gas just before it is sold. Ethene gas is produced naturally by ripe fruit. The ethene acts as a plant hormone and ripens the unripe fruit.

Summary

1. Plants are sensitive to light, moisture and gravity.
2. Phototropism is when plants respond to light.
3. Geotropism is when plants respond to gravity.
4. Plants produce hormones which co-ordinate and control growth.
5. Plant hormones are used to ripen fruit, kill weeds and stimulate root growth in cuttings.

Questions

1. What is the difference between phototropism and geotropism?
2. Explain why a plant placed near to a window grows towards the light.
3. A gardener put a foil cap on the tip of a seedling and shone a light from the side. In which direction did it grow? Explain your answer.

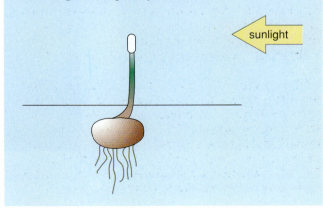

19 Adaptation

LIVING THINGS ARE ADAPTED TO THEIR SURROUNDINGS

The place where something lives is called its **habitat**. The type of animal or plant living in a habitat depends on physical factors. Temperature, the amount of sunlight, water and type of soil are all physical factors. These factors help decide what animals and plants will live in a habitat. Only the plants and animals which are adapted to a certain habitat will live there.

Birds are adapted to a life in the air. They keep away from predators by building nests high in the trees.

The plants of the undergrowth are shaded by the trees. They are adapted to grow quickly in early spring before the tree leaves appear. They flower and produce seeds in early spring.

The squirrels are adapted to live high in the trees out of the reach of predators such as foxes. They have a long tail to balance, good eyesight and strong claws for hanging on to branches. When they do come down to the ground they are alert and move quickly and carefully.

Foxes are predators with good eyesight. They are well camouflaged and so can sneak up on unsuspecting rodents. They move quickly and quietly.

These photographs show other examples of adaptations to a way of life.

Sundew grows in areas with little nitrogen in the soil. It catches flies on its sticky leaf surface. It gets the nitrogen it needs by digesting the fly.

A seal is streamlined. It is adapted to swimming quickly to catch its prey.

This tick has claws to grasp the wool of a sheep and piercing mouthparts to suck its blood.

A desert habitat

Cactus plants have special adaptations to cope with a lack of water. Their leaves are just thin spines. Such a small surface area means they lose little water by transpiration. The spines also trap a layer of moisture near the plant stem. The plants store water in their swollen stems, which also photosynthesise. Cactus plants avoid losing water by only opening their stomata at night to get carbon dioxide for photosynthesis.

A large hawk can easily spot movement below and swoop down to make a kill.

The temperature is so high that small mammals such as this kangaroo rat live in burrows during the day, only coming out to feed at night. They have specially adapted kidneys designed to absorb as much water as possible since water is scarce.

Small lizards hide from predators under rocks during the day.

Lizards are reptiles. They are cold blooded. During the day they lie in the sun and warm up. They are active when they are warm, and feed by hunting insects. During the cold night time they are inactive.

Checking water pollution

The distribution of animals can be used to check water pollution. The animals living in fresh water are very sensitive to pollution. Animals such as caddis fly larvae, mayfly nymphs and water fleas only live in water which contains enough oxygen. Bloodworms and rat-tailed maggots are **adapted** to tolerate low oxygen levels. They are able to absorb oxygen through special gills and through their skin.

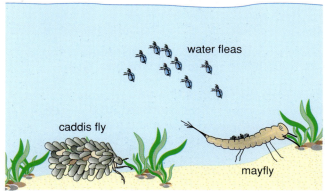

Fresh water with normal oxygen content

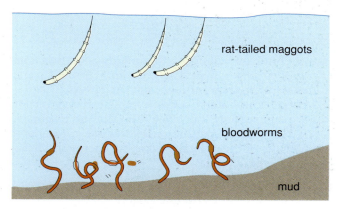

Polluted water with low oxygen content

If a river is polluted, it will be full of bloodworms and rat-tailed maggots. The pollution uses up the oxygen, so water fleas, mayfly nymphs and caddis fly larvae cannot live there. Only animals adapted to low oxygen levels can survive.

Summary

1 Physical factors affecting organisms include
   a temperature
   b light
   c water
   d oxygen and carbon dioxide
   e mineral salts in the soil.
2 Living things are adapted to the surroundings they live in.

Questions

1 Give three examples of ways in which animals in a woodland are adapted to their surroundings.
2 How is a cactus adapted to a desert environment?
3 Name two animals that are adapted to life in water which is low in oxygen.

20 Food chains

The surface of our planet receives its energy from the Sun. Only a small amount of this energy is absorbed by plants and used to make sugars. The energy from the Sun is trapped inside the sugar molecules. The energy has been transferred into the sugar. Plants use the sugars to make more molecules. This is how they grow. Animals eat plants. The energy in the plants is transferred into the animals. Some animals eat other animals. The energy they get from their food can be traced back to the Sun.

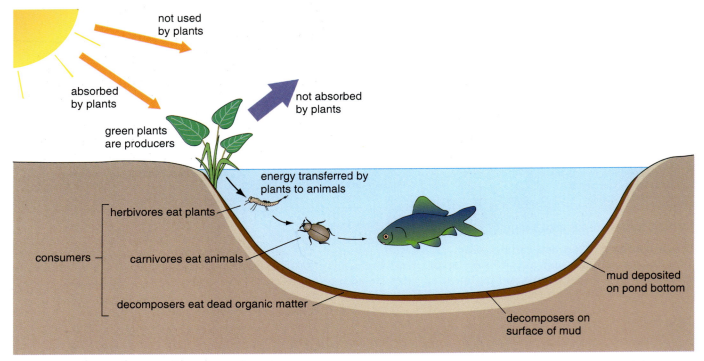

In this pond you will notice that plants only use a small amount of energy from the Sun. They use some of this energy themselves, mainly to grow and reproduce, and some is transferred into the animals which eat them. Animals which eat plants are called *herbivores*.

Herbivores are eaten by *carnivores*. The energy is transferred again, from the herbivores to the carnivores. It is the same energy that came from the Sun originally. Carnivores are eaten by other carnivores and the energy is transferred again, but the carnivores use some energy each time, for growth, reproduction and movement.

When any of the organisms die, the energy inside their bodies is not wasted. It is transferred when *decomposers* feed on the dead bodies.

FOOD CHAINS

We draw food chains to show which organisms eat each other. Food chains always begin with green plants. This is because they use sunlight energy and carbon dioxide to make sugars. The energy is trapped in the sugars. Plants are *producers*. *Consumers* are the organisms which feed on the producer.

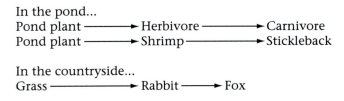

FOOD WEBS

Consumers often eat more than one thing. Herbivores eat different plants: carnivores often eat many different animals. When we draw all the animals and plants in one habitat, we can connect them with arrows showing what they feed on. The result is called a *food web*.

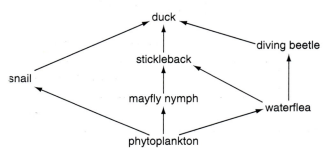

Pyramids of energy

Energy is lost at each stage of a food chain as the organisms use energy to move, reproduce, keep warm and grow. We can see this loss of energy in a pyramid diagram. To draw a pyramid diagram we count how many organisms live in a habitat. We draw a block to represent the numbers of each organism, starting with the plants at the base. We put the plants at the base because they are the producers.

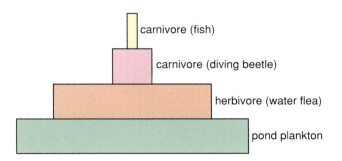

In a woodland, the producers are large and there are fewer of them compared with the numbers of animals that feed on them. The pyramid diagram is a different shape for a woodland.

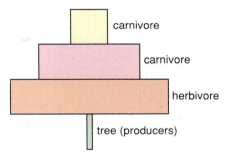

Pyramids of biomass

A better way of showing how much energy flows through a system is to draw a pyramid of biomass. The pyramid for the woodland makes it look as though the producers do not contribute a lot of energy to the system. If we measure the mass of all the organisms, then draw a block to represent the mass, we get a pyramid shape. Pyramids of biomass show how much energy is at each level more clearly.

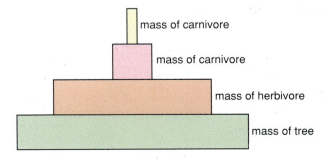

Nutrient cycles

Living things remove materials from their surroundings. When animals eat plants the material in the plant gets into the body of the animals. Plants absorb minerals from the soil and carbon dioxide from the air. The materials taken from the surroundings of an animal or plant are not lost forever. When living things die, the materials inside them get back into the environment. This happens naturally when things decay. For example, when a rabbit dies in a wood, a few months later only a few remains are left. Microbes (such as bacteria and fungi) from the soil digested the material the rabbit was made from. The microbes move back into the soil. The material that the rabbit was made from has been moved back into the soil.

The carbon cycle is an example of a nutrient cycle. The carbon containing materials which are removed are balanced by processes which return materials.

Summary

1. Food chains show which organisms eat other organisms. Food chains begin with green plants (producers) which provide food for animals (consumers).
2. Food chains can be connected together to form food webs.
3. The number or mass of organisms at each stage in a food chain can be shown as a pyramid.
4. Nutrient cycles, such as the carbon cycle, are processes in which the materials removed from the environment are returned.

Questions

1. Which of the following organisms would be placed at the beginning of a food chain? Give your reason.
   lion, insect, grass, pigeon, snail, mouse
2. Draw a food chain using these sea life examples: crab, periwinkle (snail), octopus, seal, seaweed.
3. The amount of carbon dioxide in the atmosphere is usually constant at about 0.03% even though carbon dioxide is used by plants. Explain why.

21 Populations and competition

HOW POPULATIONS GROW

There are three populations in the diagram. The two populations of plants: bracken and grass, compete for growing space, water, and nutrients in the soil. The bracken survives best in the deep soil on the hill side. The rabbit population feeds mainly on the grass because bracken is poisonous. The rabbits live in burrows. They compete with each other for living space, food and water.

POPULATION GROWTH

Populations of animals and plants usually grow in the same way. The first rabbits to arrive in the area dug burrows and began to reproduce. Rabbits reproduce quickly. They can produce four or five young at a time. The young mature quickly and produce young of their own. Soon the numbers of young being born is very high and much higher than the numbers of rabbits dying. Counting the rabbits regularly shows how the population is growing.

You will notice the curve rises steeply showing the population growing, and then levels off. It levels off because fewer rabbits are being born. Why? The rabbits are competing with each other. Perhaps there is not enough grass to eat, or enough space to build burrows. Perhaps disease is killing the rabbits. Or perhaps predators such as birds of prey or foxes are killing them.

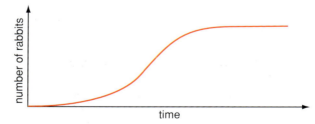

CONTROLLING POPULATIONS

Sometimes populations grow so quickly they damage crops and become pests. In a greenhouse, whitefly are pests on tomato plants. A small wasp called *Encarsia* kills whitefly. Gardeners release *Encarsia* into their greenhouses to control the whitefly population.

At one time Australia had no rabbits. Some were brought there and the population increased so much that they became pests, eating crops. There were no predators to keep them under control. Eventually someone had the idea of introducing myxomatosis, which is a deadly disease for rabbits.

The disease myxomatosis often reduces rabbit populations. It controlled the rabbit population in Australia.

PREDATORS AND PREY

It is natural for the numbers of a population to increase and decrease. Animals that hunt and eat other animals are called **predators**. The animals they kill are called **prey**. In many communities, there are never too many prey animals because predators eat them. The prey population is controlled by how many predators there are.

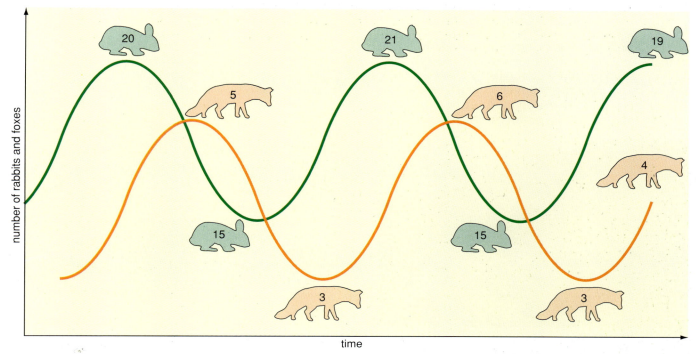

The foxes are predators. The population of foxes depends on how much food is available. Foxes eat rabbits. As the number of rabbits increases, more food is available for foxes. The number of foxes increases. When there are more foxes, they eat more rabbits, so the population of rabbits decreases.

THE HUMAN POPULATION

The human population is increasing quickly. Population growth depends on the birth rate being high and the death rate being low. We are improving our medical care all the time, so fewer people are dying. Many people are beginning to live longer. In areas of the world such as Asia, South America and Africa the population is growing quickly.

A growing world population will mean that there will be less food and space in the future.

SUMMARY

1. Plants compete with each other for space, water and nutrients in the soil.
2. Animals compete with each other for food, water and space.
3. Animals which kill other animals for food are called predators. The animals being killed are the prey.
4. A population of animals or plants can be limited by:
   a how much food or nutrients is available
   b competition for light, food or space
   c disease
   d predators.

QUESTIONS

1. Give three examples of predators and prey.
2. Why would rabbits living on the edge of a wood compete with one another?
3. Give two reasons for the rapid increase in the human population.

22 Human impact on the environment

The human population is growing and will carrying on growing for a number of years. Animals and plants need land and space to live and reproduce. As the human population increases people destroy more and more natural land...

...by building new houses, factories and roads. To make land available, builders must cut down woodland and drain ponds and lakes. Many people protest, but usually the building scheme goes ahead. There is great pressure to provide more homes, jobs and communications for an increasing population.

...by quarrying for coal. This quarry in Columbia was dug out of the rainforest. It will not be filled in when the rock has been removed. The rainforest will not return.

...by modern farming techniques. The modern method of farming is to make large fields with just one crop. This is called **monoculture**. Monoculture is cheaper than the old system because machines can be used. To make such large fields farmers remove the hedges. Hedges are the habitats for many different kinds of animals and plants. Sometimes land is drained to make large fields, so wetland habitats and hedgerows disappear, along with all the animals and plants that live there.

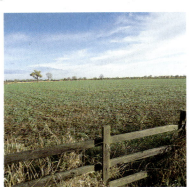

...by dumping waste. There are two kinds of waste. **Biodegradable** waste will rot away if left. Non-biodegradable wastes are made of metals and plastics which do not rot or decay. These cars will never rot away. They will always take up valuable space and look ugly.

What can we do to have less of an impact on our surroundings?
- Recycle glass, plastics and paper.
- Give grants to farmers to keep habitats with lots of wildlife.
- Make replaceable products, such as cars, of recyclable materials.
- Reclaim and renovate old houses and buildings instead of building new ones.
- Use alternatives to motor cars so that new roads are not necessary.
- Use biodegradable packages whenever possible.
- Build roads in tunnels and on bridges to avoid wildlife.

...Can you think of more?

Did you know? Some of the islands in the Pacific Ocean will disappear during the next 20 years due to sea level rises caused by global warming.

Water Pollution

All the water on our planet is recycled naturally in the **water cycle**. Water evaporates, then forms clouds and falls as rain. People may pollute the water cycle in three ways: by putting **sewage** into rivers, lakes and the sea, by using **fertilisers** on the fields and by dumping toxic chemicals in rivers and the sea. As the human population gets bigger, more and more waste is produced.

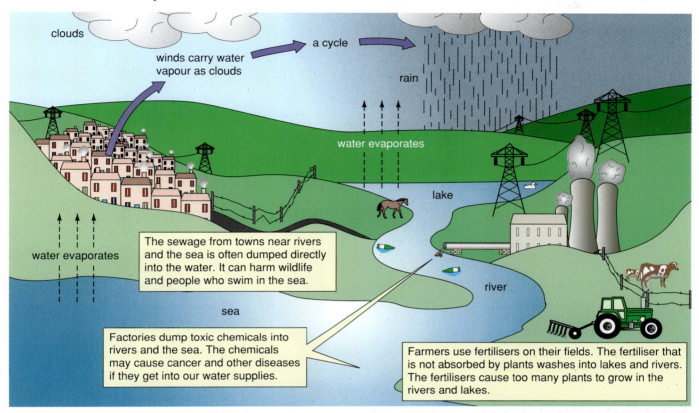

What can be done to solve the pollution problem?

Pollution of fresh water can be stopped. Farmers can use the correct amount of fertiliser so the waste is not washed away and factories can stop dumping toxic chemicals.

Often the solution involves money. Sewage wastes can be treated at a sewage treatment plant. Such a plant is expensive to build but very effective.

The sewage is screened to remove large solids.
↓
The sewage is then allowed to settle so smaller particles can be removed.
↓
The sewage is then filtered through special beds containing large numbers of microorganisms. The microorganisms get rid of all the waste by feeding on it.
↓
The fresh water is put back in the water cycle.

Summary

1. Humans destroy the habitats needed by animals and plants by:
    a building more houses, roads and factories
    b quarrying for rocks and minerals
    c some modern farming methods
    d dumping waste.
2. People pollute fresh water with sewage, fertiliser and toxic chemicals.
3. The increasing human population means that more waste is being produced.

Questions

1. Write down four ways in which humans reduce the amount of land available for animals and plants.
2. Name two biodegradable wastes and two non-biodegradable wastes.
3. Describe three ways in which people pollute the water cycle. What can be done to reduce the effects of each?

23 Pollution on a global scale

As the human population gets bigger and our standard of living gets better, we use more resources. Raw materials such as non-renewable energy resources are being used. More waste is being made. When the waste is not properly dealt with there is more pollution.

Acid rain

Non-renewable energy resources are fossil fuels such as coal and oil. When we burn them, two dangerous gases are produced: **sulphur dioxide** and **nitrogen dioxide**. Fossil fuels are burned in many factories and in power stations. The problem starts when the sulphur dioxide and nitrogen dioxide gases rise up into the atmosphere from the tall chimneys of the power station. The gases are turned into sulphuric acid and nitric acid. These acids fall onto the ground either in rain (**acid rain**), as fog, or as particles of acid.

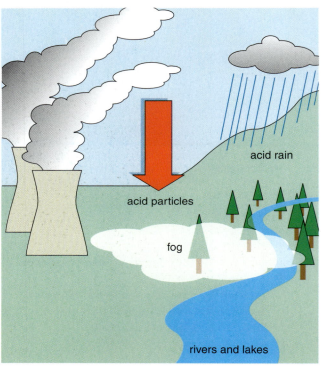

The acids have had most effect in Europe and America. Acidic rain causes fish to die in lakes and rivers: lots of trees in forests die back, and the soil in some places has become too acidic. Acidic soil interferes with normal plant growth.

The ozone layer

Ozone is a gas found naturally. When it is near the ground it can harm plants and irritate our lungs. When it is high up in the atmosphere it is a useful gas. It forms a thin layer around the world. The layer of ozone soaks up some of the dangerous ultra violet (UV) rays which would normally hit the surface of the Earth. A little UV light is good for us. It helps make vitamin D in our skin. Too much UV is dangerous. It causes skin cancer.

Scientists have discovered that the ozone layer is getting thinner in some parts of the world. If this thinning increases, more people could develop skin cancer.

What is making the ozone layer thinner?
The culprit is a gas called **CFC**. CFC gases are used in factories, in fridges and in aerosol cans. The CFC gases rise up into the atmosphere and destroy the ozone layer. The answer to the problem is for more countries to ban CFC gases.

When the Earth's population was smaller we could burn as much fossil fuel as we wanted. Waste gases such as carbon dioxide rose up into the air and disappeared into the atmosphere. Now we have a problem. Not only are we burning much more fossil fuel, we are also cutting down and burning large areas of forest. Burning on such a large scale releases carbon dioxide into the atmosphere. The effect is that the amount of carbon dioxide in the Earth's atmosphere is increasing.

The greenhouse effect

The Earth is so far away from the Sun that you would expect it to be colder than it is. In fact the carbon dioxide in our atmosphere helps to warm up the planet. It works a bit like a greenhouse. Carbon dioxide and methane gases make a greenhouse layer in the atmosphere around the planet. When the rays from the sun pass into our atmosphere they warm up the surface of the Earth. Heat bounces from the surface back into space, but the greenhouse layer reflects some of it back to Earth and the surface gets warmer. Unfortunately the greenhouse layer is getting too thick and too much heat stays near the surface. Scientists are worried that it may get too warm on our planet. Increased carbon dioxide in the atmosphere is warming up the planet.

How will global warming affect our lives?

The worst predictions are that the temperature of the Earth will rise by 4.5 °C during the next 40 years. Some of the ice caps would melt and the sea level would rise. Many animals and plants would have to live in different places.

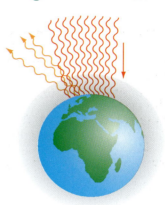

Summary

1. As the human population gets bigger more resources are used and more waste results in pollution.
2. When fossil fuels are burnt carbon dioxide, sulphur dioxide and nitrogen dioxide gases get into the atmosphere.
3. Carbon dioxide and methane cause global warming by the greenhouse effect.
4. Sulphur dioxide and nitrogen dioxide cause acid rain.
5. CFC gases are making the ozone layer thinner.

Questions

1. What is a fossil fuel? Give an example.
2. Why does burning fossil fuels cause air pollution?
3. What effect does acid rain have on wildlife?
4. What two effects can ultra violet light have on human skin?
5. What is making the ozone layer thinner?
6. Give two reasons why the amount of carbon dioxide in the atmosphere is increasing.
7. Describe how life in this country would change if global warming got worse.
8. How can we reduce global warming?

24 Variation

Animals and plants of the same type look like each other, but are never exactly the same.

Tallness or smallness, size of flower and hair colour are all **characteristics**. Many characteristics are passed from parents to their young.

There are many differences in characteristics between these beetles which were all found in the same wood. The characteristics were passed from parents to their young ones.
Some are brown, some are black, some have big spots, some have small spots. Some have red spots...but they all have six legs!

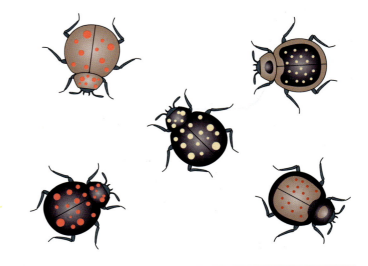

Differences between people

The differences in characteristics between members of the same species are called **variations**. You could list many variations between the people in the photograph below. When a difference is either one thing or the other (such as eye colour or gender) we call it **discontinuous variation**.

Other variations are not as clear. There are many differences in height. Some people are small, some are tall and there are many in between. We call this a range. When a variation is a range we call it **continuous variation**. Another example of continuous variation is weight.

How are characteristics passed from parents to their young?

If characteristics pass from parents to their young, they must pass in the eggs and sperm. How can so much information fit in such small things as eggs and sperm? The answer is that the information is controlled by genes. We have many genes. The genes are on our chromosomes. When eggs and sperms are made they each have a nucleus packed full of chromosomes. The chromosomes from mother and father are brought together when a sperm fertilises an egg. The fertilised egg divides and divides by mitosis until an animal or plant is made. The animal or plant is made of millions of cells. Each cell has a copy of the chromosomes and genes which came from the parents.

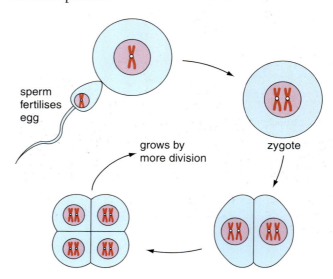

Information in the genes

Information about variation is carried by genes. Different genes control different characteristics. In the beetles, genes control the different colours and body markings. People have many different genes. We can tell that genes pass from parents to young when both parents and young have similar characteristics.

Mid-chin fissure is controlled by a gene which passes from parent to child. Also, some people have free ear lobes, others have ear lobes attached to their heads.

Genes and environment

Identical twins come from the same egg. They have the same genes and so you would expect twins to look exactly alike. These twins look slightly different. This is because their environment (surroundings) affects their characteristics.

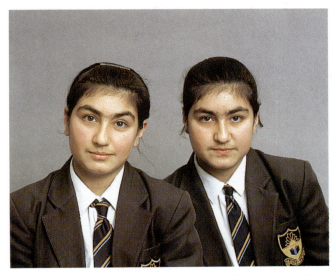

Differences between identical twins tell us that both the environment and the genes of living things control variation.

We can understand more about genes and the environment by studying bonsai trees. They are miniature versions of the trees we see around us. Gardeners produce bonsai trees by growing them in small containers. Their roots are restricted and their genes for tallness do not show through. The genes are not expressed.

How can this be an advantage for a tree? The answer is that it allows the tree to adapt to the conditions it finds itself in. If the seeds land and grow on the side of a mountain, where the environment is windy, the tree does not grow to its full height and is more able to cope with the windy conditions.

Summary

1. Animals and plants look like their parents because of information passed to them in genes.
2. Differences between living things are called variations.
3. Different genes control different characteristics.
4. Variations are due to the different genes and the effects of the surroundings.

Questions

1. Describe three characteristics of human beings that are controlled by genes.
2. How are characteristics passed from one cell to another when they divide?
3. Why do identical twins sometimes look different?

25 Genes and chromosomes

The differences, or variations, between individual animals and plants are passed from parents to their young. The variations are controlled by **genes**. The genes are carried on **chromosomes**. Chromosomes are inside the nucleus of every cell in the body.

LOOKING AT HUMAN CHROMOSOMES

To see human chromosomes we must take a dividing cell from the human body. The cell is treated in a special way so the chromosomes are easily seen. A photograph is taken of the jumbled up chromosomes, then the chromosomes are put in order. We can see that they are in pairs. One from each pair came from the person's father and one from the person's mother. Each pair is given a number. The picture of human chromosomes is called a **karyotype**.

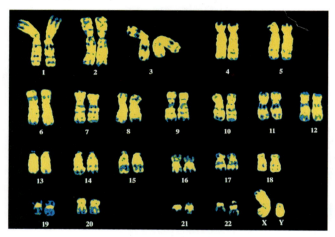

Using karyotypes

Karyotypes can be used to diagnose certain diseases. Some people have Down's syndrome. They have a face which is easy to recognise, they often find it difficult to learn and can have physical problems, such as heart disease.

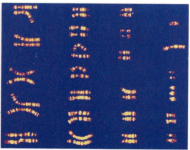

This person has Down's syndrome. The karyotype shows one extra chromosome. Can you spot it?

HOW IS THE SEX OF A BABY DECIDED?

Many couples would like to know if the baby they are expecting will be a boy or a girl. What are the chances of a boy or a girl? To answer this question look closely at a karyotype. You will see that chromosome pair 23 is very different from the others. This is the pair that decides what sex a baby will be. In a man, one of the chromosomes in pair 23 has a piece missing. We call this the **Y chromosome**. The other in the pair looks like a normal chromosome. We call this the **X chromosome**. A man has an XY chromosome pair and a woman has an XX chromosome pair as well as 22 other pairs.

When the eggs and sperm are made by meiosis, each chromosome pair separates. One from each pair will end up in each egg and one from each pair in each sperm.

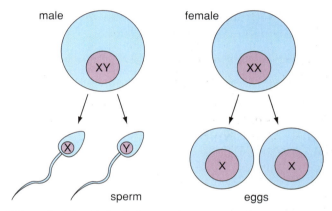

What decides if the baby is a boy or a girl? It depends on which sperm fertilises each egg. The possibilities are shown in the diagram below.

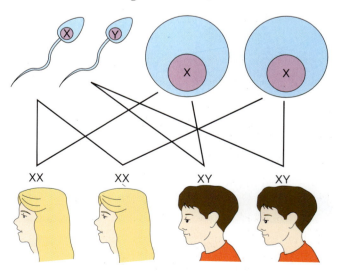

You will see that there is an equal, 50%, chance of either a boy or a girl every time a sperm fertilises an egg.

Genes control our characteristics

Every characteristic we have is controlled by a gene: eye colour, hair type. By studying certain diseases we understand how genes are passed from one generation to the next. Genes are on pairs of chromosomes.

Each gene can have more than one form. For example a gene controls whether we can roll our tongue. If you inherit the other form of the gene, you can't roll your tongue. Each form of the gene is called an **allele**.

Cystic fibrosis

Cystic fibrosis is a common disease. People who suffer from it have problems with their lungs and pancreas. The tubes in the lungs make too much sticky mucus. The lungs fill up with the mucus, making it difficult to breathe. A person without the disease makes just enough mucus.

Sally inherited the cystic fibrosis from her parents. Her parents did not know they were carriers of the disease, because they had both forms of the gene. In the diagram N represents the normal allele (form) of the gene. It is stronger (**dominant**) to the allele which causes the disease, which is shown by **n** (**n** is **recessive** to N). When N and **n** are together on a pair of chromosomes N dominates **n** and the effects of **n** do not show up.

Both Sally's parents are normal.

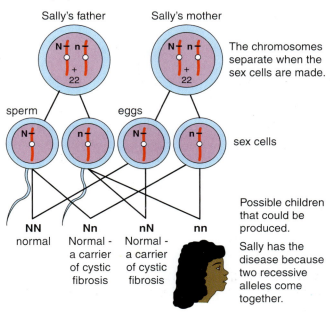

Huntingdon's chorea

This disease is a very rare disorder of the nervous system. People do not begin to suffer from it until later in their lives, when they find it difficult to co-ordinate their movements. Eventually their brain deteriorates and they die. **Huntington's chorea** is caused by the dominant form (allele) of a gene. Most people have two recessive forms of the gene for Huntingdon's chorea and do not suffer from the disease.

Mutations

Sometimes new forms of genes suddenly appear. They are called **mutations**. Mutations happen naturally when a gene changes. Mutations are more likely to happen when cells are exposed to radiation such as ultra violet light, X-rays or radiation from radioactive substances. The more radiation a cell has, the more chance there is of a mutation occurring. Mutations happen because the radiation interferes with the DNA that genes and chromosomes are made of.

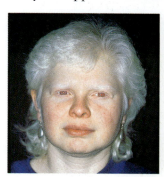

A mutation of the gene causing normal skin colour results in no skin colour at all.

Summary

1. Chromosomes are in pairs.
2. The sex of a baby is decided by special chromosomes. A man has XY sex-deciding chromosomes and a woman has XX sex-deciding chromosomes.
3. Cystic fibrosis and Huntington's chorea are inherited diseases.
4. Mutations are the result of changes to genes. They occur naturally. The chance of a mutation happening can be increased by exposing cells to radiation.

Questions

1. How many chromosomes would a person with Down's syndrome have?
2. Draw a diagram to show why there is always an equal chance of having a boy or a girl baby.
3. What are the symptoms of cystic fibrosis?
4. What is likely to increase the chances of a mutation?

26 Asexual and sexual reproduction

Imagine a group of people with the same characteristics…

They have the same genes and so they are exactly alike. Is this a nightmare or could it really happen? The answer is that we may soon have the technology to make exact copies of people. In 1997 scientists told us that exact copies or **clones** of sheep and monkeys had been made.

How scientists make clones

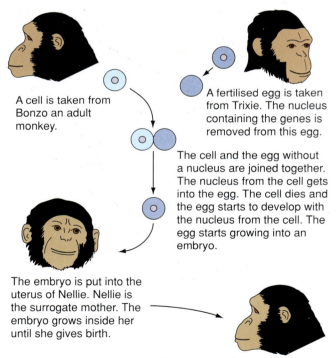

A cell is taken from Bonzo an adult monkey.

A fertilised egg is taken from Trixie. The nucleus containing the genes is removed from this egg.

The cell and the egg without a nucleus are joined together. The nucleus from the cell gets into the egg. The cell dies and the egg starts to develop with the nucleus from the cell. The egg starts growing into an embryo.

The embryo is put into the uterus of Nellie. Nellie is the surrogate mother. The embryo grows inside her until she gives birth.

The baby monkey has the same genes as Bonzo. He is identical to Bonzo. He is a clone of Bonzo.

Clones in nature

Making clones is an example of asexual reproduction. Only one individual is needed to make young ones.

Only a few animals can reproduce like this. *Hydra* is a small jellyfish which lives in ponds and lakes. It makes buds. The buds grow and then split off the parent to live by themselves. When the bud was growing the cells divided by mitosis. All the cells have the same genes and so the young are identical.

Many plants reproduce asexually. Spider and strawberry plants put out runners. The runners grow roots and soon live as separate plants. The cells in the new plant are identical to the parent.

Taking cuttings

You can easily make clones by taking cuttings. The new plants will be identical to the parent.

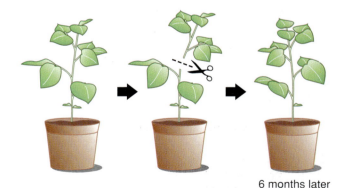

6 months later

Advantages of asexual reproduction

Asexual reproduction is useful for farmers and gardeners. When a plant is especially useful, the farmer can make many more individuals just like it.

Sexual reproduction

Sexual reproduction always involves two cells joining together. One is a cell from the male and the other is a cell from the female. These special cells have half the chromosomes that a normal body cell has. This is because they were made by meiosis. The cells are called **gametes**. Once the cells have joined by fertilisation, the new cell has the normal number of chromosomes. This cell divides and forms the new individual.

Human sexual reproduction

The sperm and eggs are gametes. They are made by meiosis. All the cells in our bodies have 46 chromosomes, so gametes have 23. When the gametes join in fertilisation the fertilised egg has 46 chromosomes. Half the chromosomes are from the father and half from the mother. This makes sure that the new person will be different from both mother and father. In this way sexual reproduction makes sure that there is variation in the human population.

The life cycle of humans

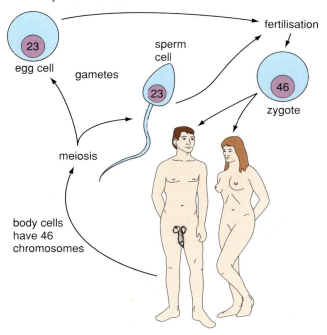

Flowering plant sexual reproduction

The gametes are inside the pollen and ovary. They have half the number of chromosomes. When pollen sticks to the stigma a tube grows to the ovary. When the tube reaches the ovary a male gamete from the pollen joins with a female gamete inside the ovary. The result is a **zygote**. It has the same number of chromosomes as the adult plant. The zygote has genes from both the male and the female. The new plant growing from a zygote has characteristics from both male and female. Plants produced by sexual reproduction have more variation than plants made by asexual reproduction.

The life cycle of a buttercup

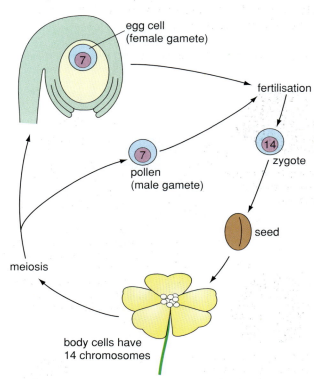

Summary

1. There are two kinds of reproduction: asexual and sexual.
2. In asexual reproduction only one individual is needed to make new ones. The new ones have the same genes as the parent. They are identical.
3. In sexual reproduction gametes are produced. They have half the chromosomes of an ordinary cell.
4. In sexual reproduction the gametes join. The new ones produced by sexual reproduction have a mixture of genetic information from the two parents.
5. Sexual reproduction produces more variation than asexual reproduction.

Questions

1. What is a clone?
2. Give three examples of organisms that can reproduce asexually.
3. In what way are gametes different from ordinary body cells?
4. How does sexual reproduction produce variation?

27 Human reproduction

THE REPRODUCTIVE ORGANS

When a human baby is born it is made of millions of cells. Its characteristics are a result of its genes. The baby is a combination of characteristics from its parents. The genes from the father and the mother get together when an egg is fertilised. The story starts when a woman's eggs are made. An egg is normally made every month by her *ovaries*. Usually the egg is released (**ovulation**) about 14 days after her period. The egg passes into the fallopian tube. It is moved along the tube by tiny hairs. Normally the egg is not used. It dies and disintegrates.

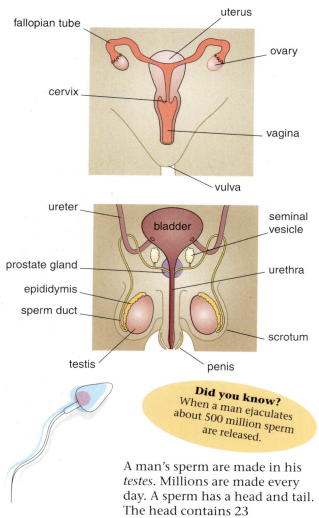

Did you know? When a man ejaculates about 500 million sperm are released.

A man's sperm are made in his *testes*. Millions are made every day. A sperm has a head and tail. The head contains 23 chromosomes. The tail uses energy to help the sperm swim. If they are not used they disintegrate. The testicles are outside the body because sperm need to be just a little bit cooler than body temperature. The glands just underneath the bladder make the *semen*. Semen contains food for the sperm. When a man's sperm are released they swim in semen.

FERTILISATION AND CONCEPTION

When a man and a woman make love the man ejaculates inside the woman. His semen, which contains his sperm, comes out into the woman's vagina near the cervix. The sperm swim into the uterus and fallopian tubes. If the woman has ovulated, there will be an egg in the fallopian tube. The egg will be surrounded by sperm. Only one sperm can fertilise an egg. The other sperms die. The nucleus in the sperm gets into the egg and joins with the nucleus in the egg. The egg now has 46 chromosomes. It is called a *zygote* and starts to divide.

The dividing cells travel along the fallopian tube and into the **uterus**. The cells are now an *embryo*. The embryo settles in the wall of the uterus.

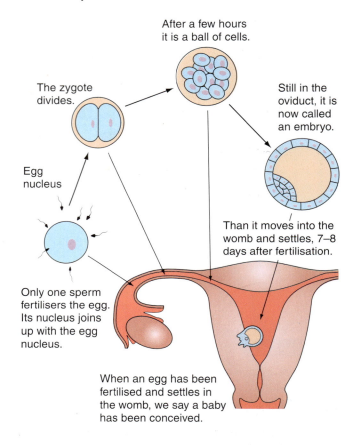

Life in the uterus

The baby develops inside the uterus. It takes about 36 weeks to grow from a single fertilised egg cell into a baby with a mass of 3.2 kg.

Once the embryo attaches to the uterus wall a *placenta* develops. The job of the placenta is to supply the embryo with food and oxygen and to remove waste. In the placenta the blood of the embryo and the mother are separated by a very thin barrier of cells. They are so close that materials can pass from one to the other by diffusion. Oxygen and food move from the mother's blood into the embryo's blood. Waste moves in the opposite direction.
A bag or *amniotic sac* grows. This is full of liquid or amniotic fluid. The fluid surrounds the embryo and protects it against infections and the movement of the mother. As the embryo gets bigger we call it a *foetus*.

Birth

When a mother starts giving birth we say she is in **labour**. The muscles in her uterus start to move and contract. At first the contractions come every 20 minutes or so. Soon they come every two or three minutes. At the same time the uterus contracts, the cervix is relaxing. We say the cervix is dilating. Eventually the cervix will relax so much that the baby's head can pass through it. The uterus is a strong muscle. Its contractions push the baby's head through the cervix and vagina and then the rest of the baby is born. Soon after the placenta is born. It is called the **afterbirth**.

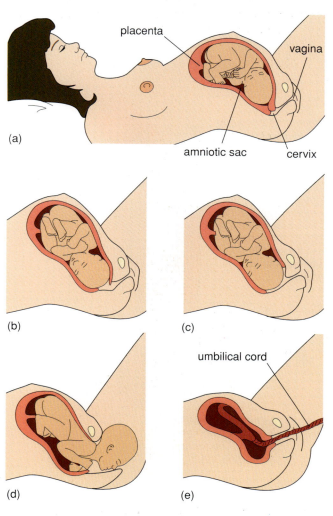

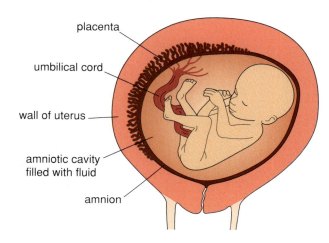

Summary

1. The male sex organs are the testes and the female sex organs are the ovaries. They produce the gametes.
2. Fertilisation happens in the fallopian tube. Only one sperm fertilises an egg.
3. The embryo develops from the fertilised egg. It grows in the wall of the uterus and develops along with a placenta and amniotic sac.
4. The embryo grows into a foetus. After 36 weeks the foetus is born.

Questions

1. Where are human eggs made?
2. Why are the testicles outside the man's body?
3. Where in the body is an egg fertilised?
4. How does an embryo gets its food and oxygen?
5. During the birth of a baby, what are contractions?
6. What is the afterbirth?

28 Controlling reproduction

A woman has a period every month. A period is the result of not becoming pregnant – it's a 'clean out' ready for the next ovulation and potential embryo. A few days after the end of one period the uterus starts getting a thicker lining. The lining gets thicker right up until the next period. If an egg is fertilised the lining stays thick, an embryo sticks to it and grows. If no egg is fertilised the lining breaks down and passes out of the body. This is the period.

Half way between two periods an egg is made. This is **ovulation**.

These monthly changes are called the **menstrual cycle**. The menstrual cycle is controlled by hormones made in the pituitary gland and the ovaries.

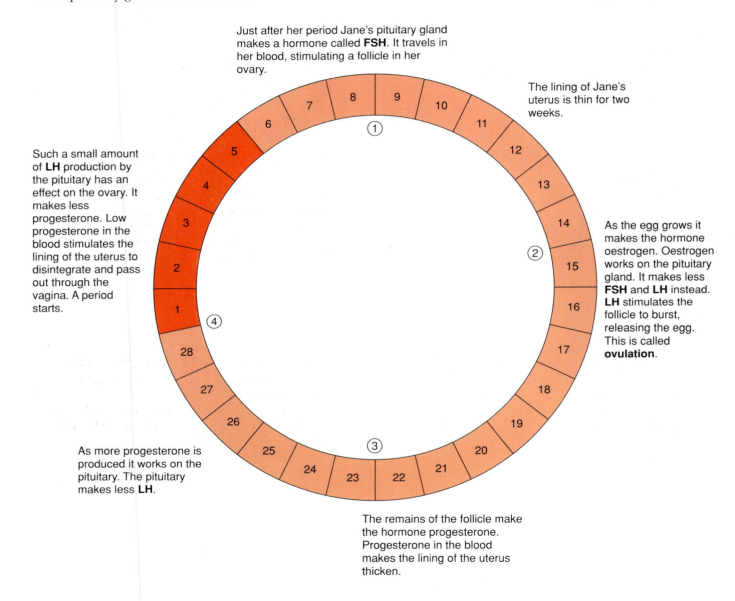

Just after her period Jane's pituitary gland makes a hormone called **FSH**. It travels in her blood, stimulating a follicle in her ovary.

The lining of Jane's uterus is thin for two weeks.

Such a small amount of **LH** production by the pituitary has an effect on the ovary. It makes less progesterone. Low progesterone in the blood stimulates the lining of the uterus to disintegrate and pass out through the vagina. A period starts.

As the egg grows it makes the hormone oestrogen. Oestrogen works on the pituitary gland. It makes less **FSH** and **LH** instead. **LH** stimulates the follicle to burst, releasing the egg. This is called **ovulation**.

As more progesterone is produced it works on the pituitary. The pituitary makes less **LH**.

The remains of the follicle make the hormone progesterone. Progesterone in the blood makes the lining of the uterus thicken.

STOPPING PREGNANCY

Doctors prescribe contraceptive pills containing oestrogen and progesterone when people wish to have sex and yet avoid getting pregnant. The high levels of these hormones in the blood stop production of FSH by the pituitary. With no FSH, ovulation does not happen. But there can be side effects. For instance, a woman on the pill may become slightly overweight or have a slightly higher risk of developing a thrombosis.

FERTILITY TREATMENT

Some women have difficulty getting pregnant. There are many possible reasons why. There could be something wrong with her partner's sperm, her fallopian tubes could be blocked or her hormone levels may be low. Whatever the reason, women can be treated with hormones to produce eggs. Usually the hormones used are FSH and LH. A doctor will give the woman injections of the hormones at the beginning of the menstrual cycle. Often the ovary produces a lot of eggs. The doctor removes the eggs with a hollow needle and then uses them for **in vitro fertilisation**. In vitro means 'in glass'. The egg and sperm are put into a glass dish where fertilisation takes place.

In vitro fertilisation

The eggs are put in a fluid which is like the fluid inside the fallopian tubes.

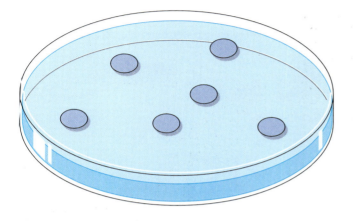

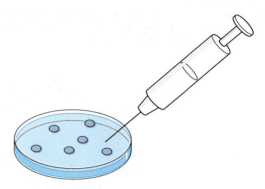

Healthy sperm from the woman's partner are added. The doctor looks to see if the eggs are fertilised. If they are, they are transferred into the woman's uterus where they will grow until they are born.

The first baby using **in vitro** fertilisation was in Great Britain in 1978. The first baby born using in vitro techniques was called a 'test-tube baby' – in fact a test-tube was not used.

SUMMARY

1. A woman's periods are controlled by hormones produced by the pituitary gland and the sex organs.
2. The contraceptive pill contains hormones.
3. Women who have problems conceiving (getting pregnant) can have fertility treatment.

QUESTIONS

1. Name the two hormones made by the ovaries.
2. How does the contraceptive pill stop people getting pregnant?
3. Some people have *in vitro* treatment to help them conceive a child. In this treatment, where does fertilisation take place?

29 Evolution

The history of our planet goes back five billion years. We will never really know what the Earth was like all those years ago, so trying to find out is a bit like detective work. The clues in our search for the history of life on Earth are fossils. From fossils we learn that animals and plants have changed since life first developed on Earth.

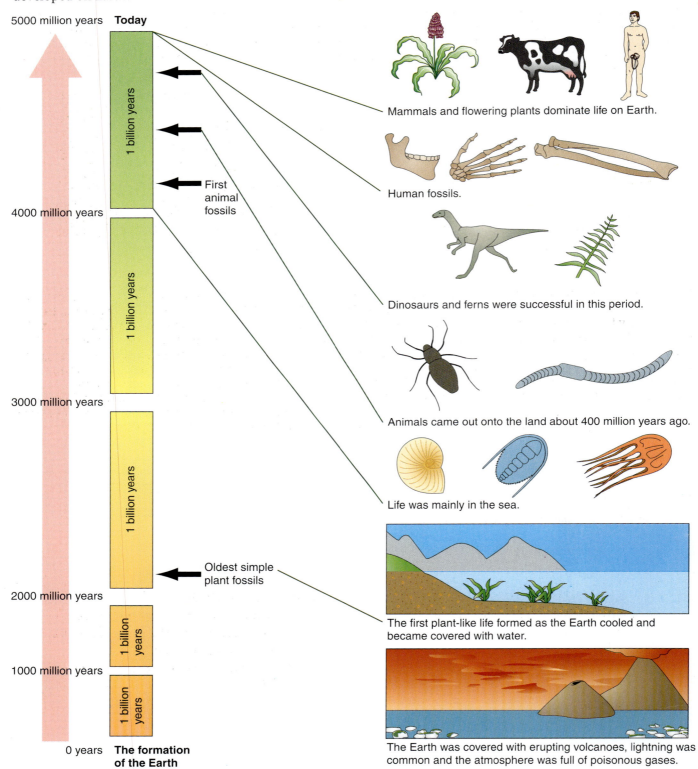

How are fossils formed

When living things die they usually decay until nothing is left. Fossils form from the hard parts of living things or when decay does not happen properly. This is usually because conditions are not right for decay. Fossils form in special conditions. When the animal or plant dies it falls in mud or silt. The mud or silt covers the body and the molecules of the body are slowly replaced by minerals as they work their way into the body. Eventually all the molecules are replaced and the body is stone. Millions of years later we find the fossil when we break open sedimentary rocks.

Sometimes an animal or plant dies and makes a mould in the soft rock. The creature decays until nothing is left, but the rock goes hard leaving the mould. Sometimes we find moulds, and sometimes the mould fills with rock making a cast. Animals also leave footprints in rocks making a mould and cast. Other animals and plants have been preserved in a substance which stops them from decaying. Many insects have been found in amber, a hard resin which forms from the soft sap leaking from a tree.

mould of ammonite fossil

fossil of Archaeopteryx

How are fossils used?

Fossils are made in sedimentary rocks. These rocks are made in layers so we can tell how old a fossil is from the layer it was found in. The deeper the layer, the older the fossil. We can also check the age of a fossil by measuring the radioactivity in the rock. Scientists use fossil evidence to reconstruct the past. One of the most important things the scientific detectives have discovered is that many of the animals and plants living on Earth have died out and become extinct. New animals and plants take over the land the others lived on. Many of the fossils we find suggest that not all of the old types of living things became extinct. Some gradually changed to suit their surroundings. This change is called **evolution**. The animals and plants we know today have evolved from the older types.

The fossil of Archaeopteryx is 150 million years old. Notice it has teeth and a long bony tail, just like a dinosaur. It also has feathers and a beak. Scientists think this is evidence for evolution. The small dinosaurs evolved into birds by losing their tails, getting more feathers and losing their teeth. It probably took millions of years.

Summary

1. Fossils are the remains of animals and plants from many years ago.
2. Fossils are formed in sedimentary rock.
3. Fossils are formed from the hard parts of living things which do not decay and from the parts which do not decay properly.
4. Fossils are made when minerals replace the molecules of the living thing or when a mould and cast is formed.
5. We use fossil evidence to support the theory of evolution.

Questions

1. How old is the Earth?
2. When did animals first appear on the Earth?
3. Describe three ways in which a fossil is formed.
4. Explain the word *evolution*.
5. Why is the fossil of *Archaeopteryx* evidence for evolution?

30 Artificial and natural selection

Many of the animals and plants we know today have been produced by artificial selection. Artificial selection takes many years. People choose animals and plants with the characteristics they want and breed them to keep the characteristics.

Certain characteristics in wild dogs are not required in domestic dogs.

By choosing dogs with the characteristics they liked and then mating them together people have produced the many breeds of dogs.

By choosing plants with large grains and then mating them together, modern varieties of wheat have been produced. The large grains are easily harvested.

ARTIFICIAL SELECTION IS USED TO INCREASE YIELDS

The amount of milk a cow produces is its *yield*. Cows are producing more and more milk. The farmer picks the cows which produce the most milk. She mates them with a bull which has genes for high milk production. She knows the calves will grow into cows which produce even more milk. Through years of artificial selection, cows are now producing more and more milk.

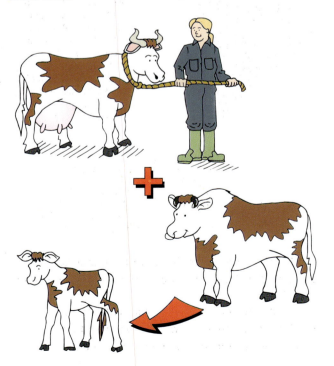

DISADVANTAGES OF ARTIFICIAL SELECTION

Often animals and plants that are related are used in **artificial selection**. This is because they share the characteristic the breeder wants. The danger is that as well as the gene the breeder wants being passed on, harmful genes may be passed on as well.

This Shar Pei dog cannot run properly.

Natural selection

Evolution means the gradual development of living things as time passes. The first person to explain how this happens was Charles Darwin. He called his theory **natural selection**.

- Most living things produce far more young than they need. There are never too many of any one kind because they compete for space and food. They are killed by disease and predators.

- Life is a struggle for survival. Many living things die before they pass on their genes.

- Because there is so much variation, some individuals will be better at surviving. They will pass on their genes before they die.

- Eventually the entire population of the species will be adapted to their surroundings. The species has changed.

Woodpecker finch

Warbler finch

Vegetarian tree finch

Ground finch

Galápagos finches adapted to their surroundings, showing adaptive radiation. Each beak is adapted to a different food source

Summary

1. We use artificial selection to produce new varieties of living things by choosing the characteristic we want and then breeding more.
2. Artificial selection can be called selective breeding. It can be used to produce plants and animals for food with increased yields.
3. Charles Darwin tried to explain evolution using the theory of natural selection.

The peppered moth

Charles Darwin did not live long enough to see his ideas tested. He died in 1882. In Britain in the 1950s, scientists studied the peppered moth.

By the 1960s there were more black moths than light ones. Evolution by natural selection had changed the moth.

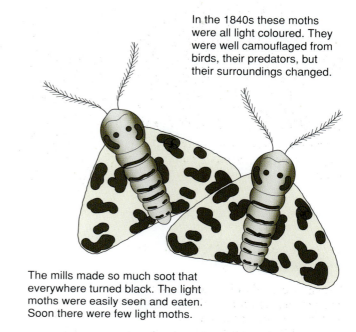

In the 1840s these moths were all light coloured. They were well camouflaged from birds, their predators, but their surroundings changed.

The mills made so much soot that everywhere turned black. The light moths were easily seen and eaten. Soon there were few light moths.

Some black moths appeared. Before the soot they were easily seen and eaten. Now they did not show up. They were adapted to their surroundings. They passed on their genes. Soon there were more black moths than light ones.

Did you know?
If beetle populations were not controlled by predators and disease, within 82 weeks there would be so many that they would weigh as much as the entire Earth.

Questions

1. Describe three examples of artificial selection.
2. How is artificial selection used to increase yields for farmers?
3. What does the word evolution mean?
4. How did Charles Darwin explain evolution?
5. Describe a modern example of evolution.

Practice questions – Life processes

1 a This diagram is of a plant cell.

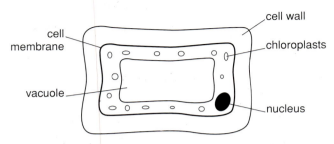

  i   Which structure in the cell is green?
  ii   Which part of the cell contains genes?
  iii Which structures are also found in animal cells?
  iv   Where do most of the chemical reactions take place in the cell?

  b Copy and complete the sentences about cell division using the words in the list below. A word may be used more than once.

  nucleus characteristics chromosomes pairs

  The information that controls the .... of a living thing is carried in the .... of each of its cells.

  When cells divide the information inside the nucleus is carried on ....

  When body cells divide the chromosomes are normally found in ....

2 a Copy this diagram of the digestive system and label it by putting the letter in the correct place.

  A: an organ which stores glucose as glycogen.
  B: the part of the system which produces hydrochloric acid.
  C: a place where bile is stored.
  D: the part where food is absorbed into the blood.

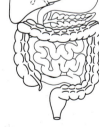

  b Copy and complete the table containing information about the components of a balanced diet.

Substance	Source	When digested is broken down into....
carbohydrate		glucose
	meat	
fat		

3 The diagram shows human blood under the microscope.

  a Which of the parts transports hormones?
  b Which is a white blood cell? Describe how white blood cells defend the body against disease.
  c The cells labelled X contain oxyhaemoglobin. Where in the body would you expect to find these cells?

4 a Copy and complete this equation for respiration.

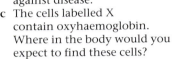

  glucose sugar + ... → .... + H$_2$O + energy

  b Give two uses for the energy released during respiration.
  c What is the meaning of the following words: thorax, trachea, bronchioles, alveoli?

5 a Name a part of the body where each of the following stimuli is sensed.
     i) temperature ii) sound iii) pressure iv) chemicals
     v) light

  b Copy and complete the following descriptions of parts of the eye.

     A: Light is focused by the c......
     B: Nerve messages are carried to the brain by the o......
     C: The light stimulus is sensed by the r......
     D: The ring of muscle which controls how much light enters the eye is called the i.....

  c Copy the diagram and label it with the letters A–D.

6 Study the diagrams below. One is a section through the skin of a person in very hot surroundings, the other is a section through the skin of the same person in very cold surroundings.

  a What would be the temperature inside of the body in each situation?
  b Which diagram is of the skin in hot surroundings?
  c Describe two features of this skin which helps the body keep its internal conditions stable.

6 *continued*
   d What is different about the skin in cold surroundings?
   e Explain why people drink more water in hot weather.

7 a Give two reasons why plants have roots.
   b The diagram is of a section through a plant leaf.

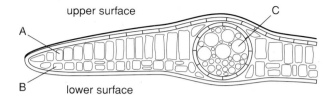

   i   Which cells specialise in photosynthesis?
   ii   Give two features of the cells which help them to photosynthesise.
   iii Name a structure which lets gases move in and out of the leaf.
   c Give two functions of plant stems.

8 a Copy and complete the following paragraph using the words from the list below.

   vapour carbon dioxide diffuses evaporates stomata

Plants lose water .... through the surfaces of their leaves. This loss of water is called transpiration. Transpiration happens when water .... through the surface of the leaf. Most of the water evaporates through tiny holes called ......
   Plants need stomata to get .... gas for photosynthesis. The gas .... into the leaf through the stomata from the atmosphere.

   b A student measured how much water two plants lost during a warm day. She plotted the results on a graph.

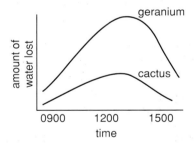

Which plant lost most water? Explain why one plant lost more water than the other.

9 a Copy and complete the table showing the difference between asexual and sexual reproduction.

	Asexual	Sexual
fertilisation		sperm and eggs join
type of young	identical to parents	
genetic material		mixture from the two parents

   b The diagram below is of an animal cell. Where are the genes situated?
   c Give two examples of characteristics controlled by genes.
   d Give an example of a disease caused by an inherited gene.

10 The diagram is of the fossil *Archaeopteryx*.
   a Explain how this fossil was formed.
   b Give two methods scientists use to give a date to a fossil.
   c The fossil has characteristics of two groups of animals: dinosaurs and birds. How does this fossil support the theory of evolution?

11 Carbon dioxide in the atmosphere produces the greenhouse effect.
   a What is the greenhouse effect?
   b How is the climate of a country such as Great Britain changed by the greenhouse effect?
   c Describe how the distribution of animals and plants may change as a result of the greenhouse effect.
   d How does cutting down and burning trees contribute to the greenhouse effect?

12 a Slugs eat leaves and frogs eat slugs.
      i   Draw a food chain from this information.
      ii Which organism is a secondary consumer?
   b Use the following information to construct a pyramid of number and a pyramid of biomass.

	Number	Biomass/g
frogs	1	150
slugs	250	10 000
leaves	25 000	300 000

13 Copy and complete the diagram of human circulation.
   a Label an artery.
   b Label a vein.
   c Label the left ventricle.
   d In which side of the heart does the blood contain oxyhaemoglobin?
   e Explain why the heart is sometimes described as two separate pumps.

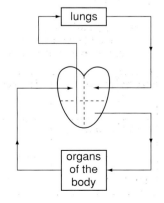

Answers to practice questions

Answers to the questions on pp.68–69

1. **a**
   i) chloroplast
   ii) nucleus
   iii) membrane, nucleus, cytoplasm
   iv) cytoplasm
   b in correct order: characteristics, nucleus, chromosomes, pairs

2. **a** A: liver
   B: stomach
   C: gall bladder
   D: small intestine
   b potatoes — protein — amino acids
   butter, oil — fatty acids and glycerol

3. **a** A
   b B; They ingest microbes and produce antibodies.
   c In blood vessels supplying tissues.

4. **a** glucose + oxygen → CO_2 + H_2O + energy
   b movement: making new molecules
   c thorax: chest
   trachea: windpipe
   bronchioles: thin tubes leading to the alveoli
   alveoli: air sacs

5. **a**
   i) temperature: skin
   ii) sound: ear
   iii) pressure: skin
   iv) chemicals: nose
   v) light: eye
   b A: cornea
   B: optic nerve
   C: retina
   D: iris
   c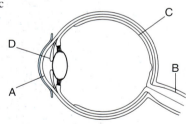

6. **a** 37 °C
   b A
   c large, dilated blood vessels, sweating
   d thin, blood vessels, no sweating
   e replace water lost as sweat

7. **a** support, absorption of water
   b i A
   ii near the surface of the leaf (light); contain chloroplast
   iii stomata
   c support, transport of water

8. **a** in order: vapour, evaporates, stomata, carbon dioxide, diffuses
   b geranium. Cactus has thick waxy layer on surface to stop evaporation.

9. **a**

	Asexual	Sexual
fertilisation	*no sperm and eggs*	sperm and eggs join
type of young	identical to parents	*different from parents*
genetic material	*same as parents*	mixture from the two parents

   b nucleus
   c examples: hair colour, eye colour
   d for example, cystic fibrosis

10. **a** The bird died and decayed. Organic material replaced by inorganic material, and mould or cast formed.
    b By dating the rock it was found in. Radioactive methods.
    c It was possible that birds evolved from dinosaur types.

11. **a** Carbon dioxide layer reflects heat back to the Earth.
    b Temperatures rise
    c Animals and plants will live in different places.
    d Releases carbon dioxide into the atmosphere.

12. **a** i leaf → slug → frog
    ii frog
    b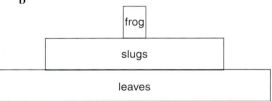

13. **a** see diagram
    b see diagram
    c see diagram
    d left
    e The left side pumps blood around the body, the right side pumps blood to the lungs.

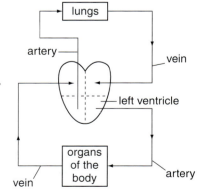

Materials and their properties

1 Everyday materials

The party scene shows common objects made from different types of materials.

Some objects are made from naturally occurring materials which are used as they are found or processed in some way. For instance, the cotton in the jeans is processed more than the wood used in furniture.

Other objects are made from synthetic or manufactured materials, for example, the plastic cutlery.

Synthetic materials are made from raw materials by changing them chemically. This is done by heating them together or reacting them with other substances.

Make lists of the naturally occurring materials and the synthetic materials shown in the picture.

Read the information below to check your lists.

Did you know?
Glass was first made thousands of years ago. Glass beads and charms have been found in Egyptian tombs dating back to 7000 BC. By 1500 BC they had made blue, green and purple glass by adding metals such as copper, chromium and manganese to molten glass.

Materials from naturally occurring substances

Non-living sources
Building materials from rocks, such as slate, marble, stone, gravel.
Metals from ores, for example, iron, copper.

Living sources
Wood from trees for buildings and furniture and for making paper and cardboard.
Canvas and rope from plants, for example, flax, sisal.
Silk, wool and cotton fibres for clothing from silk worms, sheep and cotton plants.
Rubber from the latex of rubber trees.
Leather from animal skins.

Synthetic or manufactured materials

Ceramics from clay, sand and other minerals, for example, china, concrete, bricks, tiles.

Plastics from crude oil and other substances, for example, poly(ethene), polystyrene, formica.

Glass from sand, limestone and other minerals, for example, soft soda glass, glass fibres, Pyrex glass, lead crystal.

Alloys from mixtures of metals and other substances, for example, steel, brass, bronze.

Synthetic fibres from crude oil and other substances, for example, nylon, Terylene, polyester.

Composite materials made from two or more materials, such as plastic reinforced with glass fibre for canoes, baths and plastic reinforced with carbon fibres for tennis rackets.

MATERIALS IN EVERYDAY USE

How a material is used depends on its properties. The properties of a material describe how it behaves and what it is like. The pictures below show uses of the main groups of materials and their properties.

Glass
transparent, brittle, unreactive, high melting point, non-conductor of heat and electricity.

Metals and alloys
usually hard, strong, dense, malleable, ductile and have a high melting point, conduct heat and electricity

Plastics
flexible, low density, moulded when warm, many melt easily and some burn on heating, good insulator of heat and electricity

Ceramics
brittle, hard, high melting point, unreactive, non-conductors of heat and electricity

Fibres
flexible, low density, may burn on heating, long strands

Composites
have the properties of the materials making them

MEANINGS OF THE WORDS USED TO DESCRIBE MATERIALS

Property	Meaning
Transparent	Clear, can see through it, for example, glass, some plastics
Strong	Resists the effect of forces, for example, steel
Brittle	Hard but breaks easily, for example, glass, ceramics
Dense	A large mass compared with its volume, for example, lead
Flexible	Can be bent or twisted without breaking, for example, some plastics and fibres
Malleable	Can be hammered into shape, for example, copper
Ductile	Can be drawn out into wires, for example, copper
Conductor of heat (or electricity)	Lets heat (or electricity) pass through it easily, for example, copper
Non-conductor (insulator) of heat (or electricity)	Difficult for heat (or electricity) to pass through it, for example, P.V.C.

SUMMARY

1. Some materials are made from naturally occurring substances from living or non-living sources, such as metals, cotton, wood, wool. Synthetic materials are made by heating raw materials or reacting them with other substances, e.g. plastics.
2. The use made of a material depends on its properties.

QUESTIONS

1. Name the raw materials used to manufacture the following: bricks, nylon, glass, pottery, paper.
2. Give the properties of the following materials which make them suitable for the use given:
   a glass in windows
   b plastic covering around copper electrical wires
   c wooden or plastic handle on a saucepan
   d plastic window frame
   e expanded polystyrene packaging
   f steel girders
   g wool jumper.
3. Do you think nylon or cotton thread is stronger? Plan an experiment to test your idea. Remember to make it a fair test. What results do you expect from the experiment?

2 Solids, liquids and gases

In the picture the drinks on the tray all contain some water.

The glasses of mineral water and juice contain liquid water and solid water or ice. The cups of hot coffee and tea contain liquid water with gaseous water or steam coming out of the top.

The water is present in three different physical states. It exists as a **solid**, **liquid** and **gas**. These different physical states of a substance are known as the *states of matter*.

> **Did you know?**
> Flat fish that live in the Arctic make antifreeze to stop their bodies from freezing solid. The genes for making the antifreeze are put into strawberry plants to help them resist frost.

How are solids, liquids and gases different?

Read about gases, liquids and solids below, and answer the questions.

Work out the differences between solids, liquids and gases. Compare your answers with the table on the next page.

Solids

Think about a 50 pence coin.
Does it have a certain shape?
Does it have a certain volume?
Is it hard?
Does the metal flow?

Can the solid coin easily be compressed?

Liquids

Tip a bottle of lemonade into an empty glass.
Does the liquid have a fixed shape?
Does its volume change?
Does it have any lumps?
Is the lemonade hard?
Does the lemonade flow?

Can a balloon of water be easily compressed to make it smaller?

Gases

A bad egg gives off a smelly gas.
What do you notice on entering the room containing the bad egg?
At first the gas was in the egg. Where is it once the top has been taken off?
Can you feel the gas?
Does it have a fixed shape or volume?

Can a balloon of air be squashed or compressed to make it smaller?

DIFFERENCES BETWEEN SOLIDS, LIQUIDS AND GASES

	Solids	Liquids	Gases
Volume	Fixed at a certain temperature and pressure.	Fixed at a certain temperature and pressure.	Not fixed. It spreads out and fills the container.
Shape	Fixed at a certain temperature and pressure.	Not fixed. Takes up the shape of the bottom of the container.	Not fixed. Takes up the shape of the whole of the container.
Does it flow?	Does not flow.	Flows easily.	Flows easily.
Can it be compressed?	Not easily compressed.	Compressed a little.	Easily compressed.
Expansion on heating	Low.	Medium.	High.

CHANGING THE PHYSICAL STATE

The physical state of a substance can be changed by *heating or cooling* it. The substance either gains or loses heat energy.

Put some ice on your hand.

Your hand feels cold and the ice changes to water. The heat energy from your hand is transferred to the ice. The ice melts.
  On cooling the liquid water freezes again at 0°C, to reform ice.

Heat some water in a glass beaker.

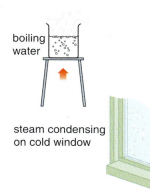

Bubbles form in the water and steam is given off. The water evaporates and eventually boils. The heat energy from the bunsen flame is transferred to the water. The water boils at 100°C to form steam.
  As it cools, the steam condenses back to liquid water.

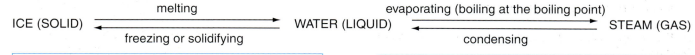

ICE (SOLID) ⇌ (melting / freezing or solidifying) WATER (LIQUID) ⇌ (evaporating (boiling at the boiling point) / condensing) STEAM (GAS)

SUMMARY

1. Matter exists as a solid, liquid or gas depending on the temperature and pressure.
2. A gas has no fixed volume or shape and is easily compressed. A liquid has a fixed volume but not shape. It is less easily compressed. A solid has a fixed volume and shape and is difficult to compress.
3. On heating, a solid melts to a liquid and a liquid boils to a gas.
4. On cooling, a gas condenses to a liquid, which solidifies or freezes to a solid.

QUESTIONS

1. What are the three states of matter?
2. Give four differences between a solid and a gas.
3. Draw a table to show which of the following are solids, liquids or gases at room temperature: jelly, flour, petrol, air, water vapour, salt, coffee granules, olive oil, mercury, copper, oxygen, a milk shake, steel.
4. What is meant by the following words: melting, freezing, condensing, boiling?

3   What is matter made up of?

Gases, solids and liquids are made up of a large number of very small particles which can move.

WHAT DO YOU NOTICE WHEN…?

- You crush garlic and move several yards away?

The small particles of gas from the garlic spread out quickly.

- You put one drop of blackcurrant juice into a glass of water?

The many small particles in the juice spread out and colour the water purple.

- You drop a small amount of green dye powder into water?

The solid dye slowly disappears or **dissolves** in the water. The small particles in the dye slowly spread out as they are hit by the moving water particles.

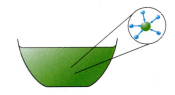

WHAT DO THESE SUGGEST?

The examples above suggest that solids, liquids and gases are made up of a large number of very small particles which can move.

HOW ARE GASES, LIQUIDS AND SOLIDS DIFFERENT?

The particles in gases, liquids and solids differ in how closely they are packed, how much they move, and how quickly they move.

Gas

moving particles

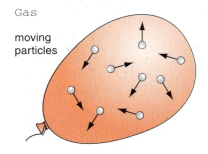

Liquid

moving particles

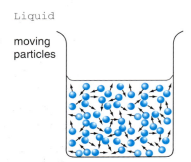

Solid

vibrating particles

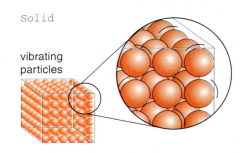

- particles are far apart
- little attraction between the particles so gases have no fixed volume
- particles move rapidly in any direction. Gases have no fixed shape
- particles easily squashed together so gases are easily compressed

- particles are closer together
- quite strong forces of attraction between the particles so liquids have a fixed volume
- particles move in the liquid. It can be poured and takes up the shape of the container
- particles not easily squashed together, so liquids are not easily compressed

- particles are very close together
- strong forces of attraction between the particles so solids have a fixed volume
- particles vibrate. Solids have a definite shape
- very difficult to squash the particles together so solids are not easily compressed

MOVING PARTICLES

Seeing the movement

When looked at through a microscope, pollen grains on the surface of water are seen to move rapidly in different directions. This is because the moving water particles collide with the pollen grains and cause them to move.

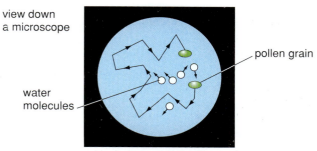

The same effect can be seen with dust particles in a beam of sunlight or smoke in a smoke cell in the laboratory. The moving air particles collide with the solid dust and smoke particles and make them move.

Diffusion

Bicycle tyres go flat after a while. What happens to the air in the tyre?

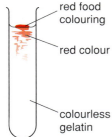

The red food colouring on top of the jelly gradually moves into the jelly and colours it red. Why?

The particles of air in the tyre move out through the rubber. The particles of the dye move through the jelly. This movement of particles from one place to another is called **diffusion**.

Lighter particles move faster and so diffuse more quickly than heavier particles.

Showing different rates of diffusion in the laboratory

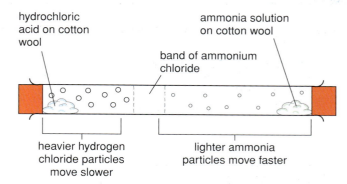

The particles of ammonia gas are lighter than those of hydrogen chloride gas, which comes from the concentrated hydrochloric acid.

The lighter ammonia particles move faster and diffuse more quickly.

A white band of the solid called ammonium chloride forms where the gases meet. The band is closer to the end of the tube which contains the hydrochloric acid.

SUMMARY

1. Solids, liquids and gases are made up of a large number of very small particles.
2. The particles in a gas and liquid move from place to place or **diffuse**. The particles in a solid vibrate.

QUESTIONS

1. Complete this table about particles in solids, liquids and gases.

	Solid	Liquid	Gas
Closeness of particles			
Forces between particles			
Movement of particles			

2. What is meant by diffusion?
3. One balloon is filled with oxygen and another with hydrogen and left. After a few days the balloon filled with hydrogen went down but the one filled with oxygen did not.
   a. What has happened?
   b. Why do you think only one of the balloons went down?
4. Explain why a bottle of lemonade goes 'flat' when the top is not screwed on tightly.

4 Speeding up and slowing down

When we feel energetic we tend to:
- move much faster
- take up more space
- bump into each other more often!

Similar things happen to the particles in a substance when it is heated. The particles move faster and take up more space so that the substance gets bigger or **expands**.

HEATING A SOLID

A tight metal top on a plastic or glass bottle can often be loosened by carefully warming it with hot water. The metal expands more than the glass or plastic. We have to be careful. If the water is too hot it may crack the bottle.

What is happening?

When a solid is heated, the heat energy is transferred to the particles. They vibrate more energetically and take up more space. The solid **expands**. When the solid is cooled, the particles vibrate less and the solid gets smaller or **contracts**.

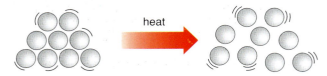

When substances expand they can produce large forces. Engineers leave small gaps in bridges to allow for expansion in hot weather. Without these gaps, the forces of expansion would cause cracks to form.

HEATING A LIQUID

When a liquid is heated, the particles move faster and further apart. They take up more space and the liquid **expands**. As the liquid is cooled it **contracts**.

When mercury in a thermometer is heated it expands and moves up the glass tube. On cooling, heat energy is transferred from the mercury particles to the surroundings. The mercury particles slow down and the liquid contracts and moves down the glass tube. We use this change for measuring the temperature of something.

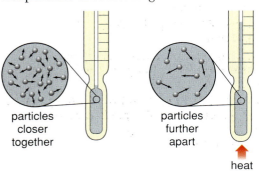

HEATING A GAS

When a gas is heated the particles move faster and further apart and the gas expands and becomes less dense. This is used in hot air balloons to make them rise.

The pressure of a gas is caused by the particles colliding with the walls of the container.

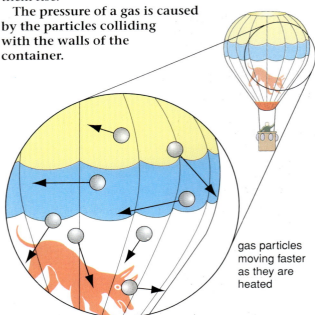

gas particles moving faster as they are heated

Why do some eggs crack when they are placed in boiling water?

Solids, liquids and gases expand by different amounts for the same change in temperature. The liquids and gases in the egg expand more than the solid shell and may cause it to crack.

Melting and boiling

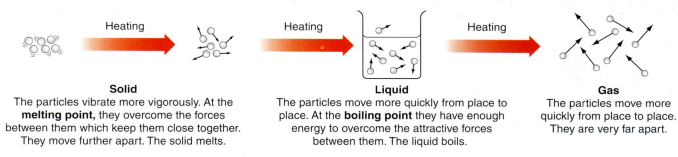

Solid
The particles vibrate more vigorously. At the **melting point,** they overcome the forces between them which keep them close together. They move further apart. The solid melts.

Liquid
The particles move more quickly from place to place. At the **boiling point** they have enough energy to overcome the attractive forces between them. The liquid boils.

Gas
The particles move more quickly from place to place. They are very far apart.

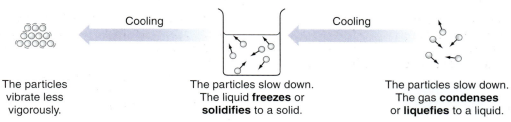

The particles vibrate less vigorously.

The particles slow down. The liquid **freezes** or **solidifies** to a solid.

The particles slow down. The gas **condenses** or **liquefies** to a liquid.

Temperature changes during melting and boiling

The ice is heated slowly until it melts and the water boils. The thermometer is read every minute. The temperatures are plotted on a graph to give a **heating curve**.

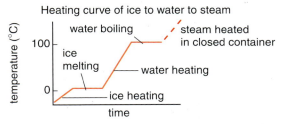

At 0°C the temperature remains constant until all the ice has melted. The heat energy is used to overcome the attractive forces holding the particles together in the solid.

At 100°C the temperature remains constant until all the water has changed to steam. The heat energy is used to overcome the attractive forces between the particles in the liquid.

If the steam is heated in a closed container then the temperature will continue to rise as shown by the dotted line.

The curve obtained as a liquid cools to a solid is called the cooling curve. Again the temperature remains constant during the change in state when the liquid solidifies.

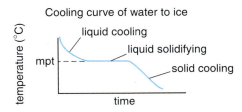

Unusual water

Water is unusual because it expands rather than contracts as it freezes. This is an advantage in ponds and rivers as the fish and plants can live underneath the ice.

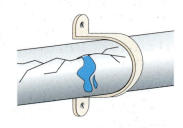

It can be a disadvantage for us if the water in our pipes freezes. The expansion can cause the pipes to crack, but we don't notice the cracks until the ice thaws and the water escapes!

Summary

1. When a solid, liquid or gas is heated, energy is transferred to the particles and the substance expands.
2. The temperature remains constant during a change in state.

Questions

1. Explain what happens to the particles in:
   a ice-cream as it melts
   b the air bubbles trapped in dough as it is cooked to make bread.
2. Why does sugar dissolve more quickly in hot than in cold tea? Explain what happens to the sugar particles.
3. Draw a cooling curve to show how the temperature of water changes as ice cubes are formed in a freezer.
   Explain the curve.

5 Simple substances

Everything in our world is made from one or more simple substances called **elements**. Elements are like building blocks. They are pure substances which cannot be split up into simpler substances.

Elements can join together to form millions of other different substances which are more complex. This picture gives the approximate percentages of the main elements present in the substances which make up the air, water, rocks and living things.

Did you know? Water makes up about 70% of the mass of our bodies.

There are over 100 known different elements with 92 occurring naturally. At room temperature and pressure, 77 of them are solids, 2 are liquids and 13 are gases.

The smallest part of an element is called an **atom**. Each element is given a **symbol** of one or two letters. The symbol represents one atom of the element, for example, O represents one atom of oxygen and Al represents one atom of aluminium.

COMMON ELEMENTS AND THEIR SYMBOLS

Liquids		Gases		Solids	
bromine	Br	oxygen	O	iron	Fe
mercury	Hg	nitrogen	N	carbon	C
		hydrogen	H	sodium	Na
		chlorine	Cl	calcium	Ca
		fluorine	F	aluminium	Al
		helium	He	potassium	K
		argon	Ar	magnesium	Mg
				copper	Cu
				zinc	Zn
				iodine	I

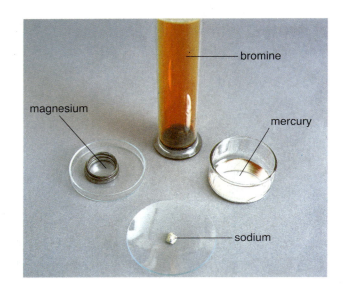

80

COMPOUNDS

Most elements do not occur on their own but combine with other elements to form **compounds**. Compounds are pure substances made by joining together atoms of two or more different elements. The smallest part of a compound is called a **molecule**.

Compounds have very different properties from those of the elements they contain. This is shown by the following examples.

Water

Water is made up of the elements hydrogen (H) and oxygen (O) both of which are colourless gases.

colourless hydrogen gas   colourless oxygen gas   colourless liquid water

Salt (sodium chloride)

Salt is made up of the reactive metal sodium (Na) and the reactive non-metal gas chlorine (Cl). Salt is a non-reactive solid.

dull solid sodium metal   pale green chlorine gas   colourless salt crystals

Limestone (calcium carbonate)

Limestone is a hard white rock. It is made up of three elements, the metal calcium (Ca), the solid non-metal carbon (C) and the gaseous non-metal oxygen (O).

dull grey solid calcium metal   black solid carbon   colourless oxygen gas   white solid limestone (calcium carbonate)

SUMMARY

1. Elements are pure substances which cannot be broken down by chemical means. The smallest part of an element is called an atom.
2. A compound contains atoms of two or more elements chemically joined together. The smallest part of a compound is called a molecule.

NAMING COMPOUNDS

In general, there are two simple rules for naming compounds although there are some exceptions.

1. Compounds ending in -ide contain two elements. Usually the first part of the name is a metal and the second part a non-metal.(The ending of the name of the non-metal is changed to -ide.)

   For example, magnesium oxide is a compound of the metal magnesium (Mg) and the non-metal oxygen (O) and zinc bromide is a compound of zinc (Zn) and bromine (Br).

   Exceptions
   a. Metal hydroxides contain three elements; a metal, hydrogen and oxygen. For example, sodium hydroxide contains sodium (Na), hydrogen (H) and oxygen (O).
   b. Ammonium compounds contain nitrogen, hydrogen and one or two other non-metals, for example, ammonium chloride contains nitrogen (N), hydrogen (H) and chlorine (Cl).

2. Compounds ending in -ate contain at least three elements one of which is oxygen, for example, sodium nitrate contains sodium (Na), nitrogen (N) and oxygen (O), potassium sulphate contains potassium (K), sulphur (S) and oxygen (O).

Being common!

Some compounds have common names such as water, salt, limestone, which do not help you work out what they contain.
Others are:
sand containing a compound of silicon and oxygen
rust which is a compound of iron, oxygen and hydrogen
methane (natural gas) a compound containing carbon and hydrogen.

QUESTIONS

1. Give the name and symbols of two liquid, four solid and three gaseous elements.
2. Make a list of five elements which are found in your home. Describe each one and give its use.
3. Arrange the following in a table to show which are elements and which are compounds: copper, water, salt, magnesium, oxygen, carbon dioxide, zinc chloride.
4. Name the compound containing:
   a. zinc and oxygen
   b. potassium and chlorine
   c. sodium, carbon and oxygen.
5. Name the elements present in:
   a. water
   b. magnesium sulphate
   c. zinc bromide
   d. calcium carbonate.

6 Mixing things together

Pure things and mixtures

When you swim in a swimming pool, you can smell and perhaps taste the chlorine in the water. When you swim in the sea, you can taste the salt it contains. Even tap water tastes different in different parts of the country.

All these samples of water are not pure water but **mixtures** of water and other things. Only the distilled water which we use in car batteries and steam irons is the pure compound water with nothing else in it. Distilled water doesn't taste of anything.

Many substances that we use, eat and find around us exist as mixtures of elements and/or compounds.

> **Did you know?**
> When Concorde travels at twice the speed of sound the fuselage heats up to 150°C – hot enough to cook your dinner!
>
> Special aluminium alloys were developed for Concorde. These had to be light but also stable enough to stand temperature changes from below freezing to 150°C.

Air is a mixture of gases, mainly the elements oxygen (O) and nitrogen (N) and the compound carbon dioxide.

Sea water is a mixture of many compounds, particularly salt (sodium chloride) dissolved in water.

Reading the labels on the prepared foods we buy shows just how many different substances are present. Some of these are chemical compounds added to preserve, colour and flavour the food. They are not really food at all. Sometimes we can see the different parts in a food mixture and even pick them out, for instance, the nuts and currants mixed in muesli.

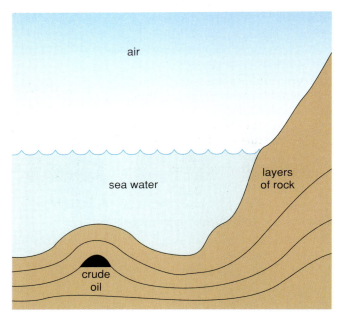

Crude oil found in certain rocks under the sea or land is a mixture of compounds called **hydrocarbons**. These contain hydrogen (H) and carbon (C). As a mixture, the crude oil is not very useful. However the separate compounds which make it up have many uses.

Changing the properties

Metals are mixed with other metals or carbon to make them look and behave very differently. **Alloys** are formed.

For example, the alloy brass is a mixture of copper (Cu) and zinc (Zn). It is harder than both the pure metals and looks different from them.

Steel is a very common alloy. It contains iron (Fe) mixed with small amounts of carbon (C) and other metals.

MIXTURES AND COMPOUNDS OF THE SAME ELEMENTS

Water is a compound of the gaseous elements hydrogen and oxygen. Water looks and behaves very differently from a mixture of these gases.

In the laboratory we can find out some of the differences between a mixture and compound of iron and sulphur by carrying out the following simple activities.

Making the mixture and the compound

Mixture
Grey iron filings and yellow powdered sulphur are mixed. There is no heat change. The mixture is a pale grey powder.

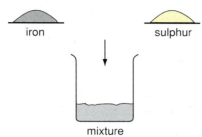

Compound
Some of the mixture is heated to start the reaction. Once started, the mixture glows red and heat is given out. On cooling a hard, grey solid compound called iron(II) sulphide is formed.

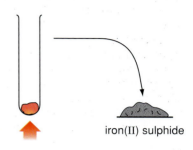

Differences between the mixture and compound

Mixture
1. The amounts of the substances in the mixture can vary as the atoms are not joined together.

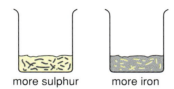

2. The substances in the mixture can be easily separated, for example, a magnet attracts the iron filings but not the sulphur.

3. The mixture has the properties of the substances in it, for example, hydrogen is given off as the iron reacts with an acid. The sulphur does not react. Hydrogen causes a lighted splint to pop.

4. Mixtures do not melt or boil at a definite temperature. For example, butter is a mixture and melts over a range of temperatures in a frying pan.

Compound
1. The amount of the substances in a compound is fixed as the atoms are chemically joined together.

1 atom of iron joined to 1 atom of sulphur

2. The elements in the compound are not easily separated.

3. The compound has new properties. For example, a gas called hydrogen sulphide is given off with an acid. It smells of bad eggs.

4. Compounds have a definite melting and boiling point. For example, pure ice melts at 0°C and pure water boils at 100°C.

SUMMARY

1. Mixtures contain elements and/or compounds mixed together.
2. Alloys are mixtures of metals and sometimes carbon.
3. A mixture and a compound of the same elements have different properties.

QUESTIONS

1. Make a list of three compounds and three mixtures found in the home.
2. A mixture of powdered aluminium and iodine was heated and a grey solid was formed. Name the solid. Is it a mixture or compound?
3. Classify the following as elements, compounds or mixtures: brass, iron, steel, water, air, salt, zinc oxide, oxygen, orange juice, ethanol, sulphur.
4. Make a table to show the differences between mixtures and compounds.

7 Metals and non-metals

There are two main types of elements: metals and non-metals.
Metals are used everywhere, either in their pure form, or as alloys, as shown in this photo of bicycles.

Three of the most common metals in everyday use are aluminium, iron and copper. Like most metals they are found in the ground combined with other substances. These compounds are called ores. The metal is first extracted from the ore before it can be used.

Aluminium
Common ores
bauxite (aluminium oxide)
Common alloy:
duralumin
(aluminium, magnesium, copper)

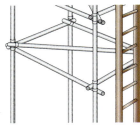

Iron
Common ores
haematite (iron (III) oxide)
Common alloy:
steel (iron, carbon, other metals)

Copper
Common ores
copper pyrites (copper sulphide)
Common alloys:
brass (copper, zinc)
and bronze (copper, tin)

How we use a metal depends on its properties and how expensive it is. For each of the metals and alloys in this table, explain how its properties are suited to the way we use it.

Metal/alloy	Uses	Properties
aluminium	Strong and low density, has a surface layer stopping it from corroding, good electrical and thermal conductor, reflects light	Foil for wrapping food, and bottle tops, window frames electrical cables, saucepans car headlamps, storage tanks
duralumin	Low density, strong, not corroded	Aeroplanes, ships, trains, buses, pistons
wrought iron (pure iron)	Tough, malleable, ductile, rusts	Gates, chains, railway carriage couplings
cast iron (impure iron)	Hard, easily moulded, brittle, rusts	Drainpipes, machinery frames, manhole covers
steel	Strong, stainless steel does not rust	Machinery, buildings, transport
copper	Good electrical conductor, corrodes on surface only, malleable, ductile	Electrical wiring, water pipes and tanks
brass	Not corroded, easily worked, yellow colour	Ornaments, taps, screws, propellers, musical instruments
bronze	Harder than copper, not corroded	Coins, statues, bells, springs, medals

GENERAL PROPERTIES OF METALS AND NON-METALS

Metals

- solids (except mercury, a liquid), 'typical' metals, for example, iron, have high melting points
- shiny when freshly cut
- 'typical' metals are dense
- 'typical' metals tend to be tough, strong, can be drawn into wires (ductile), beaten into sheets (malleable)
- good conductors of electricity and heat when solid or liquid

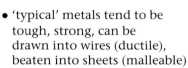

Non-metals

- gases, liquids or low melting point solids (except carbon)
- solid non-metals can be dull, glassy or sparkly.
- low density
- brittle when solid, not ductile or malleable
- poor conductors of electricity and heat (graphite conducts electricity and diamond conducts heat)

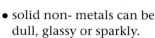
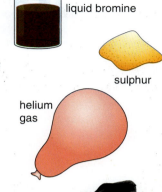

liquid bromine

sulphur

helium gas

charcoal (carbon)

Examples of metals	
aluminium Al	mercury Hg
calcium Ca	nickel Ni
chromium Cr	platinum Pt
cobalt Co	potassium K
copper Cu	silver Ag
gold Au	sodium Na
iron Fe	tin Sn
lithium Li	uranium U
magnesium Mg	zinc Zn
manganese Mn	

Expensive or cheap?

The cost of a metal depends on its usefulness, availability and how easily the ore is mined and the metal extracted.

For example, gold, silver and platinum are very expensive as they are scarce and expensive to mine. Aluminium is more expensive than lead and zinc as it is expensive to extract from its ore.

The price of metals increases as supplies of ores run out. Some metals, for example aluminium and tin, are recycled.

Materials as alternatives for metals

1. Plastics, for instance, plastic pipes, gutters and window frames.

2. Glass, for instance, glass fibres are used in telephone cables and in resins for boats.

3. New materials from compounds of elements such as boron, carbon, silicon, oxygen, nitrogen and aluminium. Some are fibres which are cheaper and lighter than steel but just as strong.

Examples of non-metals	
argon Ar	iodine I
arsenic As	krypton Kr
boron B	nitrogen N
bromine Br	oxygen O
carbon C	phosphorus P
chlorine Cl	radon Rn
fluorine F	silicon Si
helium He	sulphur S
hydrogen H	xenon Xe

Did you know? There are about 8 miles of copper wiring in an average school!

SUMMARY

1. Elements are either metals or non-metals. The uses made of a metal or its alloys depends on its properties.
2. New materials based on carbon, boron, nitrogen, aluminium and oxygen are alternatives to metals. Plastics and glass fibres are also used.

QUESTIONS

1. Suggest why silver wire is not used in electrical wires even though it is a better conductor than copper.
2. Give four general differences between metals and non-metals.
3. Mercury is a metal.
   a. Give two of its properties which are typical of a metal.
   b. Give two of its properties which are not typical of a metal.

8 What are elements made of?

All elements are made up of very tiny particles called atoms. They are much too small to be seen with ordinary microscopes but groups of atoms or very large single atoms can be seen with powerful electron microscopes. These magnify up to two million times! Atoms are extremely small. For example, you need to line up two million atoms of aluminium side by side to measure about 1 mm.

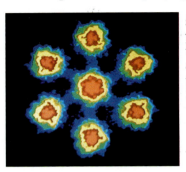

Uranium atoms seen with electron microscope

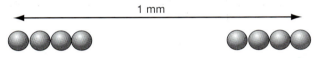

2 million aluminium atoms

All the atoms of a certain element are the same.

The atoms of one element are different from those of every other element. For example, one atom of aluminium is about 27 times heavier than one atom of hydrogen. One atom of aluminium is about nine times lighter than one atom of lead.

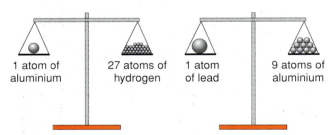

1 atom of aluminium | 27 atoms of hydrogen | 1 atom of lead | 9 atoms of aluminium

How did ideas about atoms develop?
It was first suggested that matter is made up of atoms almost 2500 years ago by a Greek called Democritus. But this idea was not generally accepted until John Dalton revived it in 1808. He thought atoms were hard – rather like billiard balls.

Early in the 20th century, other scientists including Marie and Pierre Curie and Ernest Rutherford showed that the atom itself is made up of smaller particles. These are called **protons**, **neutrons** and **electrons**.

At first it was suggested that these particles were all mixed up together with the electrons dotted about like plums in a plum pudding.

This '**plum pudding**' model was disproved by physicists working with Lord Rutherford. They fired tiny particles at a thin piece of gold. Most of them went through the gold without leaving a hole. Rutherford suggested that this showed that the atoms of gold have a lot of space in them.

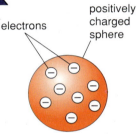

'Plum pudding' model

THE STRUCTURE OF THE ATOM

Rutherford's ideas form the basis of modern views about the structure of the atom.

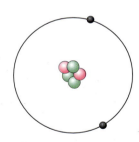

Nucleus	Relative charge	Relative mass
Proton	+1	1
Neutron	0	1
Electron	−1	Negligible

The actual masses of the proton, neutron and electron are extremely small. They are therefore given a **relative mass**. This is the mass compared with the mass of an atom of carbon. The atom of carbon is given a mass of 12 units. The charges are also given relative values.

Main points about the structure of the atom

- Most of the atom is empty space
- The protons and neutrons are at the centre of the atom called the nucleus
- The nucleus is small compared with the atom as a whole (if the atom was the size of a football pitch then the nucleus would be the size of a tiny marble at its centre)
- Most of the mass of the atom is in the nucleus
- The electrons are arranged around the nucleus
- The number of protons equals the number of electrons so that the atom has no overall charge.

Atomic number Z

The atomic number is the number of protons. Every element has a different atomic number. It is like a fingerprint for the element.

Since the atom is neutral the number of electrons also equals the atomic number.

Mass number A

The mass number is the total number of protons and neutrons in the atom.

Number of neutrons = mass number – atomic number

Did you know?
The smallest ever writing is being developed using xenon atoms. It is so small that 100 copies of the whole Bible could be written on an area the size of a postage stamp!

SUMMARY

1. Atoms are made up of protons, neutrons and electrons.
2. The protons and neutrons are in the nucleus. The electrons are arranged in shells around the nucleus.

ATOMIC SHORTHAND

The mass number is written at the top of the symbol and the atomic number at the bottom.

$$^{A}_{Z}X$$

mass number (A)
atomic number (Z)

For example, hydrogen is the simplest atom. It has a mass number of 1 and an atomic number of 1.

The atomic shorthand for hydrogen is ^1_1H

An atom of hydrogen has:
1 proton (the atomic number is 1)
1 electron (the number of electrons equals the number of protons)
1 – 1 = 0 neutrons (i.e. mass number – atomic number)

Another example

$^{23}_{11}Na$ An atom of sodium has: 11 protons, 11 electrons and (23 – 11) = 12 neutrons

QUESTIONS

1. a Explain why most of the mass of the atom is in its nucleus.
   b Why is the atom neutral overall?
2. Copy the table and fill in the gaps.

Name	Lithium		Sodium	Fluorine	Neon
Symbol	Li	N			
Atomic number	3				10
Mass number	7		23		20
Number of protons		7			
Number of neutrons		7		10	
Number of electrons				11	9

9 Arranging electrons

Electrons are arranged around the nucleus of an atom. They are in shells or energy levels. Some atoms have few shells and some have a lot. The number depends on how many electrons there are in the atom. The shells are a bit like the layers of an onion.

The electrons are arranged according to simple rules.

1. The electrons fill up the shells closest to the nucleus *first*. This is because the first shell has lowest energy. The energy of the shells increases the further from the nucleus.

2. Each shell can hold up to a maximum number of *electrons*. When one shell is full, the electrons go into the next shell.

The first shell holds a maximum of two electrons.

The simplest atom is hydrogen. It has one electron which goes into the first shell as shown here.

The next simplest atom is helium. It has two electrons which both go into the first shell. This is now full.

The second shell holds a maximum of eight electrons. Here are four examples.

Lithium has three electrons. It has two electrons in the first shell which is full. The third electron is in the second shell.

Carbon has six electrons. It has two electrons in the first shell and four in the second shell which is now half full.

Fluorine has nine electrons. It has two electrons in the first shell and seven in the second shell.

Neon has ten electrons. It has two electrons in the first shell and eight in the second shell. The second shell is full.

The third shell holds a maximum of eight electrons. Here are four examples.

Sodium has 11 electrons. It has two electrons in the first shell, eight in the second and one in the third shell.

Silicon has 14 electrons. It has two electrons in the first shell, eight in the second and four in the third shell. The third shell is half full.

Chlorine has 17 electrons. It has two electrons in the first shell, eight in the second and seven in the third shell.

Argon has 18 electrons. It has two electrons in the first shell, eight in the second and eight in the third shell. All the shells are full.

ELECTRONIC CONFIGURATION

The arrangement of the electrons in the atom is called its **electronic configuration**. The number of electrons in each shell is written in turn, separated by commas. For example, the electronic configuration of sodium is 2,8,1.

The electronic configurations of the atoms given on page 88 are shown in the table below.

The electronic configuration is very important as it determines how an atom will react.

Name	Symbol	Electronic configuration
hydrogen	H	1
helium	He	2
lithium	Li	2,1
carbon	C	2,4
fluorine	F	2,7
neon	Ne	2,8
sodium	Na	2,8,1
silicon	Si	2,8,4
chlorine	Cl	2,8,7
argon	Ar	2,8,8

You can see a pattern in the electronic configuration of some of these atoms.

For example, the outer shells of the elements fluorine and chlorine both have seven electrons. These elements have similar chemical properties. They are very reactive, poisonous gases and are both non-metals.

SUMMARY

1. The electrons are arranged in energy levels or shells around the atom.
2. Isotopes are atoms of the same element with different numbers of neutrons. They have the same atomic number but different mass number.

Isotopes

All the atoms of a particular element have the same number of protons and the same number of electrons. However, the number of neutrons can be different. Atoms like this are called **isotopes**.

Isotopes are atoms of the same element which have the same atomic number but different mass number.

The isotopes of hydrogen

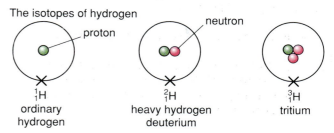

^1_1H ordinary hydrogen ^2_1H heavy hydrogen deuterium ^3_1H tritium

For example, there are three isotopes of hydrogen,

^1_1H, ^2_1H, ^3_1H which have 0, 1 and 2 neutrons respectively.

Chlorine has two isotopes:

$^{35}_{17}Cl$ number of protons = 17
number of electrons = 17
number of neutrons = (35 – 17)
= 18

$^{37}_{17}Cl$ number of protons = 17
number of electrons = 17
number of neutrons = (37 – 17)
= 20

Normal chlorine is 75% $^{35}_{17}Cl$ and 25% $^{37}_{17}Cl$.

The isotopes of chlorine

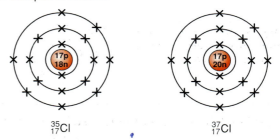

$^{35}_{17}Cl$ $^{37}_{17}Cl$

QUESTIONS

1. Where are the electrons found in the atom?
2. Boron has an atomic number of 11. How many protons and how many electrons does the boron atom have? Draw a diagram to show how the electrons are arranged.
3. There are two different atoms of carbon: $^{14}_6C$ and $^{12}_6C$.
   a. What is the name given to these two atoms?
   b. Give the numbers of protons, neutrons and electrons in each atom and their electronic arrangement.

10 Arranging elements – looking for patterns

People in the same family often look alike. There is a family resemblance. So you, your brother and sisters may show some resemblance to each other and your parents.

In a similar way, elements that are alike can be grouped together in families. So far we have only classified elements as metals or non-metals. Knowing which family an element is in helps us to predict how it will behave. For example, if we are told that an element is a metal then we can predict that it will conduct electricity.

However, there are other ways of grouping elements which help us predict more about them.

Can you spot the family likenesses?

ATTEMPTS AT ARRANGING ELEMENTS

Various attempts have been made by scientists to arrange elements in patterns. These have led to the development of a very useful chart called the Periodic Table (see page 92).

1. Newlands' Law of Octaves

In 1865, John Newlands arranged the elements which were known at the time in order of their increasing atomic masses. He noticed that every eighth element was similar.

For example, the metals lithium (Li), sodium (Na) and potassium (K) came 2nd, 9th and 16th in his series. These metals are similar as they are very reactive, even reacting with cold water.

Newlands thought this was rather like music where one note resembles the note eight places or an octave away. He therefore called his arrangement the **Law of Octaves**.

An octave apart

Unfortunately Newlands' Law of Octaves only worked for the first 16 elements because:
- some of the atomic masses he used were inaccurate
- at that time, some elements had not been discovered. When they were discovered it was found that there was no room for them in his series, for example the noble gases.

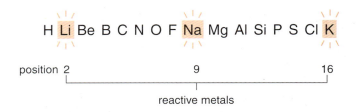

Newland's Law of Octaves

M10a2 Essential Science

2. Dmitri Mendeleev

The Russian chemist, Mendeleev published his classification of the elements in 1869. Like Newlands, he arranged the elements in ascending order of their atomic masses. He placed similar elements underneath each other in the same vertical column. At the time only 63 elements were known.

Mendeleev's table

Mendeleev's arrangement is rather like laying out the suits from a pack of cards. When one suit has been arranged, a new row is started. In this way all the cards with the same value are placed under each other.

Mendeleev called the rows **periods** because at regular periods another very similar element fitted under the first. Similar elements were in the same vertical column. Mendeleev called these columns **groups** (like a family group).

Mendeleev's classification worked because:

- he left gaps in the table for undiscovered elements and even predicted what they would be like
- he changed the order when an element was obviously in the wrong place according to its properties. For example, the atomic mass of the element tellurium (Te) is greater than that of iodine (I). But Mendeleev placed tellurium before iodine as he realised that iodine resembled bromine and should therefore be in the same group.

At the time Mendeleev did not know about the noble gases. Only helium had just been discovered, the others were unknown as they are very unreactive. When they were discovered they were put in Group 0.

The modern version of Mendeleev's table is called the **Periodic Table**. It is similar to Mendeleev's table except that the elements are arranged in *ascending order of their atomic number* (see page 92). This removes the problem of some elements being misplaced when the arrangement is based on atomic masses.

Mendeleev's table of the elements

> **Did you know?**
> The noble gas helium was first detected in 1868 in the gases around the Sun. The name helium comes from the Greek word *helios* meaning sun.

Summary

1. There have been various attempts to arrange the elements so that their properties can be predicted. The most important are those by Newlands and Mendeleev.
2. Mendeleev's table led directly to the development of the modern chart which is called the Periodic Table.

Questions

1. Why did Newlands call his arrangement of the elements the Law of Octaves? Give two problems with this arrangement.
2. Outline Mendeleev's arrangement of the elements. Give two reasons why Mendeleev's arrangement was better than Newlands' Law of Octaves.

11 Arranging elements – an introduction to the Periodic Table

Mendeleev's arrangement of the elements forms the basis of the modern chart called the **Periodic Table**. In it the elements are arranged in ascending order of their atomic numbers instead of in ascending order of their atomic masses. This removes the problem that Mendeleev found of some elements being in the wrong order. For example, the **atomic numbers** of tellurium and iodine are 52 and 53. So it is correct to place tellurium before iodine even though its atomic mass is greater (see page 91).

The Periodic Table shown below lists the 107 known elements. Ninety-two of them occur naturally, the other fifteen have been made artificially.

Period	Group 1	2												Group 3	4	5	6	7	0
1	H 1																		He 2
2	Li 3	Be 4												B 5	C 6	N 7	O 8	F 9	Ne 10
3	Na 11	Mg 12				Transition elements								Al 13	Si 14	P 15	S 16	Cl 17	Ar 18
4	K 19	Ca 20	Sc 21	Ti 22	V 23	Cr 24	Mn 25	Fe 26	Co 27	Ni 28	Cu 29	Zn 30		Ga 31	Ge 32	As 33	Se 34	Br 35	Kr 36
5	Rb 37	Sr 38	Y 39	Zr 40	Nb 41	Mo 42	Tc 43	Ru 44	Rh 45	Pd 46	Ag 47	Cd 48		In 49	Sn 50	Sb 51	Te 52	I 53	Xe 54
6	Cs 55	Ba 56	La 57	Hf 72	Ta 73	W 74	Re 75	Os 76	Ir 77	Pt 78	Au 79	Hg 80		Tl 81	Pb 82	Bi 83	Po 84	At 85	Pn 86
7	Fr 87	Ra 88	Ac 89	Unq 104	Unp 105	Unh 106	Uns 107	?	?	?	?								

Lanthanides

Ce 58	Pr 59	Nd 60	Pm 61	Sm 62	Eu 63	Gd 64	Tb 65	Dy 66	Ho 67	Er 68	Tm 69	Yb 70	Lu 71

Actinides

Th 90	Pa 91	U 92	Np 93	Pu 94	Am 95	Cm 96	Bk 97	Cf 98	Es 99	Fm 100	Md 101	No 102	Lw 103

Artificial elements

Key: H (Symbol), 1 (Atomic number – number of protons)

The main blocks of elements which resemble each other are shown below.

Metals are found on the left-hand side and centre. The most reactive metals are in Group 1 and called the **alkali metals**.

Non-metals are found on the right-hand side. The most reactive non-metals are in Group 7 and called the **halogens**.

Elements in Group 0 are very unreactive gases called the **noble gases**.

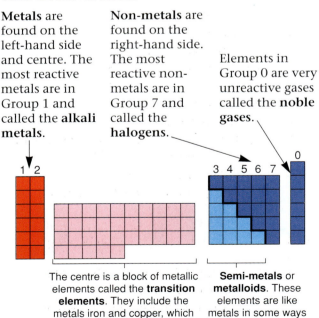

The centre is a block of metallic elements called the **transition elements**. They include the metals iron and copper, which are useful as they are hard and not reactive.

Semi-metals or **metalloids**. These elements are like metals in some ways and non-metals in other ways.

Using the Periodic Table

The position of an element in the table helps us predict how it will behave.

1 Going down a group, *metals increase* in reactivity and *non-metals decrease* in reactivity.

   For example, potassium, K, is more reactive than sodium, Na; iodine, I, is less reactive than bromine, Br. The most reactive metal is francium, Fr. The most reactive non-metal is fluorine, F.

2 Going across a period there is a gradual change from metals to non-metals.

   For example, in period 3 the metals decrease in reactivity from sodium, Na, to Magnesium, Mg, and aluminium, Al. The rest of the elements are non-metals. The non-metals increase in reactivity from silicon, Si, to chlorine, Cl. The noble gas argon, Ar, is unreactive.

HOW IS THE PERIODIC TABLE RELATED TO THE ELECTRONIC STRUCTURE OF THE ELEMENTS?

The table shows the electronic structure of the first 20 elements.

1 H							2 He
2,1 Li 3	2,2 Be 4	2,3 B 5	2,4 C 6	2,5 N 7	2,6 O 8	2,7 F 9	2,8 Ne 10
2,8,1 Na 11	2,8,2 Mg 12	2,8,3 Al 13	2,8,4 Si 14	2,8,5 P 15	2,8,6 S 16	2,8,7 Cl 17	2,8,8 Ar 18
2,8,8,1 K 19	2,8,8,2 Ca 20						

WHAT DOES THE TABLE TELL US?

By answering the following questions you will notice some patterns between the electronic structure and the position of an element in the table. The answers to the questions are given at the bottom of the page.

1. How is the number of electrons in the outer shell or energy level related to the group number?

2. What do you notice about the electronic structure of the noble gases?

3. How does the position of an element in the table relate to the number of protons in the atom and to the total number of electrons?

4. How many electrons do metals have in their outer energy level?

5. How many electrons do non-metals have in their outer energy level?

You will find these patterns useful for understanding why and how atoms join together. When they combine they try and obtain the electronic arrangement of the nearest noble gas as this is stable. Atoms do this by gaining, losing or sharing electrons.

Answers
1 They are the same except for the noble gases.
2 They have full outer energy levels.
3 They are the same.
4 1, 2 or 3 electrons.
5 4 or more electrons.

SUMMARY

1. The Periodic Table is an arrangement of the elements in ascending order of atomic number. Elements in the same group are similar.
2. The table is useful for predicting the properties of a particular element.

QUESTIONS

1. Give the symbols of:
   a. the noble gases
   b. two transition elements
   c. two alkali metals
   d. two halogens
   e. the most reactive non-metal
   f. the most reactive metal.

2. Find the element with the symbol Mg in the table.
   a. Which group and period is it in?
   b. Is it a metal or non-metal?
   c. How many protons and electrons does it have in its atom?
   d. How many electrons in its outer energy level?

3. An element has 7 electrons in its outer energy level.
   a. Which group of the Periodic Table is it in?
   b. Is it a metal or non-metal?
   c. It is the least reactive element in its group. Give its symbol.

12 Joining atoms together – the ionic bond

To form compounds, atoms must 'stick' together when they collide. In science, we say they form bonds with each other.

In some compounds, when the atoms collide they form particles called **ions**. These ions have opposite charges and are attracted together to form an **ionic compound**. The compound has **ionic bonds** between the ions. A common example is salt or sodium chloride. This contains *positive sodium ions* and *negative chloride ions* attracted together.

How and why are the ions formed?

Let us start by looking at the elements sodium and chlorine. Sodium is a silvery metal found in Group 1 of the Periodic Table and chlorine is a greenish gas found in Group 7. They are both very reactive and to become more stable need to obtain the same number of electrons as the nearest noble gas.

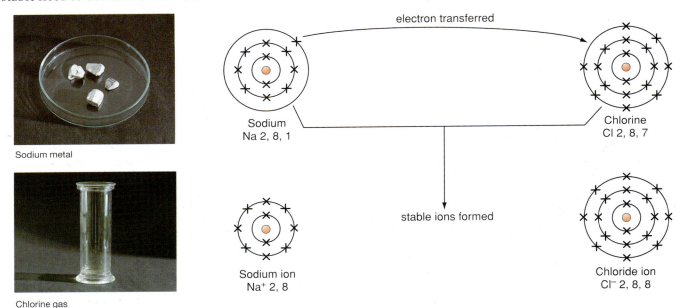

The sodium atom *loses* the one electron in its outer energy level and forms the sodium ion which has a charge of +1. It has the electronic structure of the noble gas neon.

The chlorine atom *gains* an electron in its outer energy level to form the chloride ion which has a charge of –1. It has the electronic structure of the noble gas argon.

Both the ions formed are stable.

How are the ions attracted together?

The positive and negative ions are attracted together in a regular pattern to form a giant structure or **crystal**. Overall the crystal is uncharged as there are the same number of positive and negative charges.

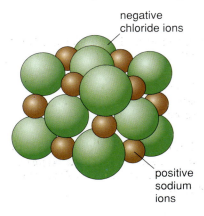

The formula gives the ratio of the ions present. The formula of sodium chloride is NaCl. It contains Na^+ and Cl^- ions arranged in the ratio of 1:1, i.e. one sodium ion to every one chloride ion.

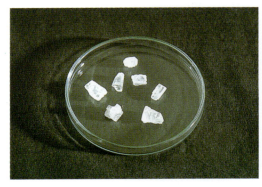

Cubic crystals of sodium chloride

WHAT ARE THE PROPERTIES OF SALT AND OF OTHER IONIC COMPOUNDS?

1. Ionic compounds are solids with high melting points and high boiling points. This is because the ions are held together by strong forces of attraction. For example, sodium chloride melts at 801°C.

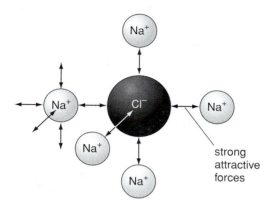

strong attractive forces

2. Some ionic compounds dissolve in water. This is because water molecules surround the ions and keep them apart. The water molecules can do this as one end of the water molecule is slightly positive and the other slightly negative.

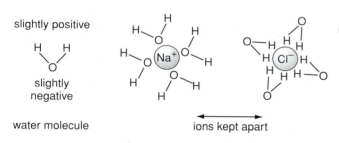

slightly positive / slightly negative / water molecule / ions kept apart

3. Solutions of ionic compounds and melted ionic compounds conduct electricity. This is because the ions can move and carry the current.

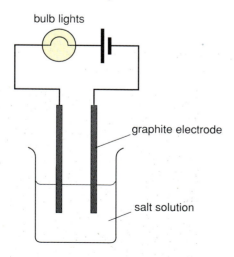

bulb lights / graphite electrode / salt solution

What other compounds are ionic?

The Periodic Table helps us predict which compounds will be ionic.

In general, metals lose electrons to form positive ions; non-metals gain these electrons to form negative ions; the ions formed have the electronic structure of the nearest noble gas and so are stable.

Most metals in Group 1, 2 and some of those in Group 3 and in the transition series form ionic compounds with non-metals from Group 6 and 7.

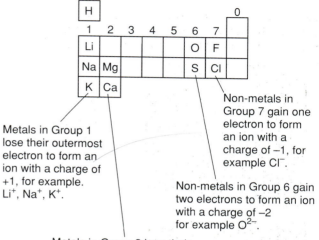

Metals in Group 1 lose their outermost electron to form an ion with a charge of +1, for example. Li^+, Na^+, K^+.

Metals in Group 2 lose their two outermost electrons to form an ion with a charge of +2, for example. Mg^{2+}, Ca^{2+}.

Non-metals in Group 7 gain one electron to form an ion with a charge of –1, for example Cl^-.

Non-metals in Group 6 gain two electrons to form an ion with a charge of –2 for example O^{2-}.

Did you know?
There is so much salt dissolved in the oceans that if they all dried up a wall of salt 180 miles and 1 mile thick could be built around the world.

SUMMARY

1. In ionic bonding metals lose electrons to form positive ions. Non-metals gain electrons to form negative ions. The ions have the electronic configuration of the nearest noble gas.
2. The ions are attracted together to form a giant structure or crystal.

QUESTIONS

1. Give the symbol and charge of the ions formed by the following: potassium, calcium, chlorine, oxygen, lithium, bromine, iodine, magnesium.
2. Draw diagrams to show the electronic structure of the following ions and in each case name the noble gas with the same electronic structure: Ca^{2+}, F^-, Na^+, O^{2-}, S^{2-}.
3. A compound has a high melting point and its solution conducts an electric current. What type of bonding is present in the compound? Explain why it has a high melting point.

13 More about ionic compounds

ALL IN A FLASH

In the early days of photography, there were no electronic flashlights on cameras. Magnesium ribbon was burnt to provide extra light.

When magnesium burns it joins with oxygen from the air to form the ionic compound magnesium oxide. The light given out is so intense that it can damage your eyes if you stare at it directly.

WHAT IONS ARE PRESENT IN MAGNESIUM OXIDE AND HOW ARE THEY FORMED?

You can find out about the structure of magnesium oxide by answering the questions. The diagrams below show the answers.

1. Magnesium is in Group 2 of the Periodic Table. How many electrons are in its outer energy level?

2. Oxygen is in Group 6 of the Periodic Table. How many electrons are in its outer energy level?

3. How many electrons does the magnesium atom lose to get the electronic structure of the nearest noble gas?
What is the charge on the magnesium ion?
Which noble gas has the same electronic structure?

4. How many electrons does the oxygen atom gain to get the electronic structure of the nearest noble gas?
What is the charge on the oxide ion?
Which noble gas has the same electronic structure?

The two outer electrons on the magnesium atom are transferred to the oxygen atom. The ions formed both have the electronic structure of the noble gas neon and so are stable. They are attracted together to form a giant ionic structure or lattice.

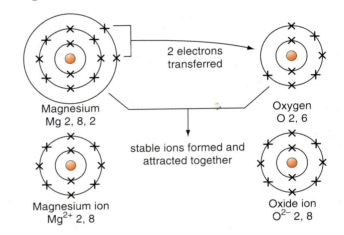

Calcium chloride, another ionic compound

In a similar way, you can work out which ions are present in calcium chloride and how they are formed.

The calcium atom loses its two outer electrons to form the calcium ion. It has the electronic structure of argon.

Each chlorine atom accepts one electron to form a chloride ion. The chloride ions have the electronic structure of argon.

The ions are attracted together to form a giant ionic structure.

The formula of calcium chloride is $CaCl_2$.

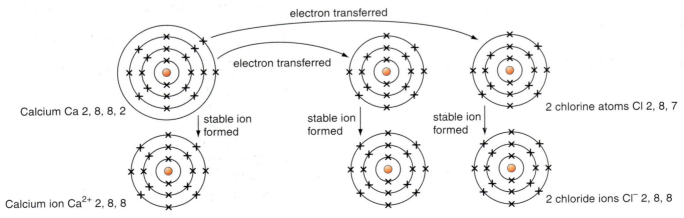

96

Formulae of ionic compounds

The formula of an ionic compound gives the simplest ratio of the ions present in the giant structure. For example, the formula of sodium chloride is NaCl. Since the compound is neutral, the total number of positive charges must equal the total number of negative charges. For example, $CaCl_2$ contains one Ca^{2+} and two Cl^- ions. The total positive charge is 2 and the total negative charge is also 2 so the compound is neutral.

Some ions contain more than one atom. These are called groups and each group has an overall charge. For example, the sulphate group in calcium sulphate contains one sulphur and four oxygen atoms and has an overall charge of −2. It is written as SO_4^{2-}.

Common ions and their charges are given below. You will notice that the metal called iron can form two different ions. In compounds such as iron(II) sulphate it has a charge of +2 and in others, such as iron(III) chloride it has a charge of +3.

Simple ions

+1	+2	+3	−1	−2
lithium Li	magnesium Mg	aluminium Al	fluoride F	oxide O
sodium Na	calcium Ca	iron(III) Fe	chloride Cl	sulphide S
potassium K	barium Ba		bromide Br	
silver Ag	zinc Zn		iodide I	
hydrogen H	iron(II) Fe			
	copper Cu			
	lead Pb			

Common groups

+1	−1	−2	−3
ammonium NH_4	hydroxide OH	sulphate SO_4	phosphate PO_4
	hydrogencarbonate HCO_3	carbonate CO_3	
	nitrate NO_3		

Working out formulae

You can easily work out the formula of an ionic compound if you remember two simple rules:
- make sure the total number of positive charges equals the total number of negative charges
- place brackets around a group where there is more than one of the group present. Put the number of the groups present after the bracket.

For example

Magnesium oxide
Ions present Mg^{2+} O^{2-}
The charges balance.
The formula is MgO.

Calcium hydroxide
Ca^{2+} OH^-
Two OH^- ions are needed to balance the charges.
The formula is $Ca(OH)_2$.

Ammonium sulphate
NH_4^+ SO_4^{2-}
Two NH_4^+ ions are needed to balance the charges.
The formula is $(NH_4)_2SO_4$.

Summary

1. The formula of an ionic compound gives the ratio of the ions present.
2. Overall, an ionic compound is neutral. The total positive charge equals the total negative charge.

Questions

1. An ionic compound XY contains a metal X and a non-metal Y. X is found in Group 1 of the Periodic Table and Y in Group 7.
   a. How many electrons are in the outer energy level of X?
   b. What will be the charge on the ion formed by X?
   c. How many electrons are in the outer energy level of Y?
   d. What will be the charge on the ion formed by Y?
   e. Why is the formula of the compound XY?
2. Work out the formulae for
   a. calcium chloride
   b. sodium sulphate
   c. zinc bromide
   d. ammonium sulphate
   e. magnesium carbonate
   f. iron(II) sulphate.

14 Joining atoms together – the covalent bond

Some atoms 'stick' together by sharing electrons in their highest energy levels. This is called **covalent bonding**.

A covalent bond is strong but the forces between the covalent molecules are weak. Sometimes giant covalent molecules are formed (see page 100).

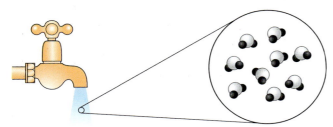

Water is a runny liquid. There are weak forces between the molecules.

Weak forces between molecules.

Covalent molecules

Hydrogen is an example of a covalent molecule with atoms of the *same* element. Each hydrogen atom shares its electron with the other hydrogen atom. They obtain the electronic structure of the noble gas helium and so are stable.

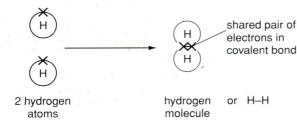

2 hydrogen atoms

hydrogen molecule or H–H

shared pair of electrons in covalent bond

Other elements with covalent bonding between the atoms in their molecules are fluorine F_2, chlorine Cl_2, bromine Br_2, iodine I_2, oxygen O_2, and nitrogen N_2.

Ammonia is an example of a covalent molecule with atoms of different elements. Ammonia has three covalent bonds. These are in definite directions so the molecule of ammonia has a definite shape. One pair of electrons is not used in bonding but takes up space. Ammonia is therefore pyramidal.

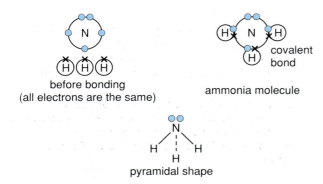

before bonding (all electrons are the same)

ammonia molecule

covalent bond

pyramidal shape

What are the properties of covalent compounds?

1 Covalent compounds without giant structures are gases, liquids or solids with low melting and boiling points. This is because the forces between the molecules are weak though the covalent bonds within the molecule are very strong. For example, if grey solid iodine crystals are heated they **sublime** at a low temperature to form a purple vapour.

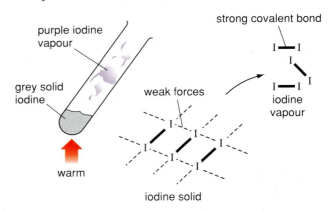

2 Covalent molecules are often insoluble in water but soluble in solvents such as tetrachloromethane and ethanol. For example, iodine is insoluble in water but dissolves in ethanol to form a brown solution.

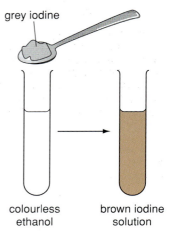

colourless ethanol

brown iodine solution

3 Covalent compounds do not conduct an electric current when liquid or in solution because the molecules do not have an overall charge.

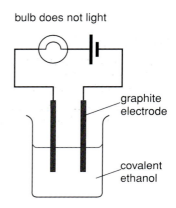

> **Did you know?**
> Hydrogen molecules are so small that there is room for about two million of them side by side on a pin head!

OTHER COVALENT COMPOUNDS

Covalent compounds are formed when atoms of non-metals join together. Non-metals in Groups 4, 5, 6, and 7 of the Periodic Table form covalent bonds when they join with

- themselves, for example, nitrogen
- each other, for example, carbon dioxide
- hydrogen, for example, ammonia.

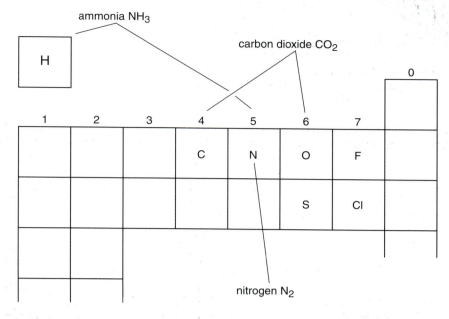

Methane CH_4
(colourless gas)

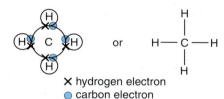

× hydrogen electron
○ carbon electron

Methane has four covalent bonds. Each bond contains one electron from the carbon atom (2,4) and one electron from each of the hydrogen atoms (1).

The electronic structures of carbon and hydrogen atoms in methane are (2,8) and (2) – those of the noble gases neon and helium.

Shape
tetrahedral

Water H_2O
(colourless liquid)

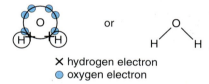

× hydrogen electron
○ oxygen electron

Water has two covalent bonds. Each bond contains one electron from the oxygen atom (2,6) and one electron from each of the hydrogen atoms (1).

The electronic structures of oxygen and hydrogen atoms in water are (2,8) and (2) – those of neon and helium.

Shape
V-shaped

The oxygen has a slight negative charge and the hydrogens a slight positive charge.

Hydrogen chloride HCl
(colourless gas)

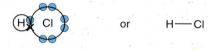

× hydrogen electron
○ chlorine electron

Hydrogen chloride has one covalent bond. The bond has one electron from the chlorine atom (2,8,7) and one from the hydrogen atom (1).

The electronic structures of chlorine and hydrogen atoms in hydrogen chloride are (2,8,8) and (2), those of argon and helium.

Shape
linear

H—Cl

The chlorine has a slight negative charge and the hydrogen a slight positive charge.

SUMMARY

1. Atoms of non-metals join together by forming covalent bonds. In covalent bonds electrons are shared between the atoms.
2. Covalent compounds are usually gases, liquids or solids with low melting points.

QUESTIONS

1. Which of the following compounds has covalent bonding: sodium chloride, oxygen, water, ammonia, iron, methane, bromine?
2. Explain why covalent molecules have a definite shape.
3. Sugar easily melts when it is heated, and it dissolves in water. Sugar solution does not conduct an electric current. Do you think sugar is a covalent or an ionic compound? Explain your answer.

15 Structures

We have already seen how salt is made up of a large number of ions arranged in a regular pattern to form a giant structure or crystal. Other giant structures also exist which do not have ions. These include giant covalent structures and metallic structures.

Giant covalent structures

Diamond and graphite are both made of only carbon atoms but look and behave very differently. We say that 'diamonds are for ever' as they are very hard and don't wear out. They also look very attractive and are clear and shiny.

In contrast, the graphite in your pencil is dull and black and very soft. Graphite easily wears away by leaving a mark on the paper.

Why are diamond and graphite so different?

This is because the carbon atoms in the structures are arranged differently.

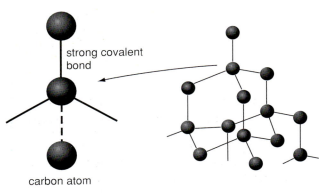

diamond

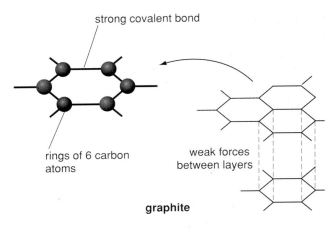

graphite

In diamond each carbon atom is joined to four other carbon atoms with strong covalent bonds. A diamond crystal is therefore one giant structure with the carbon atoms arranged tetrahedrally.

In graphite each carbon atom is joined to three other carbon atoms with covalent bonds. Layers of carbon atoms are formed with weak forces between the layers. The carbon atoms are arranged in hexagons.

Properties and uses

Diamond is the hardest known naturally occurring substance as the covalent bonds are very strong and difficult to break. It also has a very high melting point.

Diamonds are used in cutting and grinding tools. When cut, diamonds appear brilliant as they reflect light. They are therefore used in jewellery.

Properties and uses

Graphite is soft as the layers of carbon atoms can easily slide over each other. There are free electrons between the layers so that graphite conducts electricity.

Graphite is used for making electrodes, the 'lead' in pencils and the rods in nuclear reactors.

Metallic structures

The structure of metals gives them their special properties.
- The atoms are packed closely together in a regular pattern to form a giant structure. This causes many metals to be dense.
- The electrons in the outer energy levels of the metal atoms are able to move around the structure. Metals therefore conduct electricity.
- The forces holding the atoms together are strong. Most metals do not dissolve in solvents and have high melting and boiling points, for example, iron melts at 1535°C.

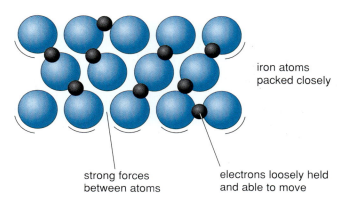

iron atoms packed closely

strong forces between atoms

electrons loosely held and able to move

Getting metals into shape

When you hammer a piece of lead or copper, it is quite easy to change its shape. The rows of atoms slide over each other but 'stick' in the new position when you stop hammering.

Metals are easily beaten into sheets or pulled into wires.

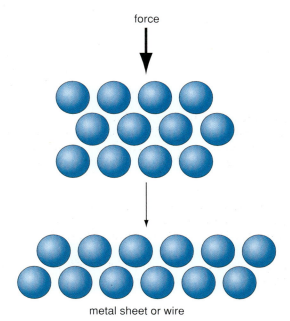

force

metal sheet or wire

Making alloys

The properties of metals are changed by adding small amounts of other metals or carbon to make alloys.

The atoms of the added substance have a different size. This makes it more difficult for the layers to slide over each other. This usually makes the alloy harder than the pure metal.

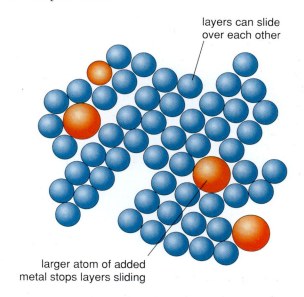

layers can slide over each other

larger atom of added metal stops layers sliding

Did you know? Eye surgeons use knives with diamond blades for many eye operations as the blades are extremely sharp.

SUMMARY

1. Giant structures are covalent, ionic or metallic.
2. Diamond and graphite both have giant covalent structures of carbon atoms. Diamond is harder than graphite. Graphite conducts electricity.
3. In metals the atoms are packed closely together in a regular pattern. The outer electrons can move so metals conduct electricity.

QUESTIONS

1. Arrange the following in a table to show which have giant covalent, giant ionic or metallic structures: sodium chloride, zinc, graphite, calcium chloride, diamond, copper, iron.
2. Graphite and iron conduct electricity but diamond does not. Explain why this is so.
3. Brass is an alloy of copper and zinc. Explain why brass is harder than pure copper.
4. Gold can be easily hammered into very thin sheets called gold leaf. Draw diagrams to show what happens to the atoms in the gold as this is carried out.

16 Solutions

> **Did you know?**
> It is possible to walk on the surface of Lake Magadi in Kenya! So much water has evaporated that the crust of salts which have crystallised out is so thick in places that it can support your weight.

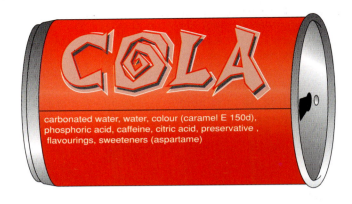

Looking at the label on a can of fizzy drink tells you that it is not a pure liquid. It contains water with flavourings, sugar, preservatives, colouring and carbon dioxide gas dissolved in it. Coke is an example of a **solution**.

Forming solutions

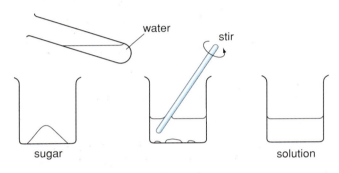

Solid sugar disappears into water when it is stirred.

The water **dissolves** the sugar and is called the **solvent**. The sugar is called the **solute**. The solute can not be removed by filtering the solution.

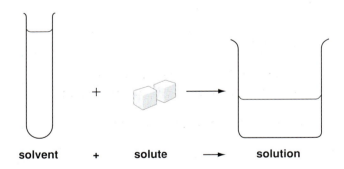

Water is a common solvent which dissolves many substances. For example, water in our blood and cells has many different substances such as sugar and salt dissolved in it. Many ionic compounds dissolve in water.

How pure is tap water?

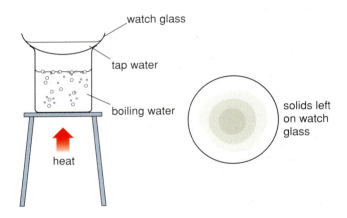

The tap water evaporates leaving pale rings of solids on the watch glass. These solids had been dissolved in the water.

Tap water also contains dissolved air and chemicals such as chlorine which are added to kill germs.

How do solids get into tap water?

Solids dissolve in water as rivers flow over certain rocks, particularly limestone (calcium carbonate). The rock dissolves very slowly over the years. Some of these solids are left inside kettles and hot water pipes when water is heated.

Water dissolves rocks leaving potholes and caves. Stalagmites and stalactites form as drops of water evaporate leaving the dissolved solids.

Making solutions of different concentrations

The washing-up liquid is a concentrated solution of detergent in water. When squirted into the bowl of water a dilute solution is formed.

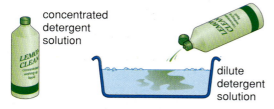

A **dilute solution** contains less solute dissolved in a certain volume of solvent than a **concentrated solution**.

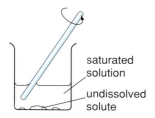

A **saturated solution** contains as much solute dissolved in it as possible at that temperature. The undissolved solute in the bottom means the solution is saturated.

The **solubility** of a solute is the amount of solute that saturates 100 grams of solvent at a certain temperature. Different solutes have different solubilities. For example, sugar has a higher solubility than salt at room temperature as more sugar than salt dissolves in a cup of water.

Improper solutions!

Suspensions

Muddy water contains some larger particles which do not dissolve. Suspensions are opaque (cannot be seen through). When left to stand the solids slowly settle.

Colloids

We can find many colloids in the home. They have tiny gas, liquid or solid particles spread out in a liquid, solid or gas. They do not settle on standing.
Aerosols (liquid or solid particles in a gas), for example, fog, smoke, deodorant sprays.
Emulsions (insoluble liquid drops in another liquid), for example, salad cream.
Foams (gas trapped in liquids or solids), for example, sponge, beer froth, expanded polystyrene.
Gels (liquid in solid network), for example, hair gel, jellies.
Sols (solid particles in liquid), for example, paints, toothpaste.

Helping solutes dissolve more quickly

Solids dissolve more quickly if they are crushed and if the mixture is stirred and warmed.

More of the substance usually dissolves on heating. The solubility of *most* solids increases with temperature.

When a hot saturated sugar solution is cooled some of the sugar comes out of solution as the solubility decreases. **Crystallisation** occurs. The slower the cooling, the larger the crystals.

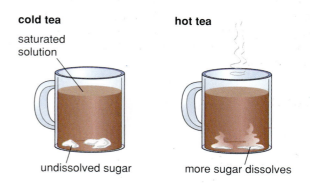

More sugar dissolves in hot tea!
The solubility of sugar in water increases with temperature.

Solvents other than water

Try washing a greasy plate in water. The grease does not dissolve. Other solvents dissolve grease and oil. They are called organic solvents
- ethanol dissolves biro, ink and perfume
- propanone dissolves nail varnish
- white spirit, turps, trichloroethane and tetrachloromethane dissolve grease, oil, wet varnish and paint.

Summary

1. Solutes dissolve in solvents to form solutions.
2. Water dissolves many ionic but not covalent compounds.
3. Organic solvents dissolve many covalent compounds.

Questions

1. Make a table to show which of the following dissolve in water, trichloroethane or are insoluble in both: salt, grease, sugar, sand, wax, sodium nitrate, graphite, varnish, oil, butter, zinc bromide?
2. Explain the difference between dilute, concentrated and saturated solutions. What happens when a hot saturated sugar solution is cooled?

17 Separating mixtures of solids

1. Making a solution, filtration and evaporation

Whenever we use a tea strainer, chip pan or even a net for removing insects from the surface of a pond, we are separating something solid from a liquid.

In a laboratory this process is called **filtration** and a filter funnel and filter paper are used.

Filtration is useful for separating solids from solutions, for example, in the purification of rock salt. Rock salt contains salt mixed with sand and other impurities. Water is added to dissolve the salt: the impurities which do not dissolve are filtered off.

The rock salt is crushed in a mortar.

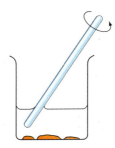

When stirred in water only the salt dissolves.

The mixture of sand and salt solution is filtered. The sand is left on the filter paper.

The filtrate is the salt solution. It is boiled to evaporate nearly all the water and then left to cool.

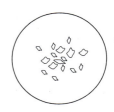

Crystals of salt form in the dish.

Obtaining salt on a large scale

Salt is obtained from underground deposits as well as from the sea.

In Cheshire, salt is obtained from underground deposits by dissolving it in water and evaporating the solution. In hot countries, sea water is run into large pools and the heat from the Sun evaporates the water. Salt is left.

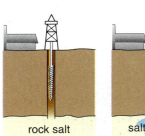

A hole is bored into the salt deposit.

Two pipes are lowered. Water is pumped down one pipe. The salt dissolves.

Salt solution or brine is pumped up the second pipe.

Using solvents other than water

Sometimes neither of the solids dissolves in water. Organic solvents can be used, for example, separating of a mixture of iodine and sulphur.

The ethanol is removed by distillation as it is inflammable and intoxicating! (page 106)

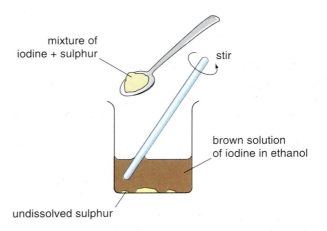

Ethanol is added. The iodine dissolves but not the sulphur, which is filtered off.

104

2. Chromatography

If you try to get a black ink spot off a cotton shirt with only a small amount of water, the mark spreads out and makes a mess.

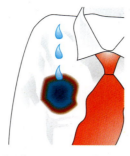

If the black ink contains a mixture of coloured compounds, these may separate out.

A process called **chromatography** has occurred and you have obtained a chromatogram on the shirt!

Chromatography is used to separate mixtures of solids and to identify the substances present.

For example, a deep blue dye often contains a mixture of different coloured dyes. To find the dyes present, the blue dye is first dissolved in a solvent such as water.

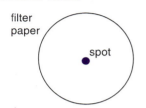
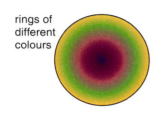

A spot of the solution of the dye is placed in the centre of the filter paper and left to dry. Drops of water are added slowly.

The different dyes present spread out at different rates. Rings of different colours are formed.

Other ways of carrying out paper chromatography are shown below.

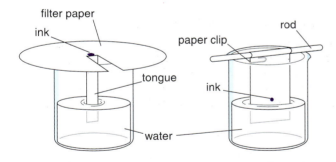

Identifying the dyes present

The chromatogram obtained for a deep blue dye and for four separate pure dyes is shown.

The results show that the deep blue dye is a mixture of the dark blue, purple and green dyes.

For mixtures which are insoluble in water, solvents such as ethanol are used.

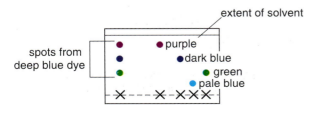

3. Using a magnet

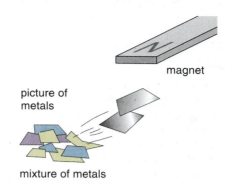

Magnets attract iron and steel, but not metals such as zinc, copper and aluminium. They are therefore used to extract iron and steel from scrap metals and household rubbish.

How pure is the solid?

A pure solid melts at a definite temperature called its melting point. Impurities lower the melting point.

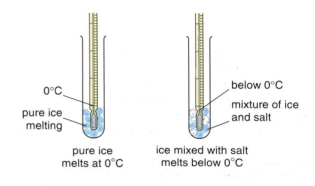

Did you know? Gold can be separated from other materials in the sediment from rivers by 'panning'. The unwanted material is washed away leaving the denser gold.

Summary

1. Mixtures of solids can be separated by: preparation of a solution, filtration and evaporation; use of a magnet; chromatography.
2. A pure solid melts at a temperature called its melting point. Impurities lower the melting point.

Questions

1. Some rice is accidentally tipped into a jar of salt. How would you separate the rice from the salt?
2. How would you show that a sample of ice is pure?
3. A black dye is a mixture of coloured substances. The dye is soluble in ethanol but not in water. How would you find out which coloured substances are present?

18 Separating mixtures of liquids

Many different mixtures of liquids are found in the home. In some cases the liquids mix together, in others they do not. Many of the liquids also contain dissolved solids and gases.

Did you know? Rose oil is expensive. Only 0.5 kg is obtained by distillation from 1000 kg of rose petals

liquids that do not mix (or **immiscible liquids**)

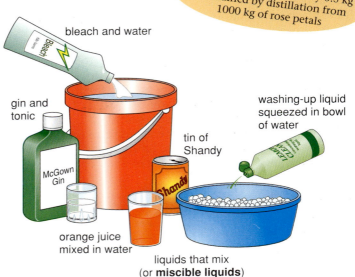

liquids that mix (or **miscible liquids**)

A CLOSER LOOK AT SALAD DRESSING

The main ingredients of salad dressing are oil and vinegar. Sometimes the presence of other substances such as mustard help to keep the small drops of oil separate. A stable **emulsion** is formed.

SEPARATING IMMISCIBLE LIQUIDS

Immiscible liquids are separated by pouring the mixture into a **separating funnel**.

The lower layer is run off first by opening the tap. This is the denser liquid. The upper layer is left in the funnel.

For example, glycerol and water are immiscible. The density of glycerol is 1.26 g cm^{-3} and of water is 1 g cm^{-3}. Which liquid will form the lower layer?

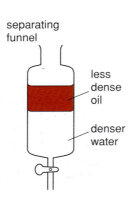

A CLOSER LOOK AT GIN AND TONIC

When gin and tonic are added together no layers are visible. The liquids have mixed together. The main ingredients are ethanol (alcohol) and water.

SEPARATING MISCIBLE LIQUIDS

Miscible liquids, such as a mixture of ethanol and water, are separated by **distillation**.

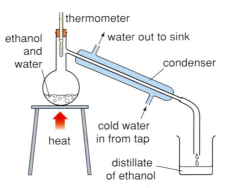

The boiling point of ethanol is 78°C and of water is 100°C. The ethanol boils off first and the vapour is cooled in the condenser. The ethanol vapour condenses and collects.

This is called the **distillate**. When the ethanol has been removed the temperature rises and the water boils at 100°C.

Better separation is obtained using fractional distillation (see page 108).

106

Pure water from dirty water

In some parts of the world there is little drinking water, but plenty of sea water. Pure water can be obtained from the sea water by **distillation**. But this process needs a lot of fuel for heating. It is therefore only carried out where oil is cheap, for example, in the Persian Gulf.

In the past, distillation, using the apparatus shown on page 106, was used in laboratories to obtain very pure water. This is called distilled water.

Cheaper methods using ion exchange columns are now used to obtain pure water. The ions forming the impurities in the water are exchanged for the hydrogen and hydroxide ions which are on the column.

Pure water is needed for topping up car batteries and in certain industries such as dyeing where impurities in the water cause problems.

Reusing solvents

Distillation is used to obtain solvents from solutions where the solvent is poisonous, inflammable or expensive, for example, the 'dry cleaning' solvent trichloroethane.

EMULSIONS

Making an emulsion

Emulsifying agents are added to mixtures of immiscible liquids to keep the liquids mixed. Detergents are common emulsifying agents.

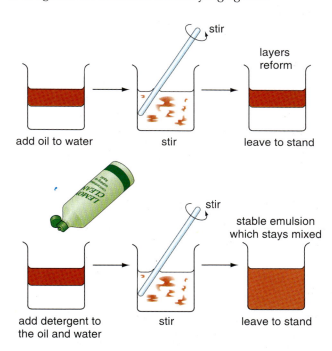

How do detergents work?

The detergent molecule has two parts. The head is 'water-loving'. The tail is 'grease-loving'. The tails of the molecules dissolve in the grease. In water, the heads of the molecules have a negative charge. The drops of oil are therefore kept apart as the charges repel each other.

Soaps are also emulsifying agents.

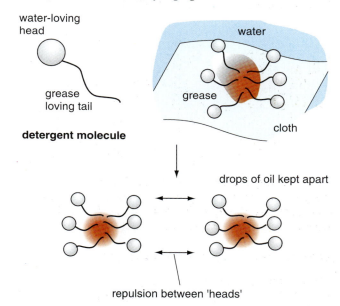

Summary

1. Immiscible liquids are liquids which do not mix. They can be separated using a separating funnel.
2. Miscible liquids are liquids that do mix. They are separated by distillation. Distillation is also used to obtain a solvent from a solution.
3. Emulsifying agents such as detergents are used to form stable emulsions.

Questions

1. Make a list of three pairs of immiscible and three pairs of miscible liquids.
2. Some water is accidentally poured into a bottle of cooking oil. What does it look like? How would you separate the liquids?
3. Draw a labelled diagram to show how you would obtain pure water from salty water.

19 Purifying liquids

How pure is a liquid?

A pure liquid boils at a definite temperature called its **boiling point** (b. pt.)

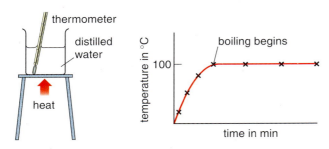

Distilled water starts to boil at 100°C and remains at this temperature until the water has boiled away.

Boiling points and pressure

An increase in pressure raises the boiling point.
In a pressure cooker a heavy weight is placed on the lid to keep in the steam. The pressure increases and the boiling point rises, so food cooks more quickly. A decrease in pressure lowers the boiling point.

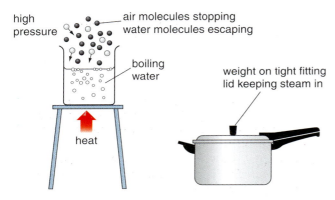

At the top of a mountain the air pressure is lower than at the bottom. The water boils at a lower temperature. It takes much longer to hard boil an egg.

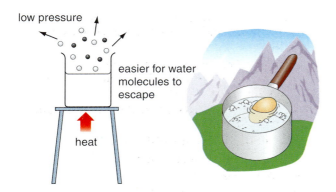

Boiling points and impurities

Impurities raise the boiling point.

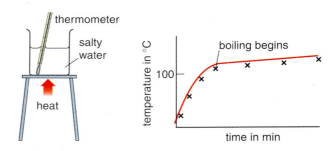

Salty water boils at about 105°C. The boiling point rises as boiling occurs because the solution becomes more concentrated as the water boils away.

Fractional distillation

A mixture of ethanol and water is difficult to separate completely by distillation as their boiling points are very close.
Fractional distillation using the apparatus below gives a better separation. The process happens in the following stages:

- the mixture boils when heated ethanol and water vapour is given off, heating up the column
- the ethanol vapour passes up through the column as the temperature is above its boiling point of 78°C
- the water vapour condenses to water on the glass beads of the column as the beads are below 100°C
- the water drips back into the flask
- All the ethanol is removed and only water remains in the flask. The temperature then rises to 100°C.

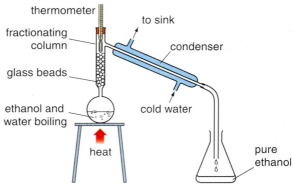

Fractional distillation is used in industry to separate liquids with close boiling points, for example, liquid air is fractionally distilled to obtain nitrogen and oxygen and crude oil is separated into different fractions.

CRUDE OIL

Crude oil is a mixture of a large number of different compounds with different boiling points.

Most of the compounds are molecules made up of carbon and hydrogen only called **hydrocarbons**. In its raw state crude oil is not very useful. Fractional distillation is used to separate it into different fractions.

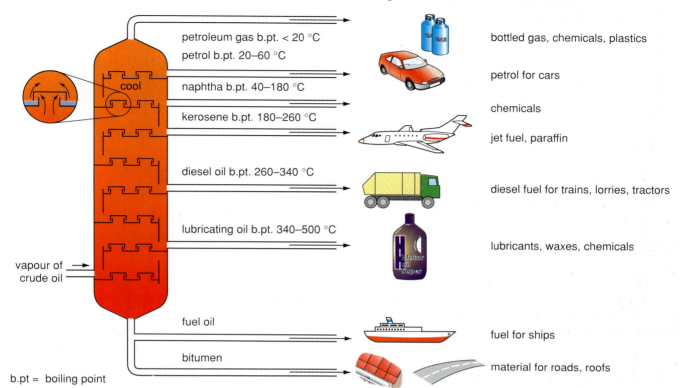

b.pt = boiling point

The fractional distillation of crude oil occurs in the following stages:
- the crude oil is heated and boils
- the vapours given off condense at different temperatures to produce different fractions
- each fraction is a mixture of substances which boil at similar temperatures and has specific uses
- the fraction with the lowest boiling point range is collected at the top of the column
- the fraction with the highest boiling point range remains at the bottom of the column.

The boiling point of a particular hydrocarbon depends on the size and shape of its molecules. The larger the molecule or the greater the number of carbon atoms it contains, the higher the boiling point. The size and shape of the molecule also affects other properties.

Summary

1. A pure liquid boils at a temperature called its boiling point. Impurities raise the boiling point. An increase in pressure raises the boiling point and vice versa.
2. Fractional distillation is used to obtain pure liquids and to separate mixtures of two or more liquids, for example, crude oil.

Questions

1. You expect a particular liquid to boil at 78°C but find it actually boils at 81°C. Give two possible reasons.
2. A sample of ethanol contains some water. Draw a diagram to explain how you would obtain a sample of pure ethanol.
3. State the method which could be used to obtain the following:
   a. oil from its mixture with water
   b. pure water from tap water
   c. petrol from crude oil
   d. the separate dyes in coloured ink.

20 Physical and chemical changes

The picture shows Michael making his breakfast.

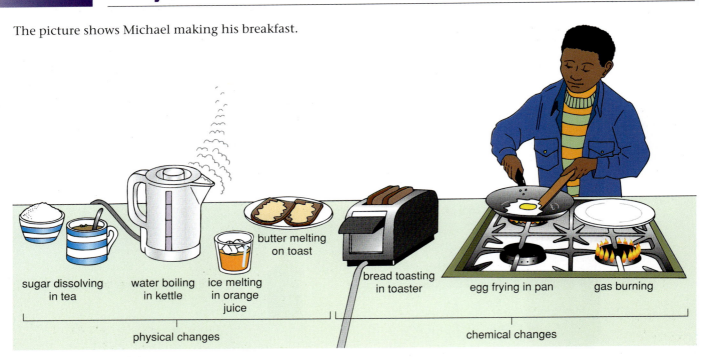

What is a physical change?

1. No new substances are formed

When the ice melts, liquid water is formed. When the water boils it changes into steam. Water molecules are present in all three states. No new substance is formed.

When sugar dissolves you can still taste it. No new substance is formed.

2. The change is reversible

When the water is cooled ice forms again. When the steam is cooled it condenses back into liquid water. When melted butter cools it becomes hard again although it changes shape.

The reactions are reversible. The only energy change involved relates to the change in state.

> **Did you know?**
> Diamonds are made from graphite by a physical change. At high temperatures and pressures graphite changes into diamonds.

What is a chemical change?

1. One or more new substances are formed

When Michael fries the egg it goes hard and its edges turn pale brown. New substances are formed.

When he toasts bread, its surface goes brown as it becomes charred. A new substance called carbon is formed.

2. The change is difficult to reverse

When the hot cooked egg is cooled, it does not become uncooked egg. When the toast is cooled it does not change back into untoasted bread.

The reactions are irreversible.

3. Energy usually transfers between substances during a chemical change

When the gas burns, heat and light energy are transferred to the surroundings. The gas burns to carbon dioxide and water. The heat change is not related to a change in state but to the formation of new substances.

Summary

1. Physical changes are reversible and no new substances are formed.
2. Chemical changes are irreversible and result in the formation of new substances. Energy is often taken in or given out during chemical changes.
3. Chemical changes include neutralisation, corrosion, combustion, precipitation, fermentation, displacement, thermal decomposition, synthesis, catalytic decomposition, electrolysis.

Summary of different types of chemical reactions

Precipitation

acid added to cream causes the protein to precipitate out

- two solutions mixed to give an insoluble substance

Fermentation

baking bread

- yeast acting on sugar to form ethanol and carbon dioxide

Thermal decomposition

toasting bread

- starch in the bread decomposes to water and black carbon
- the breakdown of compounds when heated

Catalytic decomposition

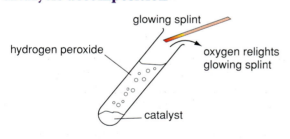

manganese (IV) oxide speeds up or catalyses the decomposition of hydrogen peroxide to water and oxygen

- the breakdown of a compound by the action of a catalyst

Synthesis

ammonia for making fertilisers is made or synthesised from nitrogen and hydrogen

- elements joining together to form a single new compound

Electrolysis (electrolytic decomposition)

extracting aluminium from its ore

- decomposition of liquids and solutions using an electric current

Displacement reactions (oxidation and reduction)

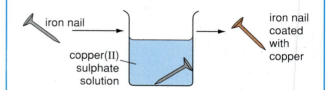

copper coats an iron nail when it is placed in copper(II) sulphate solution

- one substance pushes out another substance from its solution and takes its place

Combustion (oxidation and reduction)

natural gas burns and transfers heat energy to the surroundings

- substances burning using the oxygen in the air

Corrosion

the iron frying pan has rusted or corroded

- metals reacting with air and/or moisture

Neutralisation

indigestion tablets neutralise the excess acid in the stomach

- acids reacting with alkalis to form a neutral substance

Questions

1. **a** Give two physical and five chemical changes which occur in your home. For each of the chemical changes give the type of change.
   b Give two ways in which the physical and chemical changes differ.

21 Chemical reactions and equations

1. Combustion of magnesium ribbon

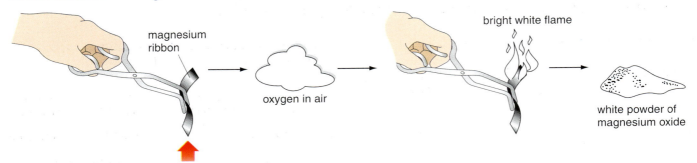

The changes can be summarised in a chemical equation.

magnesium(s) + oxygen(g) ⟶ magnesium oxide(s)

reactants   **product**

The physical state of the substances is indicated by symbols. The symbols (s) and (g) stand for *solid* and *gas*. The other symbols are l (liquid) and aq (aqueous solution) (solution in water).

2. Thermal decomposition of copper(II) carbonate

The green copper (II) carbonate decomposes to form black copper (II) oxide. The carbon dioxide gas gives a white precipitate when bubbled through limewater.

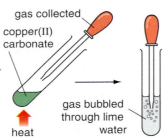

Equation
copper(II) carbonate(s) → copper(II) oxide(s) + carbon dioxide (g)

3. The reaction between silver nitrate solution and salt solution

The solutions of silver nitrate and salt (sodium chloride) are colourless. Added together they form a white precipitate of silver chloride.

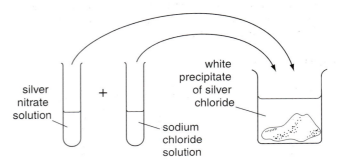

Equation

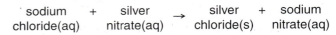

sodium chloride(aq) + silver nitrate(aq) → silver chloride(s) + sodium nitrate(aq)

The metals have swapped partners. The sodium nitrate is soluble and is left in solution.

HAZARD SYMBOLS

Hazard symbols warn us about the dangers of substances we use.

Corrosive materials
Concentrated acids and dishwasher powder burn clothes and skin.

Poisonous or toxic substances
Arsenic and many pesticides may poison us or even kill us if they get inside the body.

Flammable materials
Ethanol, petrol, turps and some paints burn very easily.

Harmful substances
Many household cleaners are harmful even though they may not be toxic

Oxidising substances
Some weedkillers and chemicals such as potassium chlorate help things burn easily.

Irritants
Household bleach may cause a rash on the skin.

MAKING EQUATIONS BALANCE

Equations using formulae show how many molecules of each substance are used up, or produced. Atoms are not created or destroyed during a chemical reaction so there must be the same number of atoms of each element in the reactants as in the products. The equation is then said to *balance*.

The balanced equations for the reactions on the opposite page are given below.

1. Combustion of magnesium ribbon

magnesium(s) + oxygen(g) ⟶ magnesium oxide(s)
Mg O_2 MgO

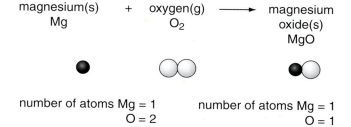

number of atoms Mg = 1   number of atoms Mg = 1
O = 2   O = 1

There are two oxygen atoms on the left-hand side of the equation but only one on the right-hand side. The equation does not balance. To make it balance, two molecules of magnesium oxide must be produced to use up both oxygen atoms and two atoms of magnesium are needed.

Balanced equation

$2Mg(s) + O_2(g) \longrightarrow 2MgO(s)$

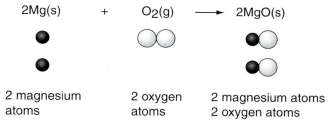

2 magnesium   2 oxygen   2 magnesium atoms
atoms   atoms   2 oxygen atoms

The balanced equation tells us that two atoms of solid magnesium react with one molecule of oxygen gas to form two molecules of solid magnesium oxide.

2. Thermal decomposition of copper(II) carbonate

copper(II) carbonate(s) → copper(II) oxide(s) + carbon dioxide(g)
$CuCO_3(s)$ → $CuO(s)$ + $CO_2(g)$

Number of atoms   Number of atoms
Cu = 1   Cu = 1
C = 1   C = 1
O = 3   O = 1+2 = 3

The number of atoms are the same on each side of the equation. The equation is balanced.

3. Reaction between silver nitrate and salt solution

sodium chloride(aq) + silver nitrate(aq) → silver chloride(s) + sodium nitrate(aq)

$NaCl(aq) + AgNO_3(aq) \rightarrow AgCl(s) + NaNO_3(aq)$

Number of atoms   Number of atoms
Na = 1   Na = 1
Cl = 1   Cl = 1
Ag = 1   Ag = 1
N = 1   N = 1
O = 3   O = 3

The number of different atoms are the same on both sides of the equation. Note that the nitrate group does not break down. The equation is balanced.

SUMMARY

1. Word equations summarise a chemical reaction.
2. Balanced symbol and formulae equations show how many molecules of the reactants and products are formed.

QUESTIONS

1. Give word equations for the following reactions
   a. carbon burning in oxygen to form carbon dioxide
   b. the decomposition of calcium carbonate to calcium oxide and carbon dioxide on heating
   c. the addition of potassium chloride solution to silver nitrate solution to give a precipitate of silver chloride.
2. Draw the hazard symbols for petrol and for concentrated hydrochloric acid.

22 How much?

WEIGHING ATOMS

Atoms are much too small to be weighed individually. For example, one atom of hydrogen has a mass of 0.000 000 000 000 000 000 000 000 17 g. Even if it could be weighed this is a very difficult number to use! Atoms are therefore compared with each other using a special scale.

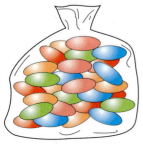
500 g smarties

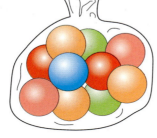
500 g gob stoppers

WHAT IS THE SCALE?

A relative scale is used which has a standard against which the masses of all the other atoms are compared.

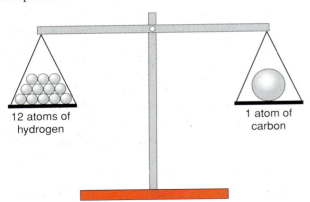

12 atoms of hydrogen

1 atom of carbon

The standard is an atom of carbon which is given a value of 12.
 The carbon atom is 12 times heavier than an atom of hydrogen. The value for an atom of hydrogen is therefore 1. This value is known as the **relative atomic mass** (A_r) of hydrogen.

Relative atomic mass (A_r)

The A_r values of some common atoms are given in the table. Some of these values are not whole numbers, for example, chlorine. This is because chlorine exists as two isotopes, chlorine-35 and chlorine-37 (page 89). The A_r value is an average value for chlorine which depends on the amounts of each isotope present.

Relative formula mass (M_r)

The M_r of a compound is calculated from its formula. It is found by adding up the relative atomic masses of the atoms in the compound as given in its formula.

For example,
carbon dioxide CO_2
M_r of CO_2 = 12 + 16 + 16 = 44

When the formula contains brackets around a group remember to multiply the *whole* group by the number after the bracket.

For example,
magnesium nitrate $Mg(NO_3)_2$
M_r of $Mg(NO_3)_2$ = 24 + 2 (14 + 16 + 16 + 16)
= 24 + 2 (62)
= 24 + 124
= 148

Some crystals have molecules of water in the crystal structure. Be careful to include all the molecules.

For example the formula of blue copper(II) sulphate crystals is $CuSO_4.5H_2O$. This means that for every $CuSO_4$ there are five molecules of water.
M_r of $CuSO_4.5H_2O$
= 64 + 32 + 16 + 16 + 16 + 16 + 5 (1 + 1 + 16)
= 160 + 5 (18)
= 160 + 90
= 250

Element	Symbol	A_r
hydrogen	H	1
helium	He	4
carbon	C	12
nitrogen	N	14
oxygen	O	16
fluorine	F	19
sodium	Na	23
magnesium	Mg	24
aluminium	Al	27
phosphorus	P	31
sulphur	S	32
chlorine	Cl	35.5
potassium	K	39
calcium	Ca	40
iron	Fe	56
copper	Cu	64
zinc	Zn	65
lead	Pb	207

Percentage of substances in a compound

It is often useful to know how much of a particular substance is in a compound. This is usually calculated as a percentage.

Percentage of the substance = $\dfrac{\text{mass of substance in the compound}}{\text{mass of compound}} \times 100\%$

1. Finding the percentages of a metal in metal ores

Haematite (Fe_2O_3) and magnetite (Fe_3O_4) are important ores of the metal iron. The iron content in the ores can be compared by finding the percentages.

M_r Fe_2O_3 = 56 + 56 + 16 + 16 + 16
       = 160

160 g of haematite contain (56 + 56)g or 112 g of iron.

% of iron in haematite = $\dfrac{112}{160} \times 100\%$
                       = 70.0%

M_r Fe_3O_4 = 56 + 56 + 56 + 16 + 16 + 16 + 16
       = 232

232 g of magnetite contain (56 + 56 + 56)g or 168 g of iron.

% of iron in magnetite = $\dfrac{168}{232} \times 100\%$
                       = 72.4%

Magnetite contains a higher percentage of iron in its ore than haematite. This suggests that it would be more economical to use magnetite provided that all other costs are the same.

Summary

1. The relative atomic mass A_r of an atom is used to compare its mass with that of other atoms. The mass of compounds can be compared using the relative formula mass M_r.
2. The percentage of a substance in a compound = $\dfrac{\text{mass of the substance in compound}}{\text{mass of compound}} \times 100\%$

Questions

1. Calculate the M_r of the following: sodium chloride NaCl, zinc carbonate $ZnCO_3$, ammonium sulphate $(NH_4)_2SO_4$.
2. Calculate the percentage of:
    a aluminium in the ore bauxite, Al_2O_3
    b nitrogen in ammonium carbonate, $(NH_4)_2CO_3$
    c water in copper(II) sulphate crystals, $CuSO_4$ $5H_2O$.

2. What is in a fertiliser?

Fertilisers are added to soil to provide extra minerals for plants, in particular, nitrogen N, phosphorus P and potassium K. The percentage of each of these three elements in the fertiliser is known as its NPK value. The nitrogen is usually provided by adding ammonium chloride NH_4Cl or ammonium nitrate NH_4NO_3.

M_r of NH_4Cl = 14 + 1 + 1 + 1 + 1 + 35.5
              = 53.5

53.5 g of ammonium chloride contains 14 g of nitrogen.

% of nitrogen = $\dfrac{14}{53.5} \times 100\%$
              = 26.2%

$M_r NH_4NO_3$ = 14 + 1 + 1 + 1 + 1 + 14 + 16 + 16 + 16
              = 80

80 g of ammonium nitrate contains (14 + 14)g or 28 g of nitrogen

% of nitrogen = $\dfrac{28}{80} \times 100\%$
              = 35.0%

A fertiliser containing ammonium nitrate provides more nitrogen, but this may not be suitable for all plants.

3. Expensive water in bath cystals

In most cases, bath crystals are crystals of washing soda ($Na_2CO_3.10H_2O$) which have been coloured and perfumed. They contain a lot of water as ten molecules of water are bound to every molecule of sodium carbonate.

M_r of $Na_2CO_3.10H_2O$
    = 23 + 23 + 12 + 16 + 16 + 16 + 10 (1 + 1 + 16)
    = 106 + 10(18) = 106 + 180
    = 286

286 g of washing soda crystals contain 180 g of water.
% of water in the crystals = $\dfrac{180}{286} \times 100\%$
                           = 62.9 %

When we buy washing soda crystals we are buying quite a lot of expensive water!

23 Fossil fuel

When we are cold we may...

- turn on an electric fire or fan heater,
- burn coal or smokeless fuel on a fire,
- light a gas fire or a stove fuelled with calor gas or paraffin,
- turn on the central heating system, which runs on gas, oil, solid fuel or electricity.

Either directly or indirectly, all of these forms of heating use up fuels known as **fossil fuels**. These include natural gas, oil and coal. Smokeless fuels are made from coal and in this country most of our electricity is generated by burning fossil fuels although other energy resources are also used.

How are fossil fuels formed?

Fossil fuels form from the decay of plant and animal remains (called organic matter) over millions of years. The organic matter is covered by layers of sedimentary rock. In the absence of air, bacteria cause it to decay. The fossil fuels slowly form as a result of the effect of heat and pressure on the decayed material.

Coal is mainly formed from plants and animals which lived on the land. Oil and natural gas are formed from plants and animals which lived in the sea.

Coal

Plants and trees use energy from the sun to photosynthesise and grow. Dead plants and animals are covered by water. They are broken down by bacteria in the absence of oxygen.

layers over coal seam

Layers of mud and rock are deposited over the remains. After millions of years they become coal.

Shafts are dug through the rocks to the coal seams. The coal is mined.

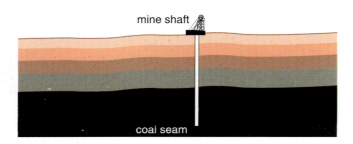

Oil and gas

Plants and tiny creatures living in the sea die and are buried under mud. They are broken down by bacteria in the absence of oxygen.

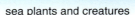

Layers of mud cover the remains and over millions of years they become oil and gas. The mud becomes rock.

Earth movements fold the layers of rock. Oil and gas move up through **porous** rocks, which have small holes in them. The oil and gas is trapped below **non-porous** rock which has no holes in it.

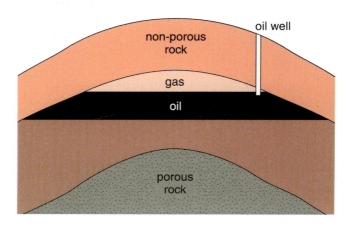

How long will fossil fuels last?

Fossil fuels are non-renewable. They take millions of years to form and are used up much faster than they can be replaced by nature. As well as being a fuel, oil is a very important raw material for the chemical industry. The amount used each year has increased rapidly.

It is predicted that the known supplies of oil and gas will soon be used up, in fact within the next 50 years! This is unless new supplies are found or more efficient methods of extraction are used. Supplies of coal are predicted to last longer, but then only about 300 years.

It is important to conserve supplies of fossil fuels. This can be done by using more energy from renewable sources, using fuels more efficiently and recycling substances made from oil.

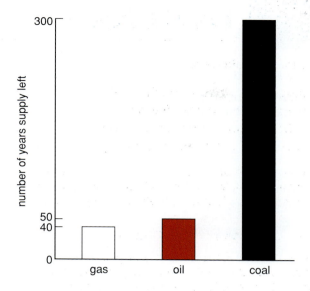

Using fossil fuels

Coal contains carbon and impurities such as compounds of sulphur. Oil and natural gas contain compounds of carbon and hydrogen called **hydrocarbons**. They also have impurities containing sulphur. When fossil fuels are burnt in air they use up oxygen and release energy. This is called combustion. Other products are formed as shown. Some of these are harmful and called **pollutants**.

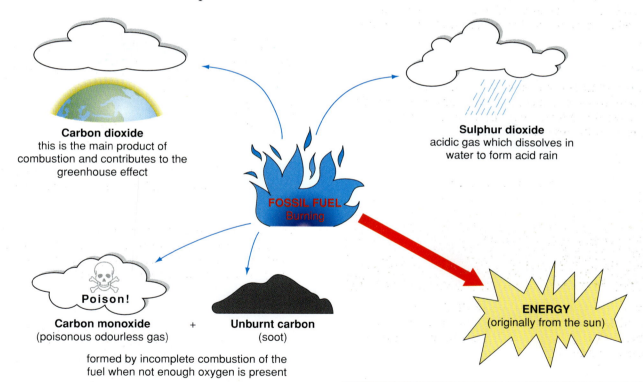

Summary

1. Fossil fuels include natural gas, oil and coal. They are non-renewable.
2. When fossil fuels are burnt they use oxygen from the air and release energy. Some of the gases formed are pollutants.

Questions

1. Explain how natural gas is formed.
2. Give reasons why it is important not to waste fuels. Describe ways in which your school could save fuel.
3. What is formed when coal is burnt? Explain why the energy transferred comes originally from the Sun.

24 Crude oil and its uses

HOW DO THE CRUDE OIL FRACTIONS DIFFER?

The three useful substances shown below come from different fractions from crude oil. They all contain hydrocarbons but the molecules in each fraction differ in size.

Gas in the gas stove
Natural gas is the simplest hydrocarbon and is called methane, CH_4. It has the lowest boiling point, $-164°C$.

Petrol
The main hydrocarbon in petrol contains eight carbon atoms in its molecule. Petrol is a liquid, boiling at about 40°C.

Candle wax
The hydrocarbons in candle wax are much larger with around 50 carbon atoms per molecule. The wax is a solid and its boiling point is high, above 350°C.

Hydrocarbons are part of a family called the alkanes. The first part of each name tells us the number of carbon atoms in the molecule and the last part ends in **-ane**. The first four members are shown in the table.

Name	Formula
methane	CH_4
ethane	C_2H_6
propane	C_3H_8
butane	C_4H_{10}

Comparing three liquid fractions of crude oil

The fractions petrol, diesel and lubricating oil contain hydrocarbons of increasing size. The ease with which they ignite (**flammability**) and the ease with which they flow (**viscosity**) can be compared.

Ease of flow (Viscosity)

The time taken for the same amount of liquid to run through the same size tube is compared.
Petrol takes the shortest time so is least viscous. Lubricating oil takes the longest time so is most viscous.

petrol   diesel   lubricating oil

Flammability

Small but equal amounts of each liquid are used. The time taken for each liquid to catch alight is compared.
Petrol catches alight most easily so is most flammable. Lubricating oil is the hardest to light so is least flammable.

	Number of carbon atoms in each molecule	Boiling point °C
petrol	6 to 9	40
diesel	16 to 22	250
lubricating oil	30 to 32	310

The size and boiling points of the three fractions.

Changes in the properties of hydrocarbons

With an increase in the size of the hydrocarbon molecule there is:
- decrease in flammability
- decrease in ease in forming a vapour (volatility)
- increase in boiling point
- increase in viscosity.

GETTING MORE FUEL FROM CRUDE OIL

There is a higher demand for petrol than for the heavier fractions of crude oil, which are less flammable. Hydrocarbons with larger molecules are broken down or '**cracked**' by passing the hot vapour over catalysts. The smaller molecules formed are used as fuels and in making chemicals.

Plastics

Plastics are everywhere. Some of the most common are poly(ethene), (usually called polythene), PVC, polystyrene and polypropylene. The uses made of plastics relate to their properties.
In general, they are:
    lightweight, relatively strong, easily moulded or cut, quite cheap, unable to rot or corrode, good insulators of heat and electricity, easy to colour.

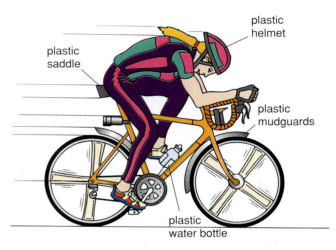

Important uses:
poly(ethene): carrier bags, insulation around cables
PVC: plastic guttering, plastic coverings for seats
expanded polystyrene (polystyrene containing small bubbles of air): packaging and insulating materials.

Some new plastics are fire resistant and so can be used more widely. Others are very strong, up to five times stronger than steel, and are used in bulletproof vests and car engines.

Making plastics

Plastics are polymers and made from some of the molecules obtained from **cracking** the heavier fractions of crude oil. The smaller molecules join together in a process called **polymerisation**.

For example, poly(ethene) is made by joining a large number (often millions) of ethene molecules together. Poly means 'lots of'.

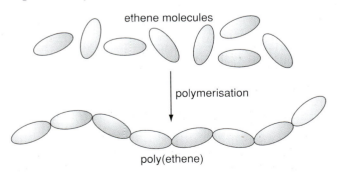

Problems with plastics

Because most plastics do not rot or break down they may cause litter. Some take over 200 years to decompose.

Recycling plastic is difficult as there are so many different types. At present in the UK, only about 1% is recycled and is mainly made into containers such as milk crates.

Other useful products from crude oil

Many important chemicals and substances are made from crude oil. These include solvents, dyes, medicines, paints and fibres such as Terylene, nylon, polyester. Crude oil is therefore a very valuable substance. It is essential that supplies are conserved and other renewable sources of energy are used.

Summary

1. The different crude oil fractions contain alkanes with different sizes of molecules. The properties relate to the size of the molecules.
2. Larger alkanes are broken into smaller molecules by cracking. The smaller molecules are used as fuels and to make other chemicals and plastics.
3. Plastics are made by polymerisation.

Questions

1. Name three different plastics and give two uses of each. Relate each use to a property of the plastic.
2. What is meant by cracking? Why is it used?
3. Two alkanes X and Y are both liquids. X has larger molecules than Y. How would you expect the boiling points, flammability and viscosity of X and Y to differ?

25 The air

Air is a mixture of gases and the approximate amounts are given below. The actual amounts vary slightly from day to day and place to place.

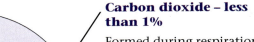

Nitrogen 78%
Unreactive gas diluting the oxygen in the air making it more suitable for breathing.
Uses:
- as a liquid, to freeze blood, sperm
- as a gas, to stop food from going off, for instance, crisps
- in the manufacture of ammonia, nitric acid, fertilisers.

Oxygen 21%
Oxygen is needed for respiration and combustion.
Uses:
- as an aid for breathing, for example, in hospitals
- for combustion, for example, welding, rocket fuel
- to remove impurities from iron in making steel (page 135).

Carbon dioxide – less than 1%
Formed during respiration and when fuels burn. Used up during photosynthesis.
Uses:
- in fizzy drinks, fire extinguishers
- for preserving food
- as a solid (dry) ice for cooling and special effects.

Pollutants and solid particles
The type and amount of pollutants present varies.

Water – less than 1%
The amount of water vapour in air varies from place to place. It partly determines the weather.

Noble gases 1%
Noble gases are unreactive (inert). They have many uses, for example, neon is used in lights.

Separating the gases from the air
Liquid air is separated by fractional distillation.

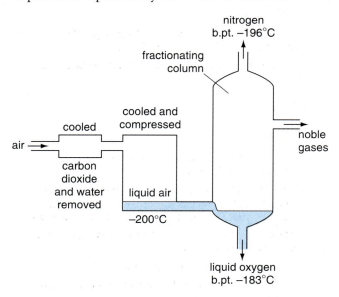

The stages in the process are:
- carbon dioxide and water vapour are removed by cooling. Otherwise, they solidify and block the pipes
- the rest of the air is liquefied by compressing and cooling to about –200°C
- the liquefied air is fractionally distilled. Nitrogen gas, boiling point –196°C, comes off at the top of the column. The noble gases are taken out half way down. Liquid oxygen, which has the highest boiling point (–183°C), is left at the bottom of the column.

REACTING SUBSTANCES WITH OXYGEN

When things burn they use oxygen and form new substances called oxides. Energy transfers to the surroundings as heat and sometimes light. The reaction is called combustion (see page 122).

Substance + Oxygen $\rightarrow$ Oxide + Energy

Did you know?
Healthy people breathe 16 000 litres of air in and out every day. That's a lot of air!

Reaction of metals with oxygen

When metals react with oxygen, metal oxides are formed.

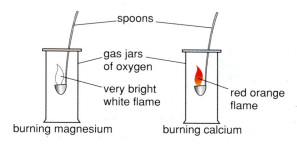

metal + oxygen $\rightarrow$ metal oxide

Magnesium forms the white solid, magnesium oxide.
magnesium(s) + oxygen(g) $\rightarrow$ magnesium oxide(s)

Calcium forms the white solid, calcium oxide.
calcium(s) + oxygen(g) $\rightarrow$ calcium oxide(s)

If the metal oxide dissolves in water an alkali is formed. For example, calcium oxide dissolves in water to form calcium hydroxide. This is a weak alkali and is commonly called limewater.

Reaction of iron in air

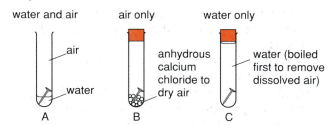

To demonstrate that iron rusts in air, three test tubes containing iron nails were set up as shown in the diagram. They were left for one week. Only the nail in test tube A rusted. This shows that both water and air are needed for iron to rust.

Rust is hydrated iron(III) oxide. Iron needs oxygen and water to corrode or rust.

Reaction of non-metals with oxygen

When non-metals react with oxygen, non-metal oxides are formed. The oxide formed depends on the substance burnt.

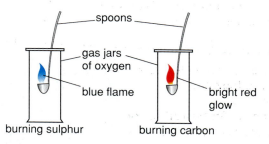

non-metal + oxygen $\rightarrow$ non-metal oxide

Sulphur forms the poisonous gas called sulphur dioxide.
sulphur(s) + oxygen(g) $\rightarrow$ sulphur dioxide(g)

Carbon forms the gas carbon dioxide.
carbon(s) + oxygen(g) $\rightarrow$ carbon dioxide(g)

If the non-metal oxide dissolves in water an acid is formed. For example, sulphur dioxide dissolves in rain water and eventually forms 'acid rain', which contains sulphuric acid.

SUMMARY

1. Air is a mixture of gases which are separated by fractional distillation of liquid air.
2. When substances react with oxygen, oxides are formed.

QUESTIONS

1. Make a table to show the percentage of the gases in the air and their uses.
2. What is formed when the following are burnt in oxygen: carbon, sulphur, sodium, magnesium, calcium? Give word equations for these reactions.
3. A pair of shears went rusty when they were left in damp grass for a week.
   a. What is rust and how is it formed?
   b. How could you protect a pair of shears from rusting?

26 More about combustion

WHAT DO RESPIRATION AND A BURNING GAS FIRE HAVE IN COMMON?

In both cases fuels are reacting with oxygen to give out energy. In respiration, the fuel is glucose from the food which has been eaten. In a gas fire, the fuel is natural gas. Both are examples of **combustion**.

When combustion occurs substances react with oxygen and oxides are formed. Combustion is also an example of **oxidation**.

WHAT IS FORMED WHEN FUELS ARE BURNT?

Fuels such as natural gas and candle wax are made of hydrocarbons. These are compounds containing carbon and hydrogen.

During combustion, the hydrogen in the hydrocarbon is oxidised to water and the carbon to carbon dioxide. Energy is transferred to the surroundings.

hydrocarbon + oxygen → water + carbon dioxide + energy

Carbon dioxide and water vapour are colourless. Simple tests are used to show they are formed.

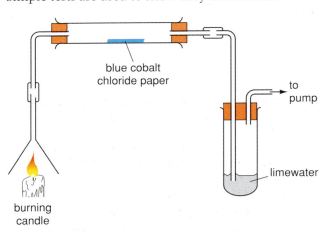

The water vapour turns the blue cobalt chloride paper pink. The carbon dioxide forms a white precipitate in the limewater.

The simplest hydrocarbon is methane or natural gas.

methane(g) + oxygen(g) → carbon dioxide(g) + water(l) + energy

The balanced equation for combustion of methane is:

$CH_4(g) + 2O_2(g) \rightarrow CO_2(g) + 2H_2O(l)$ + energy

This tells us that when one molecule of methane is burnt completely, two molecules of oxygen are used up.

WHAT IS FORMED DURING RESPIRATION?

The food is eaten and broken down or digested into smaller molecules such as glucose. This is carried by the blood to the body tissues.

Respiration occurs in the cells when glucose reacts with oxygen. Energy is transferred to other substances in the cells.

glucose(aq) + oxygen(g) → carbon dioxide(g) + water(l) + energy

The carbon dioxide is carried to the lungs and exhaled. The energy is needed for our body processes and to keep us warm.

What is formed during incomplete combustion?

When the Bunsen burner is lit with the air-hole closed the flame is yellow. A black layer of soot or carbon forms on the glass on the bottom of the beaker.

With the air-hole closed, the burning gas cannot get enough oxygen to burn completely and incomplete combustion occurs.

The poisonous gas called carbon monoxide, CO, is also formed. Carbon monoxide has no smell or colour so is very dangerous. If you breathe it in it makes you feel sleepy and can eventually kill you. It is important to have gas heaters serviced regularly. There are also special carbon monoxide detectors.

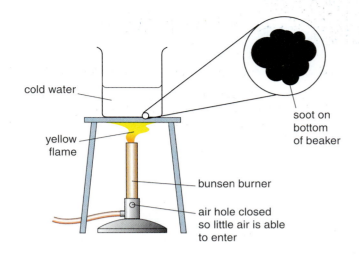

Pollutants

Carbon monoxide is one of several harmful gases released into the air. They are called pollutants. The harmful effect of a pollutant may take many years to appear.

Pollutant	Cause	Effect	Solution
carbon monoxide	incomplete combustion of fuels	poisonous, causes headaches, tiredness and sometimes death	service gas appliances regularly, ensure an adequate air supply when burning fossil fuels
sulphur dioxide	burning fossil fuels, for example, in gases from power stations and exhaust gases from engines	contribute to breathing problems such as asthma and bronchitis; dissolve in water to form 'acid rain'. This damages stonework and metal work, harms plants and animals in lakes and rivers, affects growth of trees and plants	clean exhaust gases, use fuels other than fossil fuels
nitrogen oxides	high temperature engines, for example, diesel engines cause nitrogen and oxygen in the air to react and form nitrogen oxides		
hydrocarbons	unburnt fuel from engines and spillages in garages	possible cause of some cancers and contribute to breathing problems	clean exhaust fumes, reduce spillages
lead compounds	car exhaust from leaded petrol	poisonous, damages nervous system particularly of young children	change car engines to use unleaded fuel
gases reacting with ozone	gases, for example chlorofluorocarbons (CFCs), used in refrigerators, aerosols and solvents react with ozone in the upper atmosphere	the ozone layer protects us from the Sun's dangerous rays. Holes in the layer let the rays through and contribute to skin cancers and eye problems	use less harmful chemicals, dispose of old fridges safely

Carbon dioxide is not in itself poisonous but together with methane from natural sources and rubbish dumps contributes to the 'greenhouse effect' and global warming.

Summary

1. During combustion fuels burn in oxygen to form carbon dioxide and water. Energy is released. Oxidation occurs.
2. Pollutants include carbon monoxide, oxides of sulphur and nitrogen, CFCs, hydrocarbons and lead compounds.

Questions

1. What is formed when a fossil fuel burns in plenty of air. Why should a gas boiler be serviced regularly?
2. From the following: sulphur dioxide, carbon monoxide, oxides of nitrogen, carbon dioxide, nitrogen. Name:
   a two gases causing acid rain
   b the gas forming most of the air
   c the gas formed by incomplete combustion of fuels.

27 Nitrogen and its uses

Nitrogen gas does not easily react. However, at certain temperatures and pressures, it can be made to react to form useful compounds. It is therefore an important raw material.

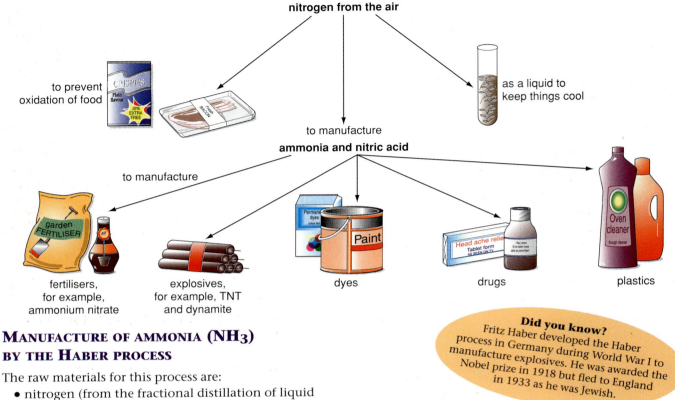

MANUFACTURE OF AMMONIA (NH_3) BY THE HABER PROCESS

The raw materials for this process are:
- nitrogen (from the fractional distillation of liquid air
- hydrogen (from passing a mixture of methane and steam over a catalyst).

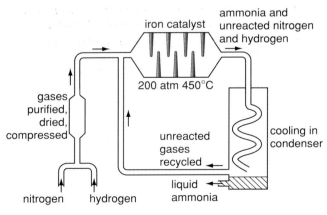

The reaction takes place when the purified gases are passed at a high pressure (200 atmospheres) and a high temperature (450°C) over a catalyst of iron. Some of the nitrogen and hydrogen react.

nitrogen(g) + hydrogen(g) ⇌ ammonia(g)
$N_2(g) + 3H_2(g) \rightleftharpoons 2NH_3(g)$

Did you know?
Fritz Haber developed the Haber process in Germany during World War I to manufacture explosives. He was awarded the Nobel prize in 1918 but fled to England in 1933 as he was Jewish.

The reaction goes in both directions. It is a **reversible reaction**. Only 10 – 15% of the gases become ammonia.

The ammonia is removed as a liquid by cooling the mixture. The unreacted gases are recycled.

USES OF AMMONIA

Most of the ammonia produced is used to make fertilisers.

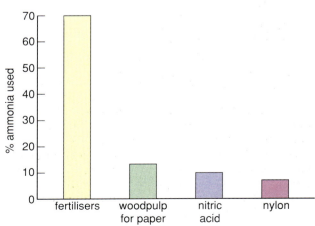

Oxidation of ammonia to nitric acid (HNO_3)

The raw materials for this process are:
- ammonia from Haber process
- air as the source of oxygen.

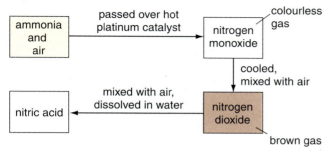

The reaction takes place when the gases are passed over a hot platinum catalyst. Nitrogen monoxide, NO, is formed.

The nitrogen monoxide is mixed with air and cooled. Nitrogen dioxide, NO_2, is formed.

The nitrogen dioxide is mixed with air and dissolved in water. Nitric acid, HNO_3, is produced.

Manufacture of ammonium nitrate (Nitram)

Ammonium nitrate is the most widely used fertiliser in Great Britain. It is prepared by neutralising nitric acid with ammonia.

nitric acid(aq) + ammonia(g) → ammonium nitrate(aq)
$HNO_3(aq)$ + $NH_3(g)$ → $NH_4NO_3(aq)$

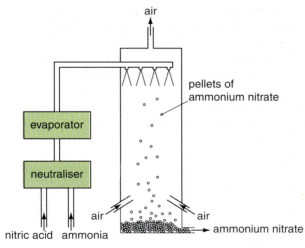

The ammonium nitrate solution is evaporated. Solid ammonium nitrate is melted and sprayed down a tall tower as air is blown up. Small pellets of Nitram are formed. This is the fertiliser which is spread on fields.

Nitram is often mixed with ammonium phosphate and potassium chloride to produce NPK fertilisers (see page 115). Good deposits of potassium chloride are found near Sheffield and Teesside.

Problems with fertilisers

Excess fertilisers are washed off into rivers. This causes algae to grow more rapidly or 'bloom'. When they die and decay the oxygen in the water is used up. **Eutrophication** is said to occur.

Summary

1. Ammonia is manufactured by the Haber process.
2. Nitric acid is produced by oxidation of ammonia.
3. Most ammonia is used to make fertilisers.

Questions

1. **a** Name the raw materials and outline the process for manufacturing ammonia and nitric acid.
   b How are these two compounds used to make fertilisers?

28 Acids and alkalis

Solutions of substances in water are acidic, alkaline or neutral.

ALKALIS	ACIDS	NEUTRAL SOLUTIONS
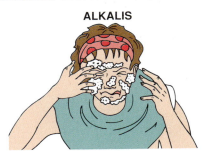		
soapy water stings our eyes; oven cleaners can harm our skin	lemon juice, rhubarb and vinegar taste sharp or sour	pure water is not sharp nor does it sting our eyes; solutions of salt and sugar are not sharp

Detecting acids

Some solutions are poisonous so it is not a good idea to taste them to find out if they are acids. Instead we use **indicators**. These are dyes which turn different colours in acids and alkalis.

Litmus is a common indicator, made from a plant. Litmus turns red in acids and blue in alkalis. It is purple in neutral solutions.

How acidic and how alkaline?

The pH scale is used to show how acidic and how alkaline a solution is. It gives the strength of the acid or alkali.

```
0  1  2  3  4  5  6  7  8  9  10  11  12  13  14
 Strong   Weak   Neutral   Weak      Strong
  acid    acid             alkali    alkali
 ←── Increasing acid strength    Increasing alkali strength ──→
```

The pH of a solution can be found using **universal indicator**. This contains a mixture of dyes. It gives a different colour for the different pH values. The colours are given in this table.

Dangerous solutions

Many acids and alkalis are harmful or corrosive. The hazard symbol is a warning to use the solution with care.

Acids and alkalis in the laboratory

The common acids used in the laboratory and in industry are:

   nitric acid HNO_3
   sulphuric acid H_2SO_4
   hydrochloric acid HCl

The common alkalis used in the laboratory and in industry are:

   sodium hydroxide $NaOH$
   potassium hydroxide KOH
   ammonia solution NH_4OH
   lime water (calcium hydroxide) $Ca(OH)_2$

pH	Colour of universal indicator	Examples in the home	Examples in the laboratory
1, 2	red	acid in car batteries and in the stomach	sulphuric, nitric, hydrochloric acids
3, 4	orange	lemon juice, vinegar	citric acid, ethanoic acid
5, 6	yellow	soda water	carbonic acid
7	green	water, ethanol, sugar and salt solution	water, sugar and sodium chloride solutions, ethanol
8, 9	blue	bicarbonate of soda, soap, toothpaste	sodium hydrogencarbonate
10, 11, 12	navy blue	washing soda	sodium carbonate, ammonia solution, limewater
13, 14	purple	oven cleaner	sodium hydroxide, potassium hydroxide

Acids and alkalis working for us

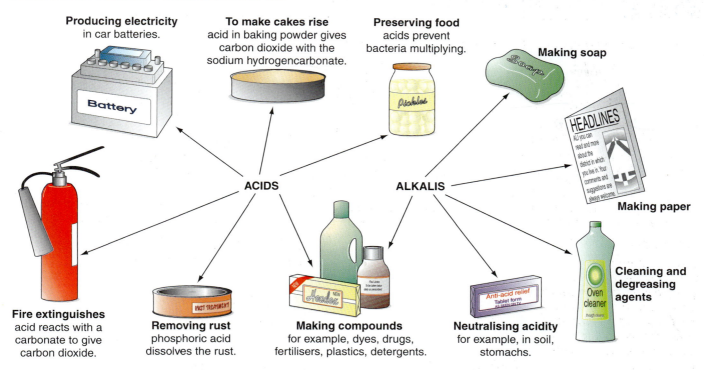

Producing electricity in car batteries.

To make cakes rise acid in baking powder gives carbon dioxide with the sodium hydrogencarbonate.

Preserving food acids prevent bacteria multiplying.

Making soap

Making paper

Fire extinguishes acid reacts with a carbonate to give carbon dioxide.

Removing rust phosphoric acid dissolves the rust.

Making compounds for example, dyes, drugs, fertilisers, plastics, detergents.

Neutralising acidity for example, in soil, stomachs.

Cleaning and degreasing agents

Reacting acids and alkalis together

Eating a piece of lemon leaves a sour taste in your mouth. If you put a small amount of bicarbonate of soda on your tongue the sourness disappears. **Neutralisation** has occurred.

Alkalis are often used to neutralise acids as they are at the opposite ends of the pH scale.

Acid	+	Alkali	→	Salt	+	Water
pH below 7		above 7		neutral 7		neutral 7

Examples of neutralisation

Excess acid in the stomach can cause stomach ache. Anti-acids are alkalis. They neutralise the excess acid. Toothpaste is alkaline. It neutralises the acid on teeth produced by bacteria.

Ant bites and bee stings are acidic. They are neutralised with an alkali such as sodium bicarbonate (sodium hydrogencarbonate).

Acidity in soil and lakes is neutralised by using limestone (calcium carbonate) or slaked lime (calcium hydroxide).

Sulphur dioxide in gases from power stations is removed by limestone.

Making acids and alkalis

Some acids are made by dissolving soluble oxides of non-metals in water, for example:

sulphur dioxide + water + air → sulphuric acid
carbon dioxide + water → carbonic acid
nitrogen dioxide + water + air → nitric acid

Alkalis are formed when soluble oxides and hydroxides of metals dissolve in water.

sodium oxide + water → sodium hydroxide solution
calcium oxide + water → limewater

Summary

1. All solutions are either acidic, alkaline or neutral.
2. Indicators give different colours with alkalis and acids. The pH scale is used to measure their strength.
3. Neutralisation occurs when an acid reacts with an alkali to form a salt and water.

Questions

1. Name two weak and two strong acids and alkalis.
2. What is meant by neutralisation? Give two examples of neutralisation reactions.

29 More about salts

Many salts are very useful.

table salt
sodium chloride

fertiliser
for example,
ammonium nitrate

Epsom salts
magnesium sulphate

chalk
calcium carbonate

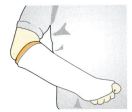
Plaster of Paris
calcium sulphate

The name of a salt is made up of two parts: the first part is the ammonium group or the name of a metal, the second part is from an acid.

Acid	Salt
hydrochloric acid	chloride
sulphuric acid	sulphate
nitric acid	nitrate
carbonic acid	carbonate

MAKING SALTS

All acids contain hydrogen which can be replaced by a metal or the ammonium group to form a salt. This can be done in various ways, as shown here:

1. Reacting acids with alkalis (neutralisation)

acid + alkali → salt + water

for example:
sodium hydroxide + hydrochloric acid → sodium chloride + water

 + →   +

2. Reacting acids with metals

metal + acid → salt + hydrogen

for example:
magnesium + sulphuric acid → magnesium sulphate + hydrogen

 + → +

3. Reacting acids with carbonates

carbonate + acid → salt + carbon dioxide + water

for example:
copper(II) carbonate + nitric acid → copper(II) nitrate + carbon dioxide + water

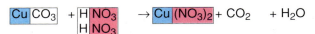

Carbon dioxide forms a white precipitate when it is bubbled through limewater.

Did you know?

A barium 'meal' is given to patients before X-rays are taken of their stomach and intestines. The 'meal' is the insoluble salt barium sulphate which shows up on X-rays.

SUMMARY

1. Salts are compounds made from acids in a number of ways.
2. The first part of the name of a salt is a metal or ammonium group and the second part is from an acid.

QUESTIONS

1. Name the acid from which the following salts can be made: sodium chloride, iron(II) sulphate, zinc nitrate, calcium sulphate.
2. Describe how you would make some dry crystals of table salt. Give the word equation for the reaction.
3. What gas is given off when:
   a zinc is added to hydrochloric acid
   b calcium carbonate is added to nitric acid?
   Give tests for the gases.

Details of making salts

1. Reacting acids with alkalis

This is used for making salts of sodium, potassium and ammonium. For example, preparation of potassium nitrate.

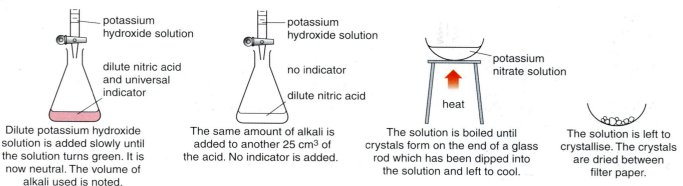

Dilute potassium hydroxide solution is added slowly until the solution turns green. It is now neutral. The volume of alkali used is noted.

The same amount of alkali is added to another 25 cm³ of the acid. No indicator is added.

The solution is boiled until crystals form on the end of a glass rod which has been dipped into the solution and left to cool.

The solution is left to crystallise. The crystals are dried between filter paper.

2. Reacting acids with metals

Metals such as magnesium, zinc and iron react with dilute sulphuric and hydrochloric acids to form a salt and hydrogen. The method is used to prepare the sulphates and chlorides of magnesium, zinc and iron. For example, preparation of magnesium sulphate shown here.

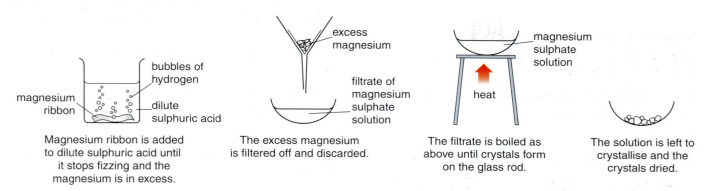

Magnesium ribbon is added to dilute sulphuric acid until it stops fizzing and the magnesium is in excess.

The excess magnesium is filtered off and discarded.

The filtrate is boiled as above until crystals form on the glass rod.

The solution is left to crystallise and the crystals dried.

The method cannot be used to prepare:

- salts of very reactive metals such as sodium or calcium, because they react explosively
- salts of unreactive metals such as copper, because they do not react to give hydrogen
- nitrates, because nitric acid does not react in this way.

3. Reacting acids with carbonates

This method can be used to make any soluble salts of metals provided that the carbonate used is insoluble. (All carbonates are insoluble except those of lithium, sodium, potassium and ammonium.)
For example, preparation of copper(II) nitrate.

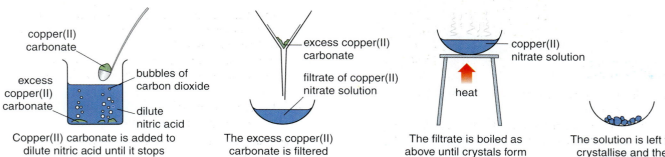

Copper(II) carbonate is added to dilute nitric acid until it stops fizzing and the copper(II) carbonate is in excess.

The excess copper(II) carbonate is filtered off and discarded.

The filtrate is boiled as above until crystals form on the glass rod.

The solution is left to crystallise and the crystals dried.

30 Limestone – a useful rock

Limestone is a common rock with many uses. It has been quarried and used in buildings for thousands of years but is also important for making other substances.

Limestone blocks are used as a building material.

Limestone chips are heated with coke and iron ore to make iron.

Limestone lumps are used as chippings for roads and mixed with tar to make Tarmac.

Powdered limestone is added to lakes and rivers, and spread on soil to neutralise acidity.

Chalk is another form of limestone. Both limestone and chalk are made up of calcium carbonate.

Limestone and chalk are formed from the shells and bones of sea creatures which lived millions of years ago. On dying they sank to the bottom of the sea and were covered by layers of sediment. The pressure eventually changed these sediments into rock. Limestone and chalk are known as **sedimentary rocks**.

With more heat and pressure, limestone changes into marble. This is called a **metamorphic rock** and is harder than limestone.

Did you know?
The term 'in the limelight' relates back to the time when quicklime was used in theatres to light the stage. The quicklime was heated and glowed very brightly to give off the 'limelight'.

REACTING LIMESTONE

1. Reaction with acids

Limestone, chalk and marble fizz with dilute hydrochloric acid. The salt calcium chloride is formed. Carbon dioxide is given off which forms a white precipitate with limewater.

calcium carbonate + hydrochloric acid → calcium chloride + carbon dioxide + water

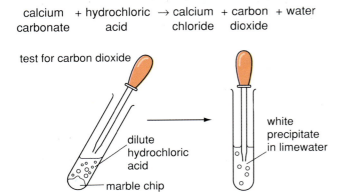

test for carbon dioxide

dilute hydrochloric acid
marble chip

white precipitate in limewater

2. Heating limestone

Limestone breaks down or decomposes when it is heated. Carbon dioxide is given off and calcium oxide is formed.

calcium carbonate → calcium oxide + carbon dioxide
$CaCO_3$ → CaO + CO_2

Calcium oxide is called quicklime and is corrosive. It reacts quickly with water giving out heat and forming slaked lime (calcium hydroxide).

calcium oxide + water → calcium hydroxide

Slaked lime is a cheap alkali which is spread on acid soil and used in making soaps and bleach. It is also used in mortar for building walls.

Useful products from limestone

Limestone is such a useful rock that over 130 million tonnes a year is quarried in Great Britain. Much of it is used in making glass, cement and concrete.

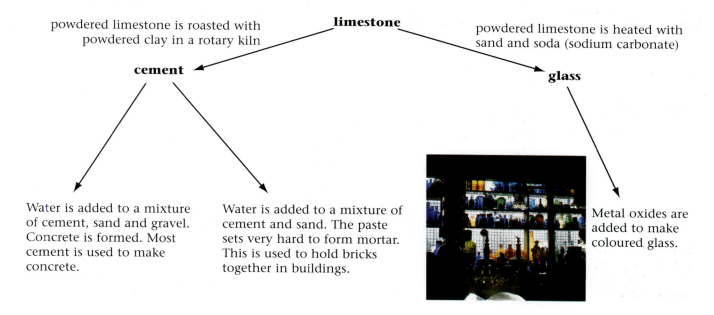

More about concrete

Concrete is used everywhere – in buildings, foundations, bridges, pavements – even lamp posts. It is a very important building material.

Concrete is made from a mixture of sand, crushed rock (gravel) and cement. When water is added a slurry is formed. This can be poured into moulds and after a few hours sets to a hard, stone-like mass.

By itself, concrete is not a very strong material. A downward force on it can cause it to crack and break. The concrete is made stronger by putting in steel rods. This composite material is called **reinforced concrete**.

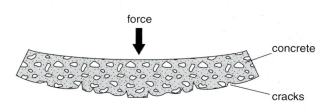

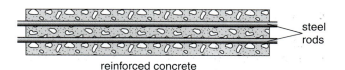

reinforced concrete

Summary

1 Limestone is a very useful rock used in buildings and to make materials such as glass, cement and concrete.
2 The main chemical in limestone, chalk and marble is calcium carbonate.

Questions

1 Name the chemical in limestone. What gas is given off when dilute acid is added to limestone? Describe a test for the gas.
2 Explain why limestone is such an important material.
3 Devise an experiment to find how the strength of concrete depends on the ratio of sand to cement used when it is made.

31 Metals from ores

Most metals are found in the Earth's crust as compounds called **ores**. Ores are usually metal oxides or sulphides and are mixed with other rocks. However, some metal compounds are found in sea water. All the metals except aluminium and iron occur in very small amounts in the Earth's crust.

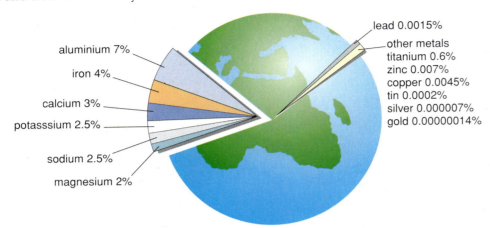

There are six main stages in getting useful metals from rocks.

1. *Finding deposits of the ore*. Many ores are found in bands.
2. *Mining*. The ore is obtained by tunnelling or using open cast mines.
3. *Concentration*. The ore is concentrated by removing the non-useful waste rock. This is done where the ore is mined to save transport costs.
4. *Extraction*. The metal is extracted or 'pulled away' from the non-metal in the ore. The method used depends on the reactivity of the metal.
5. *Purification*. The metal is often purified before it is used.
6. *Manufacturing*. The raw metal is changed into an object.

EXTRACTION OF METALS

Ores often contain the metal oxide or a substance which is easily changed to the metal oxide. The oxygen must be removed from the compound to leave the metal. This process is called **reduction**.

The method used to extract a metal depends on its reactivity. The more reactive the metal, the harder it is to extract it from its ore.

Metals can be listed in order of their reactivity. The most reactive metal is first. The least reactive metal is last. The list is called the **reactivity series**.

All the metals below carbon in the reactivity series can be obtained from their ores by reduction with carbon. Those above carbon must be obtained by electrolysis.

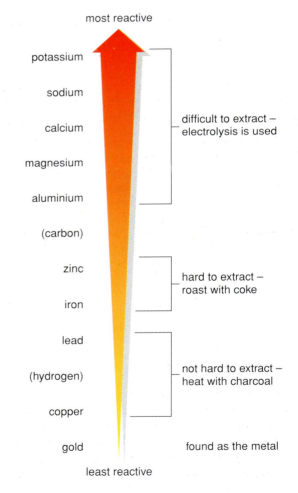

Metals through the ages

Unreactive metals were discovered and used first. They do not react with other substances and so are found as the pure metal and not as a compound. The oldest metal objects are therefore made of gold.

More reactive metals found as compounds are harder to extract and so were extracted later. For example, although aluminium is a common metal it was not extracted until just over 100 years ago when electricity was invented.

The extraction of metals has influenced history. For example, aircraft need to be built with light metals or alloys. Their development therefore depended on the availability of aluminium and its alloys.

Metal	Approximate date first extracted	Uses
gold	5000 BC	jewellery
copper	3000 BC Bronze Age	pots, pans, jewellery
iron	1000 BC Iron Age	tools, swords
aluminium	1870s	planes, light vehicles
uranium	1940s	nuclear power, nuclear weapons

Extracting metals in the laboratory

Only the least reactive metals can be extracted in the laboratory. Copper(II) oxide is reduced to copper by heating it in a stream of laboratory gas or hydrogen.

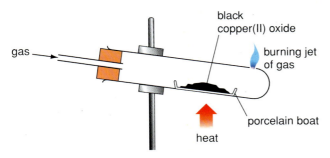

copper(II) oxide + hydrogen → copper + water
$$CuO + H_2 \rightarrow Cu + H_2O$$

Points about the experiment
- The tube slopes downwards. This stops water running back and cracking the hot tube.
- The jet of gas is not lit until the air inside the tube has been pushed out. This is because mixtures of gas and air could explode when lit.
- When the black copper(II) oxide has been reduced to brown copper, the heat is switched off. The gas is passed over the copper until it is cool. This stops the hot copper from being oxidised by the air.

Showing a metal has been formed

Copper(II) oxide does not conduct an electric current. The bulb does not light up.

After the reaction, the substance left conducts a current. The bulb lights up. This shows it is a metal.

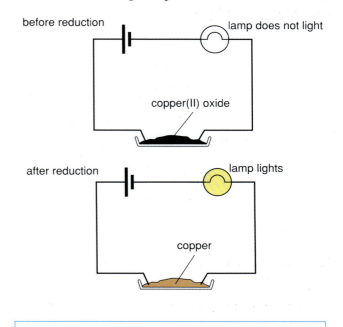

Summary

1. Metals are extracted from their ores by reduction.
2. Metals higher in the reactivity series are harder to extract than metals lower in the series.

Questions

1. To answer **a** to **d** choose the most suitable metals from the following list: aluminium, iron, sodium, copper, gold.
   a. a metal found uncombined in the Earth
   b. two metals extracted from their ores by electrolysis
   c. the least reactive metal
   d. a metal which can be obtained from its oxide by reduction in the laboratory with gas.
2. Draw a flowchart to show how iron is obtained from rocks.

32 Iron and its uses

With the discovery of iron 3000 years ago, life changed considerably. Iron was first used for tools, weapons and knives, and later in buildings, transport and machinery. Even with the development of plastics and other materials, iron and steel are still widely used.

The blast furnace

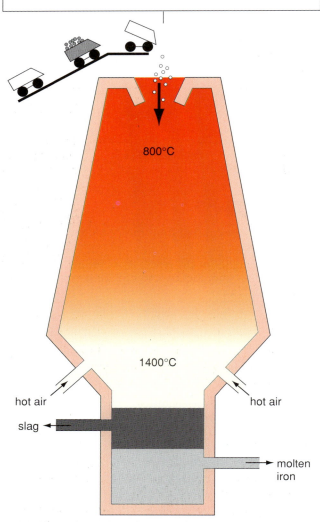

Iron is extracted in the blast furnace. Raw materials for this process are iron ore, limestone and coke.

Reactions

Iron ore contains iron and oxygen joined together. The gas carbon monoxide pulls oxygen away from the iron. It reduces the ore to iron. The process during which oxygen is removed from a compound is called **reduction**. The carbon monoxide is the reducing agent.

The reaction occurs in stages.
1 Coke burns in the hot air and gives out more heat.

carbon + oxygen → carbon dioxide
$$C + O_2 \rightarrow CO_2$$

2 Carbon dioxide reacts with hot coke to make carbon monoxide.

carbon dioxide + carbon → carbon monoxide
$$CO_2 + C \rightarrow 2CO$$

3 The carbon monoxide reduces the iron oxide to iron.

carbon monoxide + iron oxide → carbon dioxide + iron
$$3CO + Fe_2O_3 \rightarrow 3CO_2 + 2Fe$$

The carbon dioxide reacts with more coke to make more carbon monoxide. The molten iron trickles to the bottom of the furnace.

4 The limestone removes most of the acidic impurities. These are mainly sand mixed with the ore.

limestone + acidic impurities → slag

The molten slag settles on the top of the molten iron at the bottom of the furnace.

Products

The molten iron is run out. It is converted into steel, or solidified in moulds to make 'pig iron' or cast iron. Cast iron is brittle as it is impure. The impurities are mainly carbon, phosphorus and sulphur.

The slag is run off and solidifies. It is used in making roads and for foundations of buildings.

The furnace is kept working day and night and makes up to 7000 tonnes of iron each day. The waste gases heat the fresh air blown in at the bottom of the furnace to help save energy.

Making steel

Most iron is changed into the alloy **steel** to make it stronger and give it different properties.

Iron from the blast furnace contains impurities. Most are burnt away by passing oxygen into the steel-making furnace. The furnace is loaded with 70% molten iron and 30% scrap iron and oxygen is blown into the molten iron under pressure. Some of the sulphur and phosphorus and most of the carbon form acidic oxides in the waste gases. These are treated before being released. Limestone is added to remove other acidic impurities and forms slag.

Various amounts of carbon or other metals are then added to the pure iron to make the required type of steel.

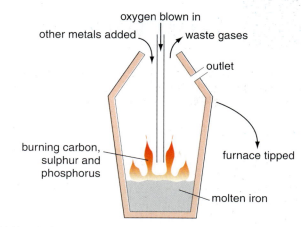

Making steel

What types of steel are there?

There are different types of steel for different purposes. In general, carbon makes a steel harder but less flexible. Steels with more than 1% carbon are very hard but also brittle (less strong).

Type of steel	Composition	Special properties	Uses
carbon steels			
• mild steel	less than 0.5% carbon	flexible sheets	cars, ships, springs, 'tin' cans
• medium steel	0.5 to 1% carbon	harder than mild steel	railway lines, girders, hammers
• high-carbon steel	1 to 1.5% carbon	very hard, less strong than medium steel	knives, razor blades, drill bits, scissors
other steels			
• stainless steel	up to 18% chromium and 8% nickel	does not rust	cutlery, industrial works, washing machine drums, sinks,
• tungsten steel	up to 18% tungsten	very tough	tools, armour plate

Stopping iron and steel rusting

Besides making stainless steel there are other ways of stopping iron and steel rusting:
- coating with tin (for instance, tin cans) or zinc (galvanised iron)
- covering with plastic, such as steel wire
- painting or greasing.

Where are blast furnaces and steel works built?

- Near ports and good transport
- Near deposits of coal and limestone
- Near water supplies (200 tonnes of water are needed to make 1 tonne of steel).

Environmental considerations

- After quarrying, land should be returned to its natural state
- Dust and acidic gases such as sulphur dioxide should be removed from waste gases
- Waste water is acidic and should be treated before it enters sewers or is recycled.

Summary

1. In the blast furnace, iron ore is reduced to iron with carbon monoxide. Cast iron is formed.
2. Cast iron is brittle and not as useful as steel.
3. Steel is mainly iron with small amounts of carbon or other metals.

Questions

1. List the raw materials used in the blast furnace and explain why each is added. Give an equation for the reduction of the iron ore.
2. Give two disadvantages of the cast iron obtained from the blast furnace. How could the properties of cast iron be altered to make it suitable for use in a sink?

33 Aluminium and its uses

Aluminium has many uses. Unlike iron it doesn't rust and appears to be unreactive. However, from its position in the reactivity series we would expect it to react more than it does.

WHY IS ALUMINIUM UNREACTIVE?

Aluminium has an oxide layer on its surface. It acts like a shield and protects it from further reaction.

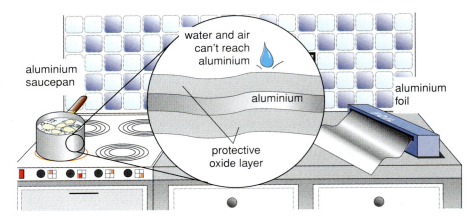

EXTRACTING ALUMINIUM

The main ore of aluminium is bauxite or aluminium oxide. Aluminium oxide is an ionic compound with positive aluminium ions tightly bound to negative oxide ions. A powerful method of reduction is needed to remove the oxygen.

The method used is **electrolysis**. During electrolysis a substance is broken down into simpler substances by an electric current.

Raw materials

Deposits of bauxite are mined in many countries such as Australia, New Guinea, Jamaica, Indonesia, India and Brazil. The ore is concentrated and purified at the site of mining to cut transport costs.

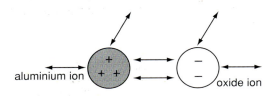

ions held together by strong forces

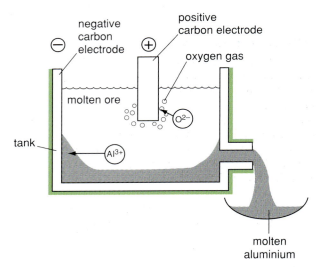

Electrolysis reaction

When the current is switched on, one electrode becomes positive and the other negative.

At the *negative electrode* positive aluminium ions are attracted. Aluminium is formed and collects in the bottom of the tank.

At the *positive electrode* negative oxide ions are attracted. Oxygen gas is formed. Some of the hot carbon electrode burns away so they have to be frequently replaced.

The aluminium oxide is split up or decomposed by the electric current into aluminium and oxygen.

The aluminium oxide is melted before it is electrolysed. It melts at a very high temperature, 2000°C. Another mineral called cryolite is added and lowers the melting point to about 900°C. This saves energy and therefore cost.

In the solution the positive aluminium ions and negative oxide ions are able to move and carry the current. Electrodes made of graphite carry the current into and out of the solution.

AN EXPENSIVE METAL

Although aluminium ore is more common than iron ore in the Earth's crust, aluminium is about six times more expensive. This is because a large amount of energy is needed to obtain it from its ore. Aluminium is therefore extracted in countries with cheap supplies of electricity, for example, near hydroelectric power plants in Canada and Scotland.

WHY IS ALUMINIUM SO USEFUL?

Aluminium has special properties which make it useful for many things.

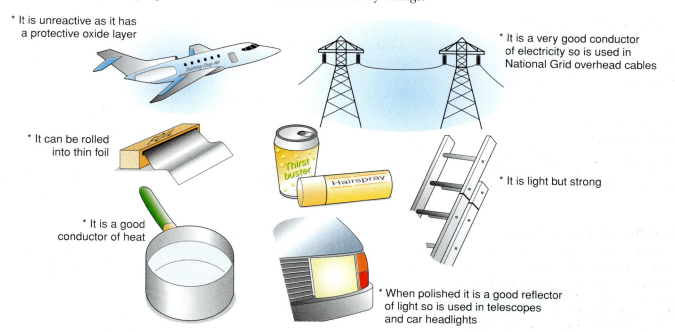

* It is unreactive as it has a protective oxide layer
* It is a very good conductor of electricity so is used in National Grid overhead cables
* It can be rolled into thin foil
* It is light but strong
* It is a good conductor of heat
* When polished it is a good reflector of light so is used in telescopes and car headlights

UNREACTIVE ALUMINIUM

Find aluminium in the reactivity series. It comes below magnesium but above zinc. So we expect it to be less reactive than magnesium but more reactive than zinc.

The reactivity of the three metals can be compared by seeing how easily they react with dilute hydrochloric acid. To make it a fair test, the same volume of acid is added to the same amount of metal. Each metal has the same size pieces.

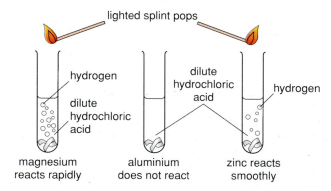

The magnesium fizzes very rapidly, the zinc less rapidly. In each case, hydrogen gas is given off which causes a lighted splint to pop.

magnesium + hydrochloric acid → magnesium chloride + hydrogen

zinc + hydrochloric acid → zinc chloride + hydrogen

The aluminium does not react even when the acid is warmed. The oxide layer stops the acid reaching the metal.

RECYCLING ALUMINIUM

It is cheaper to recycle aluminium than to extract more of it from its ore. This is why aluminium cans and tops are recycled.

Did you know? A typical aluminium factory uses as much energy in a day as a typical home uses in two or three years.

SUMMARY

1. Aluminium is extracted by electrolysis.
2. It has an oxide layer which stops it reacting.

QUESTIONS

1. A metal X is obtained from its ore by heating with coke, and a metal Y from its ore by electrolysis. Which metal is more reactive? Name a metal which could be Y, give its ore and explain how it is extracted from this ore.
2. Give four uses of aluminium. For each give the properties of aluminium which make it useful.

34 Copper and its uses

Compared with aluminium, copper is a very 'ancient' metal. People were able to extract it over 5000 years ago as it is unreactive and easily obtained from its ore. The heat of an open fire is enough to extract copper from a mixture of its ore and charcoal. The alloy bronze was made by mixing tin with copper and ancient bronze tools dating from this Bronze Age have been found.

Extracting copper

Copper is found in ores such as malachite as shown in this photograph. This is a green colour and contains copper(II) carbonate. Another common ore is copper pyrites which contains copper (II) sulphide and iron(II) sulphide.

The ore is roasted in a small amount of air to give impure copper. This often contains small amounts of precious metals such as silver and platinum as well as other impurities. The copper is purified before it is used.

Purifying copper

Electrolysis is used to purify copper. The liquid carrying the current (the electrolyte) is a solution of the ionic compound copper(II) sulphate in water. The positive electrode is the lump of impure copper. The negative electrode is a strip of pure copper.

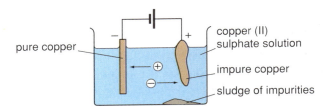

At the negative electrode
Positive ions including the copper ions are attracted. Copper is formed and deposited on the electrode as a layer of pure copper.

At the positive electrode
Negative ions are attracted. Copper from the impure lump dissolves into the electrolyte. It replaces the copper ions deposited at the negative electrode. A sludge is left underneath which contains small amounts of the other metals.

The current is carried through the solution by the movement of the ions.

Making a metal object silver!

The method for purifying copper can be used to plate metal objects with an unreactive metal such as silver or copper. This is called electroplating.

For example, coating a metal object with silver. The electrolyte is silver nitrate solution. The object is made the negative electrode. A strip of silver is made the positive electrode.

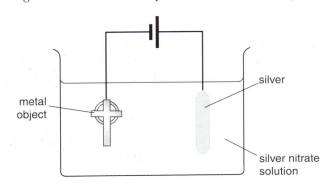

For best results, the object should be very clean. A small current should be used so that the silver is deposited slowly.

138

Unreactive copper

Copper is very low in the reactivity series. It is therefore very unreactive. However, in damp air it reacts slowly to form a green compound. This occurs much more slowly than the rusting of iron.

Did you know?
Copper was used to cover the bottoms of wooden sailing ships to protect the wood from insects and rotting. It led to the phrase 'copper-bottomed guarantee' – a promise that would not be broken.

Comparing the reactivities of copper and magnesium

1. Reaction with dilute hydrochloric acid

Unlike magnesium, copper does not react with dilute acids to give hydrogen even when heated.

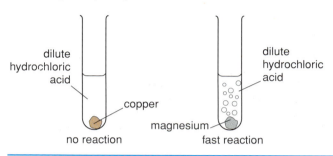

2. Heating in air

Magnesium burns with a bright white flame. Copper does not burn, but after some time forms a surface layer of black copper(II) oxide which can be scraped off.

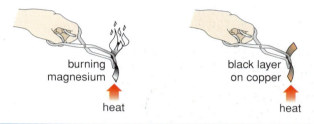

Using copper

Unreactive metal easily bent and shaped

Copper doesn't corrode or dissolve in water. It is used in water tanks and gas pipes.

Good conductor of electricity and heat

Copper is used in wiring and in the bottom of saucepans.

Attractive metal

Copper can be polished and remains shiny because it is unreactive. It is used in jewellery and ornaments.

> ### Summary
> 1. Copper is an unreactive metal purified by electrolysis.
> 2. It is very useful by itself and in alloys.

Using copper in alloys
Hardening gold

Copper is mixed with gold to make the gold harder. Twenty-four carat gold is pure gold and very soft. Nine carat gold has more copper than eighteen carat gold and is much harder.

9 carat gold   18 carat gold   24 carat gold

Hardening copper

Brass containing copper and zinc is harder and more yellow than copper. It is a good conductor, does not rust and is used in plugs, nails, taps, locks and ornaments.

Making it pink

Bronze containing tin and copper is a hard alloy, which is pinkish in colour. It is used in ornaments, and coins.

> ### Questions
> 1. Give reasons why copper is used in electrical wires whereas the pins in plugs are made of brass. Give another alloy of copper, what it is made of and its uses.
> 2. Explain how you would purify a lump of copper.
> 3. Metal X burns in air with a bright white flame and gives gas Z with dilute hydrochloric acid which pops when lit. Metal Y is a pink colour, does burn and does not give gas Z with the acid. Identify X, Y and Z and explain the reactions.

35 Reactivity of metals

We have already seen that metals can be arranged in order of their reactivity to form the reactivity series. The table compares the reactivity of common metals in the reactivity series with air, water and dilute acids.

Metal	Air	Water	Dilute hydrochloric or sulphuric acid
potassium	when heated **burns** with a lilac flame to a white **oxide** forms a white **oxide layer** rapidly in **cold air**	reacts very vigorously with **cold** water to give **potassium hydroxide** and **hydrogen**	reacts explosively to give a **salt** and **hydrogen**
sodium	when heated **burns** with a yellow flame to a white **oxide** forms a white **oxide layer** rapidly in **cold air**	reacts vigorously with **cold water** to give **sodium hydroxide** and **hydrogen**	reacts explosively to give a **salt** and **hydrogen**
calcium	when heated **burns** with a red flame to a white **oxide** forms a white **oxide layer** rapidly in **cold air**	reacts smoothly with **cold water** to give **calcium hydroxide** and **hydrogen**	reacts very vigorously with dilute hydrochloric acid only to give **hydrogen** and a **salt**
magnesium	when heated **burns** with a bright white flame to a white **oxide** forms a thin white **oxide layer** in cold air	when hot reacts with **steam** to give **magnesium oxide** and **hydrogen**	reacts vigorously to give **hydrogen** and a **salt**
aluminium	when heated strongly **burns** with a white flame to a white **oxide** forms a thin white protective **oxide layer** in cold air	when heated strongly in **steam** gives **aluminium oxide** and **hydrogen**	**no reaction** even with hot dilute acids because of the oxide layer
zinc	when heated strongly **burns** with a pale blue flame to a white **oxide** which is yellow when hot forms a thin white **oxide layer** in cold air	when heated strongly in **steam** gives **zinc oxide** and **hydrogen**	reacts smoothly to give **hydrogen** and a **salt**
iron	when heated strongly **burns** with an orange flame to a black **oxide** forms brown **rust** in **moist air**	when hot reacts **reversibly** with **steam** to give **iron oxide** and **hydrogen**	reacts slowly, faster **when warmed**, to give **hydrogen** and a **salt**
copper	does not burn but forms a black **oxide layer** which can be scraped off forms **green layer** in **moist air**	**no reaction**	**no reaction**
gold	**no reaction**	**no reaction**	**no reaction**

A CLOSER LOOK AT REACTIONS WITH WATER

1. Calcium and water

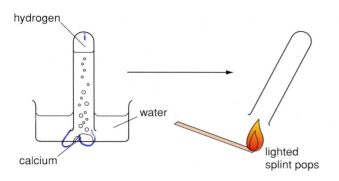

The calcium sinks and fizzes. The hydrogen gas is collected by displacing the water in the test tube. It is tested with a lighted splint and pops. The water turns cloudy as calcium hydroxide is only slightly soluble.

calcium + water → calcium hydroxide + hydrogen

2. Magnesium and steam

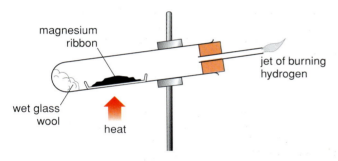

The magnesium is heated strongly. The jet of hydrogen is lit after air has been pushed out of the tube to avoid an explosion. The magnesium burns in the steam with a bright white flame.

magnesium + steam → magnesium oxide + hydrogen

A similar reaction occurs when aluminium and zinc are heated very strongly in steam but it is less vigorous.

With iron the reaction is reversible. It goes in both the forward and backward directions.

iron + steam ⇌ iron oxide + hydrogen

SUMMARY

1. Metals are arranged in descending order of their reactivity in the reactivity series.
2. A more reactive metal will displace a less reactive metal from its compound.

DISPLACEMENT REACTIONS

A more reactive metal will displace a less reactive metal from its compound. The compound can be in the solid form or in solution.

1. Replacing iron with aluminium in iron(III) oxide (the Thermit reaction)

Powdered aluminium mixed with powdered iron(III) oxide is heated strongly in a crucible. A violent reaction occurs and a lot of heat is given out.

aluminium + iron(III) oxide → aluminium oxide + iron

The reaction is used to weld railway lines together.

2. Displacement reactions in solution

When an iron nail is dropped into a blue solution of copper(II) sulphate the colour of the solution fades. A brown layer of copper forms on the iron nail.

A displacement reaction occurs as iron is more reactive than copper. It pushes it out of solution.

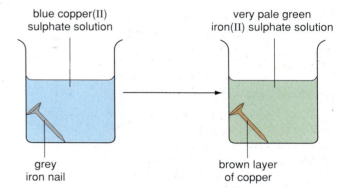

iron + copper(II) sulphate → iron(II) sulphate + copper

If a piece of copper is placed in iron(II) sulphate solution, no displacement reaction occurs as copper is less reactive than iron.

QUESTIONS

1. Arrange the following metals in order of their reactivity with the most reactive metal first: copper, zinc, sodium, magnesium. From the list give a metal:
   a. which reacts explosively with dilute acids
   b. which burns with a bright white flame
   c. which does not give hydrogen with acids
   d. displaced from a solution of its salt by iron.
2. A piece of zinc is dropped into a solution of copper(II) sulphate. What do you expect to happen? Explain your answer.

36 Different types of rocks

Rocks differ in appearance, age and composition. There are three main types: igneous, sedimentary and metamorphic.

igneous	sedimentary	$\xrightarrow{\text{high temperature}}$ metamorphic
granite speckled grey or pink-grey, large crystals	**sandstone** yellow-brown, small sand-like grains, soft	**quartzite** white rock, layered, very hard, crystalline
basalt dark coloured, hard, small crystals	**limestone** ⟶ pale coloured, soft	**marble** pale coloured, very hard, crystalline, glassy
crystals, no fossils, no grains of sediment, no layers	**mudstone** dark, unlayered, soft, crumbly, grains too small to be seen	**slate** grey or deep purple, hard and brittle, split into thin layers
	shale like mudstone but more layered	**schist** silvery coloured layers, flaky crystals
	conglomerate rounded pebbles cemented in clay	**gneiss** light and dark bands, crystalline
	grains, layers, sometimes fossils	**crystals, sometimes layers, no fossils**

IGNEOUS ROCKS

Igneous rocks are usually the oldest rocks on the Earth's surface. Four and a half billion years ago the Earth was a ball of hot molten rock called **magma**. As it cooled, crystals started to grow and formed a crust of igneous rocks around its surface. These rocks still form when hot magma from inside the Earth comes to the surface and solidifies, for instance, when volcanoes erupt.

Igneous rocks differ from sedimentary rocks as they don't contain fossils or grains of sediment and do not have any layers in them.

Granite

Granite is a hard, speckled rock with a mixture of large crystals which are several millimetres across. *They grow as magma cools slowly.* The crystals include glassy quartz and grey or pink feldspar arranged in a random pattern. The tors of Dartmoor and much of the Highlands of Scotland are made of granite.

Basalt

Basalt is a hard black rock with smaller crystals than granite. These can be seen with a microscope. Basalt is made when *magma cools very quickly*. This happens when magma comes out of volcanoes as lava. The air is much cooler than the inside of the Earth so the molten rock solidifies quickly.

The Giant's Causeway, Northern Ireland, is made of basalt.

VOLCANOES

As you go deeper into the Earth the temperature rises. When it is over 1000°C the rocks melt to form magma. In certain places this hot magma may be forced to the surface through cracks and flows out as molten lava. Sometimes this occurs under the ocean where the crust is thinner. A volcano forms as the lava cools quickly and turns to rock. This is mainly basalt. Often the lava contains dissolved gases which bubble out as the magma reaches the surface. Some volcanic eruptions are therefore explosive and dangerous but can be very spectacular.

Volcanoes bring many useful elements from the inside of the Earth to the crust as metal ores. The rocks that form on the surface like this are called extrusive igneous rocks.

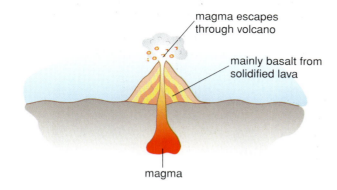

An active volcano forming extrusive igneous rocks.

SUMMARY

1. Rocks are of three main types: igneous, sedimentary and metamorphic.
2. Igneous rocks are formed when molten rock, called magma, solidifies.
3. Volcanoes are formed where molten rock comes out of the surface of the Earth as lava.

COOLING INSIDE THE CRUST

Below volcanoes and newly-formed mountains, most of the molten rock does not reach the surface as lava. It stays trapped deep within the crust surrounded by hot rock and cools very slowly. Over thousands of years, large crystals grow and granite forms.

Rocks that form inside the crust in this way are called intrusive igneous rocks.

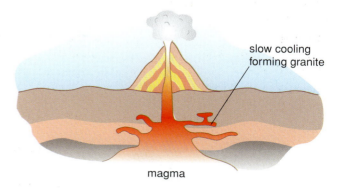

Formation of intrusive igneous rocks.

LARGE AND SMALL CRYSTALS

If crystals in a rock are small, the magma from which the rock formed cooled quickly. If crystals are large the magma cooled more slowly.

Did you know?
The volcano called Mount Vesuvius near Naples in Italy erupted violently in AD79. The explosion blew off the top of the mountain and buried the nearby cities in mud, cinders and ash. In Pompeii, the ash preserved the city, even the people were buried while they were running away.

QUESTIONS

1. The diagram shows two igneous rocks.

   a. What is the name of the molten rock from which they were formed? Where did it come from?
   b. Which rock solidified more quickly? Explain your answer.
   c. What type of igneous rock is X and what type is Y?

2. Draw a labelled diagram of a volcano. On it show where you expect granite and where you expect basalt to be found. Why are the soils around a volcano very fertile?

37 Sedimentary and metamorphic rocks

Sedimentary rocks

Sedimentary rocks are made up of layers of rock containing grains or fragments cemented together. They are formed from layers of sediment built up in the sea. The sediment comes from eroded rock brought down by rivers or from the shells and bones of sea creatures deposited on top of each other on the sea bed.

The weight of the layers squeezes out the water. The particles of sediment are cemented together as salts crystallise out of the water. Eventually, after millions of years, sedimentary rocks are formed. They are pushed to the surface by forces within the Earth.

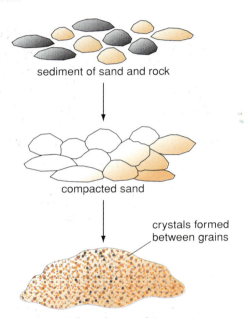

Sedimentary rocks include:

- **sandstones** – made from grains of sand cemented together
- **limestone** – made from the shells and bones of living organisms
- **mudstone** – made from clay or tiny rock particles which are much smaller than sand grains and deposited rapidly
- **shale** – made from clay which is deposited slowly
- **conglomerate** – like natural concrete containing pebbles which are often rounded and are cemented in clay, such as Hertfordshire pudding stone.

Fossils

Fossils are often found in sedimentary rocks, particularly limestone and shale. They form when animals and plants die and fall to the sea floor where they are squashed into sediments. The soft parts rot away but the hard parts remain and gradually turn into sedimentary rock.

Using fossils for dating

The life forms have changed steadily over millions of years. The fossils found in a particular rock therefore act as a 'time fingerprint' and can be used to date the rock.

For example if a rock contains a fossil ammonite then we know it is about 225 million years old. But this is only a very approximate value. A more accurate but expensive method of finding the age of a rock is to use carbon dating.

This is a rock containing fossil fish.

Metamorphic rocks

At high temperatures and pressures sedimentary rocks can change into metamorphic rocks. When this happens the rocks do not melt but the minerals in them recrystallise. This makes the rocks harder although they still contain the same composition. For example, limestone changes to marble but they both contain calcium carbonate.

Showing a carbonate is present

Dilute hydrochloric acid is added. Both the limestone and marble fizz and give off carbon dioxide which gives a white precipitate with lime water. This is a useful test for these rocks.

What causes the high temperatures and pressure?

Metamorphic rocks are found in both present-day and ancient mountain belts. As mountains are formed, high temperatures and pressures occur. Movements in the Earth (tectonic activity), cause sedimentary rocks to get buried deep underground. The deeper they are buried, the hotter they become. A range of metamorphic changes can therefore occur depending on the temperature and pressure of the rocks.

Mudstone and shale can undergo a series of metamorphic changes.

mudstone or shale ⟶ slate ⟶ schist ⟶ gneiss

Relatively low temperatures and pressures squash and harden the rock to form slate. This can be split into thin layers.

Increasing pressures and temperatures form schist. This has wavy, sparkling layers.

At higher temperatures and pressures gneiss is formed. The banding is coarser and new minerals like garnet may form from the old.

Differences between metamorphic and igneous rocks

Although granite and gneiss can be made of the same minerals, they look different. Gneiss has bands or layers but granite does not. This is because the sedimentary rock does not melt when it changes to a metamorphic rock but new crystals grow and line up against the pressure to form layers.

Statues and buildings made from metamorphic and igneous rocks are harder and do not wear away as quickly as sedimentary rocks.

Wearing down rocks

When mountains and cliffs wear away they are said to erode. **Erosion** is caused by many things but particularly the weather. It includes the action on rocks of water, wind, acid gases and acid rain and vegetation.

Summary

1. Sedimentary rocks are formed from layers of sediment under the sea. They often contain fossils which can be used to date the rocks.
2. Sedimentary rocks change to metamorphic rocks with high temperatures and pressures.

Questions

1. Place the following rocks under the three headings igneous, metamorphic, sedimentary: slate, gneiss, granite, schist, conglomerate, limestone, marble, mudstone, basalt.
2. How are metamorphic rocks made? Which of the following rocks would be most suitable for making an outdoor statue – marble, slate or limestone? Give reasons for your answer.

38 The Earth and its structure

The Earth is roughly spherical with an outer crust, inner core and a mantle filling the space between the crust and core. The thin outer crust of solid rocks is mainly covered by sea. The crust is about 40 km thick under the land and about 10 km thick under the sea.

The materials inside the Earth are denser and different from those in the crust. Pieces of a broken-down planet which used to orbit the Sun between Mars and Jupiter have struck the Earth's surface as meteorites. Some of these meteorites were found to be made of a basalt-type rock, possibly like the rocks in the mantle of the Earth. Other meteorites are denser and made of nickel and iron. Scientists think they are similar to the core of the Earth.

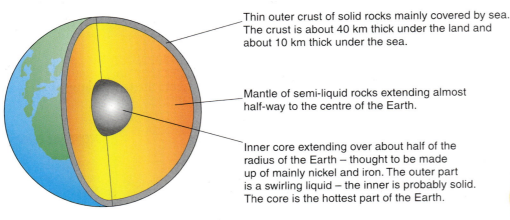

Thin outer crust of solid rocks mainly covered by sea. The crust is about 40 km thick under the land and about 10 km thick under the sea.

Mantle of semi-liquid rocks extending almost half-way to the centre of the Earth.

Inner core extending over about half of the radius of the Earth – thought to be made up of mainly nickel and iron. The outer part is a swirling liquid – the inner is probably solid. The core is the hottest part of the Earth.

Did you know?
A meteorite, which landed on Earth from Mars, was found to contain carbon. This suggests there could possibly have been some form of life on Mars.

THE ROCK CYCLE

Rocks change from one form to another. Rocks on the surface of the Earth are worn away and deposited as sediments elsewhere. The sedimentary rock formed from the sediments changes to metamorphic rock under high temperatures and pressures. At even higher temperatures and pressures, metamorphic rocks melt to magma. When magma cools igneous rocks are formed and the cycle begins again. The whole cycle takes millions of years to complete.

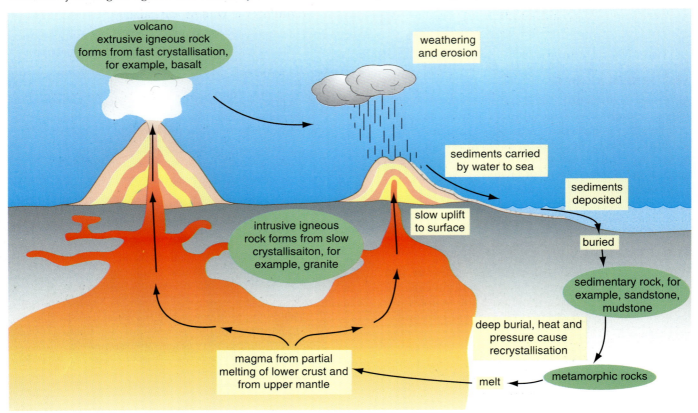

FOLDING AND FAULTING

Movements in the Earth's crust cause the layers of rocks to fold and breaks to occur. The breaks are called faults.

SQUEEZING ROCKS TOGETHER

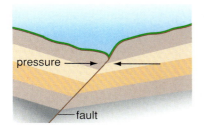

A sudden fault may occur and result in a shock wave or an earthquake. The layers of rock have breaks in them.

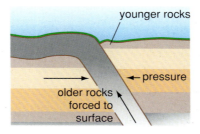

Some rocks may be forced up over other rock so that older rocks come to the surface, such as in the Alps.

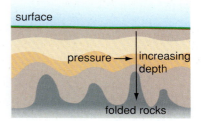

Deep in the Earth at high temperatures and pressures the rocks become like plastic. When squeezed, they form folds. Many metamorphic rocks are folded in this way.

PULLING THE ROCKS APART

If the crust is stretched then cracks may appear and the central block sinks to form a rift valley. An example of this is the Midland valley in Scotland.

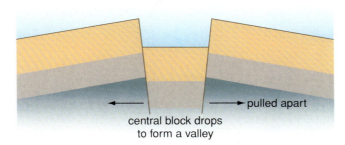

Other clues

1. Rocks that are over 200 million years old in North America are found to be very similar to those in Europe.

2. Fossils found in America of plants and animals living 200 million years ago are similar to those found in Europe. Younger rocks have different fossils.

3. Fossils of pouched mammals such as kangaroos are found all over the world. Now they are only found in the wild in Australia.

MOVING CONTINENTS

In 1912 Alfred Wegener, a German scientist, suggested that millions of years ago the continents were joined together to form one huge supercontinent. He suggested that the continents slowly moved apart until they reached their present positions. This movement is called the Continental Drift and is still happening today at the rate of a few centimetres each year – about the rate at which our nails grow.

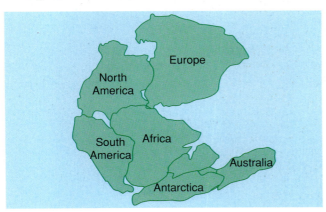

SUMMARY

1. The Earth is made up of a crust, mantle and core.
2. The rock cycle shows how the rocks in the crust slowly change from one to the other.
3. The rocks are folded and faulted in different ways.
4. Continents were once joined together, but are still moving apart.

QUESTIONS

1. Draw a flow chart to show how sedimentary rocks change to metamorphic and igneous rocks.
2. Give reasons why it is thought that all the continents were once joined together and then moved apart.

39 Movements in the Earth

The shape and surface of the Earth is altered by movements in its crust. The movement causes earthquakes and volcanoes and pushes up mountain ranges.

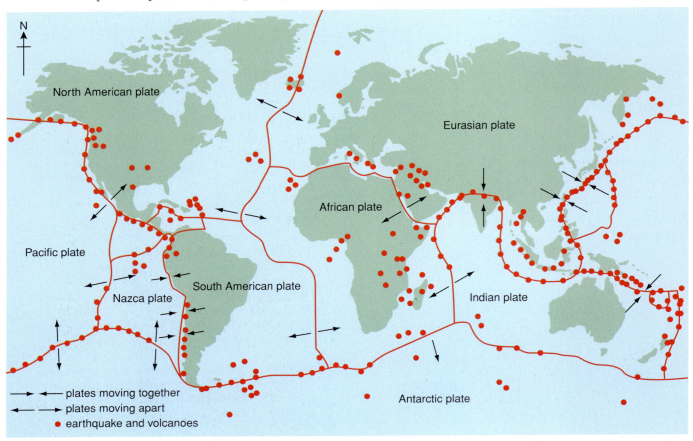

The map shows where there are volcanoes and major earthquakes. You can see that they happen in certain places a lot but not at all in others.

Scientists have suggested that this is because the Earth's crust is made up of large moving segments called **plates**. These fit together like jigsaw pieces and float on the liquid mantle below the crust. The theory of the movement of these plates is called plate tectonics.

WHY DO THEY MOVE?

The plates move slowly due to convection currents set up inside the mantle. Heat is released in the Earth by natural radioactive processes and the hotter material near the core is pushed up by cooler slightly denser magma. The convection currents formed move very slowly so the plates also move slowly – just a few centimetres each year. The continents are carried on the plates.

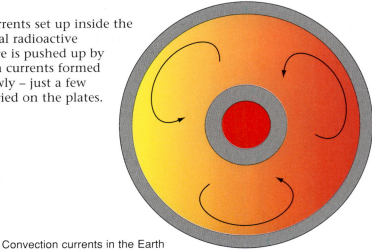

Convection currents in the Earth

Plate boundaries

The map shows that most earthquakes and volcanoes happen where two plates meet or at the **plate boundaries**. There are three types of boundaries.

Plates moving apart

Plates are moving apart in the middle of the oceans. Hot liquid magma from inside the Earth pours out through the gap. It cools and forms a ridge of new igneous rocks made mainly of basalt. This is happening in the middle of the Atlantic Ocean.

Plates colliding head on

When moving plates collide together, the land shakes. An earthquake results and one plate is pushed down under the other. The plate going into the Earth gets hotter and the rocks melt to form magma. If the pressure increases then the magma will escape upwards creating a volcano.

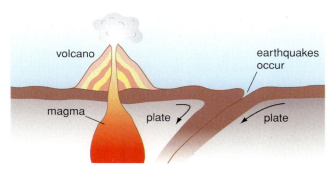

Plates sliding past each other

When plates slide past each other, huge forces may be suddenly released and the land shakes. An earthquake results and faults are formed, such as the San Andreas Fault in California.

Evidence for the theory

In the 1950s and 1960s scientists examined the ocean floor in the middle of the Atlantic Ocean. They made two important finds. Firstly, a chain of volcanic mountains runs under the ocean along its centre. There is a symmetrical pattern to the Earth's crust beneath the ocean. Secondly, the Earth's magnetic field reverses every half million years or so and its direction is recorded in a symmetrical pattern in the rocks either side of the mountain ridge.

Other evidence comes from looking at the similarity between rocks and fossils in the different continents.

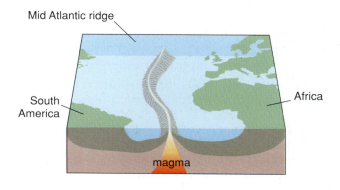

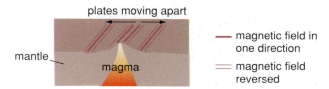

THE SHRINKING EARTH – AN EARLIER IDEA

About 100 years ago scientists thought that the Earth must have shrunk as it cooled. They thought the crust wrinkled up to form mountain ranges like the Alps and Himalayas. This theory has now been replaced by the theory of plate tectonics.

SUMMARY

1. The Earth's crust is made up of moving plates which carry the continents. The theory is called plate tectonics.
2. Volcanoes and earthquakes occur where the plates collide.
3. New rock is formed where the plates move apart.

QUESTIONS

1. Explain why earthquakes are rare in Britain but more common along the west coasts of the Americas and in Japan.
2. What is happening when a volcano erupts?
3. The Red Sea is gradually getting wider. Explain what might be happening.

40 Patterns in the Periodic Table, Group 1 and Group 0

GROUP 1 METALS

The elements in Group 1 of the Periodic Table are metals. They are good conductors of heat and electricity but differ from metals like iron and copper in the following ways.

They are:
- extremely reactive and must be kept under oil
- so soft that they can be cut with a knife
- very light and float on water as well as reacting with it.

The metals appear dull and grey as they react rapidly with air. When freshly cut, the new surface is bright and shiny but quickly tarnishes again in the air.

Why are Group 1 metals so reactive?

The reason is best explained by looking at the arrangement of the electrons in the atoms. The metals are similar as they each have one electron in their outer energy level. This electron is easily lost to form a positive ion with a charge of +1. This is stable as it has the electronic arrangement of a noble gas.

The electron is accepted by a non-metal to form a negative ion. The ions are attracted together and an ionic compound is formed.

Going down the group, the atoms get bigger. The outer electron gets further from the positive nucleus and is more easily lost. The metals get more reactive.

Potassium is more reactive than sodium.
Sodium is more reactive than lithium.
Lithium is the least reactive metal in Group 1 but is still very reactive.

The increase in reactivity going down the group is shown by their reaction with water (see opposite page).

Other changes down the group:
- the melting points decrease
- the boiling points decrease
- the metals get softer.

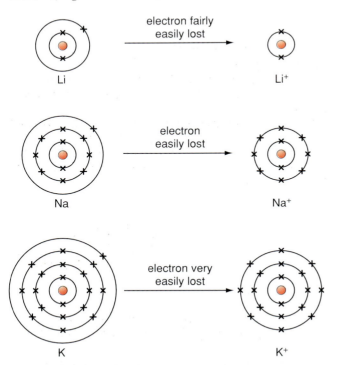

Metals	Melting point °C	Boiling point °C	Hardness
lithium	180	1340	soft
sodium	98	880	very soft
potassium	63	760	very soft

Using the Group 1 metals

Sodium is used in street lighting and in the liquid form as a coolant in nuclear reactors. Lithium and potassium are used in a few specialist alloys. Many of the compounds of the metals have important uses.

Reacting with water

Group 1 metals float on water, react vigorously and give off hydrogen. A metal hydroxide is formed which dissolves in the water to form an **alkali** and turns red litmus paper blue. For this reason the Group 1 metals are called the **alkali metals**.

Lithium
Lithium fizzes and moves around the surface. When lit, the hydrogen burns with a red flame. Lithium hydroxide is formed.

Sodium
Sodium reacts more vigorously. It melts to a silvery ball. When lit, the hydrogen burns with a yellow flame. Sodium hydroxide is formed.

Potassium
Potassium reacts even more vigorously. It melts to a silvery ball. The hydrogen lights itself and burns with a lilac flame. Potassium hydroxide is formed.

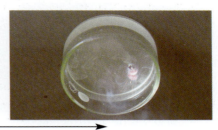

Increasing reactivity →

The equations for the reaction are similar:

metal + water → metal hydroxide + hydrogen

for example, sodium + water → sodium hydroxide + hydrogen

GROUP 0 ELEMENTS

The elements in Group 0 have few reactions and are known as the **noble gases**. They are so unreactive that they exist as single atoms. Other gaseous elements have two atoms joined together in each molecule, for example, Cl_2. The noble gases are extracted from liquid air by fractional distillation.

Why are the noble gases so unreactive?

Again, it is useful to look at the arrangement of the electrons in the atom.

Helium He

Each gas comes at the end of a row in the Periodic Table.

Neon Ne

The outer energy level is full. Electrons are not lost or gained.

Argon Ar

The noble gases are therefore stable and unreactive.

Uses of the noble gases

The noble gases have many uses.

Helium is lighter than air. It is used in weather balloons and air ships. It is used instead of nitrogen in diving gases.

Neon lights are used everywhere. The gas glows red when an electric current is passed through.

Argon is used to fill electric light bulbs. It is unreactive and stops the metal wire or filament from burning and breaking.

Did you know?
Liquid helium is used in brain scanners. It cools the giant electromagnet to create large magnetic fields.

SUMMARY

1. The alkali metals in Group 1 are very soft and reactive. They give off hydrogen when in contact with cold water.
2. The noble gases in Group 0 are unreactive. They exist as single atoms.

QUESTIONS

1. Explain why the Group 1 elements are metals. What properties make them different from other metals?
2. What are the trends in the physical and chemical properties of the Group 1 elements as you go down the group?
3. What are the elements in Group 0? Why do they exist as single atoms?

41 Patterns in the Periodic Table, Group 7 and the transition metals

GROUP 7 ELEMENTS

The elements in Group 7 are reactive non-metals called the **halogens**. They are poisonous and have a strong smell.

Fluorine is a pale yellow gas, chlorine a pale green gas, bromine is a red-brown liquid and iodine a grey solid.

When warmed, bromine readily forms a red-brown vapour and iodine a purple vapour.

Why are the halogens so reactive?

The reactivity of the halogens is easily explained by looking at the arrangement of their electrons.

The halogens all have seven electrons in their outer energy levels. They need one more electron to fill the level and obtain the electronic arrangement of a noble gas. The level can be filled in two ways:

- an electron is gained from a metal and a negative ion is formed with a charge of –1, for instance, in ionic salts with metals such as sodium chloride
- a pair of electrons is shared with the atom of another non-metal to form a covalent compound. An electron comes from each of the atoms, for instance, hydrogen chloride.

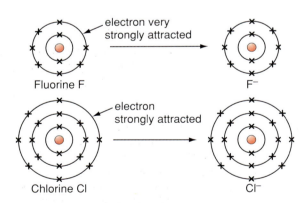

Going down the group the atoms get larger. The electrons are further from the positive nucleus and so it becomes less easy to attract an electron.

The non-metals become less reactive going down the group. Iodine is less reactive than bromine, which is less reactive than chlorine, which is less reactive than fluorine. Fluorine is the most reactive non-metal.

Displacement reactions

A more reactive halogen pushes out or displaces a less reactive halogen from an aqueous solution of one of its salts. Fluorine is so reactive it even displaces the other halogens from their solid salts.

For example, chlorine displaces bromine from potassium bromide solution. The colourless solution turns orange brown.

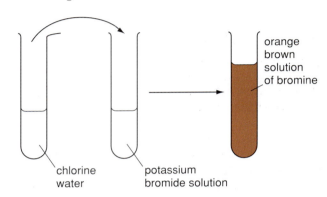

chlorine + potassium bromide → bromine + potassium chloride

For example, bromine displaces iodine from potassium iodide solution. The colourless solution turns dark brown and a grey precipitate of iodine forms.

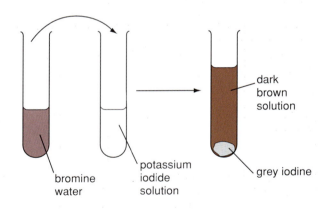

bromine + potassium iodide → iodine + potassium bromide

152

Changes in physical properties of the halogens

Going down the group the atoms get bigger so melting and boiling points increase.

Chlorine is used to kill bacteria in water, to make bleaches, household cleaners and the plastic PVC.

Iodine is milder and used in antiseptics to kill germs. It is needed in the diet for the thyroid gland.

Fluorine compounds are added to toothpaste and water to strengthen teeth.

Halogen	Appearance	Melting point °C	Boiling point °C
fluorine	pale yellow gas	−220	−188
chlorine	pale green gas	−101	−35
bromine	red-brown liquid	−7	59
iodine	purple grey solid	114	184

THE TRANSITION METALS

Most of the common metals we meet in everyday life are found in the central block in the Periodic Table. They are called the transition metals, for example, iron, cobalt, nickel and copper.

The transition metals have certain characteristics:
- they are good conductors of heat and electricity
- they have high melting points, boiling points and densities compared with the alkali metals
- their compounds are frequently coloured and they may form more than one ion, for example, iron forms Fe^{2+}, Fe^{3+}
- the metals and their compounds are used as catalysts to speed up chemical reactions, for instance, iron in the manufacture of ammonia, nickel in the manufacture of margarine from oils.

Metal	iron	cobalt	nickel	copper	sodium
Melting point °C	1540	1492	1452	1084	98
Boiling point °C	2750	2900	2837	2570	880
Colour of compounds	green or brown	pink or blue	green	blue or green	colourless

Testing for iron and copper in solutions of their compounds

1 Test for copper(II) ions Cu^{2+}
Aqueous ammonia solution is added.

A pale blue precipitate is first formed. With more ammonia solution it dissolves to give a deep blue solution.

2 Test for iron(II) ions Fe^{2+}
Sodium hydroxide solution is added.

A pale green jelly-like precipitate is formed.

3 Test for iron(III) ions Fe^{3+}
Sodium hydroxide solution is added.

A brown jelly-like precipitate is formed.

Did you know? Chlorine was used in World War I as a poison gas. It caused soldiers to choke and attacked their lungs.

SUMMARY

1 The halogens in Group 7 are reactive non-metals. Fluorine is the most reactive.
2 The transition metals are found in a central block in the periodic table.

QUESTIONS

1 Where are the halogens found in the Periodic Table? How are they similar? Why are they reactive non-metals?
2 What do you see when chlorine is passed into sodium bromide solution? Why does a reaction not occur when bromine is added to sodium chloride solution?
3 Manganese is a transition metal. What properties do you expect it to have?
4 Sodium hydroxide solution was added to a pale green solution of a metal compound. A dark green precipitate was formed. Give the metal ion present.

42 Compounds of halogens and their uses

SALT, AN IMPORTANT SUBSTANCE

We add it to our food, need it in our body fluids and use it to make other chemicals. Salt or sodium chloride is a very important substance. It is obtained from underground deposits or from the sea.

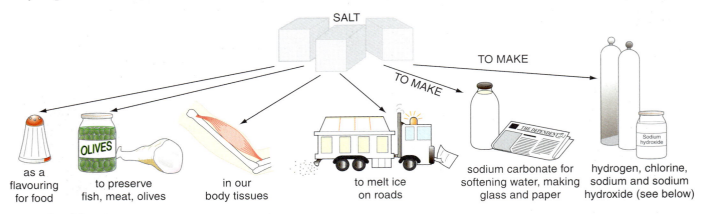

BREAKING UP SALT

Sodium chloride is an ionic compound. It can be decomposed by using an electric current. This is done by passing the current through molten salt or brine. Brine is a solution of salt in water.

Electrolysing molten sodium chloride

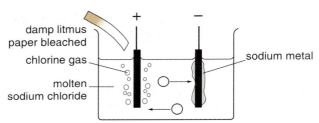

Ions present: sodium Na+ and chloride Cl−

At the positive electrode (anode)
Chloride ions attracted, **chlorine gas** given off. The chlorine bleaches damp litmus paper.

At the negative electrode (cathode)
Sodium ions attracted, **sodium metal** produced.

Electrolysing a concentrated solution of sodium chloride

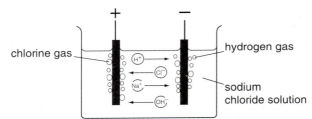

Ions present: sodium Na+ and chloride Cl− from the salt; hydrogen H+ and hydroxide OH− from the water

At the anode
Chloride and hydroxide ions attracted, **chlorine gas** given off.

At the cathode
Sodium and hydrogen ions attracted, **hydrogen gas** given off (sodium is not given off as it is more reactive than hydrogen).

USEFUL PRODUCTS FROM ELECTROLYSING MOLTEN SALT AND BRINE

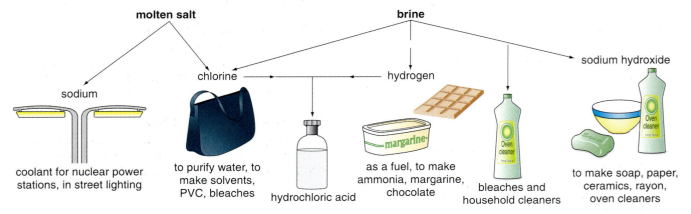

Test for chlorine: it bleaches damp litmus paper.

TAKING A PHOTOGRAPH AND MAKING A PRINT

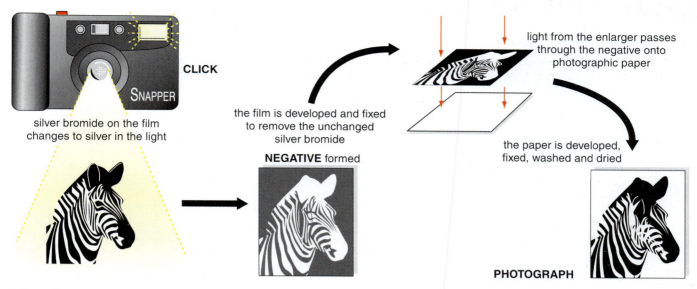

Silver chloride, bromide and iodide (silver halides) are used in photographic film and paper. They are reduced to grains of black silver metal by the action of light, X-rays and the radiation from radioactive substances. This forms a negative. A positive image is made when light is shone through the negative onto photographic paper. X-ray photographs are usually recycled to get back the silver.

MAKING ACIDS FROM HALOGENS

Hydrogen halides dissolve in water to form acid solutions. Hydrogen chloride is more stable than hydrogen bromide and iodide.

The hydrogen chloride gas dissolves in the water to form hydrochloric acid.

WHAT MAKES THE SOLUTION ACIDIC?

Hydrogen chloride gas has a covalent bond and is not acidic. It does not affect pH paper.

In water the covalent bond breaks. H^+ and Cl^- ions are formed which are surrounded by water molecules. They are written as $H^+(aq)$ and $Cl^-(aq)$. The $H^+(aq)$ ions cause the solution to be acidic and turn pH paper red. All acidic solutions contain $H^+(aq)$ ions.

> #### SUMMARY
> 1. Salt is an important raw material with many uses.
> 2. Hydrogen chloride dissolves in water to form an acid.

> #### QUESTIONS
> 1. Name the substances formed when brine is electrolysed. Give a use of each.
> 2. You have two solutions, one contains salt and the other sodium sulphate. Describe two tests to identify them.

REACTIONS OF HYDROCHLORIC ACID

1. Metals

Reactive metals such as magnesium and zinc fizz and give hydrogen gas. The hydrogen causes a lighted splint to pop.

For example:
magnesium + hydrochloric → magnesium + hydrogen
                  acid   chloride

2. Carbonates

Solid carbonates and solutions of carbonates fizz and give off carbon dioxide. Carbon dioxide gives a white precipitate with limewater.

For example:
sodium + hydrochloric → sodium + carbon + water
carbonate   acid   chloride   dioxide

TEST FOR CHLORIDE IONS

A few drops of dilute nitric acid and silver nitrate solution are added to a solution of the chloride. A white precipitate of silver chloride is formed. This turns grey in light as silver is formed.

TEST FOR SULPHATE IONS

A few drops of dilute nitric acid and barium nitrate solution are added to a solution of the sulphate. A white precipitate of barium sulphate is formed.

43 Rates of reaction

It's bonfire party time! The picture shows some chemical reactions happening in the garden.

The reactions shown take place at different rates. The explosions from the banger and Catherine wheel are very fast chemical reactions. The wood and paper also burn quickly. The potatoes take about half an hour to cook. The rusting of the iron is a much slower chemical reaction.

The rate of a chemical reaction is a measure of how fast a reaction takes place. It is a measure of how fast the substances which react (reactants) are used up. It is also a measure of how fast the substances produced (products) are formed. The shorter the time taken, the greater the rate. The longer the time taken, the smaller the rate.

MEASURING RATES OF REACTION

To measure the rate of a reaction we need to record the time taken for a particular change to occur.

1. Change in colour or appearance

In the chemical reactions which occur during the bonfire party, the products look different from the reactants.

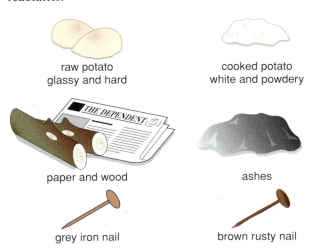

2. Formation of a solid in a solution (precipitate)

In some reactions a precipitate is formed as the reaction takes place. For example, a pale yellow precipitate of sulphur is slowly formed when dilute hydrochloric acid is added to a colourless solution of sodium thiosulphate.

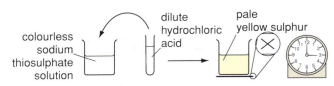

The solution turns pale yellow and is difficult to see through (opaque) as the sulphur forms. A piece of paper with a pencil cross drawn on it is placed under the beaker. The time is recorded for the cross to disappear. The shorter the time taken, the faster the reaction. The longer the time taken, the slower the reaction. *(Care: poisonous sulphur dioxide gas is also formed during the reaction.)*

3. Change in mass

The mass of reactants decreases if a gas is formed during the reaction and escapes into the air.
For example, the action of dilute hydrochloric acid on marble chips (calcium carbonate).

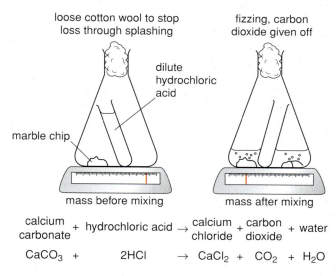

calcium carbonate + hydrochloric acid → calcium chloride + carbon dioxide + water

$CaCO_3 + 2HCl \rightarrow CaCl_2 + CO_2 + H_2O$

The reaction rate decreases as the reaction occurs. This is shown by recording the mass every few seconds. A graph is plotted of the mass against the time.

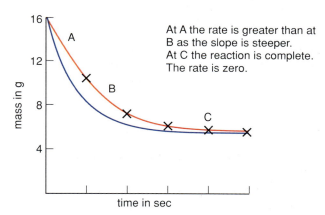

At A the rate is greater than at B as the slope is steeper.
At C the reaction is complete. The rate is zero.

The blue line shows a quicker reaction but using the same amounts of the same reactants.

Did you know?
The light given out by a firefly at night is produced by a slow chemical reaction in its body. The oxygen from the air reacts with a chemical in the firefly called luciferin.

SUMMARY

1. The rate of a chemical reaction is a measure of how fast it occurs.
2. A measure of the rate of a reaction is obtained by finding the time taken for a change to occur.

4. Change in volume

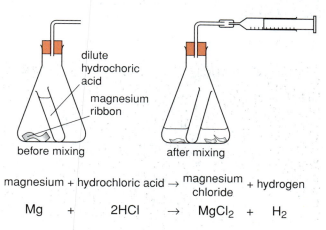

magnesium + hydrochloric acid → magnesium chloride + hydrogen

$Mg + 2HCl \rightarrow MgCl_2 + H_2$

There is an increase in volume during a reaction if a gas is formed and collected as it is produced. For example, the action of dilute hydrochloric acid on magnesium.

The reaction rate decreases as the reaction occurs. This is shown by recording the volume of hydrogen every few seconds. A graph is plotted of the volume against time.

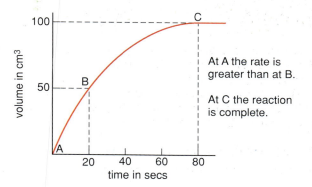

At A the rate is greater than at B.
At C the reaction is complete.

Using the graph

The time taken for the complete reaction is 80 seconds. The final volume of hydrogen is 100 cm^3. At 20 seconds, 50 cm^3 of hydrogen has formed. The reaction is half complete.

QUESTIONS

1. Give five chemical reactions which occur in the home. In each case name the reactants and products. List these reactions in decreasing order of their rate, i.e. begin with the fastest reaction.
2. What is meant by the rate of a reaction?
3. Give four changes which can occur during a reaction.
4. Draw a labelled diagram to show how you could measure the rate of a reaction in which a gas is formed. What would you measure? How could you use your results to show how the reaction rate changes during the reaction?

44 Changing rates of reactions

You are hungry and want to cook a potato quickly! You could ...

fry small pieces covered in oil   boil small pieces covered in water   fry large pieces covered in oil

Potatoes cook quicker by frying small pieces than by boiling them. This is because the hot oil is at a higher temperature than the boiling water. Small pieces of potato fry quicker than large pieces because there is a larger surface area in contact with the hot oil.

The rate of a chemical reaction depends on the conditions and whether or not a catalyst or enzyme is used.

SPEEDING UP CHEMICAL REACTIONS

1 Increasing the temperature

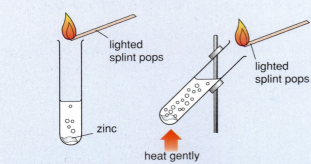

cold dilute hydrochloric acid – bubbles of hydrogen gas given off *slowly*

hot dilute hydrochloric acid – bubbles of hydrogen gas given off *quickly*

The same volume of acid and same mass of zinc is used in each case.
  The zinc reacts more quickly with the hot than with the cold dilute acid.

zinc + hydrochloric acid → zinc chloride + hydrogen
$Zn + 2HCl \rightarrow ZnCl_2 + H_2$

The reaction rate increases with temperature. The acid particles have more energy when they are hotter. They move faster and collide with the zinc particles more frequently and more energetically.

2 Increasing the concentration

The same size marble chip and same volume of acid is used in each case. The marble chip (calcium carbonate) reacts more quickly with the concentrated acid.

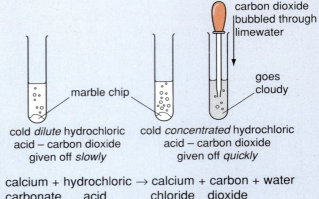

cold *dilute* hydrochloric acid – carbon dioxide given off *slowly*

cold *concentrated* hydrochloric acid – carbon dioxide given off *quickly*

calcium + hydrochloric → calcium + carbon + water
carbonate   acid   chloride   dioxide

$CaCO_3 + 2HCl \rightarrow CaCl_2 + CO_2 + H_2O$

The concentrated acid has more acid particles in the same volume of solution. They collide with the chalk particles more frequently and the rate increases. For reactions between gases, the concentration is increased by increasing the pressure. An increase in pressure increases the rate of gaseous reactions as the particles are squeezed closer together.

Did you know?
In just 15 cm³ of air there are a thousand, million, million collisions every second between the particles in the air!

SUMMARY

1. Chemical reactions only occur if the reacting particles collide together with sufficient energy. The activation energy is the minimum amount of energy that they need.
2. Reaction rates are increased by increasing the energy or the rate of collision of the reacting particles.
3. Catalysts increase the rate of certain reactions.

Why do chemical reactions occur?

Chemical reactions occur when reacting particles collide together with sufficient energy. The minimum amount of energy the particles must have for the collision to result in a reaction is called the activation energy.

The reaction rate is increased by...

...increasing the rate of collision between particles

...increasing the energy of the particles.

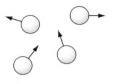

few collisions per second

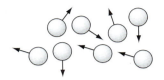

many collisions per second

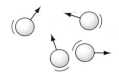

less energy, moving slower and fewer fruitful collisions

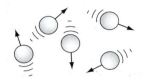

more energy, moving faster and more fruitful collisions

3 Decreasing the particle size of solids

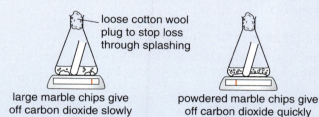

large marble chips give off carbon dioxide slowly with dilute acid

powdered marble chips give off carbon dioxide quickly with dilute acid

The mass of marble chips and volume of acid is the same in both cases. The effect of the size of the particles on the rate of reaction is shown by plotting the mass against the time.

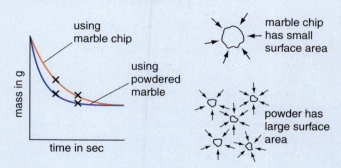

The reaction with the powdered marble chips is faster because there is a larger surface area for reacting with the acid. There are more collisions each second and so the rate of reaction is increased.

4 Using a catalyst

A catalyst is a substance that speeds up a chemical reaction but is not itself used up.

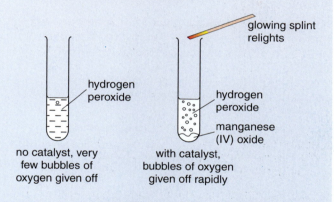

no catalyst, very few bubbles of oxygen given off

with catalyst, bubbles of oxygen given off rapidly

Manganese(IV) oxide catalyses the breakdown of hydrogen peroxide to oxygen at room temperature. The oxygen relights a glowing splint. The catalyst can be filtered off and used again.

hydrogen peroxide → oxygen + water
$$2H_2O_2 \rightarrow O_2 + 2H_2O$$

Questions

1. How can you speed up a reaction between
   a. a solid and solution
   b. two gases?
2. What is a catalyst? Give an example of a reaction which can be catalysed.
3. Why in industry is it necessary to speed up reactions?
4. How can you increase
   a. the rate of the collision between reacting particles?
   b. the energy of the reacting particles?

45 Energy changes and catalysts

GETTING WARM

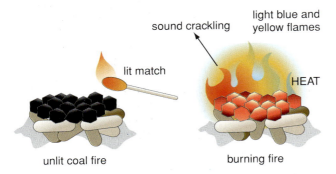

unlit coal fire — burning fire

When fuels burn, heat, light and sometimes sound energy is transferred to the surroundings. The reaction is said to be **exothermic**.

A kick start

The coal, paper, wood or gas do not spontaneously start to burn under normal conditions. They have to be lit with a spark or match. Energy has to be supplied.

An energy profile shows the energy changes occurring during the reaction.

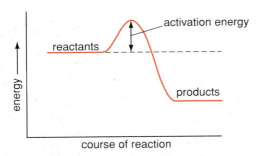

In exothermic reactions, the energy of the reactants is greater than the energy of the products. The energy supplied before the reaction begins is usually heat but may be light, electrical or sound energy. Only molecules with this energy are able to react.

The minimum energy needed before the molecules can react is called the **activation energy**. This is like a barrier. It has to be overcome before the reaction can occur.

Other exothermic reactions

1. Neutralisation.
2. Adding water to quick lime to form slaked lime.
3. Combustion, such as, burning petrol, magnesium ribbon.

COOLING DOWN

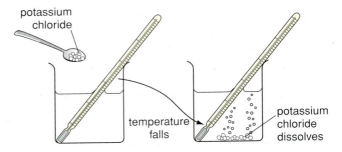

As the crystals dissolve the temperature falls. Heat energy is transferred from the water and used to break up the crystal. The reaction is said to be **endothermic**.

A kick start

Endothermic reactions also need a kick start. In this case a lot of energy has to be supplied.

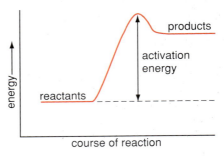

This is the energy profile for an endothermic reaction. In endothermic reactions, the energy of the reactants is less than the energy of the products. The transfer of energy from the surroundings may be heat, light or electrical energy.

The **activation energy** needed for endothermic reactions is usually larger than for exothermic reactions.

Other endothermic reactions

1. During thunderstorms, the energy in lightning causes nitrogen and oxygen to combine.
2. In photosynthesis light energy from the Sun is transferred into chemical energy.
3. The electrolysis of aluminium oxide to aluminium uses electrical energy.

> **Did you know?**
> Making a cool drink: when sodium hydrogencarbonate (sodium bicarbonate) is added to a solution of lemon juice, bubbles of carbon dioxide are formed and the solution cools. The reaction is endothermic.

More about catalysts

Catalysts are used to speed up chemical reactions. They save time and energy and therefore money.

Catalysts have the following characteristics:
- different reactions need different catalysts, such as nickel in the reaction of oils with hydrogen to make margarine
- they are often transition metals or their compounds
- they are not used up during the reaction and can be used over and over again.

Using a catalyst over and over again

Manganese(IV) oxide catalyses the breakdown of hydrogen peroxide to oxygen.

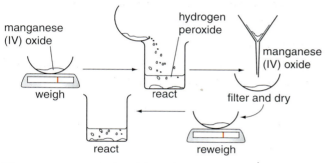

The manganese(IV) oxide is weighed, used to catalyse the reaction and then filtered off, dried and reweighed. The weight is the same. When added to another portion of hydrogen peroxide it causes it to decompose. The catalyst can be used again.

How does the catalyst work?

Catalysts lower the activation energy of both exothermic and endothermic reactions.

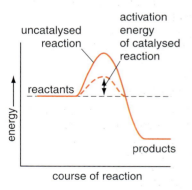

One way of doing this is to provide a different pathway for the reaction, rather like cycling through a tunnel rather than going over the top of a hill.

The products in the catalysed reaction are the same as those in the uncatalysed reaction.

Showing how catalysts speed up reactions

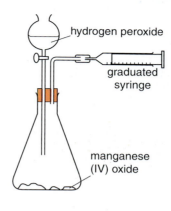

Hydrogen peroxide breaks down slowly at room temperature. The volume of oxygen formed is recorded every 30 seconds.

The experiment is repeated but manganese(IV) oxide is first added. In both cases the volume of oxygen formed is plotted against the time.

The graph for the catalysed reaction is much steeper. This shows the reaction was faster.

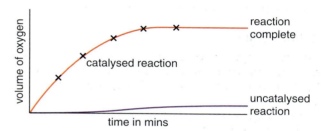

Poisoning catalysts

Catalysts are easily poisoned by impurities. This is why in industry the reactants are first purified.

In cars, catalytic converters are put in exhausts to convert poisonous carbon and nitrogen monoxides in exhaust gases to less harmful substances. The catalyst (sometimes platinum) catalyses the reaction.

carbon monoxide + nitrogen monoxide → carbon dioxide + nitrogen

If leaded rather than unleaded petrol is used by mistake, the catalyst is poisoned and no longer works.

Questions

1. Explain what is meant by the terms exothermic and endothermic reactions. Give an example of each.
2. When some hydrogen peroxide was poured into a dirty beaker, it started to fizz and the gas given off relit a glowing splint. What do you think is happening and why?
3. Explain why a gas fire has to be lit before it begins to burn.

Summary

1. In exothermic reactions energy is transferred to the surroundings. In endothermic reactions energy is transferred from the surroundings.
2. Catalysts speed up chemical reactions.

46 Biological catalysts

Without catalysts we would not be alive. All our body processes from digestion to respiration depend on the help of biological catalysts found in the cells of our bodies. These catalysts are called **enzymes**.

Many of our foods and drinks are produced by reactions using enzymes as catalysts.

The production of bread, wine and beer depend on the action of yeast on sugars. Cheese and yoghurt are made by the action of bacteria on milk. Both the yeast and bacteria contain enzymes which catalyse the reactions. Fresh pineapple has enzymes which help to break down the protein in the ham. This makes it easier to chew and digest.

THE BAKING, BREWING AND WINE MAKING INDUSTRIES

These industries are based on the action of enzymes in yeast on sugars. The enzymes catalyse the breakdown of sugar to ethanol and carbon dioxide. This process is called **fermentation**.

$$\text{sugar} \xrightarrow{\text{yeast}} \text{ethanol} + \text{carbon dioxide}$$

Brewing
Barley grains are sprouted to change the starch to a sugar, malt.

Water and hops are added and the solution is boiled. Yeast is added to the cooled mixture and it is left to ferment.

When the alcohol reaches about 4% the beer is filtered and stored in barrels. Further fermentation produces carbon dioxide which makes the beer fizzy.

Wine making
The juice from crushed grapes is left to ferment. (Other fruits or vegetables give different flavours.)

When the alcohol reaches about 12% the yeast dies. The wine is bottled and left to mature, sometimes for many years.

Baking
Yeast, flour, water and a little sugar is mixed to a dough and left in a warm place (about 35°C) to ferment. It rises as bubbles of carbon dioxide are trapped in the dough.

The dough is kneaded, left to rise and cooked. The carbon dioxide expands in the hot oven causing the bread to rise more. The heat kills the yeast.

THE DAIRY INDUSTRY

Bacteria are used to make yoghurt and cheese from milk. Enzymes in the bacteria catalyse the chemical changes.

Milk is first pasteurised by heating it to 72°C for 15 seconds and then cooling it quickly. This kills harmful bacteria.

Other bacteria are added. They use the sugar in the milk (lactose) and make an acid (lactic acid). Some yoghurt (bio yoghurt) has live bacteria in it.

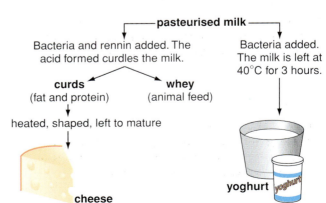

Showing enzymes are present in blood

If a drop of blood or chopped liver is added to hydrogen peroxide it fizzes and oxygen is given off. The reaction is faster than when manganese(IV) oxide is used.

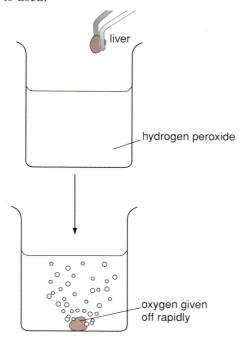

The enzyme catalase breaks down hydrogen peroxide. This reaction is important in the body as peroxides are harmful. Catalase is very effective as one molecule breaks down 40 000 molecules of peroxide each second!

How do enzymes work?

An enzyme is a large protein molecule which has a certain shape. It seems to work in a jigsaw fashion.

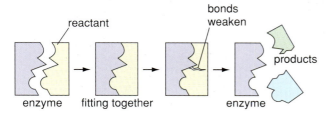

Reactants are also large molecules with certain shapes. An enzyme only fits a particular reactant, so an enzyme only speeds up one reaction.

Summary

1. Biological catalysts are called enzymes.
2. Bread, wine and beer are made by fermentation using the enzymes in yeast. Other enzymes are used to make cheese and yoghurt.

Enzymes cleaning for us

Enzymes are added to washing powders to break down or 'digest' stains from food or body fluids at moderate temperatures. Without them higher temperatures are needed.

Biological washing powders should be used at about 40°C. At higher temperatures the enzymes break down.

Stopping food from going bad

Some microbes cause food to go bad. They need air, moisture and warmth to multiply. Food is preserved by:

- killing the microbes, for example sterilisation, pasteurisation
- excluding the air and heat treating, for example canning, bottling, vacuum packing
- removing liquid water, for example drying and freezing
- using preservatives which kill microbes, for example vinegar, salt, sugar and other chemicals
- cooling, for example freezing and refrigerating.

Differences between enzymes and other catalysts

Enzymes are protein molecules. They break down above 40°C and are inactive at low temperatures. The temperature at which they work best is called the optimum temperature.

For most enzymes the optimum temperature is around body temperature. This is not surprising! The effectiveness of non-biological catalysts usually increases steadily as the temperature rises. They do not have an optimum temperature.

Enzymes

- are protein molecules
- speed up one reaction only
- work best at about body temperature
- are destroyed when too hot and inactive when cold.

Did you know? Every cell in our body contains hundreds of different enzymes, one for each of the reactions that are carried out in it. Without these enzymes we wouldn't be alive.

Questions

1. What is meant by fermentation? How is this reaction used in making wine and beer?
2. Pitta bread is a bread made without yeast. Why is it flat?
3. How do enzymes differ from non-biological catalysts?

Practice questions – Materials

1. On a camping trip you take a cool box made of expanded polystyrene, stainless steel cutlery, ceramic mugs, aluminium pans with wooden handles, plastic plates and a nylon tent.
   a. List the materials which are made from crude oil.
   b. Name an alloy.
   c. Name a metal.
   d. Give one reason for taking plastic rather than ceramic plates.
   e. Explain why the saucepans are made of aluminium but the handles are made of wood.
   f. Give a reason why the cool box is not made of metal.
   g. Expanded polystyrene contains bubbles of air trapped in the polystyrene. Why is this a better material than ordinary polystyrene for the cool box?

2. Meringue is a kind of cake made by beating air into a mixture of sugar, egg whites and a few drops of vanilla flavouring.
   a. Make a table with columns headed solids, liquids, gases and put the four ingredients into the right columns.
   b. Draw diagrams to show the arrangement of the particles in a solid, a liquid and a gas.
   c. When the meringue is in the hot oven it gets bigger as the air bubbles in it expand. Explain why this happens.

3. a. Copy and complete the following table.

Name	Relative charge	Relative mass
neutron		
proton		
electron		'almost 0'

   b. Which particles are found in the nucleus of an atom?
   c. Find sodium and fluorine in the Periodic Table. Copy the diagrams and draw in the correct number of electrons in each shell. Use a cross to represent an electron. (Not all the shells may contain electrons.)

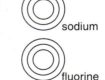

   d. Sodium and fluorine are both elements. What is an element? Which of these elements is a non-metal?
   e. Both sodium and fluorine are very reactive and can join together to form an ionic compound.
      i. What is a compound?
      ii. What is the name of the compound formed between sodium and fluorine?
      iii. Explain why both sodium and fluorine are very reactive by referring to the arrangement of their electrons.
      iv. Give the symbol and charge on each ion present in the compound. Explain how the ions are formed.
      v. Explain why the solid compound has a high melting point.

4. An atom of carbon can be written as $^{12}_{6}C$.
   a. Which number is the atomic number?
   b. How many protons, neutrons and electrons are there in the atom?
   c. Draw a diagram to show how the electrons are arranged.
   d. A different atom of carbon has the same number of protons and electrons but one more neutron.
      i. What is the name given to these two forms of carbon?
      ii. What is the atomic number of this atom?
      iii. What is the mass number of this atom?
   e. Is carbon a metal or non-metal?
   f. Carbon joins with oxygen to form carbon dioxide.
      i. What type of bonding is present in carbon dioxide?
      ii. Explain why carbon dioxide is a gas.
      iii. Give a test for showing that a gas is carbon dioxide. Give the results of the test.

5. a. A small amount of salt is dissolved in pure water. Name the solute and the solvent.
   b. More salt is added but some remains undissolved in the bottom of the beaker.
      i. How is the solution here different from the solution in a?
      ii. Draw a labelled diagram to explain how you would separate the undissolved salt from the solution.

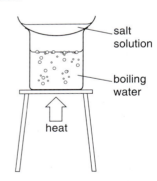

   c. A small amount of the salt solution is placed on a watch glass on top of the beaker of boiling water as shown.
      i. What happens to the water in the solution?
      ii. What is left on the watch glass?
   d. You are asked to get a sample of pure water from the salt solution. Draw a labelled diagram to show how you would do this.

6. Which of the statements i – iv below:
   a. describes a physical change?
   b. describes combustion?
   c. applies to all chemical changes?
      i. one or more new substances are formed.
      ii. the change is reversible.
      iii. the physical state of a substance always changes.
      iv. a substance always burns.

7 a Limestone and marble contain the same chemical compound but are different types of rock.
      i   Name the chemical compound.
      ii   What type of rock is limestone?
      iii What type of rock is marble?
      iv   Explain how limestone is converted to marble in the Earth.
   b A marble chip is heated strongly and forms a white solid and gives off a gas. A white precipitate is formed when the gas is bubbled through limewater.
      i   Name the gas.
      ii   Name the white solid left after heating the marble chip.
      iii Give a word equation for the effect of heat on marble.
   c Limestone is heated with other substances to make cement and glass.
      i   What other substance is used to make cement?
      ii   What other substances are used to make glass?
      iii Cement is used to make concrete. Why is concrete so useful? Give one disadvantage.

8 Ammonium phosphate $(NH_4)_3PO_4$ is used as a fertiliser.
   a Name two elements in the fertiliser which are important for plant growth.
   b Apart from its cost, give one advantage and one disadvantage of using this fertiliser.
   c Name another compound which is used in some fertilisers.
   d Use the following relative atomic masses (A_r) to calculate the relative formula mass of ammonium phosphate.
      A_r (N) = 14, A_r (H) = 1, A_r (P) = 31, A_r (O) = 16.
   e Use your answer to d to calculate the percentage of nitrogen and the percentage of phosphorus in ammonium phosphate.

9 a Crude oil is an important fossil fuel and a raw material for making many other substances.
      i   How is crude oil formed?
      ii   Name two other fossil fuels.
      iii Name one gas formed when fossil fuels burn which contributes to acid rain.
      iv   What is the effect of acid rain on the environment?
   b Crude oil is a mixture of hydrocarbons.
      i   Name the two elements in hydrocarbons.
      ii   Give the name of the method used to separate the oil into different fractions.
   c Petrol, diesel and lubricating oil are three of the fractions obtained from crude oil.
      i   Which fraction has the highest boiling point?
      ii   Which fraction has the smallest molecules?
      iii Give one use of each of the fractions.
   d Some fractions are cracked.
      i   What conditions are needed to carry out cracking?
      ii   What happens to molecules when they are cracked?
   e Ethene is made by cracking. It is then made into a plastic.
      i   What is the name of the plastic formed?
      ii   Draw a diagram to show how ethene molecules join to make the plastic.
      iii Why can waste plastic be a problem?

10 The pie chart shows the approximate composition of the air.
   a Name the gases A and B and give one use of each.
   b C includes carbon dioxide, noble gases and pollutants.
      i   Name two processes which increase the amount of carbon dioxide in the air.
      ii   Name two noble gases.
      iii Explain why the noble gases are unreactive.
      iv   Name two pollutants. Explain how they are formed.

11 From the list: sodium hydroxide, water, lemon juice, sugar solution, hydrochloric acid, soap, alcohol, vinegar, toothpaste.
   a Give the substance which has a pH of 1.
   b Name two weak acids.
   c Name three substances which will not change the colour of either red or blue litmus paper.
   d Name one weak alkali.
   e Name the two substances which will react together to form sodium chloride solution.

12 Magnesium reacts with dilute sulphuric acid at room temperature to form a salt and a gas.
   a Name the salt and the gas formed.
   b Draw a diagram of the apparatus you would use so that you could measure the volume of the gas formed with time.
   c In an experiment the volume of the gas obtained was plotted against the time as shown below.

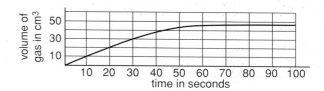

      i   At what time was the reaction complete?
      ii   What was the final volume of gas obtained?
      iii In another experiment the same amounts of acid and magnesium were used but the acid was first cooled. Say what would happen and sketch on the axes the curve you expect to obtain.
      iv   Give two other ways of altering the rate of the reaction, stating whether the reaction will be faster or slower.

13 The diagram shows a section through a volcano.
   a What is found at A?
   b What type of rock is found at B and what type at C?
   c How do the crystals in the rocks found at B and C differ? Why do they differ in this way?
   d Sedimentary rocks can be changed into another type of rock by high temperatures and pressures. Name this type of rock and give an example.

Answers to practice questions

Answers to the questions on pp.164–165

1.
   a. expanded polystyrene, plastic, nylon
   b. stainless steel
   c. aluminium
   d. It is lighter to carry.
   e. Aluminium is a good heat conductor, wood insulates heat so a wooden handle would enable you to pick up the saucepan.
   f. Metals are good heat conductors so would allow heat through.
   g. Air is a good insulator.

2.
   a.
solids	liquids	gases
sugar	egg whites	air
	vanilla flavouring	

   b. see p. 76
   c. The heat from the oven causes air to expand.

3.
   a.
name	relative charge	relative mass
neutron	0	1
proton	+1	1
electron	-1	negligible

   b. neutrons and protons
   c. see p. 93
   d. An element is a substance which cannot be broken down into a simpler substance. Fluorine is a non-metal.
   e.
      i. A compound is a substance made by chemically combining two or more elements.
      ii. sodium fluoride
      iii. Sodium has only to lose one electron to achieve a stable configuration. Fluorine has only to gain one electron to achieve a stable configuration.
      iv. Na^+ F^-
      v. The forces between the ions are large.

4.
   a. 6
   b. 6 protons, 6 neutrons, 6 electrons
   c. see diagram
   d.
      i. isotopes
      ii. 6
      iii. 13
   e. non-metal
   f.
      i. covalent
      ii. It is a gas (and not a solid) because it has a simple molecular structure and does not form giant mols.
      iii. Turns limewater a cloudy white.

5.
   a. solute is salt, solvent is water
   b.
      i. It is saturated and therefore is more concentrated.
      ii. The diagram here should show a filter funnel with filter paper.
   c.
      i. It evaporates.
      ii. salt
   d. This diagram should show a flask and a condenser.

6.
   a. The change is reversible. The physical state of the substance always changes.
   b. A substance always burns.
   c. One or more new substances are formed.

7.
   a.
      i. calcium carbonate
      ii. sedimentary
      iii. metamorphic
      iv. Limestone is changed to marble under extreme heat and pressure.
   b.
      i. carbon dioxide
      ii. calcium oxide
      iii. calcium carbonate → calcium oxide + carbon dioxide
   c.
      i. clay
      ii. sand and sodium carbonate
      iii. It can be moulded, and is relatively light. Disadvantage: it is not very strong.

8.
   a. nitrogen, phosphorus
   b. advantage: it contains 2 important elements for growth
      disadvantage: it is very soluble and easily leached, a pollutant
   c. Any suitable compound such as potassium nitrate or ammonium sulphate.
   d. 149
   e. N = 28.2, P = 20.8

9.
   a.
      i. From dead decaying plants and animals buried in sediment at high temperature and pressure.
      ii. coal, natural gas
      iii. sulphur dioxide or nitrogen dioxide
      iv. kills plants and animals
   b.
      i. hydrogen and carbon
      ii. fractional distillation
   c.
      i. lubricating oil
      ii. petrol
      iii. petrol - fuel/solvent, lubricating oil - lubrication, diesel fuel
   d.
      i. high temperature, calalyst
      ii. break into smaller chains
   e.
      i. polythene
      ii. see diagram
      iii. not biodegradable

10.
    a. A nitrogen B oxygen
    b.
       i. respiration, combustion
       ii. Any suitable example such as helium and neon.
       iii. full outer shell
       iv. Any suitable example such as nitrogen dioxide.

11.
    a. hydrochloric acid
    b. lemon juice, vinegar
    c. water, sugar solution, alcohol
    d. toothpaste
    e. sodium hydroxide, hydrochloric acid

12.
    a. magnesium sulphate, hydrogen
    b. This could be a diagram of a flask with a gas syringe attached to it.
    c.
       i. 60 s
       ii. 45 cm^3
       iii. Less steep curve, with same total volume. The rate of reaction.
       iv. By increasing concentration of acid - producing a faster reaction
           By increasing temperature of acid - producing a faster reaction
           Powdered magnesium - faster reaction

13.
    a. magma
    b. B basalt, C granite
    c. basalt, smaller crystals than granite as basalt cools more quickly
    d. metamorphic rock, such as marble, slate

Physical processes

1 The solar system

THE SOLAR SYSTEM 1

There are nine planets in our solar system. They move around the Sun in **orbits**. The orbits are not circles but squashed circles called **ellipses**. Each planet is held in its orbit by its high speed and the gravity of the Sun. The further away the planet is the smaller the effect of the gravity of the Sun. The further the planet from the Sun, the bigger its orbit and the longer it takes to orbit the Sun.

The Earth

The Earth spins on its own axis once every day (24 hours). It takes the Earth 365 days (one year) to orbit the Sun. Looking from the Earth we can see the stars at night, but we see different stars at different times of the year.

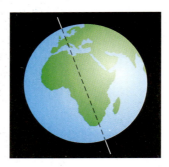

Stars

When we look at the sky at night, we see stars. Stars make their own light because nuclear reactions are happening inside them. They are like our Sun. Stars do not move away from each other, so we see them in fixed patterns. Even in ancient times people could see the fixed patterns in the stars. They gave them names. We call the patterns **constellations**.

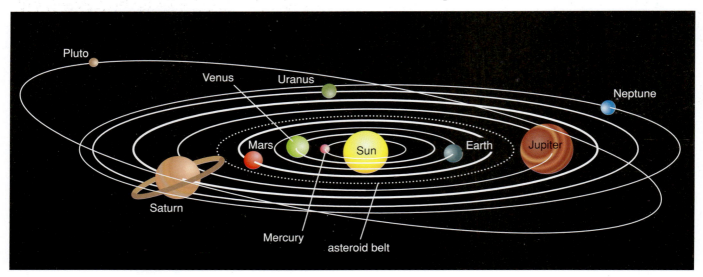

The planets

The planets do not make their own light, but we see them because they reflect light from the Sun. Because they are orbiting the Sun we can see them move across our sky. They look like stars. However they are different from the stars, which do not move from their fixed patterns. We see planets move slowly across the constellations of stars. Where we see planets in the sky depends on where they are in their orbit at that time.

The ecliptic

As the planets move around the Sun in their orbits they seem to move along one line. This is because they all move on the same plane. We call this the *ecliptic*. You can see this in the diagram.

Did you know?
The rotation of the Earth causes the water to go down your bath plug hole in a clockwise direction.

WHAT CAUSES NIGHT AND DAY?

The Sun rises in the east and goes down in the west. At midday the Sun is high in the sky and it is the hottest part of the day. It would be easy to think that the Sun is moving. In fact the Earth is. If you could look down on the Earth from above the North Pole you would see it turning round once every day. The Earth is so big you can't feel the movement, but you are moving about 36 000 km each day in an anticlockwise direction. So you are always moving towards the east.

The solar system 2

Throughout ancient times people had different ideas about the solar system.

As early as 300 BC Aristarchus of Samos said that the Earth and Moon revolve around the Sun.

But Aristarchus was not taken seriously. It is easy to see why. After all the Sun and the Moon moved across the sky, so most people thought the Earth was not moving, but the Sun and Moon were. It seemed obvious to scientists such as Aristotle and Ptolemy in AD 100 that the planets and the Sun moved around the Earth, and their calculations confirmed this. To them the Earth was the centre of the universe. The other heavenly bodies revolved around the Earth in circular paths.

The ideas of Ptolemy survived for 1500 years. The Christian Church in Europe supported the idea of the Earth being at the centre of things. Copernicus was certain that his calculations proved Aristarchus's ideas but was so frightened by the Church that he would not allow his book to be published until after his death. He was right to be frightened. In 1600 Giordano Bruno was burnt at the stake for suggesting that the Earth orbits the Sun.

Galileo made a breakthrough by using a telescope in 1609. Johannes Kepler worked out that the orbits of the planets were elliptical. Both Galileo and Kepler could see the planets using telescopes and began to support Copernicus's ideas.

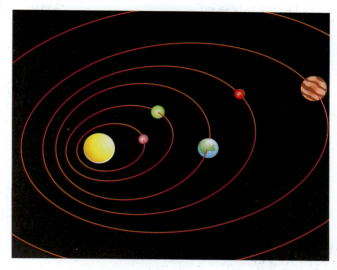

The Sun - centred solar system

By 1674 Robert Hooke and Isaac Newton had convinced many scientists that the gravity of the Sun caused the planets to move in elliptical orbits. They used models to show that their ideas fitted the observations made with telescopes.

Summary

1. The Earth spins on its own axis once every 24 hours. The Earth orbits the Sun once each year.
2. Nine planets orbit the Sun in our solar system. Their orbits are elliptical.
3. The stars in the sky stay in fixed patterns called constellations.
4. For about 1500 years people thought that the Earth was at the centre of the solar system. Observing the movement of the planets with telescopes provided evidence for the idea of the Sun being at the centre.

Questions

1. Name the nine planets in the solar system.
2. What causes the planets to orbit the Sun?
3. What is a constellation? Give two examples.
4. Planets do not make light. Explain how we see them.
5. When the Ancient Greeks looked at the night sky, they called the planets 'the wanderers'. Explain why.

2 Gravity and satellites

GRAVITY

Gravity pulls everything downwards on Earth. **Gravity** is a force. The force of gravity is strong enough to hold everything on the surface of the planet. The force of gravity is also strong enough to have an effect on objects far away from the Earth, but its force is less the further away an object is from the Earth. The gravitational field around the Earth holds objects such as the Moon and satellites in orbit around the Earth.

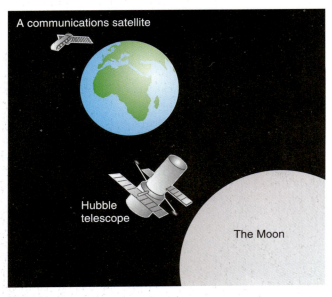

WEIGHT AND MASS

Another name for the gravitational force is **weight**. The weight of something is a combination of how much material is inside it (its mass) and the gravity pulling on it. A good example is a bag of sugar. Some people say 'a bag of sugar weighs 1 kg'. This is wrong. There is 1 kg of mass in the sugar. Gravity pulls on the 1 kg mass. Gravity pulls by 10 newtons on every 1 kg of mass. So the weight of the sugar is:
1 kg × 10 N = 10 newtons.
We can write:
    weight = mass × 10 N (gravitational force)

mass = 1kg

weight = 10 newtons

THE MOON – THE EARTH'S SATELLITE

The Moon orbits the Earth. We can tell this because each night it is in a different position and seems to change its shape a little.

The Moon orbits the Earth once every 28 days. It is held in its orbit by the force of gravity. It does not fall onto the Earth because it is moving at a speed which counteracts the force of gravity.

The phases of the Moon are when its shape seems to change. In fact its shape does not change. What we can see of the Moon changes. This is because the Moon does not make light of its own. We see the Moon by sunlight reflected from the surface of the Moon. In the diagram below, imagine yourself looking at the Moon from the North Pole. Sometimes the Sun is behind it. It is not lit up at all (a). You see nothing. Sometimes the Sun is shining on half of the Moon, you only see half (b),(d). Sometimes the Sun is shining on the whole of the side of the Moon. You see a full Moon (c).

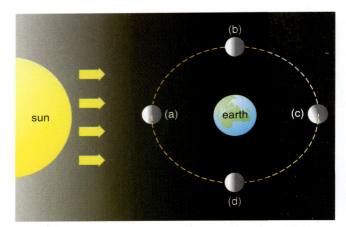

GRAVITY ON OTHER PLANETS

Wherever an object is, it has the same mass. This is because mass depends on the material inside it. If you could stand on each of the planets of our solar system you would have the same mass. Each planet has a different force of gravity. So you would have a different weight. If your weight on Earth is 500 newtons, your mass is 50 kg. On Jupiter you would weigh 50 kg × the force of gravity, which is 25 N/kg. Your weight would be 50 × 25 = 1250 newtons – more than double what it is on Earth.

On the Moon you would only weigh 85 newtons because the force of gravity is only 1.7 N/kg.

Natural satellites

The Moon is a natural satellite, which orbits the Earth. There are natural satellites which orbit the other planets in our solar system.

Saturn and its satellites

Comets

Comets orbit the Sun. Comets have a centre or core made of frozen dust and gases. As the orbit brings the comet closer to the Sun the frozen gases evaporate. The light from the Sun reflects from the frozen gases and so we see the comet and the trailing gases which we call the 'tail' of the comet. When the orbit of a comet brings it close to the Earth we can see it clearly in the sky.

Hale Bopp

Did you know?
Hale Bopp Comet could be seen by us on Earth during 1997. It last travelled past Earth in 2213 BC. It will return about AD 4300. At its closest it was 122 million miles from Earth.

Summary

1. The downward pull of the Earth is called gravity.
2. Another name for the gravitational force is weight. The weight of something is the combination of how much material is inside it and the pull of gravity on the material.
3. Satellites orbit the Earth and other planets. Satellites stay in orbit because of a combination of the pull of gravity and their speed.

Artificial satellites

Artificial satellites can be used to
- send information between places on Earth
- check on conditions on Earth
- observe the universe without the atmosphere getting in the way.

Satellites stay in orbit because of a combination of the pull of gravity and their speed.

Geostationary satellites move quite slowly compared to some satellites. They are put in a high orbit above the equator. Their speed is the same as the Earth's speed of rotation, so they orbit once every 24 hours. If you could see one, it would seem not to move at all because it is moving at the same speed as you.

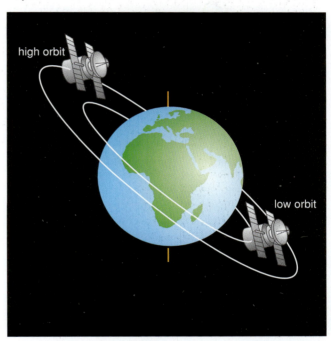

Geostationary satellites are used for television, radio and telephone transmissions.

Satellites which check up on weather and climate are put in low orbits. Because the pull of gravity is greater closer to the Earth they must move faster so that they are not pulled to Earth.

Questions

1. Why is it wrong to say 'a bag of sugar weighs 1 kg'?
2. The force of gravity on the Moon is 1.7 N/kg. What would a person with a mass of 70 kg weigh on the Moon?
3. As a comet gets nearer the Sun it speeds up. Explain why.
4. Give three uses for artificial satellites.

3 Stars

What is a star?

Our Sun is a typical star. There are millions and millions of stars. In between the stars is empty space. Each star, like our Sun, is made of hydrogen gas. Inside a star the gas is under a lot of pressure and the temperature is high. This causes nuclear fusion reactions when hydrogen atoms bump into each other and join together. A lot of energy is produced by a nuclear fusion reaction. The energy radiates into space from the star which makes it shine.

This view of a Nebula, light years away, shows stars forming. It is likely that there are planets around many of the stars in the universe.

Each star has a life

Stars are made inside a cloud of gas and dust called a **nebula**. Our Sun formed inside a nebula about 5000 million years ago when gravity pulled material inside the nebula into a lump. The gas in the lump got so hot that nuclear fusion started. Smaller lumps were not big enough for nuclear fusion to start and became the planets. The planets were attracted to the Sun by gravity.

Stars do not stay the same forever

Once started, nuclear fusion reactions carry on inside a star until all the hydrogen is used up. This will happen to our Sun in about 5000 million years. It will swell up and its outside will cool to a red glow. It will be a *red giant*. Later its outside will drift away in an explosion called a nova, leaving a hot core called a *white dwarf*. The white dwarf will use helium as energy until it runs out and the star fades away to become a dead star – a *black dwarf*.

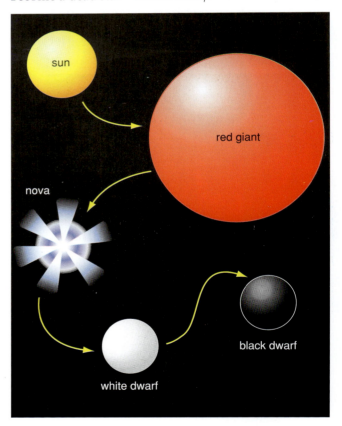

WHAT IS THE UNIVERSE?

The **universe** is the stars and the space between them. No one knows how big the universe is. We are still counting more and more stars. It is hard to understand how big the universe is. We use light years to measure distance in space. A **light year** is how far light travels in one year in space. A light year is 9 461 000 000 000 km (about six million million miles). The nearest star to us is Proxima Centauri. It is 4.3 light years away. When we see light from this star it has taken 4.3 years to reach us!

HOW WAS THE UNIVERSE FORMED?

We have no way of knowing how the universe was formed so scientists use evidence to support the idea of the **Big Bang Theory**. The idea is that everything started as a very dense hot centre made of particles. The 'Big Bang' was the largest explosion we can imagine, when the centre released all the energy and material that is in the universe today. The new universe was like a huge ball of fire, which expanded and spread out. As it spread out hydrogen particles gathered together to form stars.

There are two pieces of evidence for the Big Bang idea:
- the universe is moving away from a 'centre'
- radio telescopes have picked up microwaves coming from all directions in space which may be echoes from the Big Bang.

SUMMARY

1. Stars, including the Sun, form when gas and dust in space are pulled together by gravity. Planets form as smaller masses are attracted to the star by gravity.
2. Stars produce energy by nuclear fusion reactions. The energy radiates into space.
3. Stars do not stay the same forever because their energy is used up.
4. All the stars and the space between them is called the universe. The Big Bang Theory is used to explain the origin of the universe.

QUESTIONS

1. How is the energy produced inside a star?
2. What does the word universe mean?
3. Make a list of the things you would find in the universe.
4. Describe the formation of the universe.
5. Explain this statement made by a scientist: 'when we look at stars we are seeing the past'.

4 Observing the universe

Galaxies

About a million years after the Big Bang gravitational forces attracted some stars towards each other. Soon there were places in space where there were more stars than in others. Galaxies were formed. A **galaxy** is a group of stars. There are sometimes more than 100 000 million stars in a single galaxy. The stars in a galaxy are often millions of times further away from each other than the planets in our solar system. The universe is made of at least a billion galaxies. Each galaxy can be billions of miles away from other galaxies.

Did you know?
The Milky Way is expected to collide with the Andromeda Galaxy in ten billion years time, but people will not be around to witness this great event. Our Sun has only another 5000 million (5 billion) years left before it flares into a red giant and destroys its planets, including the Earth.

This Galaxy is light years away from the Milky Way.

The Earth is on the edge of a galaxy called the Milky Way. The Milky Way contains 200 million stars. It takes light 100 000 years to travel across the Milky Way.

The Hubble telescope

The Hubble telescope, launched in 1990, is orbiting the Earth. It carries a range of different instruments which are capable of recording events throughout the universe.

This image was taken in 1995 with a special camera on the Hubble telescope. It gave scientists their deepest ever look into space. To understand the area of the image hold a five pence piece against the night sky at the end of your outstretched arm. Now imagine the coin is 25 metres away. It would cover about the same area as this image. In the image you can see galaxies that are so far away, the light from them has taken ten billion years to travel to the camera in the telescope. We are seeing galaxies in the early days of the universe.

Summary

1. Stars are grouped together to form galaxies.
2. Our Sun is just one of millions of stars in the galaxy called the Milky Way.
3. Stars in a galaxy are millions of miles apart.
4. The universe is made up of at least a billion galaxies. Galaxies are millions of miles apart.

Questions

1. Explain the meaning of these words: galaxy, universe, star.
2. How many stars are there in a galaxy?
3. How many galaxies are there in the universe?
4. How big is the Milky Way?

5 Forces in action

We know that forces are all around us because we can see what they do.

A force is needed to move something. The arrow shows the direction of the force.

Forces can add up...
If two people push the supermarket trolley the forces combine. The effect of all the forces is called the **net force**.

Your body is pulled down by the force of gravity. The size of the force is your weight. The forces are balanced when the ground exerts an equal upward force.

The two teams are pulling in opposite directions. The teams do not move if the two forces are equal. The forces cancel each other out. They are **balanced forces**.

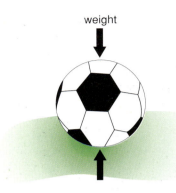

Forces subtract...
There are two forces acting on the football when it is resting on the surface. It is pulled down by the force of gravity and the ground is pushing it up. The forces **balance** each other, and the ball doesn't move. The net force is zero. Objects stay at rest like this unless an **unbalanced force** acts on them.

A stationary object like the football will move in the direction of the unbalanced force.

Stock cars travel around the track at a similar speed. The forces acting on the cars are balanced.

A force can change the direction something is moving in. If one of the stock cars is bumped in the side by another, its direction will change. It will be changed by the sideways force exerted by the other car.

The sideways force is an **unbalanced force**.

Unbalanced forces affect the movement of objects...

An object moving in the opposite direction to the force will slow down.

An object moving in the direction of the force will speed up.

MEASURING FORCES

We can use a spring balance (or force meter) to measure small forces. The spring balance pulls upwards with the same force as the weight of the bag of sugar. The greater the force, the higher the reading on the balance scale. Small forces are measured in newtons (N). For large forces we use kilo newtons (kN); 1 kN is another way of writing 1000 newtons.

A small force of 4 newtons is needed to lift this small bag of sugar.

The force on this tennis ball is 2000 newtons or 2 kN.

The force from the engines of this jet plane is about 800 000 newtons (800 kN).

The effects of a force depends on the size of the force and the mass of the object.

The car accelerates when the forces are unbalanced. The push of the engine is greater than the friction between the tyres and the road. The greater the force of the engine, the greater the acceleration. The truck needs a powerful engine because the bigger the mass of the truck, the greater the force needed to give the same acceleration as the car.

> ### SUMMARY
> 1. A force is a push or pull. Forces act in a certain direction.
> 2. The effects of forces can add up or cancel out. Balanced forces have no effect on the movement of an object. When forces do not cancel out we say an unbalanced force is acting on the object.
> 3. The effects of a force depends on the size of the force and the mass of the object.
> 4. Forces are measured in units called newtons.

> ### QUESTIONS
> 1. What forces act on a book when it is on a table or desk?
> 2. A man is pushing his car with a force of 250 N. His friend helps by pushing with a force of 300 N. What is the net force on the car?
> 3. Each engine of a jet plane with two engines exerts a force of 200 000 N. What is the net force of the engines? Give your answer in kN.

6 Speed

During the successful attempt to break the land speed record, the car took a few minutes to reach its record-breaking speed of 763.035 miles per hour. It only kept up this speed for a few seconds, so the speedometer only showed this top speed for a few seconds. Then the car slowed down and eventually stopped. Its speed was different during different parts of the journey.

A typical car journey is like a speed record attempt but slower. At times you may reach 50 miles per hour, then slow down at the traffic lights and then be held up by people crossing the road. It is the average speed of the car that decides how quickly you complete your journey. To work out your average speed you need to know how far the car has travelled. You also need to know how long it took. Speed links time and the distance travelled.

For example, if it took you 3 hours to travel 60 miles,

$$\text{the average speed} = \frac{\text{distance moved}}{\text{time taken}}$$

therefore speed $= \frac{60}{3} = 20$ miles per hour

When we work out speeds we can use the speed triangle. We can use metres and seconds to work out speeds.

The fastest car in the world with a speed of 763.035 miles per hour.

Cover the S with your finger ...speed is distance (D) divided by time (t).

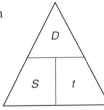

...to find the equation for D or t, cover one or the other with your finger.

A sprinter sometimes reaches speeds of 600 metres per minute during a race.
At this speed the sprinter would travel 600 metres in sixty seconds, the same time as it takes the cheetah to run 1800 metres.

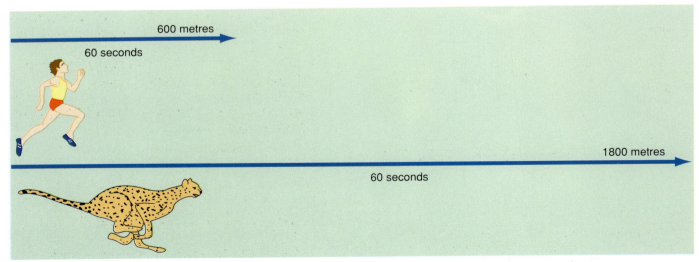

A cheetah is one of the fastest mammals. It can run at a speed of up to 1800 m/minute (30 m/s). When it is running at this speed, usually only for a small part of its journey, it could travel 1800 metres in 60 seconds.

DISTANCE–TIME GRAPHS

When a cheetah chases its prey, it sets off running quickly. It gets faster and faster at first. We say it accelerates. Soon it reaches a steady speed. Often this is its top speed. If it does not catch its prey it slows down and then stops.

A cheetah was photographed running. Drawings were made every second, so you can see its position. From its position we can tell its distance from the start.

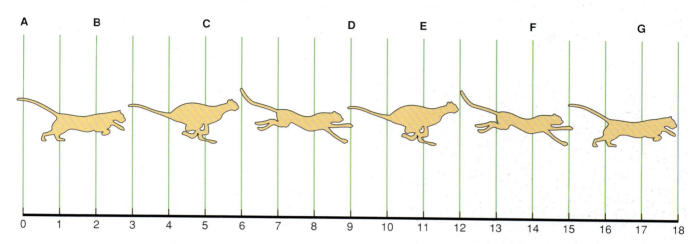

Drawing a distance–time graph for the cheetah

The distance is on the y-axis and the time on the x-axis. Photographs of the cheetah were taken every second, so each point is one second further along the graph. The photographs tell us how far away the cheetah is from the start.

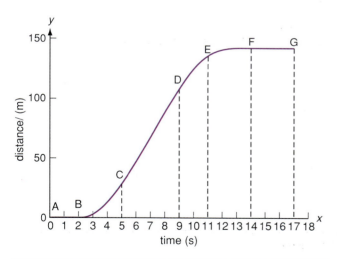

What the graph tells us

The line from A to B represents the cheetah not moving. It is accelerating between points B and C. Its speed is increasing between these points. The slope is steep. Between C and D the steepness of the graph is steady, the cheetah has a steady speed. Between D and E the cheetah slows down. The slope (gradient) is not as steep. Between E, F and G the cheetah slows down and stops. Notice that the graph is flat when the cheetah stops. Although time is still passing, it is not covering any distance.

- The steepness (gradient) of the graph tells us the cheetah's speed. The steeper the graph, the greater the speed.
- When the cheetah had a steady (constant) speed the steepness was constant. The graph was a straight line.
- When the cheetah was standing still, the gradient of the graph was zero.

SUMMARY

1. To describe how an object moves, we need to know how far it has travelled and how long it took. From this we can work out its speed.

   $$\text{Speed} = \frac{\text{distance travelled}}{\text{time taken}}$$

2. Distance–time graphs show the distance something has travelled against time.

QUESTIONS

1. A car travels 200 metres in 10 seconds. What is its speed?
2. Use the speed triangle to work out the time it would take for a woman jogging at a speed of 3 m/s, to travel 3000 m.
3. A boy sets off on his bicycle. After 10 s he has travelled 25 m, after 20 s, 45 m and after 30 s, he has travelled 65 m. Draw a distance–time graph of his journey.

7 Velocity and acceleration

Velocity

The **velocity** of an object is another way of thinking about speed. It is the speed in a certain direction. This is easy to understand if the object is a car or motorcycle. Imagine the motorcycle is travelling along a *straight road at 25 m/s* (about 56 mph). We know its *speed* and *direction*, so we say that its velocity is 25 m/s along the road. At the end of the straight road is a left turn. The motorcycle turns left and keeps its speed the same (constant) at 25 m/s. Its velocity has changed. It is now 25 m/s to the left.

The velocity of something is its speed in a particular direction.

Calculating velocities

We can use distance–time graphs to work out velocities. Imagine a cyclist travelling in a straight line along a road. The distance and time travelled are shown in the table below. We can draw a graph and use it to work out her speed.

First we draw a triangle to work out the slope of the graph. From the graph we can work out the distance she travelled, and how long it took her.

Distance (m)	5	10	15	20	25	30
Time (s)	1	2	3	4	5	6

To find the velocity between X and Y

We draw a triangle. From the triangle we can see that the distance travelled is 10 metres and the time taken is 2 seconds.

$$\text{Speed} = \frac{\text{distance}}{\text{time}}$$

$$= \frac{10 \text{ m}}{2 \text{ s}} = 5 \text{ m/s}$$

She is travelling in a straight line, so her velocity is 5 m/s along the road.

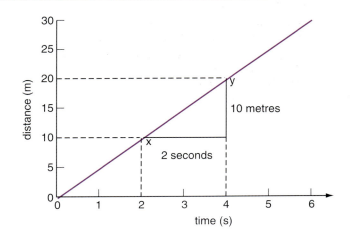

ACCELERATION

Acceleration means speeding up.

Acceleration measures the rate at which the velocity of a moving object changes. If the object is moving in a straight line, this is the same as the rate at which the speed changes.

We can work this out: acceleration = $\dfrac{\text{change in velocity}}{\text{time taken for change}}$

If a car reaches a speed of 50 m/s from a standing start after 10 s, it has *changed its velocity* from 0 m/s to 50 m/s. In other words, 50 − 0 = 50 m/s.

Its acceleration can be found by using the equation: acceleration = $\dfrac{\text{change in velocity}}{\text{time taken}} = \dfrac{50-0}{10} = \dfrac{50}{10} = 5$ m/s/s

Another way of writing this is 5 m/s^2.

VELOCITY–TIME GRAPHS

If we plot a velocity–time graph for a moving object we get another picture of a journey. Imagine two cars accelerating from traffic lights.

At first the graphs are straight lines. The line for the faster car shows us that a steeper slope of the graph shows us greater acceleration. Soon the cars reach a steady (constant) velocity and the graph shows this as a horizontal line.

In a velocity–time graph we see
- constant velocity as a horizontal line
- constant acceleration as a straight line sloping up.

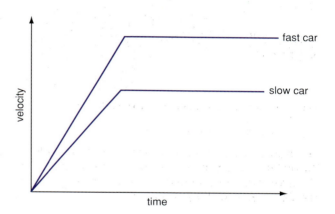

SUMMARY

1. The velocity of a moving object is its speed in a certain direction.
2. Acceleration of a moving object is how much (the rate at which) its velocity changes.
3. We can use a velocity–time graph to see constant velocity (a horizontal line) and constant acceleration (a straight sloping line).

QUESTIONS

1. Write meanings for these words: speed, velocity, acceleration, deceleration.
2. A car travels from standing still (0 m/s) to 80 m/s in 8 s. What is its acceleration?
3. What units do we use to measure:
   a. acceleration
   b. velocity
   c. speed?
4. Why is a velocity–time graph useful?

8 Forces on solids stretching

Forces can change the shape of things.

Elastic properties: material which returns to its original shape after a force is applied is said to have **elastic** properties.

The opposite of elastic is **inelastic**. This is when materials do not return to their original shape.

USING MATERIALS WITH ELASTIC PROPERTIES

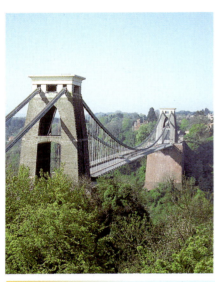

The road is suspended by steel cables. Steel is elastic, so the cables are stretched slightly by the weight of the road.

The springboard shows us an important feature of elastic material. The heavier the person, the more the springboard bends.

When this person takes off his Lycra clothes, they will go back to their original shape.

Springs are quite elastic. They return to their original shape when no force is applied.

MEASURING THE STRETCH OF A SPRING

You can investigate the stretching of a spring or metal wire by hanging weights (loads) on it. Use different weights and measure the amount by which the spring stretches. If you use 100 g masses, remember that each has a weight of 1N. To find the amount by which the spring stretches, measure the increase in the length of the spring. This is called the *extension*.

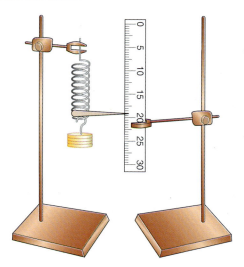

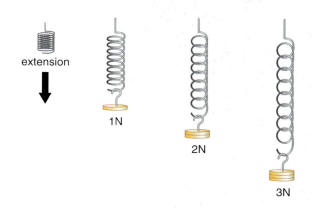

Draw a graph of extension against load to see the effects of increasing the load. You will notice that the graph is a straight line at first as the extension increases steadily as the load increases. The extension is directly proportional to the load. This means that if the load doubles the extension doubles; if the load triples, the extension triples, and so on. If the spring is removed from the experiment at any point on this line it will return to its original shape.

When the weight gets too big, the line is no longer straight. The spring has been damaged and its extension is increasing at a faster rate. The spring has been stretched too far. We say it has been stretched beyond its elastic limit. It will not return to its original shape.

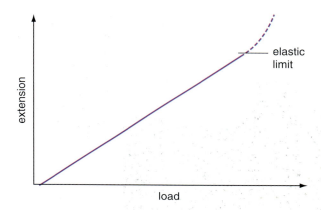

Robert Hooke 1635–1703 was famous for his microscopes. He was the first person to use the word cell. He studied forces on springs and wires and wrote about what happened to a spring when it was stretched beyond its elastic limit. He will always be remembered for Hooke's Law which describes what happens when a force is applied to a spring.

SUMMARY

1. Some solids are elastic. This means that they will return to their original shape after a force is applied.
2. The greater the stretching force on a wire or spring, the greater the extension.
3. Wires and springs return to their original shape after a force is applied although they are deformed if they are stretched beyond their elastic limit.

QUESTIONS

1. Make a list of elastic and non-elastic materials.
2. Explain why a springboard has to be made from elastic material.
3. Plan an investigation to find the elastic limit of a piece of Lycra.

9 Friction

FRICTION AND SURFACES

The force of friction always acts when two solid surfaces rub against each other. The force is caused by the roughness of the surfaces. Although some surfaces look smooth, we would see the roughness clearly if we magnified the surface.

Rub a rubber block along the table. You will feel the friction between the block and the table. The force acts in the opposite direction to the movement.

The surfaces of the rubber and the wood are rough, so the frictional forces are large.

If you rub wax on the table the rubber slides more easily. There is less friction between smooth surfaces.

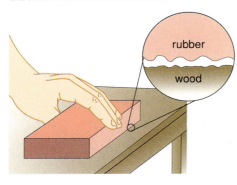
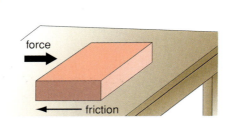
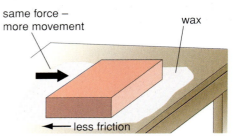

FRICTION AND HEAT

Friction causes surfaces to heat up and wear away. This is because the surfaces are rubbing against each other.

HOW BRAKES WORK

When friction acts against a moving surface, it slows it down. Brakes on cars and bicycles work in this way.

On a bicycle, the rubber brakes act on the rim of the wheel. They exert a frictional force in the opposite direction to the movement of the cycle. This makes the cycle slow down. Cycle brakes get hot and wear away. They have to be replaced regularly.

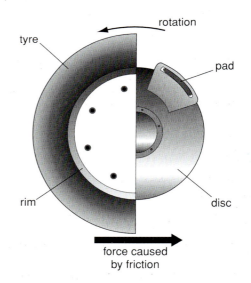
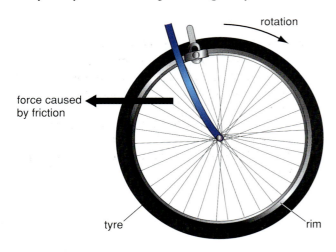

Car brakes work in a similar way to cycle brakes. They act on a special disc connected to the wheel. The brake pads push against the disc in the opposite direction to the movement of the car. This makes the car slow down. The friction causes a lot of heat. Car brake pads are made of special material that can stand high temperatures.

STOPPING DISTANCES

Some accidents are caused by cars travelling too fast. Some drivers cannot stop in time. They have not thought about **stopping distances**. The stopping distance is how far a car will travel before it stops safely.

The stopping distance is made up of two things.
- The driver's reaction time. It takes a few seconds for a driver to think before he puts his foot on the brake.
- The braking distance. This is how far the car travels when the brakes are working.

 At 20 mph it takes 12 m to stop (3 car lengths)

→ reaction time
------▶ braking distance

 At 30 mph it takes 23 m to stop (6 car lengths)

 At 40 mph it takes 36 m to stop (9 car lengths)

You will notice that the stopping distance is more if the car is travelling faster. Other things also affect the stopping distance. Weather is an important factor. Wet and icy roads, along with poor visibility, increase stopping time because reaction times are longer. Accidents can also occur when people are tired or under the influence of alcohol or drugs. This is because they misjudge stopping times. Poor tyres and worn brakes also increase stopping times.

SKIDDING

Cars skid when the road surface is wet or icy. Normally the tyre grips the road because frictional forces are large between the rubber tyre and the road. Water and ice make the road surface smooth. This reduces friction. The tyres cannot grip the road surface. The reduced friction also makes it difficult to stop the car. When the driver puts the brakes on hard, the wheels stop, but the tyres do not grip the road surface, so the car skids.

SUMMARY

1. The force of friction acts when solid surfaces slide over each other.
2. The direction of the force is opposite to the direction in which the object is moving.
3. Friction causes objects to heat up and wear out at their surfaces.
4. Brakes on cars and bicycles use frictional forces.
5. Stopping distances depend on reaction times and the distance the car travels under the braking force.

QUESTIONS

1. Why do bicycle and car brakes get hot?
2. Explain why skiers rub wax on their skis.
3. a Use the diagram of stopping distances to predict the stopping distance of a car travelling at 60 mph.
   b Explain why the stopping distance increases as the speed of the car increases.
4. Explain why motorway traffic should slow down in bad weather.

10 Frictional forces

When things move through air or water there is a force called friction which acts in the opposite direction to the movement.

The swimmer is pushing herself forward. If she doesn't swim as hard she will slow down because of the friction of the water.

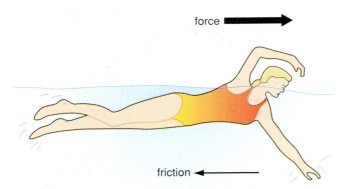

When the swimmer was moving forward the push of her swimming was bigger than the force of friction acting against her. To move at a steady (constant) speed, her push had to balance the force of friction (**balanced force**).

The force of the car engine pushes the car forward. If the engine stops, the car slows down and stops because of the force of friction between the air and the car body and the road and the car tyres.

Using friction

Chris Boardman won a gold medal for cycling in the 1992 Olympics. Many of the competitors worked hard to increase their strength and stamina and make the pushing force on their pedals more. They thought that the person winning the race would be the strongest. Chris surprised everybody by trying to reduce the force of friction.

He bent low to reduce surface area.

He had a smooth suit to reduce air flow.

He had a smooth helmet so the air flowed over it.

186

'Sky divers' use their knowledge of friction to control their descent.

After leaving the aeroplane the sky diver speeds up (accelerates). This is because the forces are unbalanced. The downward pull of gravity (her weight), is greater than the upward force of friction.

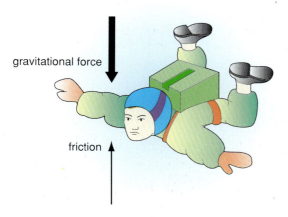

The faster an object moves through air, the greater the force of friction acting on it. As she accelerates the frictional force increases. She spreads her arms and legs. This also increases the force of friction on her body because more surface is exposed to the air. The increased friction slows her down.

Soon the upward frictional forces balance the downward force. She falls at a steady (constant) speed. This is called the **terminal velocity**.

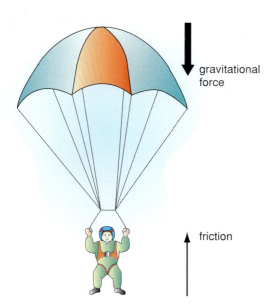

The balanced forces become unbalanced again when the parachute opens. The large surface of the parachute increases the frictional force until it is greater than her weight, so she slows down. Because she slows down, the frictional force gradually decreases until it is the same as her weight yet again. She continues falling at a steady (constant) speed.

STREAMLINING

Cars

When a car moves, frictional forces slow it down. If the frictional forces are smaller than the thrust force of the engine, the car speeds up. This is because the forces do not cancel each other out. They are unbalanced. The unbalanced force makes the car speed up.

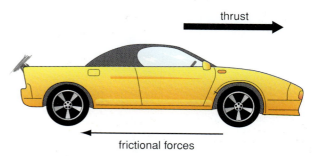

Car manufacturers are always trying to make the frictional forces small by streamlining the car. When the forces are small the engine needs less thrust and therefore uses less petrol to achieve the same speed.

SUMMARY

1. Frictional forces act when objects move through air or water.
2. The direction of the frictional force is opposite to the direction in which the object is moving.
3. The faster an object moves through air or a liquid, the greater the force of friction acting on it.
4. When an object falls it accelerates until frictional forces balance gravitational forces. When the forces balance, the object falls at its terminal velocity.
5. When a vehicle has a steady speed the frictional forces balance the driving force.

QUESTIONS

1. a The fish is swimming forward. Describe the forces which make this happen.
   b What forces will cause the fish to stop moving?

2. How did Chris Boardman reduce frictional forces?
3. Explain the meaning of: terminal velocity, streamlined, unbalanced forces.

11 Pressure

A force can have a greater effect if it is spread over a smaller area.

The pond skater floats on the surface of the water. Its weight is spread out over a large area. It does not sink.

The water scorpion weighs the same as the pond skater. Its weight is spread over less area, so it sinks. Its weight has a greater effect than the weight of the pond skater.

The two bricks weigh the same. The brick standing on its end easily sinks in the soft sand. Its weight has more effect because the end of the brick has a smaller area than the side. The other brick is put on its side. It does not sink because its weight is spread over a larger area.

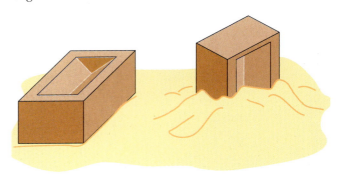

When a certain force is spread over a large area the pressure is small (we say low pressure).
When the same force is spread over a small area, the pressure is large (we say high pressure).

Keeping the area large means the pressure is low.   Keeping the area small means the pressure is high.

Snow shoes have a large area

... the explorer does not sink into the snow

The camels feet have a large area

...he does not sink into the sand

Knife blade has a small area

Pin point has a small area

CALCULATING PRESSURE

To work out pressure you need two things:
- the force – it always acts at right angles
- and the area it is acting on

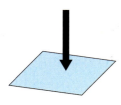

We measure the area the force is pressing on in square metres. Forces are measured in newtons.

$$\text{pressure} = \frac{\text{force}}{\text{area}}$$

Example

The pressure that brick 1 puts on the sand = $\frac{150 \text{ N}}{5 \text{m}^2}$
= 30 Pa

brick 1

The pressure that brick 2 puts on the sand = $\frac{150 \text{ N}}{2 \text{ m}^2}$
= 75 Pa

brick 2

How much is a pressure of 1 Pa?

If a force of 1 N acted at right angles on an area of 1 m², the pressure would be 1 Pa. To understand what this would feel like put a paperclip on the palm of your hand. This exerts a pressure of about 1 Pa.

188

Pressure in liquids

Deep sea divers wear special suits to protect them from the high pressures at the bottom of the sea.

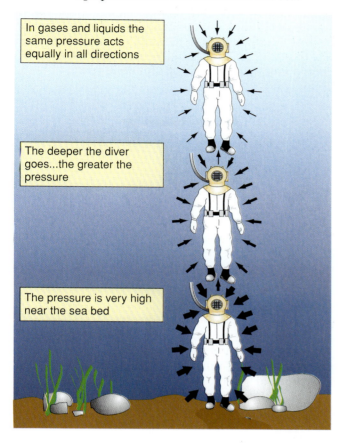

In gases and liquids the same pressure acts equally in all directions

The deeper the diver goes...the greater the pressure

The pressure is very high near the sea bed

Summary

1. Pressure, force and area are linked. We can see this in the equation:

   $$\text{pressure (Pa)} = \frac{\text{force (N)}}{\text{area (m}^2\text{)}}$$

2. A pressure of 1 Pa is exerted by a force of 1 N acting at right angles to an area of 1 m².
3. Pressure in liquids acts equally in all directions and increases with depth.
4. Hydraulics systems send forces to where they are wanted. They make forces bigger.

Questions

1. A book weighing 15 N is resting on a table. The area of the book in contact with the table is 0.3 m². What pressure is exerted on the table?
2. When dams are built to hold back water, the base is always thicker than the top. Explain why.
3. It is very difficult to burst a balloon with your finger, but easy with a pin. Explain why.

Hydraulics

In a hydraulics system a liquid is used to send a force to where it is needed.
There are two parts to a hydraulics system.

- A force is applied to the liquid inside a master cylinder. The force presses on the piston and the piston puts the liquid under pressure. The liquid cannot be squashed (liquids are incompressible)
- The liquid is trapped inside the hydraulics system, and the pressure acts equally in all directions, so the force is transmitted to all parts of the liquid. The force is carried through the liquid to the slave cylinder. Inside the slave cylinder the force pushes on the piston.

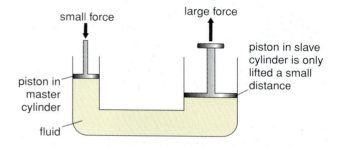

Hydraulics systems work as force multipliers

In the diagram a small force on the master cylinder piston produces a bigger force on the slave piston. This is because the area of the slave piston is much larger than that of the master piston. The slave piston pushes up for a smaller distance than the master piston is pushed down.

How do car brakes work?

Car brakes are a hydraulics system.

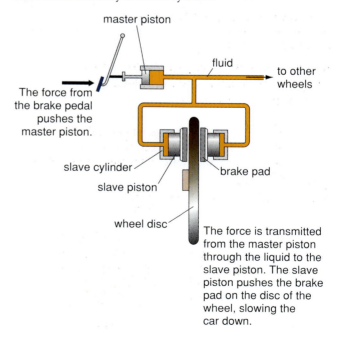

The force is transmitted from the master piston through the liquid to the slave piston. The slave piston pushes the brake pad on the disc of the wheel, slowing the car down.

12 Waves

The wave in the swimming bath is produced by a wave machine. The energy in the machine is transferred to the water and the wave carries the energy *across the swimming bath*. As the wave passes through the water, the swimmers and the water in the wave move up and down. The up and down movement is called **oscillation**. The swimmers and the water particles in the wave do not move across the swimming bath.

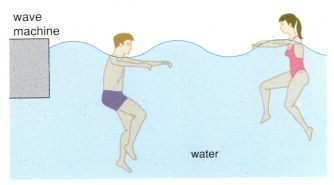

Waves like the one in the swimming baths are called **transverse waves**. Like all waves, they move from one place to another. Like all waves, the waves in the swimming baths move from one place to another. To measure one wave we measure the distance from one crest of the wave to the crest of the next. It is called the **wavelength**. We measure it in metres and use a Greek letter to represent it (λ).

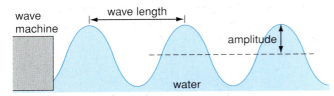

There are big waves and small ones. Big waves carry more energy than the small waves. The height of a wave is called its **amplitude**. When the wave machine works faster it makes more waves of the same size. The machine uses more energy, so more waves are needed to carry the energy away. The waves are produced more frequently. The number of waves produced in one second is called the **frequency**. It is measured in hertz (Hz).

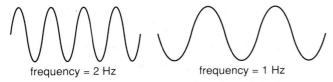

The shorter the wavelength, the greater the frequency.

TYPES OF WAVES

You can use a rope or a spring to show waves like the one in the swimming baths. If you move it from side to side or up and down, the wave travels along it. This type of wave is called a **transverse wave**.

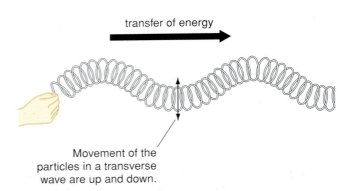

Movement of the particles in a transverse wave are up and down.

Another way of making a wave in a spring is by pushing and pulling it at the ends. The segments of the spring bunch in and pull apart making a pattern. The pattern moves from one end to the other carrying the energy of the push and pull. This is called a **longitudinal wave**.

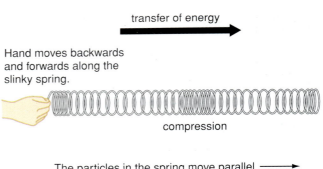

The particles in the spring move parallel to the direction the wave is travelling in

Reflection of waves

When the waves in the swimming pool hit the walls, they bounce back. They still have energy because it is not absorbed by the wall. They are reflected and travel back into the pool.

When scientists noticed this it started them thinking. They had noticed that both light and sound are reflected. Could light and sound travel as waves?

Both sound and light are reflected. This is evidence for the idea that they travel as waves.

Refraction of waves

Waves change direction when they move from deep water to shallow water. This happens when they meet the boundary between the deep water and shallow water. We would see this if we looked down on water from above. If the boundary between the deep water and the shallow water is at an angle the waves are bent. The waves move more slowly in the shallow water. The bending is caused by the speed of the waves changing. The change in direction is called **refraction**.

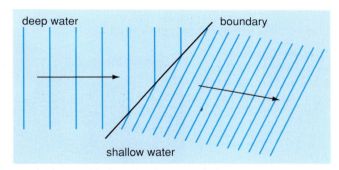

When scientists noticed that light also changed direction when it passed from one substance to another, it was even more evidence that light travels as waves.

The speed of waves

The waves in water and in the rope and spring move slowly. Light and sound travel in waves, but much more quickly.

To work out the speed we multiply the wavelength by the frequency.

$$\text{speed} = \text{wavelength} \times \text{frequency}$$
$$v = \lambda \times f$$

Light waves travel the fastest at about 300 million metres per second. Sound waves in air travel much more slowly, at 330 metres per second. This explains why the crowd at a race see the runners setting off before they hear the starting pistol. They see the runners set off first because light travels so fast. The sound travels so slowly it reaches their ears after the light reaches their eyes.

Questions

1. Which wave has the greatest amplitude?

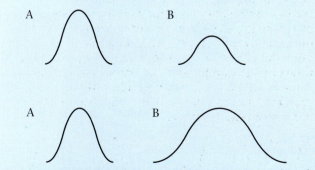

2. Which wave has the shortest wavelength?
3. Describe the difference between a transverse and a longitudinal wave.
4. What evidence is there that sound and light travel as waves?

Summary

1. When waves travel along ropes, springs and water they transfer energy, not matter.
2. The height of a wave is its amplitude, the distance between adjacent crests is its wavelength. The number of waves produced each second is the frequency.
3. Waves are reflected and refracted.
4. The behaviour of sound and light is evidence that they both travel as waves.

13 Reflection and refraction

How you see things

You see something because light moves from the object into your eye. If the object is a light source it makes light.

The light travels in straight lines. We do not draw all the lines, just enough to help you understand what is happening. We call the lines rays.

When objects do not make their own light, light rays bounce off them and into your eye. The light is reflected. You see the **reflected rays**.

Mirrors

Most mirrors are flat. We call them plane mirrors. A mirror reflects light. Draw a large number 2 on a piece of card and then look at it in a mirror. The image looks just like the number because of the reflected light. This happens because your brain knows that light travels in straight lines. It thinks that the light has come from behind the mirror! The image seems to be behind the mirror. It is the same size as the number and the same distance from the mirror, but there is a difference. The number is swapped round or **laterally inverted**.

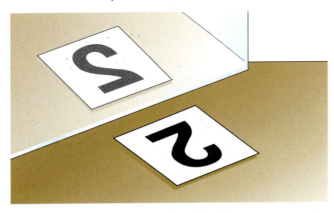

The image of the number is not real because we can't put it on a screen. We call it a **virtual image**.

Reflection from a plane mirror

We can predict the way light is reflected from a mirror. It depends on the angle of the ray arriving at the mirror. We call the ray arriving at the mirror the **incident ray**. The ray coming away from the mirror is the **reflected ray**.

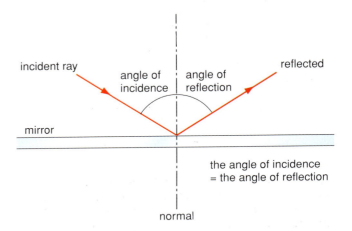

A special line can be drawn at right angles to the mirror. It is called the **normal**. The angle between the incident ray and the normal is the angle of incidence and is equal to the angle of reflection.

Using mirrors

Curved mirrors are useful to drivers. They give a wider view of the road behind them.

Summary

1. Light travels in straight lines.
2. You see things when light travels from the object to your eye.
3. With a plane mirror the angle of incidence is the same as the angle of reflection.
4. Light bends as it passes from one substance to another. This is called refraction.
5. Increasing the angle of the incident ray increases the angle of refraction.
6. If the angle of incidence is large enough, the ray is not refracted. It is reflected inside the substance. This is total internal reflection.

Refraction

Light travels as waves. Light bends as it passes across the boundary from one substance to another. For example, from air into glass. To understand this we draw a line called the **normal** at right angles to the surface of the substance. The light rays bend towards the normal as they pass from air to glass. When a light ray passes out of the block from glass into air, it bends away from the normal. Bending light this way is called **refraction**.

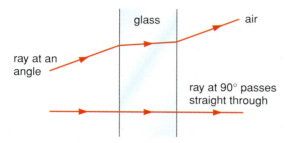

Angles in refraction

A ray arriving at a boundary between substances is called the incident ray. Increasing the size of the angle between this ray and the normal increases the size of the angle between the refracted ray and the normal.

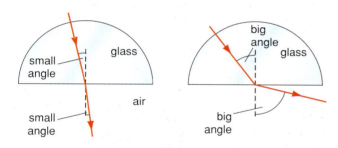

Total internal reflection

Sometimes the light ray is not refracted when it meets a boundary. The ray stays inside the block of material. The ray is reflected. The angle of incidence must be quite large for this to happen. It must be more than a certain size. This size is the critical angle. When light stays inside a block like this we call it **total internal reflection**.

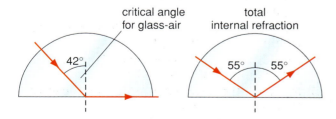

When the angle of incidence is larger than 42°, the light is totally internally reflected.

Total internal reflection is used in optical fibres. Optical fibres are thin solid fibres of glass or plastic. The light going in one end of the fibre is totally internally reflected. It stays inside the fibre, being reflected again and again along the inside until it comes out of the other end.

Optical fibres are used in endoscopes. Using an endoscope enables doctors to see inside the human body.

Light is sent down the fibre into the body. It is reflected back up the optical fibres and an image of that part of the body is obtained.

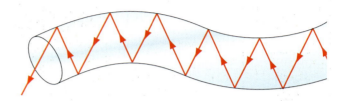

A periscope uses total internal reflection. There are two glass prisms inside.

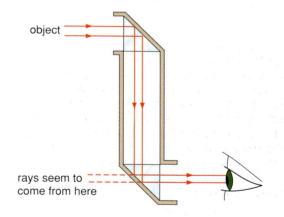

Did you know? An optical fibre can carry up to 35 000 telephone calls at once.

Questions

1. How do we see objects which do not make their own light?
2. If the angle of incidence when a light ray arrives at a plane mirror is 25°, what is the angle of reflection? Draw a diagram of your answer.
3. What is the difference between reflection and refraction?
4. Describe two uses of total internal reflection.

14 Prisms

HOW A PRISM REFRACTS LIGHT

When a ray of light passes through a triangular prism, it passes out in a different direction. We say that the ray coming out of the other side of the prism has been **deviated**.

The ray of light deviates because it is refracted twice. Once when it enters the prism, and once as it leaves the prism.

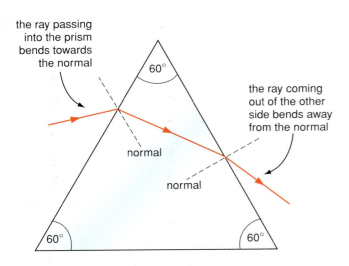

HOW A PRISM REFRACTS WHITE LIGHT

When you shine a ray of white light from a ray box through a triangular prism you get a different effect. White light is made of different colours. The different colours of light are refracted by different amounts. Red light is only refracted a little. It only bends a little as it passes into the prism. The other colours each bend by a different amount. Orange bends a little more than red and so on, with violet light being bent the most. The other colours each bend by a different amount. The colours separate as they pass through the prism. We say that the prism has dispersed the white light into a spectrum of colours.

Each colour of light has a different wavelength. Red light has a longer wavelength than violet light.

The water droplets in the air behave like prisms. The light from the sun is refracted and dispersed to produce to produce a rainbow. If the droplets are very large, you may get a double rainbow.

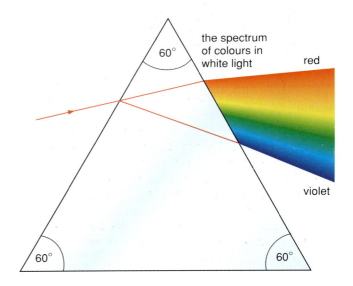

THE ELECTROMAGNETIC SPECTRUM

Light splits up into a spectrum of different colours when we pass it through a prism. It splits because white light is made up of many different waves. There are far more waves around us that we cannot see. The human eye can only sense some of the wavelengths. The invisible wavelengths have either longer or shorter wavelengths than visible light. In the electromagnetic spectrum we set out the waves in order, from the shortest wavelength to the longest.

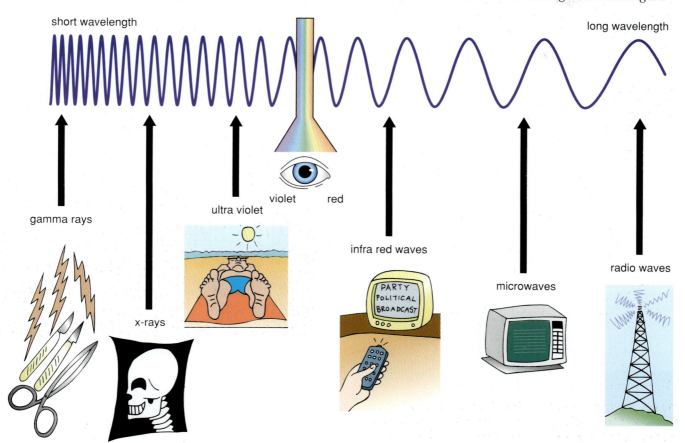

The different wavelengths in the electromagnetic spectrum.

The waves of the electromagnetic spectrum have things in common.
- They travel in straight lines and are reflected
- They all travel in space (space is a vacuum) – so they do not need material to travel through
- They travel at the same speed – the speed of light. In space this is 300 000 000 metres/second or 3×10^8 m/s
- They transfer energy from one place to another. They can be absorbed and then transfer some of their energy into the object.

SUMMARY

1 When a ray of light passes through a prism, its direction is changed.
2 A glass prism disperses white light into a spectrum of seven colours.
3 There are many types of electromagnetic radiation. Light is the only one we can see.

QUESTIONS

1 Draw a diagram to show how a glass prism deviates a ray of light.
2 Explain this sentence: 'White light is dispersed into the colours of the rainbow.'
3 At what speed do microwaves travel in space?
4 Which type of electromagnetic radiation has the shortest wavelength?

15 Using electromagnetic radiation

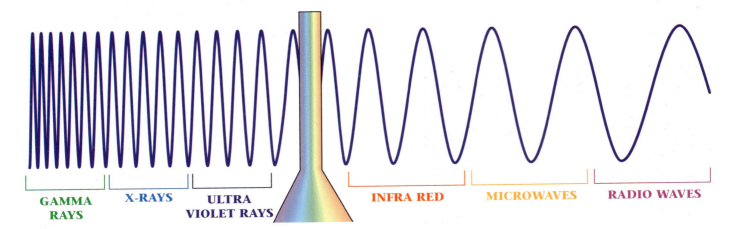

GAMMA RAYS | X-RAYS | ULTRA VIOLET RAYS | INFRA RED | MICROWAVES | RADIO WAVES

Gamma rays

Gamma radiation is very harmful to living things. It kills cells and can cause cancer. Gamma radiation is often used to sterilise equipment in hospitals. Any bacteria or other micro-organisms on the equipment are killed.

Gamma radiation is also used to kill the micro-organisms which cause food to go bad. The food is given a short exposure to the radiation. Usually food treated in this way is labelled.

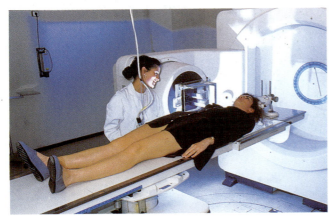

People who are suffering from cancer can be treated with gamma radiation. The radiation is focused on the cancer cells which are killed.

X-rays

X-rays do not easily pass through certain substances, such as metal and bone. They are used to make X-ray pictures of our internal organs.

X-rays are also used to scan luggage at the airport.

Ultra violet

Ultra violet radiation is produced naturally by the sun. When ultra violet radiation passes deep into the skin it can cause cancer. Skin which is darker gives some protection against the effects of ultra violet light.

People who want a sun tan may use a sun bed. The tubes in the sun bed produce ultra violet light.

196

Infra red

Infra red is given out by all objects. The hotter the object, the more infra red radiation it gives out.

Some cameras are sensitive to infra red and can pick up the radiation. Such cameras will even produce an image in very dark conditions.

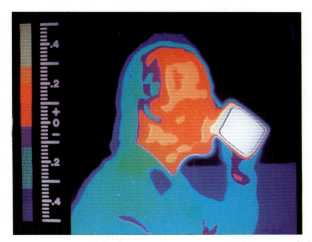

The remote controls of TV and video sets use infra red. The infra red is produced by the hand set. A receiver on the TV or video picks up the signal and decodes it.

Microwaves

Microwaves used in ovens transfer their energy to the water molecules in food. The water molecules begin to vibrate very quickly and the food gets hot. The microwaves produced by the oven would also make the water molecules inside living tissue vibrate. This would damage the tissue.

Some microwaves have wavelengths similar to radio waves. These microwaves can be used to carry information in the same way as radio waves. Speech is changed into electrical signals and then transmitted from an aerial. Some mobile telephones use this idea.

Although microwaves are similar to radio waves they have a shorter wavelength. They are not reflected by the charged layer around the surface of the Earth. Microwaves can be used to communicate to and from satellites which orbit the Earth.

Radio waves

There are both short and long radio waves. All radio waves are long compared with the other waves in the spectrum. The longest are a few kilometres long and the shortest are a few centimetres. When radio waves touch a metal conductor they make the particles of metal vibrate at the same frequency as the wave. This sets up a current in the metal which can be turned into sound or light.

Long radio waves are useful because they can be used to send messages between different points on the Earth's surface. A layer in the upper atmosphere is electrically charged. When radio waves touch this layer, they are reflected back down to a receiver. In this way radio waves travel long distances.

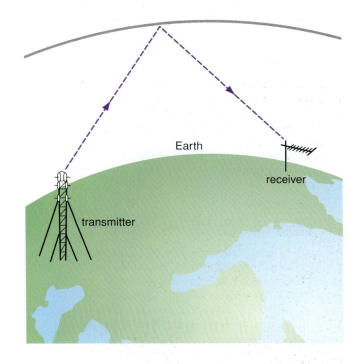

Summary

1. The various types of electromagnetic radiation make a continuous spectrum.
2. The uses of the different types of radiation depend on their properties, for example, microwaves make substances hotter when they are absorbed, so they are used for cooking.

Questions

1. Which type of radiation has
   a the shortest wavelength?
   b the longest wavelength?
2. Describe how microwaves are used to cook food.
3. Explain how radio waves travel long distances.
4. Microwaves are used for satellite communications rather than radio waves. Why?

16 Sound

Sounds are made when something is vibrating. The vibrations touch the molecules of air and in turn make them vibrate. The vibrations are carried through the air to our ears. The vibrations cause the inside of our ear to vibrate.

The drums, cymbals, guitar strings and speaker all vibrate. You can feel the vibrations if you touch them. They vibrate because of energy. The energy is transferred to the air molecules. Air molecules are good at carrying sound. They become pushed together and pulled further apart to make a sound wave. The wave transfers the energy as it travels to our ears.

Did you know? If you hold a candle next to the loud speaker in a rock concert, the sound waves will blow it out.

Sound is a **longitudinal wave**. A spring gives us a good idea of how the molecules of air carry the energy of a sound wave. The air molecules just next to the guitar string or speaker are like the first part of the spring. At first the air molecules are pushed together, then they become more spread out. This pattern repeats to make a wave.

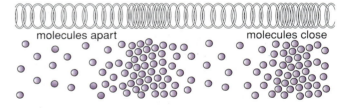

molecules apart   molecules close

Vibrating molecules

Sound waves can travel through any material if the molecules can vibrate. In space, there are no air molecules, so even if something vibrates, there is no sound. You can check this by putting a bell in a glass jar. If a pump is used to remove the air from the jar there will be a vacuum in the jar. You will not hear the bell even though you can see it ringing.

When sound passes through materials, the molecules of the material vibrate and pass the vibration on to each other. The sound is carried through the material. Sound travels more slowly in air and water than in solids such as metal. The molecules in a metal are closer together than in a gas, or a liquid such as water.

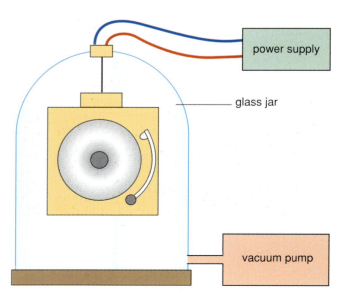

Reflecting sound

Sound waves reflect from a hard surface just like other waves. You are more likely to hear an echo if the surfaces are hard, (such as in a cave) rather than in a room where the walls are covered with wallpaper. Wallpaper absorbs some of the sound.

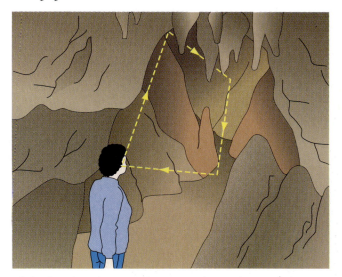

If the hard surface is a long way from the sound, the sound wave takes time to travel and there is a time delay before you hear the echo.

Refraction of sound

Sound waves are bent when the speed at which they are travelling is changed. On a warm day the air just above the ground is warm. The speed of sound is increased in warm air, so the sound waves tend to bend away from the Earth. This is why you do not hear sounds as well in very hot weather.

In cold weather, the layer of air near the ground is cold. The sound waves are bent towards the ground, so you hear them better in cold weather.

Using echoes

The time it takes for an echo to return is used in sonar. The ship sends a sound downwards towards the sea bed. The time taken for the sound to return is noted and then halved, because it travels to the bottom and back. Sound travels at 1500 m/s in water, faster than in air. A computer works out the distance of the sea bed using the speed equation:

$$\text{speed} = \frac{\text{distance}}{\text{time taken}}$$

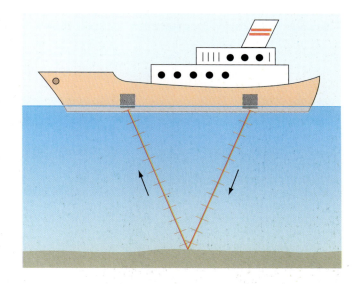

Summary

1. Sounds are waves produced when things vibrate.
2. Sound waves carry energy.
3. Sound waves travel through substances made of particles. They do not travel in a vacuum.
4. Sounds bounce (reflect) off hard objects to make echoes.
5. Sound waves are refracted when they speed up or slow down.

Questions

1. Which two materials would sound travel through most quickly: steam, concrete, milk, water, petrol, steel, oxygen?
2. Why are the walls of recording studios covered with thick wallpaper?
3. A ship's sonar does not work well when the sea bed is covered by seaweed. Why?

17 Ultrasound

We call the number of sound waves per second the frequency. It is measured in hertz. One hertz is one vibration per second or one wave per second. A guitar note with a frequency of 250 Hz will be producing 250 sound waves every second. Ultrasounds have frequencies above 20 000 Hz. Humans cannot hear ultrasound.

Sounds and their frequencies	Frequency
A dog whistle, bat and dolphin noises.	Above 20 000 Hz
The highest sound we can hear.	20 000 Hz
Guitarist playing a very high note.	10 000 Hz
Guitarist playing a high note.	5000 Hz
Person singing a high note.	1000 Hz
Person singing a low note.	100 Hz
Bass drum in a rock band.	20 Hz

Bats

Bats use sound information, called echo location, to hunt, and find their way in the dark. They make high frequency sounds with their special voice boxes. The sounds are of such high frequency that we cannot hear them. The sounds bounce off objects and are reflected back to the bat's large ears.

Using ultrasound with animals

Did you know? Bats can avoid wires less than 0.5 mm thick in complete darkness by using echo location.

Using ultrasound in medicine

Doctors use ultrasound to see inside people. An ultrasound scanner is a transducer. Transducers turn one type of energy into another. An ultrasound scanner turns electrical signals into sound. The sound is ultrasound so we cannot hear it. The ultrasound scanner is rubbed over the patient's skin. As the sound waves pass through the different tissues, they are reflected back to another transducer. Different amounts are reflected back depending on the tissue. The transducer turns the reflected sound into electrical signals. A computer turns the signals into an image on the screen.

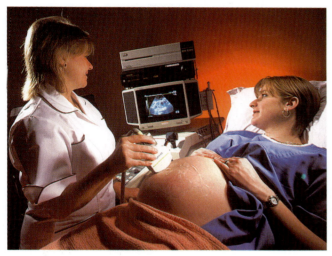

Ultrasound scans are very useful to show a developing foetus inside its mother.

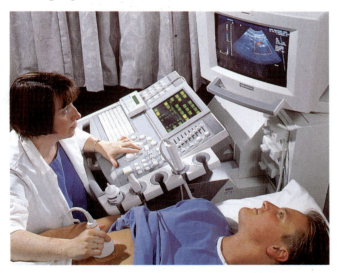

Ultrasound scans can be used to diagnose disease.

Using ultrasound in industry

Ultrasound can be used for finding flaws in metal. The flaw reflects the sound and this can be analysed to find it.

Jewellery and delicate pieces of equipment can be cleaned using ultrasound. The equipment is put in a bath of special liquid. The ultrasound passes through the liquid and it makes the equipment vibrate so much of the dirt falls off into the liquid.

Car tyres are also checked using ultrasound. Ultrasound detectors underneath the tyre pick up differences in the ultrasound signal if there is something wrong with the tyre.

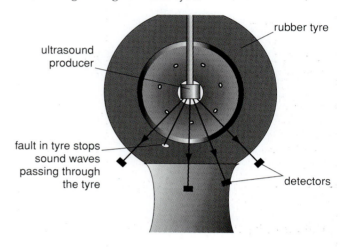

Summary

1. The frequency of sound is measured in hertz. One hertz = 1 sound wave each second.
2. Sounds above 20 000 Hz are called ultrasound.
3. An ultrasound scanner is a type of transducer which turns electrical signals into ultrasound waves.
4. Ultrasound can be used in medicine to see inside the human body or in industry to diagnose faults.

Questions

1. What does frequency mean?
2. What is the range of human hearing?
3. A dolphin uses echo location to hunt fish. Describe how this might work.
4. Describe three uses of ultrasound.

18 Seeing sound

We use a machine called an **oscilloscope** to see sound waves. You can imagine a sound wave by thinking about what happens to the molecules when a sound is made by a guitar string.

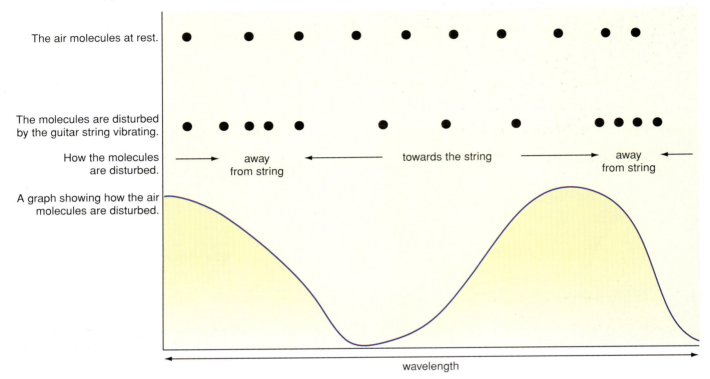

HIGH PITCH AND LOW PITCH

If a microphone is used to change sound waves into electrical signals, the signals can be fed into an oscilloscope. The oscilosope makes a picture showing how the electrical signal varies.

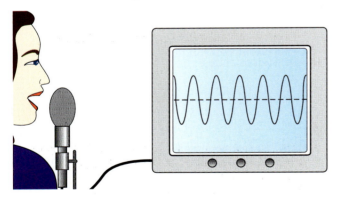

Using an oscilloscope to understand pitch and frequency.

When a guitarist plays high up the fretboard, he is plucking a short string. The string makes a high note. The pitch is high. This is because the string vibrates very fast indeed. Faster than you can see. There are many vibrations in every second, so the frequency is high. High frequency vibrations give high pitched sounds.

When the guitarist plays lower down on the fretboard the vibrating string is longer and the note is lower. It has low pitch. There are fewer vibrations per second, so the frequency is less. Low frequency vibrations give a low pitched sound.

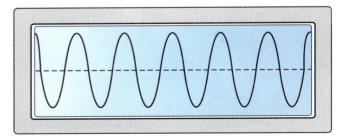

High pitch, high frequency

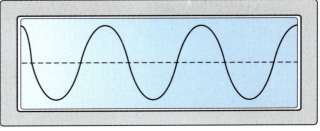

Low pitch, low frequency

LOUDER AND LOUDER SOUNDS

A big wave has high amplitude. The wave carries a lot of energy.

If we make a loud sound we see that the trace on the oscilloscope goes higher. The amplitude of the wave increases.

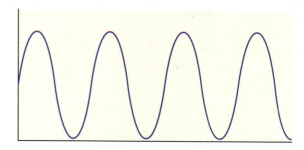

A small wave means low amplitude. The wave carries less energy.

For a quiet sound, the trace is smaller. The amplitude is less.

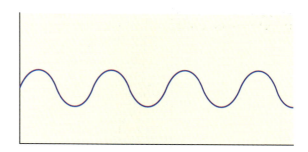

THE SPEED OF SOUND

We can measure the speed of sound by using echoes. A scientist stands 160 metres from a wall. She makes a loud noise with a machine. Her assistant starts the stop watch as soon as the sound is made. She stops the watch as soon as she hears the echo. It takes one second. The scientist uses the equation

$$\text{speed} = \frac{\text{distance}}{\text{time}}$$

$$\text{speed} = \frac{160 \times 2}{1} \quad (\times 2 \text{ because the sound travels to the wall and back})$$

$$= 320 \text{ m/s}$$

Can you think of any problems with this method? How would you improve the method if you were doing the measurements for yourself?

Summary

1. Sound can be changed into electrical signals using a microphone. We can feed the signals into an oscilloscope which makes a picture of how the signals vary.
2. High frequency vibrations produce a high pitched sound.
3. Low frequency vibrations produce a low pitched sound.
4. The amplitude of a wave is a measure of how much energy it carries. A loud sound wave has high amplitude. A quiet sound wave has low amplitude.

Questions

1. Copy the following sentences and fill in the gaps using the following words: frequency, pitch, vibrate, louder.
   Sounds are produced when objects _____. The greater the size of vibrations the _____ the sound. The number of complete vibrations each second is called the _____. The higher the frequency of a sound the higher its _____.
2. Describe the difference between a high pitched note and a low pitched note played on a violin.
3. What do we use an oscilloscope for?

19 Static electricity

Combing clean, dry hair vigorously with a plastic comb may cause it to stick out and be attracted to the comb. Small pieces of paper also stick to the hair and comb.

This effect is caused by a build up of an electric charge called an electrostatic charge on the surface of the hair and comb. The charge does not move, it is stationary or static. **Static electricity** has been produced.

What is happening?

When we comb our hair vigorously the force of friction between the hair and the comb causes electrons to be transferred from the molecules of the hair to the plastic comb.

The electrons have a negative charge. They are in energy levels around the nucleus of the atom. The nucleus has a positive charge.

Atoms join together to make up the molecules forming our hair.

The comb becomes negatively charged. The hair becomes positively charged.

The individual hairs push each other apart or repel each other.

The charged hair and comb attract small pieces of paper.

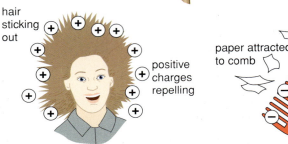

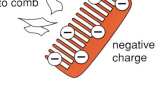

Why doesn't greasy hair work?

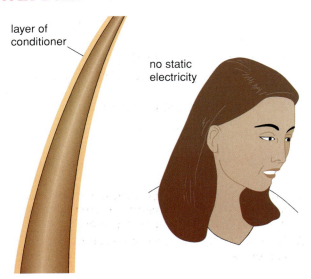

The natural oils in greasy hair stop the movement of the electrons to the comb and the formation of static electricity. Shampooing our hair removes these oils.

Conditioners coat our hair like the oils. This stops the transfer of electrons and the formation of static electricity. Our hair no longer sticks out.

Attraction and repulsion

Charge up two balloons by rubbing them on your jumper. When you hold them close together you will find that they push each other apart or repel each other. This is because both balloons have the same charge.

In the laboratory

a   Rub two thin strips of polythene with a woollen cloth. Both strips gain a negative charge as the polythene pulls electrons from the cloth. They repel each other.

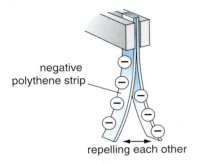

b   Rub two thin strips of acetate with a woollen cloth. Both strips gain a positive charge. The cloth pulls electrons from them. They repel each other.

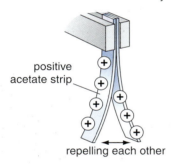

c   When a charged polythene strip is placed near a charged acetate strip, they are attracted together.

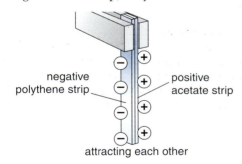

The above three diagrams show that:
   like charges repel each other
   unlike charges attract each other.

The forces between the charges are called electrostatic forces. They are quite small, but large enough to attract light uncharged objects, such as pieces of paper.

Why does the charge not move?

The charge is static because the charged material does not allow electrons to move through it. It is an **insulator**. Plastics are good insulators.

When does the charge move?

Substances which let electrons flow through them allow the charge to move and are called **conductors**. Metals and graphite are good conductors.

Semiconductors are 'in-between' materials. They are often insulators when cold, but conductors when warm. They are used in microchips.

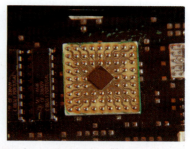

| Conductors | | Semi-conductors | Insulators |
good	poor		
metals	air	silicon	plastics, e.g. PVC
graphite	water	germanium	polystyrene, perspex
	human body		glass, rubber, cork

Conducting solutions

Ionic compounds conduct electricity when they are melted or dissolved in water. The ions have either a positive or negative charge. The current is due to the negative ions moving to the positive electrode and the positive ions moving to the negative electrode. Unlike metals and carbon, the ionic compound breaks down as new substances are formed at the electrodes. This is called **electrolysis**.

Summary

1. Static electricity is produced by friction.
2. There are two types of electric charge, positive and negative.
3. Like charges repel, unlike charges attract.

Questions

1. How can a plastic ruler be made to attract small pieces of paper? What happens when two rulers like this are suspended near together?
2. List two conductors and two insulators and give a use for each.

20 Dangers and uses of static electricity

The moving charge

1. After a car journey you may feel an electric shock when you get out and touch the car door.

2. After walking across a nylon carpet you may feel an electric shock when you touch a metal object.

3. When nylon clothes are taken out of a tumble-drier they often stick together and crackle. In the dark you can even see small sparks.

In all these cases the charge on an object is being discharged. As the charge moves a small current flows. This current is small so there is no danger of being electrocuted.

In the first two examples above, the charge flows from you, through the metal conductor to Earth and you feel a small electric shock. When you get a shock from a car door it may be because either you are charged through the friction between your clothes and the material of the car seat, or because the car is charged through friction between the car body and the air flow.

In the third example, the charge flows through the air and so produces a small spark.

Bigger sparks

During storms the huge electric sparks of the lightning can be very dangerous.

Electric charge builds up on the surface of clouds as the masses of air rub against each other. When the charge becomes large, it may discharge to Earth as lightning. This can be dangerous and can cause fires and electrocute people, as a large current flows. High buildings and tall isolated trees are at greatest risk – don't shelter under exposed trees during a thunder storm.

Damage to buildings is prevented by using a lightning conductor. This is a strip of copper which connects a spike on the top of a building to a metal plate in the ground. The copper is a good conductor and conducts the charge to Earth without damaging the building.

Did you know? The temperature of a lightning spark can be as high as 10 000°C.

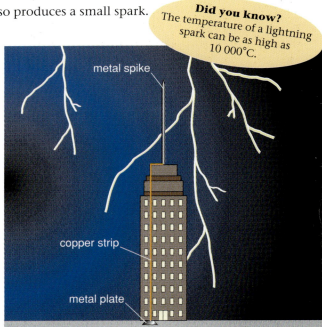

REFUELLING

A mixture of petrol vapour and air will explode if it is ignited. When aircraft are being refuelled, the fuel is pumped into the plane through a hose. Friction causes the hose to become charged and this can then charge up the plane. Sparks could jump to the ground and ignite the petrol vapour. To prevent this from happening a cable is used to connect the fuel tanker, hose and aircraft to Earth.

Similar precautions are taken at petrol stations when petrol is delivered and pumped into the storage tanks.

SPARKS IN THE LABORATORY

A Van der Graaff generator is used to store large amounts of electrostatic charge. When it is turned on, a positive charge spreads over the dome. If you stand on an insulator like a rubber mat, and touch the dome you will also become charged and your hair may stand on end. This is because the charged strands of hair repel each other.

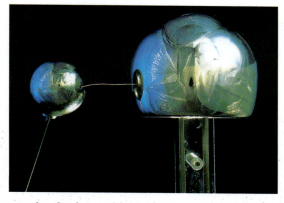

You can be discharged by touching a metal gas tap when a small shock is felt.

If the generator is switched on for a while, the charge can become so large that a spark may jump across a few centimetres of air to a metal object.

USING STATIC ELECTRICITY

Painting round corners

Painting both sides of curved surfaces such as the bodywork of cars can be difficult and waste paint. Static electricity is used to solve the problem. The droplets of paint are given a negative charge and the car panel is made positive. The paint is then attracted to both sides of the panel and doesn't fall on the floor.

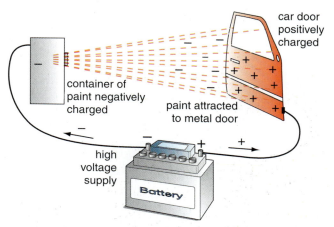

Cleaning fumes

The fumes from chimneys, such as those in power stations, often contain a lot of dust and soot and cause pollution. The dust and soot can be removed using static electricity. The fumes are passed over wires carrying a large negative charge and the dust and soot particles become charged. They are then attracted to positively charged plates in the chimney. The dust and soot sticks to the plates and is cleaned off.

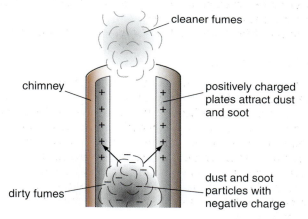

SUMMARY

1. When a static charge is discharged a spark may be formed. This can be dangerous. It is avoided by making a connection to Earth.
2. Static electricity has various uses.

QUESTIONS

1. Explain why you sometimes feel a small shock when you touch a television screen after it has been on for a while. Why does the screen tend to get dusty very quickly?
2. How can static electricity be used in painting metal railings without wasting too much paint?

21 Simple electric circuits

The simplest circuit

The simplest circuit possible is made by connecting the positive terminal of a source of electricity, such as a cell, to the negative terminal with a piece of wire.

The wire is a **conductor** and electrons flow through the wire from the end with the negative charge to the end with a positive charge. The current is regarded as flowing in the opposite direction, from the positive to the negative terminal.

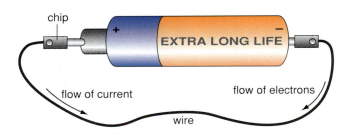

In this circuit the electrons are not doing any useful work and the cell soon gets hot and goes flat.

Making a more useful circuit

If a bulb is placed in the circuit with a switch, and the switch is turned on, then the bulb lights up. The bulb contains a filament made of a piece of resistance wire. This reduces the rate of flow of electrons and changes some of their energy into heat energy. The filament glows white hot.

Drawing the circuit

A **circuit diagram** shows how the different parts or **components** of a circuit are joined together. Each component has a special symbol. These are given in the table opposite. The direction in which the current flows is shown by the direction of the arrows in the circuit diagram.

The wires are shown as straight lines with right-angled corners. They are drawn as short as possible.

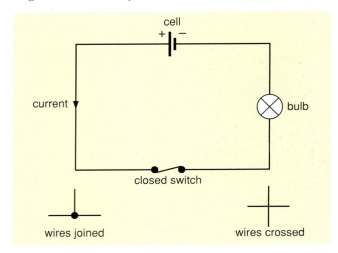

Completing a circuit

Switches are used to turn on all kinds of appliances. They are made of two pieces of metal. When the switch is turned on, the pieces of metal touch and conduct the current. The circuit is complete. When the switch is turned off, the pieces of metal no longer touch and the circuit is broken.

How much current?

A meter called an ammeter is used to measure the size of a current. The current is measured in **amperes** (symbol A).

The current is the same anywhere in the circuit, as the electrons flow all round it. The ammeter can therefore be placed at any position in the circuit.

To find the current flowing through a bulb in a circuit, the ammeter can be connected to either side of the cell as shown. It is connected to the bulb end-to-end or in series.

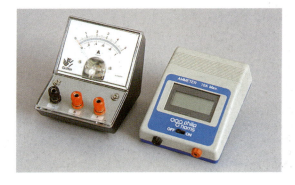

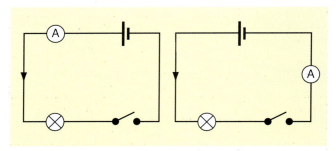

The size of the current through the bulb is measured by placing the ammeter in series with it anywhere in the circuit.

208

VOLTAGE

For an electric current to flow, there must be a source of electricity such as a cell, generator (or dynamo) or the mains supply. This gives the necessary 'push' to make the current flow. The size of the 'push' is the **voltage** of the supply of electricity. Another name for voltage is **potential difference**. The voltage is measured in volts (symbol V).

Different power supplies

Different sources of electricity have different voltages. An ordinary 'battery' you buy in a shop is just one cell with a voltage of about 1.5 V. A power supply used in the laboratory can be adjusted by turning the dial to give different voltages. The mains supply has a much higher voltage, 230 V.

Different appliances need different voltages. It is important to use the correct supply.

laptop computor with a 12 V rechargeable battery

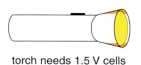
torch needs 1.5 V cells

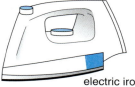
electric iron needing a 230 V supply

Joining cells together

A 'walkman' usually needs two 1.5 V cells joined together to give a voltage of 3.0 V. The cells must be connected end-to-end or in series. In this way the positive end of one cell is joined to the negative end of the other. (If they are placed in the walkman the wrong way round then they cancel each other out and no current flows.) The total voltage is then the sum of the individual voltages.

Measuring the voltage

A **voltmeter** is used to measure the voltage provided by a cell, and between two points in a circuit, such as across a lamp. The voltmeter is connected in parallel as shown.

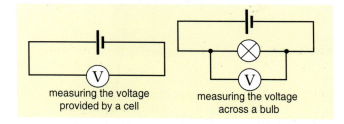
measuring the voltage provided by a cell   measuring the voltage across a bulb

Component	Symbol	Use
switch	open / closed	makes or breaks an electric circuit
cell	⊢⊢	stores chemical energy which is converted into electrical energy
battery	⊢⊢--⊢⊢	two or more cells joined together in series
lamp	⊗	converts electrical energy into light energy
diode	▷⊢	allows current to flow only in the the direction shown by the arrow
resistor	▭	used to reduce the current or to provide a particular voltage
variable resistor	▭ with arrow	a resistor which can be changed to give different currents or voltages
fuse	▭	placed in a circuit for protection
voltmeter	–Ⓥ–	measures the voltage between two points in the circuit
ammeter	–Ⓐ–	measures the current

SUMMARY

1. A current flows when a circuit is complete. A switch must be closed.
2. Current is measured in amperes, A.
3. Voltage is measured in volts, V.

QUESTIONS

1. Name and draw the symbols of the instruments used to measure the size of an electric current and the voltage across a lamp. Draw circuit diagrams to show how you would use them.

2. Draw a circuit diagram for the circuit shown. Which switch must be closed to make the lamp light up?

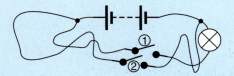

3. List four different things which require batteries, and the total voltage they each need. A lamp needs two 1.5 V cells. Draw a circuit diagram to show how the cells are connected. What is the voltage in the circuit?

22 Resistance

RESISTING THE CURRENT

If you touch a television after it has been on for a while you will find that it is warm. Electric light bulbs get much hotter, even if they have only been on for a very short time. In fact, all electrical appliances become warm when they are used as they resist the current flowing through them. They are said to have a **resistance**. Some of the electrical energy has been changed into heat energy and the current is reduced.

The higher the resistance, the more heat energy is produced and the smaller the current.

RESISTORS

Electrical components called resistors (shown in the photograph below) are placed in circuits to change the current. Their resistance is measured in **ohms** (symbol Ω).
The circuit symbol is ─▭─

The resistance of a metal wire depends on its temperature, the metal used and the length and thickness of the wire. The longer the wire, the greater the resistance as there are more obstacles to the flow of the electricity. The thinner the wire, the greater the resistance as there are fewer paths for the current to take.

VARYING THE RESISTANCE

In theatres, and sometimes in the home, dimmer switches are used to vary the brightness of lights. Turning or sliding the dimmer changes the resistance and therefore the current flowing through the bulbs. The dimmer is a **variable resistor**.

The circuit symbol is ─▱─

MEASURING RESISTANCE

The resistance R of a resistor is found by dividing the voltage V across it in volts (V) by the current I flowing through it in amperes (A)

$$\text{resistance} = \frac{\text{voltage}}{\text{current}} \quad \text{or} \quad R = \frac{V}{I}$$

For example

Voltage across a resistor = 12.0 V
current through resistor = 0.5 A

$$\text{resistance} = \frac{\text{voltage}}{\text{current}} = \frac{12.0 \text{ V}}{0.5 \text{ A}} = 24 \, \Omega$$

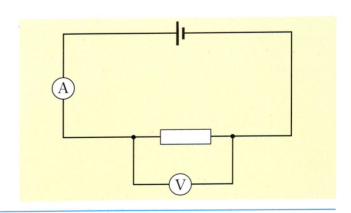

CONNECTING MORE THAN ONE RESISTOR TOGETHER

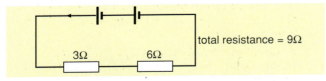

total resistance = 9Ω

Resistors in series

The same current flows through one resistor and then through the next. The total resistance equals the sum of the separate resistances.

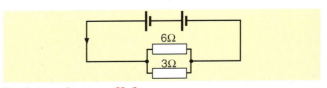

Resistors in parallel

It is easier for the current to flow through the resistors when they are connected in parallel. Some of the current flows through one of the resistors and some through the other. More of the current flows through the smaller resistor.

VARYING THE VOLTAGE ACROSS A RESISTOR AT CONSTANT TEMPERATURE

The voltage across a resistor is varied using a variable power supply as shown in the circuit diagram. For each voltage, the current flowing through the resistor is recorded. A graph is plotted of the current in amperes against the voltage in volts.

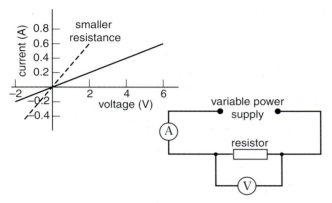

A straight line is obtained passing through the origin (if the terminals of the power supply are reversed, then the direction of the current is also reversed). This shows that the current is directly proportional to the voltage at constant temperature.

If the resistor is replaced by another resistor which has a smaller resistance then a steeper graph is obtained. This is shown with a dotted line. For a given voltage the current is always larger as the resistance is smaller.

VARYING THE VOLTAGE ACROSS A BULB

When the experiment is repeated using a bulb instead of a resistor, the graph obtained is not a straight line. The current is not proportional to the voltage.

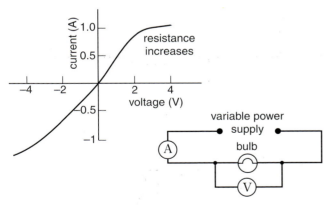

At higher voltages less current (than is expected) flows as the resistance of the bulb increases. This is because the filament in the bulb gets hotter as the bulb gets brighter. It is harder for a current to flow through a hotter wire as the metal atoms in the wire vibrate more. The collisions with the conducting electrons are therefore more frequent.

VARYING THE VOLTAGE ACROSS A DIODE

A diode will only let current flow one way in a circuit. If it is connected the wrong way round no current flows.

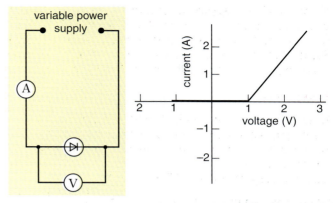

The graph of the current against the voltage shows that below a particular voltage no current flows as the resistance is very high. At higher voltages the resistance becomes very low and a large current flows. This can damage the diode.

Did you know?
Seventy percent of the people in the world do not have access to a supply of electricity.

SUMMARY

1. The resistance of a component makes it more difficult for a current to flow through it.
2. Resistance (in ohms) = $\dfrac{\text{Voltage (in volts)}}{\text{Current (in amperes)}}$
3. For resistors, the current is proportional to the voltage.
4. For light bulbs the resistance increases as the filament gets hotter.
5. Diodes will let current flow in one direction only.

QUESTIONS

1. Give the circuit symbols for a resistor, lamp and diode. Draw a circuit diagram to show how you would find how the current through a bulb depends on the voltage across it. Draw a graph showing the results you would expect. How would the graph change if a diode, rather than the lamp, is in the circuit?
2. A current of 0.5 A flows through a bulb with a voltage of 20 V across it. What is the resistance of the bulb?
3. Draw a circuit diagram to show two 5 Ω resistors connected in series in a circuit. Include an ammeter to measure the current and a voltmeter to measure the voltage of the battery. What is the total resistance of the resistors in series?

23 Series and parallel

Lights in series

In the past, most sets of Christmas tree lights were connected in such a way that all the bulbs went out when one blew.

The bulbs were connected in series. When the filament in one bulb broke the circuit was broken and all the lights went out.
It was therefore difficult to find the broken bulb.

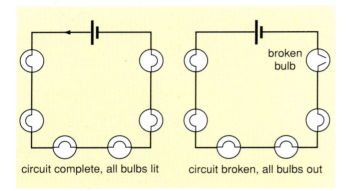

circuit complete, all bulbs lit   circuit broken, all bulbs out

Components in series

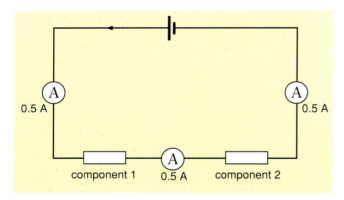

Measuring the current

All three ammeters show the same current. The same current flows through each component.

Lights in parallel

In wall lights one switch may control two bulbs. When one of the bulbs blows, the other still works. The bulbs are connected in parallel. If the bulbs have the same resistance, then the current divides in two. Half flows through one bulb and half through the other. When one bulb breaks the current still flows through the other bulb.

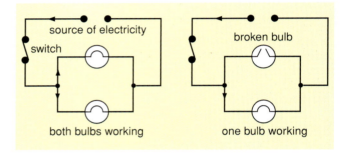

both bulbs working   one bulb working

Components in parallel

Measuring the current

The current is shared between the components. The amount through each depends on the resistance. The greater the resistance the smaller the current. The total current in the circuit is the sum of the currents through the separate components.

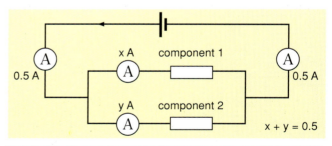

$x + y = 0.5$

Summary

1. Components in series are connected end-to-end. The *same current flows* through each component. The total voltage is shared between them.
2. Components in parallel are connected side-to-side. The current through each is not the same unless they have the same resistance. There is the *same voltage* across each component.

COMPONENTS IN SERIES

Measuring the voltage

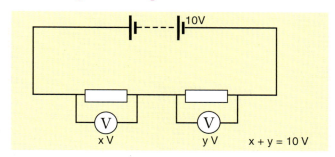

x + y = 10 V

The voltage across each component is different unless they have the same resistance. The sum of the voltages across the components equals the voltage of the energy supply.

When components are in series
- the same current flows through them all
- their total resistance is the sum of their separate resistances
- the voltage across each component is different.

The sum of the voltages equals the voltage of the energy supply.

CELLS IN SERIES

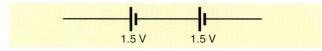

The total voltage is 3.0 V.

PUTTING MORE LAMPS IN SERIES

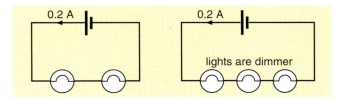

The voltage is shared between the lamps. If more of the same lamps are added, they have the same resistance and are therefore as bright as each other. But the voltage across each one is smaller. *All the lights are dimmer.*

The lights cannot be switched on and off separately. If one is switched off they all go off.

COMPONENTS IN PARALLEL

Measuring the voltage

The voltage across each component is the same and equal to the voltage of the energy supply.

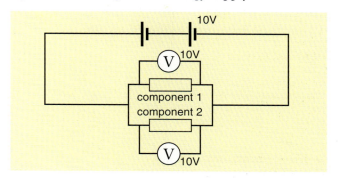

When components are in parallel
- the current through each component differs unless they have the same resistance. The total current in the circuit is the sum of the currents through each component
- the total resistance is not the sum of the separate resistances of the components
- there is the *same voltage* across each component.

CELLS IN PARALLEL

The total voltage is 1.5 V.

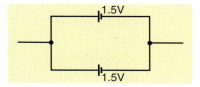

PUTTING MORE LAMPS IN PARALLEL

The voltage across each lamp is the same. If more of the same lamps are added they will have the same brightness. *The lamps do not go dimmer.* More current is used and the battery is exhausted more quickly.

Each light can be switched on and off separately. House lights are connected in parallel.

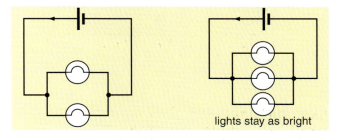

QUESTIONS

1. In a model of a school, when one bulb blows the others also go out. Are the bulbs in series or parallel? Draw a circuit diagram to show the wiring. Does the model accurately show the wiring of the lights in a school? Explain your answer.

2. Copy out the following circuits and fill in the missing values of the current in the ammeters (A).

24 Using electricity

Our homes are full of appliances powered by electricity. They change or transfer electrical energy into other more useful forms of energy quickly and cleanly.

All energy is measured in joules, (symbol J).

Did you know? The temperature of the filament in an electric light bulb can be as high as 3000°C.

HEAT ENERGY

Electric fires, irons, toasters and other appliances transfer electrical energy into heat or **thermal energy**. Some light energy may also be produced.

Most electrical appliances get warm when they are used.

SOUND ENERGY

Radios, stereos and electric bells transfer electrical energy into sound energy.

Most appliances with electric motors also make a noise when they are on.

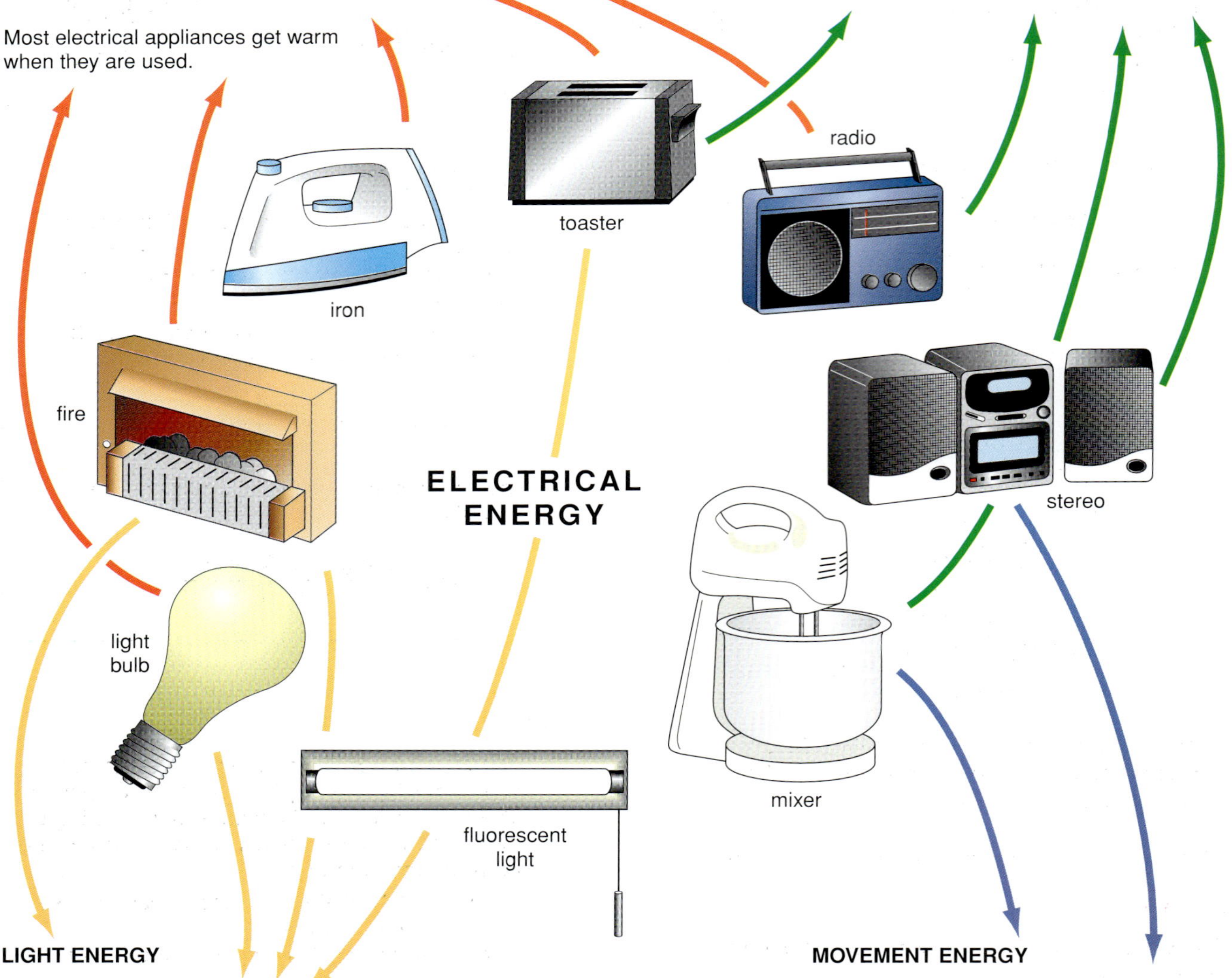

ELECTRICAL ENERGY

- toaster
- iron
- fire
- radio
- stereo
- light bulb
- fluorescent light
- mixer

LIGHT ENERGY

The filament in a light bulb glows white hot when the light is switched on. Electrical energy is transferred to light and heat energy.

Fluorescent lights do not get as hot as filament bulbs. They transfer most of the electrical energy into light energy. The gas in the tube glows when the electricity is switched on.

MOVEMENT ENERGY

Any appliance which produces movement when it is switched on, transfers electrical energy to movement or **kinetic energy**. Most of these appliances have a motor.

In stereo systems, CDs, tapes and records are made to go round. Some of the electrical energy is also transferred to sound energy.

214

How much electricity?

It is much more expensive to leave an electric fire on for an hour than a table lamp. This is because the fire uses more electricity during that time than the bulb in the lamp. The fire has a higher *power rating* than the bulb and so uses energy more quickly. Different appliances have different power ratings.

The power of an appliance is measured in **watts** (W) or kilowatts (kW), 1 kW = 1000 W.

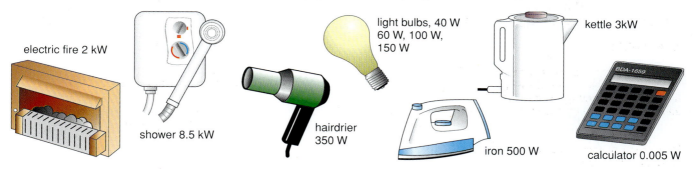

electric fire 2 kW
shower 8.5 kW
hairdrier 350 W
light bulbs, 40 W 60 W, 100 W, 150 W
iron 500 W
kettle 3kW
calculator 0.005 W

A power of 1 watt means that 1 joule of energy is used in 1 second.

The fire in the picture has a power rating of 2 kW or 2000 W. It therefore uses 2000 J of electrical energy every second when it is switched on.

Power in watts = $\dfrac{\text{energy transferred in joules}}{\text{time in seconds}}$

Calculating the power of an appliance

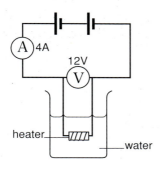

The power of an electrical appliance is calculated by multiplying the voltage across it in volts by the current through it in amperes.

Power in watts = voltage in volts × current in amperes

Example:

a Calculate the power of the water heater shown in the diagram.
b Calculate the energy transferred if the heater is on for 10 minutes.
   a Power (W) = voltage (V) × current (A)
      The power of the heater = 12 × 4 = 48 W
   b Energy transferred (J) = power (W) × time (s)
      The energy transferred = 48 × 60 × 10 = 28 800 J

Summary

1 Electrical energy can be transferred into heat (thermal energy), light, sound and movement (kinetic energy). **Energy** is measured in **joules** (J).

2 The power in watts (W) of an appliance is the voltage (V) multiplied by the current (A).

   Power (W) = voltage (V) × current (A)

3 The power is the energy (J) transferred in a second (s).

   Power (W) = $\dfrac{\text{energy transferred (J)}}{\text{time (s)}}$

Questions

1 Look at the labels on three of the appliances in your home. List the appliances with their power ratings in order from the highest power rating to the lowest. Which appliance uses the most energy if it is run for 10 minutes?

2 A bulb uses 60 J of electrical energy each second. What is its power rating?
What is the electrical energy transferred into?

3 Find the power of a car headlamp if it is run off a 12 V battery and draws a current of 3 A. How much energy does it use if it is run for 5 minutes?

4 Which of the following has the highest power rating
   a an electric heater (current 4 A, voltage 230 V)
   b an electric iron with a power rating of 1200 W?

25 Electricity in the home

MAINS ELECTRICITY

The mains electricity supplying our homes, schools and other buildings has a voltage of 230 volts. It must be used safely as the current it can push through us is big enough to kill, particularly if our skin is wet.

Bathrooms are often wet so extra safety precautions are taken. There are no mains sockets in modern bathrooms.

Skin condition	Current flowing through person touching the mains
dry skin with a thick insulator under foot, for example, shoes with rubber soles	1 milliamp (a thousandth of an amp). Gives a nasty shock.
wet skin with bare feet on a wet floor	30 milliamps – enough to kill

CABLES AND PLUGS

Most appliances are connected to the mains using a cable and a three-pin plug. To make them safe the cable and plug are made of special materials and connected together carefully.

The cable is made of:
- two or three inner wires of copper (a good electrical conductor) each covered with plastic (a good insulator)
- an outer layer of tough flexible plastic.

The plug has:
- a plastic or rubber case, as both materials are good insulators
- brass pins, as brass is a good conductor. The pins are often half-covered with plastic to stop us touching the metal when putting in the plug. One of the pins is an earth pin
- a fuse which 'blows' if the current is too high
- a cable grip so that the wires can't be pulled out.

Fitting a plug

The wires in the cable are colour-coded to make sure they are fitted to the right pin.

The cable must be secured under the cable grip.

Colour	Terminal
blue	neutral
brown	live (via a fuse)
green/yellow	earth

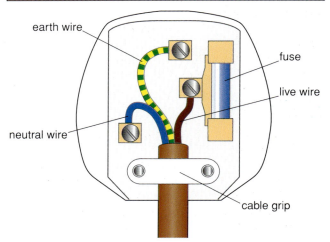

The correct fuse recommended by the manufacturer should be fitted (usually 3 A or 13 A). The fuse has a slightly higher value than the current which flows through the appliance when it is working normally.

Earthing appliances

All electrical appliances with metal parts have an earth wire fitted as a safety precaution. One end of the earth wire is connected to the metal and the other to the ground through the earth pin of the plug. If a fault occurs in the appliance and the live wire carrying the current touches the metal then the current flows to earth and not through you.

Fuses

Fuses are safety devices. They stop wires from overheating and so protect us against fires and electric shocks. If a fault occurs in an appliance and the live wire touches the metal casing then the large current flowing to earth through the casing will be greater than the current rating of the fuse. The wire in the fuse gets hot and melts. The fuse 'blows' and breaks the circuit, switching off the current.

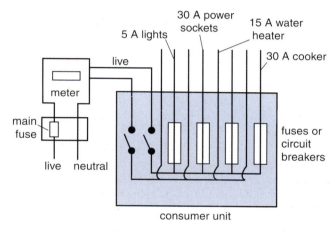

The mains electricity supply

The mains supply to a house goes through a meter and then a consumer unit containing fuses or circuit breakers. Each of these protects a particular circuit in the house from overload. Appliances such as cookers and water heaters which use a large current have their own fuse or circuit breaker in the consumer unit.

> ### Summary
>
> 1. Mains electricity has a voltage of 230 V and must be used safely.
> 2. Plugs must be wired correctly and fitted with the right fuse. The earth wire protects us if the metal case of an appliance becomes live.
> 3. The current from a battery is a direct current. The current from the mains is an alternating current.

Direct current (d.c.) and alternating current (a.c.)

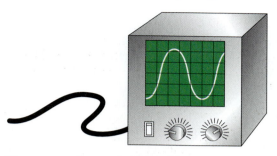

The current from a battery flows in one direction from the positive to the negative terminal. It is called a **direct current (d.c.)**.

The electric current from the mains supply is continually reversing. It flows back and forth along the wires, 50 times every second and is called an **alternating current (a.c.)**. It has a frequency of 50 cycles per second or 50 hertz (Hz). The oscilloscope shows how the voltage changes with time. The current follows a similar variation.

Be safe

- don't plug too many appliances into one socket
- make sure plugs and flexes are in good condition
- don't poke metal objects into sockets
- keep sockets and switches dry
- put the correct fuse for the appliance in the plug.

How many hazards can you spot?

> ### Questions
>
> 1. Draw a diagram of the inside of a plug.
>   a. Label the names and colours of the wires.
>   b. Why are the pins of a plug made of brass?
>   c. Why is the case made of plastic?
> 2. Copy out the sentence filling in the names of the correct wires. In an electric fire the current flows in through the ____- wire and out through the ____- wire. The metal case is connected to the ____- wire.

26 Paying for electricity

How much electricity?

The amount of electricity we use at home is measured with a meter. This records the amount of electricity used in **units**.

The meter is read every three months. The number of units used is calculated by subtracting the last meter reading from the present reading.

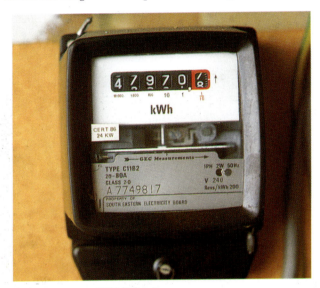

This meter reading is 47970 kWh units.

Checking your electricity bill

The bill shows the two meter readings; the number of units of electricity used and the cost of each unit, usually about 7p.

cost of the electricity used = number of units × unit price

A quarterly charge known as a standing charge, and VAT is added to give the final cost.

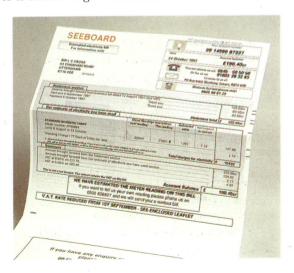

How many units?

The number of units of electricity that we use depends on the power of our appliances and how long we use them. One unit of electrical energy is used by a 1 kW appliance which is run for 1 hour. 1 Unit of electricity is 1 kilowatt hour (kWh).

A 3 kW heater which is run for 4 hours uses 3 × 4 or 12 units of electricity.

Energy transferred (kWh) = power (kW) × time (h)
Units used = power (kW) × time (h)

Remember that when calculating the number of units used, the power is in kW and the time in hours.

Note To convert the power in W to kW, divide by 1000.
To convert the time in minutes to hours, divide by 60.

What is the cost?

Typical power ratings of different appliances are given below.

kettle	2.2 kW
fire	2 kW
desk lamp	60 W
fridge-freezer	150 W
hi-fi	200 W
television	130 W
immersion heater	3.5 kW

Appliances which transfer electrical energy to heat energy have a higher power rating. They are therefore more expensive to run.

Example

a Calculate the number of units of electricity used when a 100 W lamp is left on for 120 minutes.
b What is the total cost if one unit costs 7p?

a Power of the lamp = 100 W = $\frac{100}{1000}$ kW = 0.1 kW

Time the lamp is left on = 120 min = $\frac{120}{60}$ h = 2 h

Energy transferred (kWh) = power (kW) × time (h)
= 0.1 × 2 = 0.2 kWh
Number of units used = 0.2

b Cost = 0.2 × 7 = 1.4p.

An expensive fuel!

It is more expensive to use electricity than coal, oil or gas for heating our homes. The table compares the approximate cost of 1 unit of energy supplied by the different fuels.

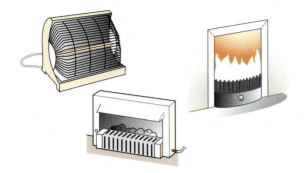

Which is the most expensive fuel to use?

Energy source	Cost of 1 Unit/pence
coal	1.0
gas	1.5
oil	1.4
electricity	7.0

Most of our electricity is generated by burning coal, oil or gas but a lot of energy is wasted in the process. This makes electricity the most expensive fuel.

Cheaper electricity

The amount of electricity used during the day varies. There can even be a noticeable surge in demand during the break in a popular match or film on TV when we all switch on our kettles for a cup of tea!

But electrical energy cannot be stored and the power stations cannot be turned off and on very easily. We are therefore encouraged to use electricity during the night, when demand is low by making it cheaper. A special meter is installed to measure the amount of off-peak electricity used. This is a more economical way of heating if storage heaters and well-insulated water tanks are used.

Summary

1. The amount of electricity used is measured in units. 1 unit is 1 kWh.
2. The energy used = power × time
   (Units)   (kW)   (h)
3. Cost = number of Units × cost per Unit.
4. Electricity is the most expensive fuel.

How many joules in a unit of electricity?

The amount of energy used (in joules) is calculated by multiplying the power (in watts) by the time (in seconds).

Energy (J) = power (W) × time (s)

The energy in 1 unit of electricity = 1 kWh
$$= 1000 \times 60 \times 60 \text{ J}$$
$$= 3,600,000 \text{ J}$$

A lot of joules are used in running a 1 kW fire for 1 hour!

Questions

1. The meter readings taken from the meter at the beginning and end of a holiday in a rented cottage are

   First reading   05275
   Second reading   05425

   a How many units were used during the holiday?
   b If each unit is charged at 8p, what is the total cost?

2. Explain why it is more expensive to turn on an immersion heater for 1 hour than to leave a 60 W light bulb on for the same time.

3. A 2 kW fire is turned on for 30 minutes. How many units of electricity are used? How many joules of energy are transferred?

4. Using the table showing the cost of 1 unit of energy supplied by different fuels
   a draw a bar chart to show the information
   b give the cheapest fuel.

27 Magnets and electromagnets

There are two kinds of magnets in this kitchen – permanent magnets and electromagnets.
Permanent magnets are magnetic all the time, for instance, the magnets in the magnetic clips.
Electromagnets are magnetic only when the current is switched on. When the current is switched off they are not magnetic. Electromagnets are used in motors and electric bells.

Permanent magnets

Permanent magnets can have various shapes, such as bar, horseshoe or U-shaped. They have the following properties.

- Magnets attract iron, nickel, cobalt and steel. These metals are said to be magnetic and can be magnetised
- A magnet settles in a north–south direction when suspended in air.
  Magnets are therefore used in making compasses. The end of the magnet pointing north is called the north-seeking pole.
  The end of the magnet pointing south is called the south-seeking pole
- The like poles of two magnets repel each other. The unlike poles of two magnets attract each other
- There is a magnetic field around a magnet which affects any magnetic material in it. Lines of force force are drawn to show the pattern of the field. The arrows go from the north to the south pole. A compass is used to find the direction of the forces in the magnetic field.

Did you know?
The North Pole and magnetic north pole of the Earth are not in the same place. The magnetic north pole is currently on the Arctic coast of North America at the Boothia Peninsula.

While sailing around parts of Greenland, a compass needle will appear to point west not north!

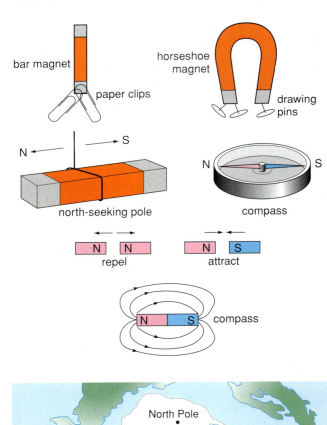

ELECTROMAGNETS

Producing a magnetic field around an electric wire

When an electric current flows through a wire, a magnetic field is formed round the wire.

When the current is turned off there is no magnetic field.

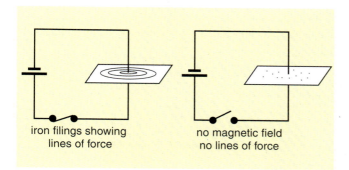

What is the effect of the magnetic field?

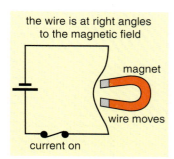

The wire is passed between the poles of a horseshoe magnet. When the current is turned on the wire moves. This is because the magnetic field around the wire interacts with that of the magnet. This effect is used in making electric motors.

When the current is turned off there is no field around the wire so it returns to its original position.

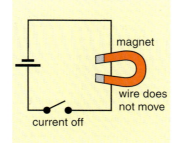

Making an electromagnet

A coiled wire acts like a bar magnet when a current is passed through it. One end is a north-seeking pole and the other is a south-seeking pole.

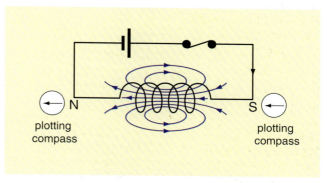

The strength of the electromagnet is increased by:
- placing an iron rod inside the coil
- increasing the number of turns on the coil
- increasing the current through the coil.

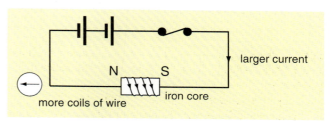

If the direction of the current is reversed then the poles are reversed.

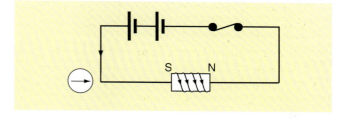

SUMMARY

1. Magnets have a north-seeking pole and a south-seeking pole.
2. Like poles repel, unlike poles attract.
3. The magnetic field around a magnet attracts magnetic materials.
4. An electromagnet is a coil of wire with an electric current flowing through it. When the current is switched off it is no longer magnetic.

QUESTIONS

1. Go round your home and list three uses for permanent magnets and three for electromagnets.
2. Explain how you would show that there is a magnetic field around:
   a a bar magnet
   b an electric wire carrying a current.
   In each case draw a diagram to show the field.
3. Give two ways of increasing the strength of an electromagnet.

28 Using electromagnets

Electromagnets are used in many everyday devices. Some of the more common ones include circuit breakers, electric bells, loudspeakers and relays. They are also used in monorail trains.

Circuit breakers

Circuit breakers are safety devices which protect us in case the electrical equipment we are using is faulty. They do the same job as a fuse but are more convenient to use.

Trip switch

Trip switches switch off the power if the current is too high and so are used in school laboratories as well as in equipment such as power supplies.

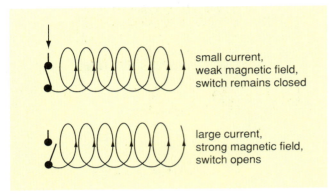

small current, weak magnetic field, switch remains closed

large current, strong magnetic field, switch opens

The switch has an electromagnet. If the equipment is faulty then the current flowing in the circuit may be very large. The electromagnet creates a sufficiently strong magnetic field to pull the switch open. This breaks the circuit and stops the flow of the current.

When the fault has been repaired a reset button is pushed to close the switch and complete the circuit again.

Strong electromagnets

Electromagnets are used to separate metals.

The electric bell

When the button is pushed, the circuit is completed and the current flows. The electromagnet attracts the iron arm. The hammer hits the bell and makes a noise.

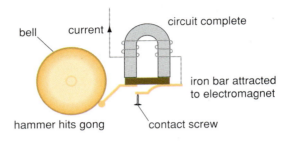

bell — current — circuit complete — iron bar attracted to electromagnet — hammer hits gong — contact screw

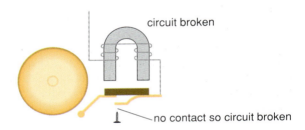

circuit broken — no contact so circuit broken

The iron arm moves away from the contact screw and the circuit breaks. The current stops flowing so that the electromagnet is no longer magnetic. The hammer returns to its original position.

The process is repeated continually until the button is not pressed any more.

RCD (residual circuit device)

Another type of circuit breaker is an RCD. This is used in lawnmowers and power tools.

An RCD compares the current in the live and neutral wires. If they are not the same then some of the current could be flowing through the person using the tool. An electromagnet pulls the switch open and breaks the circuit.

The relay (electromagnetic switch)

The relay uses an electromagnet in one circuit to turn on a switch in a second circuit. This means that a small current in a circuit with thin wires can be used to switch on a much larger current flowing through a circuit with thicker wires.

Relays are used in many devices such as in switching on outside security lights, starting powerful machines and the starter motors in cars.

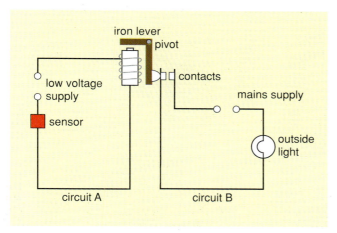

In outside security lights, the sensor is activated by movement. Someone walking past the house causes circuit A to be completed. The electromagnet attracts the iron lever. This closes the contacts in circuit B and the light goes on.

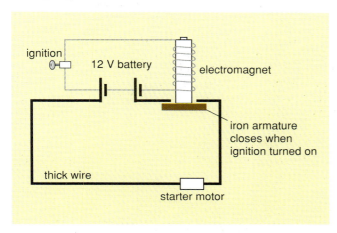

The starter motor in a car needs a current of over 100 A (amperes or amps). It is turned on by a relay when the ignition key is turned.

Summary

Electromagnets are used in many devices. These include electric bells, relays, circuit breakers and loudspeakers.

The loudspeaker

The loudspeaker has a cardboard cone attached to a coil of wire. The coil can move in and out.

When the amplifier in your radio, CD player or stereo passes a current to the coil, it becomes an electromagnet. Its magnetic field interacts with that of the permanent magnet. This causes the coil and cone to move.

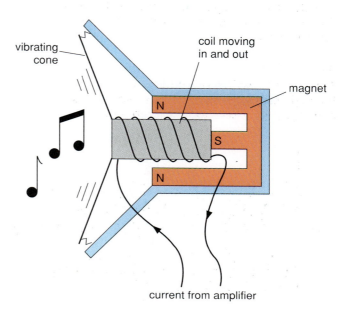

As the current varies, the movement of the cone makes the air in front of it vibrate. We hear the vibrations as sound or music.

Did you know? Powerful electromagnets are used in hospitals to remove metal splinters from eyes.

Questions

1. Make a list of the appliances in your home which you think will probably have a relay for switching them on. Explain why relays are used.
2. You are working in the laboratory and using an electric power supply when suddenly the current stops flowing. The trip switch has switched it off.
   a. What is a trip switch and how does it work?
   b. Why do you think the trip switch switched off the current?
   c. What might have happened if the laboratory had not been fitted with trip switches?
3. You replace the power supply with another one and reset the trip switch. The current now flows. What does this tell you about the first power supply?

29 Electric motors and generators

Motors change electrical energy into kinetic energy and generators change kinetic energy into electrical energy. Generators and motors are therefore essential for the operation of many machines, appliances, and some vehicles.

Motors transfer
electrical energy into kinetic energy.

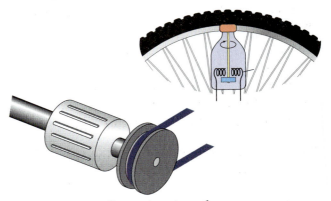

Generators transfer
kinetic energy into **electrical energy**.

ELECTRIC MOTORS

A force is exerted on a wire carrying a current when it is placed in a magnetic field. This force is used in the electric motor to produce a turning effect.

Direction of the force

If the current is at right angles to the magnetic field, the direction of the force on the wire which produces motion is found using the Left-Hand Rule. The rule:
 if the **F**irst finger is in the direction of the **F**ield,
 and the se**C**ond finger is in the direction of the **C**urrent,
 then, the thu**M**b points in the direction of the **M**otion.
The fingers and thumb are all at right angles to each other. The direction of the force is reversed by reversing either the magnetic field or the direction of the current.

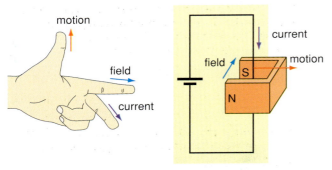

The current, magnetic field and direction of motion are at right angles to each other.

Increasing the force

The size of the force is increased by increasing the strength of the magnetic field or the size of the current.

The d.c. motor

A simple motor contains a coil of wire mounted between the poles of a magnet or electromagnet.
 When the d.c. current is switched on there is a force on each side of the coil causing it to turn in an anti-clockwise direction. The forces are equal to each other but in opposite directions (the Left-Hand Rule). The turning effect is reversed when the coil passes the vertical position so this would not make a very useful motor. To keep the loop turning in the same direction, a device called a split-ring commutator is used. This reverses the current in the loop every half revolution.

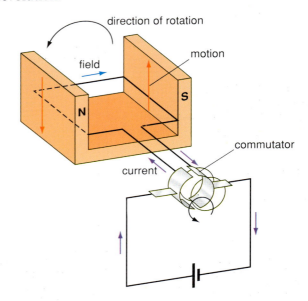

Practical motors have several coils of wire and an electromagnet rather than a permanent magnet. Some are also designed to work using an alternating current from the mains.

224

GENERATORS

Generators and dynamos depend on the fact that electricity is produced when a magnetic field around a wire changes. A voltage is produced in the wire and the process is called **electromagnetic induction**.

Inducing a voltage

A small current flows when the magnet is moved into the coil.

The size of the induced voltage and current is increased by:
- increasing the strength of the magnet
- increasing the number of turns on the coil
- moving the magnet more quickly.

The induced current flows in the opposite direction if:
- the magnet is moved out of the coil, or
- the other pole of the magnet is moved into the coil.

A voltage is induced in a similar way if the coil of wire is moved rather than the magnet.

Dynamos and generators

In a bicycle dynamo the magnet rotates as the bicycle wheel turns. This causes the magnetic field to change direction. An alternating voltage is generated in the coil. A current flows in the circuit and the bicycle lamps light. It is harder to pedal when the dynamo is working as you have to supply energy to make the dynamo spin. This energy is then transferred into electrical energy.

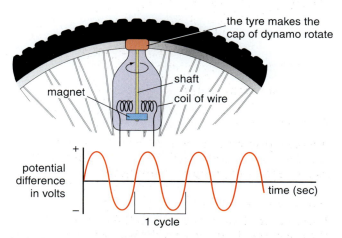

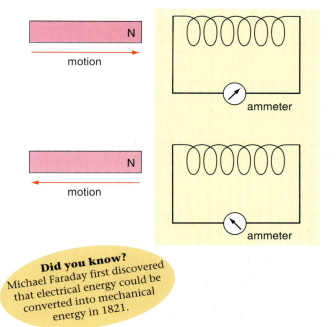

In power stations, powerful generators are used rather than dynamos. These have electromagnets rather than permanent magnets which are rotated by turbines driven by steam.

SUMMARY

1. Motors convert electrical energy into kinetic energy. They contain a coil of wire carrying a current between the poles of a magnet.
2. Dynamos and generators convert kinetic energy into electrical energy by moving a magnet in a coil of wire. A voltage is induced in the wire. Electromagnetic induction occurs.

Did you know?
Michael Faraday first discovered that electrical energy could be converted into mechanical energy in 1821.

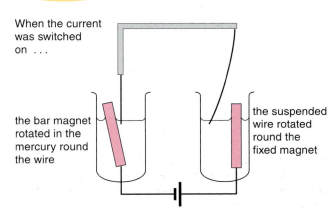

QUESTIONS

1. Both a motor and a dynamo contain a coil of wire placed between the poles of a magnet. How do they differ?
2. Give three ways of making an electric motor more powerful.
3. Explain what is meant by electromagnetic induction. How can the induced voltage be increased? What use is made of electromagnetic induction?

30 Power around the country

Generating electricity

Mains electricity is generated in many power stations using heat from burning fossil fuels or nuclear reactions to produce steam to drive the turbines. An alternating current is produced which flows back and forth along the wires 50 times each second. Its frequency is 50 hertz (50 Hz).

A typical generator produces a very large current of 20 000 A or 20 kA at a voltage of 25 000 V or 25 kV.

Power station

Getting electricity into our home

Each power station generates enough electricity for about a half a million homes, but we don't receive our electricity directly from one station. Instead, the electricity from all the stations is fed into a network of overhead cables known as the National Grid. This takes electricity round the country to the consumer.

The cables carrying the current are held high above the ground by pylons. This is so that no-one can reach them as they carry a large current at a very high voltage and can therefore be very dangerous.

Thick cables

When a current flows through a wire some of the electrical energy is transferred into heat energy and there is a loss in power. The amount of heat transferred increases with the size of the current and the resistance of the wires. Thin wires have a higher resistance than thick wires and so get hotter. Less heat energy is produced when smaller currents and thicker wires are used.

The large currents generated in power stations would need very thick cables to reduce the amount of heat produced. But thick cables are expensive and heavy to support above the ground on pylons.

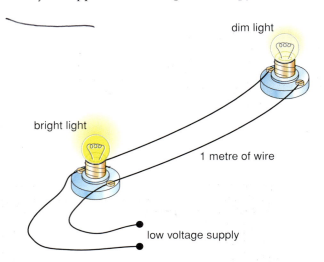

Reducing the current

Transformers are used to change the voltage and current of an a.c. supply. At the power station, step-up transformers increase the voltage and decrease the current before it is transmitted. The voltage is increased from 25 kV to 275 kV or 400 kV and the current is decreased from 20 kA to 1.25 kA. Less power is lost as less electrical energy is transferred to heat energy. Thinner cables can also be used.

The cables carrying the current have no insulation as the air gap between them and the ground is large enough to prevent sparking. The air also cools the cables and prevents them from overheating.

If the cables were underground they would have to be cooled by oil flowing around them. This would be very expensive.

Power to the consumer

It would be much too dangerous to have a 400 kV electrical supply in our homes. The voltage is reduced in stages in substations using step-down transformers. The railways and some industries use electricity supplies at voltages between 11 and 33 kV. For example, hospitals receive 11 kV supplies which are stepped-down inside the building.

The last stage in the step-down process is at a sub-station close to the home. This reduces the voltage to 230 V, a much safer level for domestic supplies but still dangerous if it is not used properly.

Transformers in the home

Many everyday electrical appliances have transformers in them, or in the mains adaptor which is plugged into the socket.

The transformer in a train set reduces the voltage to 12 V to make it safe to use. Voltage from the transformer is carried to the electric motor in the train through the rails. They are therefore safe to touch. Many electronic devices like calculators have transformers to reduce the voltage to 9 V.

Did you know?
Televisions have both step-down and step-up transformers. The voltage is stepped-down to about 12 V for the electronic circuit and stepped-up to provide the 15 kV needed to accelerate the electrons in the picture tube.

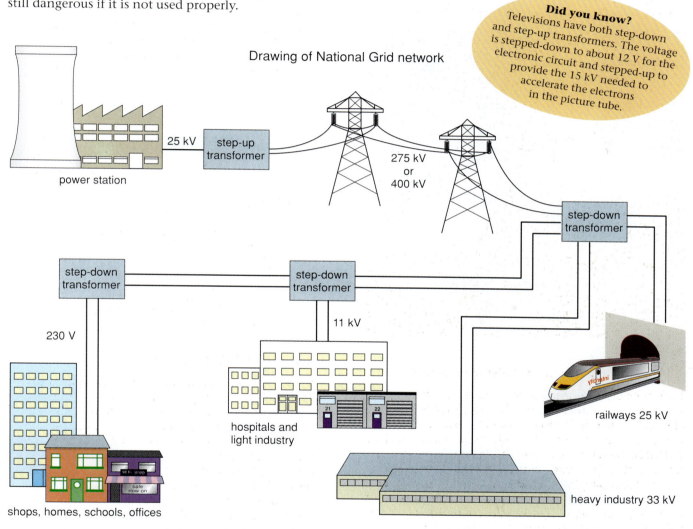

Drawing of National Grid network

Summary

1. The National Grid carries electricity from the power stations to the consumer. The electricity is at a very high voltage.
2. Step-up transformers are used to increase the voltage of an alternating current (a.c.) supply and reduce the current. Step-down transformers decrease the voltage and increase the current.

Questions

1. Explain why electricity supply cables
   a. are thick and have no insulation
   b. are carried high in the air on pylons and not buried underground.
2. What is used to alter the voltage of an a.c. current? How and why is the voltage of the mains supply changed first at the power station and then again before it reaches you in your home?

31 Where does energy come from?

Without energy nothing would happen. We get our energy from the food we eat but where does the energy in the food come from?

Most, but not all, of the energy comes originally from the Sun. It is continually being converted from one form into another and is not created nor destroyed.

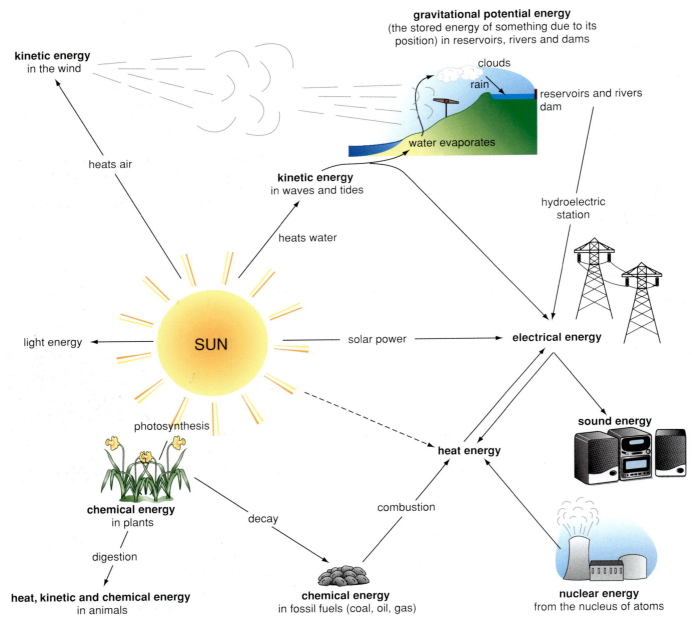

Nuclear energy does not come from the Sun but from the nucleus of atoms.

Some energy transfers occur naturally, for example, the evaporation of water from the seas and lakes. Others only occur when we allow them to, for example, when we switch on an electric fire to convert electrical energy into heat energy.

What happens to the Sun's energy?

Most of the energy from the Sun reaching the Earth is returned directly to space. Only about a quarter of it is converted into forms of energy which we use.

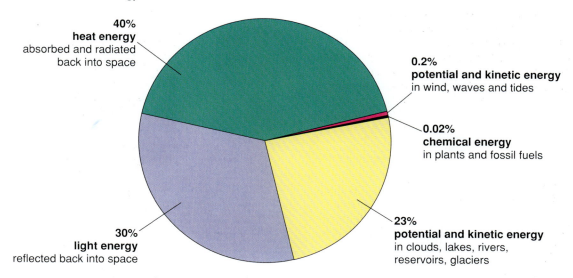

Just less than a quarter of the energy from the Sun is used in the evaporation of water to form clouds and then rain as part of the water cycle. This also leads to the formation of air and water currents. As a result of these processes, energy from the Sun is transferred into kinetic energy or gravitational potential energy.

Only a tiny percentage of the Sun's energy is used by plants in photosynthesis and stored as chemical energy in their leaves and roots.

Energy conversions

Many activities involve several energy changes. Think of the changes undergone when a child uses a clockwork toy. The main energy changes are shown in the energy chain.

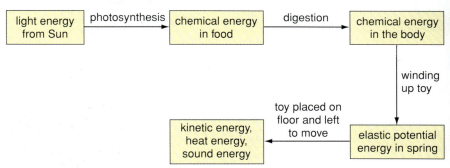

Did you know? Only one fifth of 1% of the electricity in the UK comes from wind power.

Summary

1 Most of the energy we use comes directly or indirectly from the Sun. A small amount comes from nuclear reactions.
2 Energy is converted from one form to another. It cannot be created or destroyed.

Questions

1 In each case give two examples of something which possesses
   a chemical energy
   b kinetic energy
   c gravitational potential energy.
2 Work out the energy conversions that occur as you climb a hill. Start with the energy from the Sun.
3 Explain why we depend on plants for our energy, and where the energy in the plants comes from.

32 How hot is it?

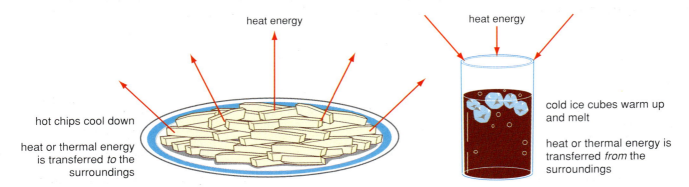

A substance has more thermal energy when it is hot than when it is cold. When things are heated they often begin to glow. For example, the metal element in an electric toaster or fire glows 'red hot' when it is switched on. At higher temperatures it goes orange and then paler in colour.

As a substance is heated its particles (atoms or molecules) move faster. Their average kinetic energy increases.

Temperature and its measurement

The temperature of a substance tells us how hot or cold it is. It is a measure of its thermal energy or the average kinetic energy of its particles. Temperature is measured in degrees Celsius (°C). Water normally freezes at 0°C and boils at 100°C. On this scale, 'red hot' iron is about 500°C and the temperature of the sun about 6000°C.

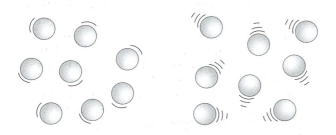

cold particles moving more slowly

hot particles moving more quickly

Mercury thermometers contain mercury in a narrow glass tube, marked with a scale. As the mercury gets warmer it expands and moves up the tube. The distance it moves gives a measure of the temperature which is read from the scale.

Clinical thermometers have a fine tube so that the mercury moves a long way when it expands. It is used to measure body temperature. When the thermometer is placed under the tongue, the mercury expands and is forced past the constriction and along the tube. When the thermometer is taken out of the mouth, the bulb cools and the mercury contracts. The column of mercury breaks at the constriction and is left in the tube so that its position can be read. The average body temperature is 37°C. The thermometer is reset by shaking the mercury back into the bulb.

Liquid crystal thermometers change colour at different temperatures. Electronic thermometers are useful for recording temperature changes as they can be connected to a computer.

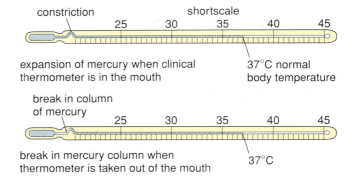

Getting hot and cooling down

Thermal energy is transferred from hotter to cooler substances. As something cools, the average kinetic energy of its particles falls. As it gets hot, the average kinetic energy of its particles increases.

The transfer of thermal energy takes place by **conduction**, **convection** or **radiation**.

CONDUCTION

Conduction is the transfer of thermal energy without the substance itself moving. It is the main method of transferring thermal energy in solids. It occurs less readily in liquids and hardly at all in gases.

Metal handles and spoons get very hot. Plastic or wooden handles and spoons remain cool.

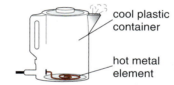

The metal element transfers heat energy to the water. The plastic container is much cooler than the boiling water.

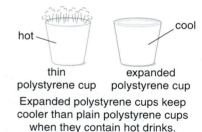

Expanded polystyrene cups keep cooler than plain polystyrene cups when they contain hot drinks.

Some materials transfer thermal energy by conduction better than others. They are good **conductors**. Substances which do not readily conduct thermal energy are called **insulators**. The examples above suggest that metals are good conductors and plastic, wood and the air trapped in the expanded polystyrene are poorer conductors. Air is a better insulator than plastic.

How good a conductor?

The different rods have the same diameter. The heat-sensitive paper changes colour at a particular temperature. The heat-sensitive paper on the rod that conducts heat best will change colour first.

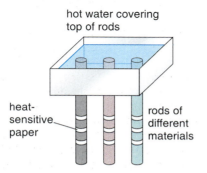

silver	good conductor
copper	
aluminium	
brass	decreasing
iron, steel	conductivity
concrete	
glass	
brick	
wood	
plastic	
foam	poor conductor
air	good insulator

Many materials that are used for their insulating properties contain trapped air, for instance, expanded polystyrene. Woolly clothes trap air between the fibres. The air insulates us so that we keep warm in cold weather.

How does conduction work?

All materials conduct some heat by passing energy from particle to particle. In metals the atoms are close together and the electrons are loosely held. At the hot end, the electrons have more kinetic energy and diffuse quickly through the metal. They also collide with adjacent electrons causing them to move more. The energy is therefore transferred through the metal.

In liquids, fewer molecules touch each other so conduction is slower. In gases, the molecules are very far apart and energy is only transferred when they collide. Gases are therefore poor conductors.

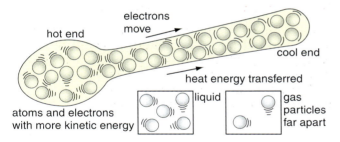

SUMMARY

1. The temperature of a substance gives a measure of its thermal energy. Temperature is measured in °C.
2. Thermal energy is transferred by conduction, convection or radiation.
3. Solids are better conductors than liquids or gases.

QUESTIONS

1. Give examples of two good conductors and two good insulators and a use of each which relates to this property.
2. The filament in a light bulb glows white and the element in a toaster glows red. Which is hotter? Where does the thermal energy come from? Give two other appliances with elements.
3. Explain how thermal energy in a hot cup of tea travels to the end of a metal teaspoon used to stir it. Why do metal teapots often have plastic handles?
4. Arrange the following in decreasing order of conductivity: copper, oxygen, glass, silver, water.

33 Convection and radiation

CONVECTION

The transfer of thermal energy in gases and liquids can occur by convection. **Convection currents** are set up.

You can feel the current of cold air around your feet when you open the freezer door.

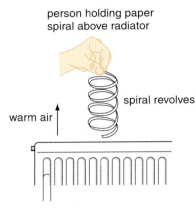

A paper spiral moves in the convection current in the air above a warm radiator.

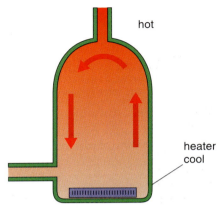

The water in the top of the water tank is hotter than that in the bottom when the immersion heater is switched on.

What is happening?

When a gas or liquid is heated, the molecules gain energy. They move faster and get further apart. The gas or liquid expands and becomes less dense. It therefore rises and is replaced by cooler gas or liquid. A convection current is set up.

Seeing the convection currents

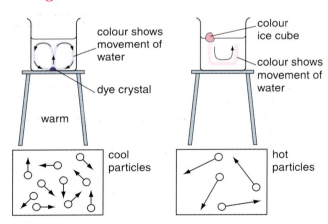

Convection currents in the home

Convection currents are set up around fires and radiators as well as in water heating systems.

In gas or coal fires the hot waste gases formed by combustion pass up the chimney. They are replaced by cooler air which is drawn into the fire. This is necessary to provide the oxygen needed for combustion.

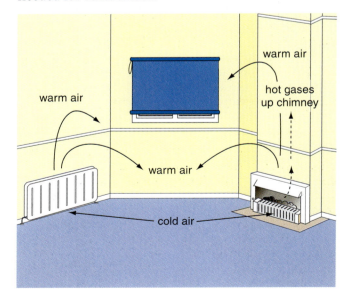

Thermals, winds and ocean currents

Convection currents form over areas of land which are warmer than the land around. The currents are called **thermals** and are used by birds and gliders to gain height.

On a large scale, uneven heating of the Earth's surface by the Sun causes air pressure differences and the formation of winds.

Large convection currents in the oceans have a big influence on climate. For example, the UK has mild winters because the North Atlantic Drift carries warm water from near the equator across the Atlantic to Western Europe.

Radiation

If someone is feverish or sunburnt we can feel heat energy radiating out from their skin. The hotter they are the more heat is radiated. Anything that is hot transfers heat energy by radiation.

When we are sunburnt we radiate out more heat.

The Earth absorbs radiation from the Sun and warms up.

The hot coals on a barbecue radiate thermal energy and the food cooks.

What is the radiant energy?

The transfer of thermal energy by radiation differs from conduction and convection as it does not need a substance to travel through. The radiant energy travels through air or empty space mainly as infra red radiation. This is part of the electromagnetic spectrum and has a larger wavelength (lower frequency) than visible light. However, it can be 'seen' using a heat-sensitive camera.

Thermal energy is continually being transferred to and from objects by radiation. The rate at which it is given out and absorbed depends on the colour and surface of the object.

Good and bad radiators

Black matt surfaces radiate thermal energy faster than shiny white surfaces.

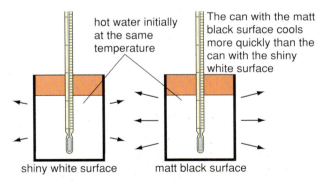

Using radiant energy

Greenhouses and some water heating systems use the radiant energy from the Sun for heating. The Sun gives off radiation of all wavelengths and glass allows visible light and infra red light with a short wavelength to pass through it.

The greenhouse and blackened panel behind the water pipes are cooler and only give off long-wave infra red radiation. Glass does not allow this to pass through, so the thermal energy is trapped inside.

Good and bad absorbers

Black matt surfaces absorb thermal energy faster than shiny white surfaces. Shiny white surfaces are better reflectors of the radiation.

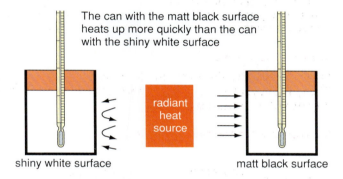

Summary

1. Convection currents in gases and liquids carry thermal energy from place to place.
2. Thermal energy is transferred through the air or a vacuum by infra red radiation.
3. Black matt surfaces are better emitters and absorbers of infra red radiation than shiny white surfaces.

Questions

1. Draw a diagram to show the convection currents around a hot baked potato taken from the oven. Why does the potato cool?
2. Explain why heat energy can be transferred through a vacuum by radiation but not by convection.
3. a Why is the inside of an oven painted matt black?
   b Why are accident victims and runners at the end of a marathon often wrapped in shiny foil blankets?

34 Saving energy and being efficient

We have seen how thermal energy moves from hotter to cooler areas. Warm houses will therefore lose heat to the surroundings. Different parts of a house transfer thermal energy at different rates.

Although area for area windows lose energy at the greatest rate, in general, the total amount of heat lost through windows is less than that transferred through the walls and roof.

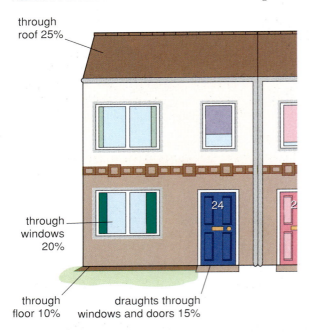

through roof 25%
through windows 20%
through floor 10%
draughts through windows and doors 15%

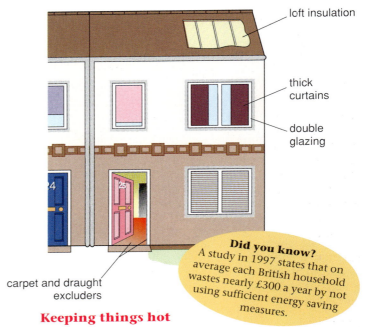

loft insulation
thick curtains
double glazing
carpet and draught excluders

Did you know? A study in 1997 states that on average each British household wastes nearly £300 a year by not using sufficient energy saving measures.

SAVING ENERGY

Energy costs money. There is also concern about how quickly the Earth's energy supplies are being used up. So, it makes sense to reduce the amount of heat energy lost from our homes and other buildings. Various methods are used. They mainly reduce loss of heat by conduction and convection and include:

- *insulating lofts with rockwool.* This traps air between its fibres. Air is a good insulator
- *double glazing windows.* The air between the layers of glass is an insulator
- *filling cavity walls with foam.* The foam has bubbles of trapped air in it. Both the foam and air are insulators
- *fitting draught excluders round doors*
- *insulating the floor by using thick carpets*
- *insulating hot water pipes by lagging them*
- *using thicker curtains or shutters across windows*
- *using low-energy light bulbs*
- *building a porch.*

Energy from the Sun is free! New houses are usually built with larger windows on the south facing walls to capture more infra red radiation from the Sun. Windows on the north side are smaller.

Keeping things hot

Thermos flasks keep things hot or cold.

air-filled plastic stopper stops evaporation and is a good insulator
vacuum between glass walls reduces conduction and convection
silver lining reflects radiant heat back into the flask
glass walls reduce conduction
Containers made of expanded polystyrene keep food hot

Keeping things cold

The inside of a fridge is cooler than the air outside. Heat energy leaks in slowly and has to be removed. The fluid in the pipes is forced to evaporate in the pipes in the freezer compartment. This process takes in heat energy and cools the air in the fridge.

BEING EFFICIENT

Not all the energy we use goes where we want it to go. We say that the energy has been 'wasted' if it is transferred in a way which is not useful for us.

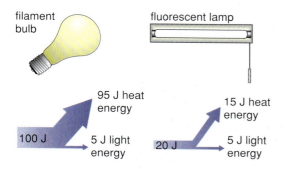

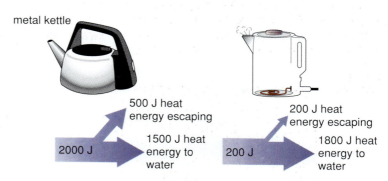

Whenever we use any electrical appliance, heat energy is always produced. Radios, televisions and any machines with motors get warm when they are used. Computers usually have fans to keep them cool. In fact, all the energy which is usefully or not usefully transferred eventually ends up as heat energy in the surroundings. The energy becomes more spread out as it is transferred. Less of the energy stays in a form which can be used.

What happens when you switch on a 'walkman'?

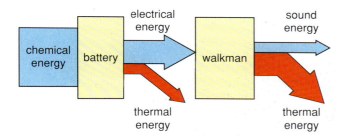

The batteries are a useful source of chemical energy. This is changed into electrical energy when the 'walkman' is turned on. A series of energy changes occur and at each stage some thermal energy is produced. Only a small amount of the chemical energy actually ends up as sound energy.

Efficiency

The efficiency of an appliance is the fraction of the energy which is supplied to the appliance which is usefully transferred.

$$\% \text{ efficiency} = \frac{\text{useful energy transferred by device}}{\text{total energy supplied to the device}} \times 100$$

Comparing efficiencies

The two different types of light bulbs shown above have very different efficiencies.

Filament bulb
$$\% \text{ efficiency} = \frac{\text{useful energy}}{\text{total energy}} \times 100$$
$$= \frac{5}{100} \times 100 = 5$$

Fluorescent bulb
$$\% \text{ efficiency} = \frac{\text{useful energy}}{\text{total energy}} \times 100$$
$$= \frac{5}{20} \times 100 = 25$$

The fluorescent bulb is five times more efficient than the filament bulb.

> ### SUMMARY
> 1. Many houses lose a lot of heat energy. This can be reduced in many ways.
> 2. Energy is said to be wasted if it is transferred in a way which isn't useful to us.
> 3. The efficiency of a device is the fraction of the supplied energy which is usefully transferred.
> 4. Energy which is transferred ends up as heat energy.

> ### QUESTIONS
> 1. Explain three ways in which a caravan could be insulated so that it wastes less heat energy when it is used in winter.
> 2. Two ovens X and Y each use 6000 J of energy. X wastes 4000 J and B wastes 2000 J.
>   a. Calculate the percentage efficiency of each oven.
>   b. Which of the two ovens do you think is a microwave and which is a conventional oven?
> 3. Explain how energy is wasted when a metal pan is used on a cooker ring.

35 Energy sources and power stations

We need energy for transport and heating as well as for generating electricity. There are two types of energy sources:

Non-renewable

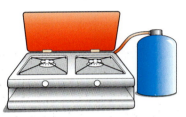

- fossil fuels, coal, gas, oil
- nuclear fuels

Renewable

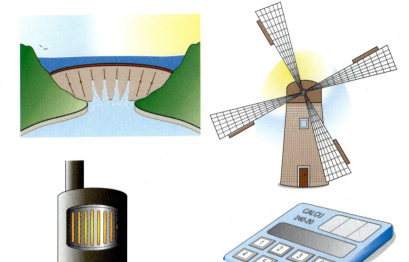

- wind, waves, tides, rivers, hot rocks, the Sun
- biomass fuels such as wood, straw, quick-growing crops, sewage, rubbish

Where does our energy come from?

At present, in the UK about 90% of the total energy we use comes from **fossil fuels**. A large amount of fossil fuel is burnt in power stations to produce electricity. However, supplies of fossil fuels are limited. The use of renewable energy sources is increasing and being encouraged by the Energy Act of 1989. This requires electricity suppliers to obtain a certain amount of their electricity from renewable sources of energy.

Burning fuels

Fossil fuels and biomass fuels are stores of chemical energy. This is changed into heat energy when the fuel is burnt. Fast growing trees such as willows and poplars are planted to provide **biomass fuels**. They grow quickly and after five years are large enough to be cut down and burnt. In England, some power stations have been built to burn rubbish and old car tyres.

Sewage and other organic matter is broken down by bacteria and produces gas which can be refined and burnt as a fuel for cooking and heating.

Sugar is fermented to produce ethanol. This is mixed with petrol to form a fuel called 'gasohol' for use in cars. Some cars with modified engines can run on pure alcohol.

Pollution from fuels

All fuels produce waste gases when they are burnt. Many of these are pollutants and all of them produce carbon dioxide which contributes to global warming. Catalytic converters are used to reduce pollutants in car exhausts. Other methods are used to clean waste gases from power stations.

Power stations

All power stations for generating electricity have a turbine and a generator. The turbine is turned by the high pressure flow of a gas (air from wind, combustion gases, steam) or water (from rivers, reservoirs or the sea) past its blades. The turbines turn the generator to produce electricity.

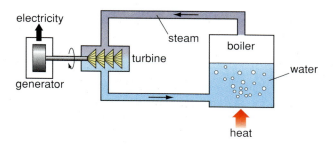

Most of the electricity in the UK is generated using steam-driven turbines. The steam is obtained from:
- burning fossil fuels or biomass, such as rubbish, straw
- nuclear reactions in a nuclear reactor.

The amounts of electricity obtained by each method in the mid-1990s are shown below. As you can see, as yet very little electricity is obtained from renewable sources.

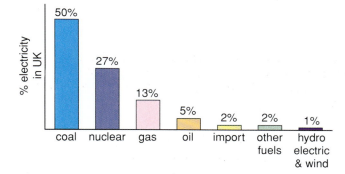

Burning fossil fuels

When we burn fossil fuels various combustion products are formed which can pollute the atmosphere. The amounts produced depend on the fuels used. The main pollutants are:
- dust particles, removed by electrostatic precipitation
- sulphur dioxide and nitrogen oxides causing acid rain – can be removed by passing the gases through a mixture of crushed limestone in water, but this is expensive
- carbon dioxide, a 'greenhouse gas' contributing to global warming.

Nuclear power stations

The fuel for nuclear power stations is uranium or plutonium. This undergoes radioactive decay and gives out heat to produce steam. The reactions are carefully controlled. Although nuclear power stations produce no waste gases they have several disadvantages:
- they are expensive to build and dismantle
- the radioactive fuels and waste must be transported and stored safely. Storage can be difficult and expensive
- any nuclear accidents can be very serious and contaminate large areas of land and affect the health of many people.

When the nuclear reactor at Chernobyl in the former Soviet Union blew up, soil and sheep in Wales and the Lake District were contaminated.

Cooling the steam

Power stations using steam-driven turbines need ways of cooling the used steam to condense it. If river water is used, the cold water taken in is returned at a higher temperature causing thermal pollution. If river water is not used then huge cooling towers are built to cool the steam.

Whether we like it or not there are always environmental costs when we use energy.

Summary

1. There are renewable and non-renewable energy sources.
2. Power stations use mainly fossil fuels or nuclear fuels.
3. The use of renewable energy sources is increasing.

Questions

1. Explain what happens in the furnace, boiler, turbine and generator in a power station.
2. Name the type of energy
   a. stored in nuclear fuels
   b. stored in natural gas
   c. generated in a power station
   d. wasted in a power station.
3. What is meant by the term renewable energy source? Give three examples. Why is it important to develop power stations using these renewable sources?

36 Power from renewable energy sources

Water

Hydroelectric power stations use the flow of water from a higher level to a lower level, rather than steam, to turn the turbines. The kinetic and potential energy of the water is transferred into electrical energy. Water from rivers is usually stored in a reservoir behind a dam and the power station is built in the dam.

Some hydroelectric power stations are used to store energy, for example, the station at Dinorwig in North Wales. It is expensive to switch steam-driven power stations on and off, so sometimes more power is supplied to the National Grid than is needed. To store the power, some of the excess electricity is used to pump water back up into the reservoir. The water gains potential energy which can be converted back into electricity using the hydroelectric power station when it is needed.

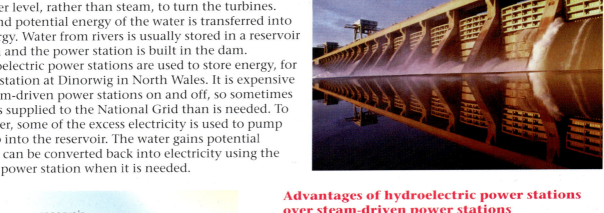

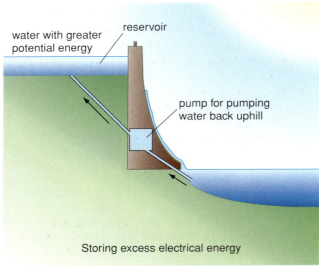

Storing excess electrical energy

Advantages of hydroelectric power stations over steam-driven power stations

- very efficient as very little energy is wasted as heat
- use renewable energy source
- no polluting gases produced
- can be switched on and off easily (usually within a few minutes)
- can be used to store energy.

Disadvantages

- usually have to be built in hilly areas with reliably high rainfall
- reservoirs cause flooding of large areas of land which are often of great natural beauty
- the local climate, plant and animal life can be affected.

Tidal power stations work in a similar way to hydroelectric power stations. A barrage is built across the mouth of a river where there is a large difference between high and low tides, for instance, the river Rance in northern France. When the tide comes in, the reservoir behind the barrage is filled with water. As the tide goes out, the stored water is used to turn the turbines to generate electricity. As yet there are no tidal power stations in the UK.

Advantages of tidal power stations

- efficient
- use renewable energy source
- no polluting gases.

Disadvantages

- affects shipping and has an environmental impact on plants and animals
- expensive to construct
- since high tides occur every 12 hours 25 minutes the time at which the station can generate electricity varies on a daily basis.

Wave power generators are planned to use the movement of the waves to drive turbines. They are still in the early stages of development.

THE SUN

Using heat energy directly

It is easy to burn a hole in paper by concentrating the rays of the Sun on a small area. This heating effect is used on a large scale in places where there is a lot of sunlight, such as southern Europe. The Sun's energy is focused on a furnace by thousands of computer-controlled mirrors which move as the Sun moves. The steam produced drives turbines to generate electricity. This method is not very suitable in the UK for generating electricity as the amount of Sun we have is not usually sufficient.

Solar cells

Many calculators are powered by **solar cells**. When light falls on the cells, the Sun's energy is converted directly into electrical energy. This is convenient for low-power devices. But solar cells are only about 15% efficient and are expensive. They are used in hot countries for generating small amounts of electricity and are used to power equipment in satellites.

Solar heating

Solar panels are used to heat domestic water supplies.

HOT SPRINGS AND UNDERGROUND ROCKS

In some places, such as Iceland, there are hot rocks just under the surface of the ground, and hot lakes and springs. This geothermal energy is used to generate electricity and to heat buildings. At present **geothermal energy** is not used in this country although hot granite rocks exist just a few kilometres below the surface in Cornwall. They are heated by radioactive decay.

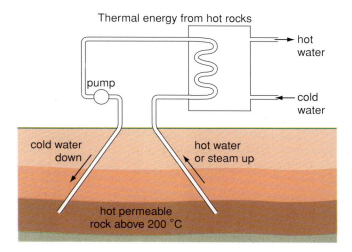

WIND

Modern windmills use the kinetic energy of the wind to turn turbines and generate electricity. Many wind generators grouped together are called a **wind farm**.

Advantages

- no polluting waste gases
- use renewable energy source.

Disadvantages

- each windmill generates only about 1 MW of electricity compared with a coal-fired station which produces up to 2000 MW
- each wind farm has 20 to 30 wind turbines and so large areas of land are needed – some people think they spoil the landscape
- the windmills can affect local TV reception and can be noisy
- the amount of wind is unpredictable.

> ### SUMMARY
> 1. Energy from the sea, rivers, wind, Sun and underground rocks can be used to generate electricity. All these sources of energy are renewable.

QUESTIONS

1. For each of the energy sources give the type of energy which can be transferred into electrical energy
   - a Wind
   - b Hydroelectric
   - c Tidal
   - d the Sun
   - e hot rocks.
2. Give three reasons why solar cells are not used to produce much electricity in the UK. In what situations are they useful?
3. Explain why there might be problems if the supply of electricity in the UK depended mainly on wind farms.
4. Suggest one main advantage of hydroelectric power stations.

37 Radioactivity

What is radioactivity?

Some materials release energy as invisible radiation. We call them radioactive materials. In 1896 the French scientist Henri Becquerel was amazed when he left a substance called uranium in a dark drawer. He left the uranium on top of a photographic plate, with paper in between. When he took the photographic plate out of the drawer, it had turned black even though there was no light near it. The only explanation was that the uranium produced invisible rays which affected the plate.

Radioactivity is natural

Radiation is produced by many things around us. Some gases in the air are radioactive: substances found in rocks, such as uranium and radium are also radioactive. Other rocks such as granite produce a little radioactivity. Sometimes these rocks are used for buildings. Some of the natural radioactivity around us is absorbed by the plants and animals we eventually eat. Radiation from space also bombards the Earth. All in all, we are exposed to small amounts of radiation every day. Scientists can measure this radiation. For most people the exposure is about 3 millisieverts (radioactivity units) per year.

Is radioactivity a risk to our health?

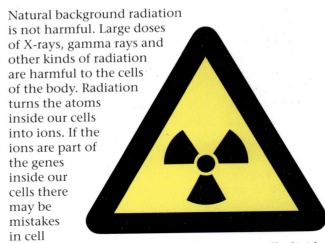

Natural background radiation is not harmful. Large doses of X-rays, gamma rays and other kinds of radiation are harmful to the cells of the body. Radiation turns the atoms inside our cells into ions. If the ions are part of the genes inside our cells there may be mistakes in cell division. This may cause mutations. Some cells divide without stopping, forming a cancer. Other cells die. The effects are more severe if the dose of radiation is larger. For example, the larger the dose of radiation, the greater the risk of cancer.

Workers in hospitals and their patients wear protection to avoid the risks of exposure to radiation.

Unnatural radiation

We are all exposed to this natural or **background radiation**. Some people are exposed to more radiation than others. If you have an X-ray, you will be exposed to about 0.02 millisieverts.

When there was an accident at the nuclear power station in Chernobyl in 1986, radioactive materials were released into the atmosphere. Radioactive materials were also released when nuclear weapons were dropped on Japan in 1945. Radioactivity is released when nuclear weapons are tested. Some of this radioactivity is still in our surroundings. We call it **fallout**. Fallout adds about 0.02 millisieverts to our yearly exposure.

Some people work with radioactivity. During their normal jobs radiographers and nuclear power industry workers may be exposed to between one and two extra millisieverts per year.

THREE TYPES OF RADIOACTIVITY

There are three kinds of radioactivity given out (emitted) by radioactive materials. They are named after Greek letters.

- Alpha radiation (α) is a stream of particles from the radioactive substance. The particles are actually helium nuclei (two protons and two neutrons). When the stream hits nearby atoms, it turns them into ions by knocking off their electrons. This is why it is called *ionising* **radiation**. Alpha radiation does not pass far into other substances.
- Beta radiation (β) is also a stream of particles. The particles are electrons, so beta radiation has different properties from alpha. It is less ionising than alpha radiation. Beta radiation can pass through paper.
- Gamma radiation (γ) is a type of electromagnetic radiation. It travels long distances and can pass through certain metals, but not lead or thick concrete.

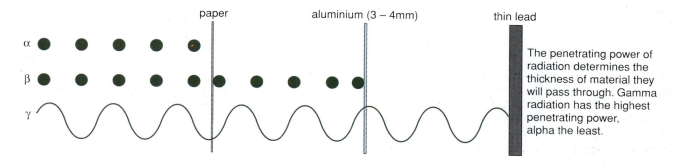

The penetrating power of radiation determines the thickness of material they will pass through. Gamma radiation has the highest penetrating power, alpha the least.

HOW RADIOACTIVITY IS USED

Radiation is useful for measuring the thickness of materials such as metals. A radiation detector called a Geiger–Müller tube is used. The tube is connected to a counter which counts the radiation. The thicker the sample material, the more radiation will be absorbed. A thin material gives a high radiation count and a thick material gives a low count.

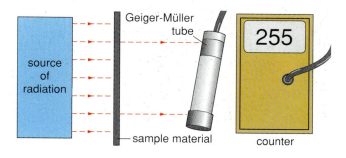

Doctors use radiation to see inside the human body. For example to see the gut, the patient drinks a liquid containing a small amount of gamma radiation. The X-ray detects where the radiation is inside the patient.

A smoke alarm is another use for radioactivity. A source of alpha radiation is used with a detector. Alpha particles have low penetrating power, but they can travel across the inside of the alarm to the detector. The alarm is off. If smoke gets inside the alarm, it stops the particles reaching the detector and the alarm switches on.

Did you know? Traces of radioactive materials were found in British sheep ten years after the Chernobyl accident.

SUMMARY

1. Radioactive substances give out radiation all the time.
2. There are three types of radiation emitted by radioactive materials
   - alpha particles
   - beta particles
   - gamma radiation.
3. We are all exposed to background radiation.
4. Radiation ionises atoms. If the atoms are inside living cells, it can cause damage, including cancer.

QUESTIONS

1. Where does background radiation come from?
2. What is fallout?
3. Make a table to summarise the properties of the three types of radiation.
4. Why is exposure to radiation a health risk?
5. Describe three uses of radioactive materials.

38 Radioactive isotopes

Atoms and isotopes

The atoms of all elements have a nucleus with electrons around the outside of it. The nucleus of each atom is made of protons and neutrons. The protons are an important part of an atom. Protons give an element its chemical properties. They have mass. They also have a positive charge which balances the negative charge of the electrons. When the negative and positive charges balance, the atom is neutral. Neutrons are inside the nucleus, but don't have any charge. They have the same mass as protons. They help hold the nucleus together.

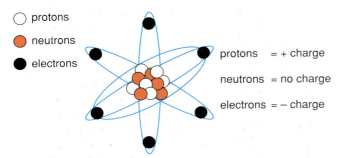

Isotopes

Some elements have isotopes. Isotopes are different forms of the same element. Atoms of the isotope have the same number of protons, but a different number of neutrons from other atoms of the element. We can tell a lot about isotopes by looking at their atomic mass numbers. This number is the number of protons added to the number of neutrons in the nucleus of the atom.

Take carbon as an example. It has six protons and six electrons. The protons give carbon its chemical properties. Three isotopes of carbon exist. Each isotope has the same number of protons, but a different number of neutrons. They have similar chemical properties because of the six protons, but behave in a slightly different way.

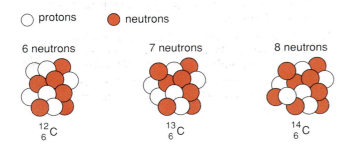

Radioactive decay

Many isotopes are stable. They do not produce radiation. An example is carbon-12. Other isotopes are unstable because they have too many neutrons. When an atom is unstable the nucleus is likely to split up or decay. We call it **radioactive decay**. The nucleus splits and energy is released as radiation. An example is carbon-14. It emits beta radiation when the nucleus splits and a neutron changes into a proton. The atom now has seven protons and seven neutrons. It is now nitrogen-14, which is stable. Carbon-14 takes a long time to decay.

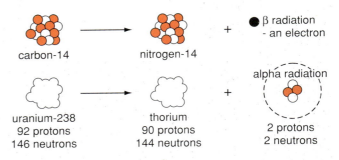

Nuclear fuel

Nuclear power stations like the one in the photograph can make enough power to supply a city. In the power station the heat from radioactive uranium is used to make steam. The steam turns turbines which make electricity.

Uranium is found in rocks. It contains two isotopes, uranium-238, and uranium-235 which is used in power stations. The atoms of this isotope can split up very quickly, releasing energy. When they split, we call it **spontaneous fission**. The atoms split into two, releasing two neutrons. The neutrons shoot quickly out of the nucleus and hit other atoms of uranium-235. This makes the other atoms split and they release energy and neutrons. A **chain reaction** has started. As the atoms split, the bits bump into other atoms making them move faster. The energy in the nucleus is being changed into heat energy which is used to make steam.

CARBON DATING

Scientists were amazed to find a human fossil skull in the rocks of the East African Rift Valley. They knew the rocks were old, but how could they put a date on the skull? The answer was found by using **carbon dating**. When the ancient human died, most of the carbon in his food was the stable C^{12}. Some was unstable C^{14}. As time goes by C^{14} decays. Half of the C^{14} disappears every 5770 years. The amount of C^{14} left in the fossil tells the scientist how old the fossil is.

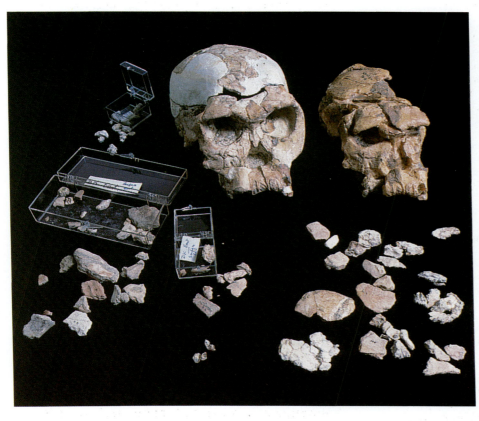

Half lives

Carbon-14 can be used to date rock because we know its half-life is 5770 years. A half-life is how long it takes for the number of atoms in a sample of a radioactive substance to fall to a half.

If we started with 40 carbon-14 atoms, 5770 years later we would be left with 20, then 5770 years later, 10 and so on. Radioactive substances have different half-lives; strontium-90 is 28 years and radon-222 is 4 days.

Knowledge of half-lives helps us to use radioactivity safely. Radioactive substances used in medicine have short half-lives to reduce the risk of damage to healthy cells by radioactivity.

Nuclear power stations produce radioactive waste containing strontium-90 and plutonium-239. They are both very dangerous to human cells. Strontium-90 has a half-life of 28 years, so the waste should be safe after three or four half-lives. Plutonium-239 will have to be stored for a long time before it is safe, its half-life is 24360 years.

SUMMARY

1. Atoms of the same element which have different numbers of neutrons are called isotopes.
2. Radioactive isotopes are atoms with unstable nuclei.
3. When an unstable atom decays (splits up), it emits radiation.
4. When α or β radiation is given off atoms of a different element are formed.
5. The older a radioactive material, the less radiation it emits. We can date materials using this knowledge.
6. The half-life of a radioactive substance is the time taken for half of the atoms to decay.

QUESTIONS

1. What is the difference between the three isotopes of carbon?
2. Explain how atoms of nitrogen are formed from atoms of carbon.
3. The half-life of radioactive iodine-131 is 8 days. Starting with 1000 atoms, how long will it take to reach a safe number of less than 100 atoms?
4. The older a radioactive material is, the less radiation it emits. How can we use this idea to date rocks?

Practice questions – Physical Processes

1. The following is a list of electrical components: voltmeter, ammeter, switch, cell, diode, variable resistor.
   a. Give the circuit symbol for each of the components.
   b. In each case give the component from the list which:
      i. measures the size of a current
      ii. breaks a circuit
      iii. produces a voltage
      iv. is used to alter the current in a circuit.

2. a. When a plastic pen is rubbed with a woollen cloth electrons are transferred from the pen to the cloth and both become charged.
      i. What is the charge on an electron?
      ii. Name the force which caused the pen and cloth to become charged.
      iii. What type of electricity was produced?
      iv. What is the charge on the pen?
   b. A polythene strip was rubbed with the woollen cloth and was attracted to the pen when it was held near to it.
      i. Why was the polythene strip attracted to the pen?
      ii. What is the charge on the polythene strip?

3. A radio runs on mains electricity in the UK and takes a current of 3 amps. Select the correct number from the list to complete the following statements.
   3, 5, 50, 230, 690
   a. The voltage of mains electricity is .... volts.
   b. The frequency of mains electricity is .... hertz.
   c. The power of the radio is .... watts.
   d. The fuse fitted in the plug should be .... amps.

4. Part of an electricity bill is shown below.

Meter reading		Units used
present	previous	
3100	900	
Cost per unit of electricity = 7p		

   a. What is the number of units used?
   b. What is the total cost of the electricity used?

   You use electricity for heating water and heating your flat. A friend suggests that it would be cheaper to use 'off-peak' electricity.
   c. What is meant by 'off-peak' electricity?
   d. Name and briefly describe the type of fires which are designed to use 'off peak' electricity.

   Your flat is in the top floor of a house.
   e. Give three ways in which heat energy is transferred from your flat to the surroundings.
   f. Give four ways of reducing the transfer of heat energy from your flat to the surroundings.

5. a. The diagram shows the inside of a 3-pin plug. Match the words from the list to each of the labels on the diagram.

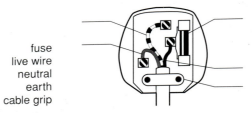

   fuse
   live wire
   neutral
   earth
   cable grip

   An electrical appliance did not have an earth wire.
   b. Suggest an appliance which does not need an earth wire.
   c. Explain why an earth wire is not needed.

6. Look at the circuit diagram below which is used to find the resistance of a bulb.

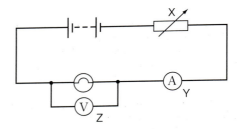

   a. Name the components X, Y and Z.
   b. If the voltage across the bulb is 4.0 V and the current through it is 2.0 A, calculate the resistance of the bulb.
   c. If the resistance of the bulb does not change what would be the current through it when the voltage is 12 V?

   The actual current through the bulb was found to be less than expected when the voltage across the bulb was 12 V.
   d. Explain what is happening at the higher voltage.

   A graph is plotted of the current through the bulb against the voltage across it as the voltage is altered.

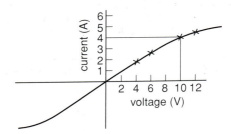

   e. How is the voltage across the bulb varied?
   f. Use the graph to find the current through the bulb when the voltage is 10 V.
   g. What is the power of the bulb when the voltage is 10 V?
   h. How many units of electricity are used if the bulb is left on for 2 hours 30 minutes using the power rating you calculated in g. (1 unit of electricity is 1 kilowatt hour.)

7 Electricity can be generated by different methods.
   a Explain how the energy in coal is transferred to the generators in coal-fired power stations.
   b Give two disadvantages of coal-fired power stations.
   c What drives the turbines in hydroelectric power stations?
   d Explain how hydroelectric power stations can be adapted to store electrical energy.

8 A coil of wire carrying an electric current is placed in a magnetic field as shown.

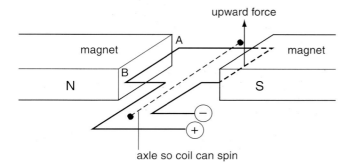

   a Draw the force which acts on the part AB of the coil.
   b What effect do the forces have on the coil?
   c What component is this idea used in?
   d What happens if more coils of wire are placed between the poles of the magnet?

9 a Many years ago scientists used the 'Earth-centred model' to describe our solar system.
      i   Describe this model.
      ii What model replaced the Earth-centred model?
   b The Earth orbits the Sun. Explain the following:
      i   night and day
      ii a year.
   c Although planets do not produce light, we can see them at night. Explain why.
   d Give the meaning of the following words:
      universe galaxy star Big Bang Theory

10 a A girl throws a javelin. Her friend measures the distance it travels and how long it takes before it lands. It travels 60 metres and lands 20 seconds after she throws it. What is the speed of the javelin?
   b A world-class sprinter is training. His coach times him as he runs 100 m. Use the figures in the table to plot a distance–time graph for the sprinter.

Time (s)	Distance (m)
1	10
2	20
3	30
4	40
5	50
6	60
7	70
8	80
9	90
10	100

11 The diagram shows the real depth of a fish under the water and (A) the apparent depth of the same fish as seen by the person shown. Copy the diagram and explain why this happens by using ray diagrams.

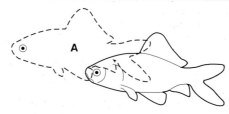

12 The diagram shows an oscilloscope trace of a wave. Use the diagram to explain the following words:
   wavelength amplitude
   frequency

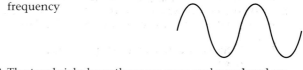

13 The two bricks have the same mass and are placed on wet sand. One brick is put on its side and one on its end.
   a Which brick sinks into the sand more quickly? Explain why.
   b Calculate the pressure exerted on the floor by a box with an area of 0.5 m² and a weight of 1000 N.
   c The apparatus in the diagram is filled with water. Explain why water coming from each tube travels a different distance.

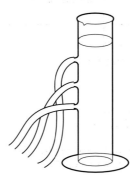

14 The smoke alarm in the diagram uses a small radioactive source. Explain how it works.

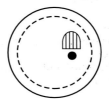

Smoke alarm

Answers to practice questions

Answers to the questions on pp.244–245

1. **a** see p. 209
   b i ammeter
   ii switch
   iii cell
   iv variable resistor

2. **a** i negative
   ii friction
   iii static
   iv positive
   b i Electrons transferred to polythene strip from cloth. Strip has opposite charge to pen.
   ii negative

3. **a** 230
   b 50
   c 690
   d 5

4. **a** 2,200 units
   b £154
   c electricity supplied outside peak hours - overnight
   d storage heater - stores heat overnight. This is insulated and gives out heat during the day.
   e convection, conduction, radiation
   f double glazing, loft insulation, draught excluder, insulation in cavity walls, carpets.

5. **a**

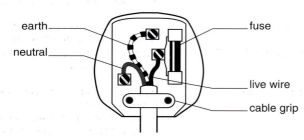

   b Anything with a plastic case (such as a plastic kettle) or a case which has double insulation.
   c The live wire cannot touch the outside case.

6. **a** X - variable resistor
   Y - ammeter
   Z - voltmeter
   b $R = \frac{V}{I} = \frac{4}{2} = 2\Omega$
   c $I = \frac{V}{R} = \frac{12}{2} = 6A$
   d Resistance is increasing.
   e Using a variable resistor.
   f 4A
   g W = Amps v Volts = 4 x 10 = 40W
   h 0.1 units

7. **a** Coal burns, heat is produced and turns water to steam. Steam drives the turbine which turns magnets in the generators.
   b They are polluting and expensive.
   c falling water
   d Water can be pumped back up to reservoir at off-peak timer.

8. **a** downward force on AB
   b turning effect on coil
   c electric motor
   d stronger turning effect - more powerful motor

9. **a** i The planets orbit the Earth.
   ii The planets (including the Earth) orbit the Sun.
   b i Earth makes one rotation on its axis every 24 hrs. The part of the Earth facing the Sun has day and that facing away from the Sun has night.
   ii The time taken for the Earth to orbit the Sun which is 365 days.
   c They reflect light from the Sun.
   d Universe: everything that exists including the particles, objects and energy.
   Galaxy: a large group of stars separated from other groups.
   Star: a huge ball of glowing gases which gives off light and heat.
   Big Bang: the theory that the universe started as a small very dense ball that exploded.

10. **a** $S = \frac{D}{t} = \frac{60}{20} = 30$ m/s
    b a suitable graph

11.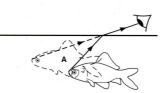

12. wavelength: the distance from one crest of a wave to the next
    amplitude: the height of a wave
    frequency: the number of waves produced in one second.

13. **a** A - greater pressure
    b Pressure $= \frac{F}{A} = \frac{1000}{0.5} = 2000$ Pa
    c Pressure increases with depth

14. Radioactive source gives out radiation. This is received by the detector. Smoke particles stop radiation hitting the detector and the buzzer circuit is switched on.

Glossary

A

acceleration	Speeding up and going faster.
acid	A solution with a pH value of less than 7. Acids turn litmus paper red.
acid rain	Rain containing dissolved gases such as sulphur dioxide.
activation energy	The minimum energy which has to be supplied to the reactants before they can react together.
adapt	When a species changes over time to suit particular conditions.
addicted	When the body relies so much on a drug that to do without would cause illness.
adrenal gland	Gland just above the kidney, which secretes the hormone adrenaline.
adrenaline	Hormone secreted when a person is frightened or excited, to help the body react quickly in emergencies.
aerobic respiration	Getting energy from food using oxygen.
afterbirth	The placenta which is born after the baby.
air resistance	A force due to the air which pushes against something as it moves through the air.
alimentary canal	Long tube which carries food through the body. It is where food is digested and absorbed.
alkali	A solution with a pH value of greater than 7. Alkalis turn litmus paper blue.
alkaline metals	The reactive metals found in group 1 of the Periodic Table
alkanes	A group of hydrocarbons with the same general formula. The name of each member ends in 'ane' and the first member of the group is methane
allele	Different form of the same gene
alloys	A mixture of metals and sometimes carbon such as bronze, steel.
alpha radiation	A stream of helium nuclei released by some radioactive substances.
alternating current (a.c)	An electric current which flows backwards and forwards along a wire.
alveoli	Tiny sacs in the lungs where gases diffuse in and out of the blood
ammeter	The meter used to measure the size of an electric current.
amniotic sac	A bag of tissue which surrounds a developing foetus.
amperes (amps A)	The unit of electric current
amplitude	The height of a wave from the middle to the top.
anaerobic respiration	Getting energy from food without using oxygen.
antibodies	A type of protein produced by white blood cells which binds with and de-activates antigens on bacteria and viruses.
aorta	A large artery distributing oxygenated blood from the left ventricle of the heart.
aqueous solution	A solution of a substance in water.
artery	A blood vessel carrying blood away from the heart.
artificial satellite	A man-made satellite orbiting the Earth.
artificial selection	Changing a species by breeding.
asexual reproduction	When animals and plants reproduce without fertilisation.
atom	The smallest part of an element which cannot be split up by chemical means.
atomic number	The number of protons found in the nucleus of the atom. It is also the number of electrons in the atom.
atrium	One of the top two chambers in the heart.
auxin	A plant hormone.

B

background radiation	The natural radiation produced by our surroundings and arriving from space.
bacteria	Very small living things which have a cell wall and cytoplasm.
balanced diet	A diet containing all the essential nutrients in the correct proportions.
balanced forces	When forces act on an object and it does not move.
battery	A source of electrical power usually made of two or more cells joined together.
beta radiation	A stream of electrons released by radioactive substances.
Big Bang Theory	An explanation of how the universe formed from a large explosion.
bile	The food substances a living thing needs to keep healthy.
biodegradable	A substance which decays naturally.
biomass fuel	Recently grown trees and plants which are used as fuels.
boiling point	The temperature at which a liquid changes to a gas.
brittle	A substance which is hard but breaks easily such as glass, ceramics.
bronchitis	A disease of the tubes leading to the lungs.

C

capillary	A blood vessel connecting arteries to veins which has a thin wall to allow diffusion of substances to and from the blood.
carbohydrase	A carbohydrate digesting enzyme.
carbohydrate	A substance made by plants containing carbon, hydrogen and oxygen.
carbon dating	Using the amount of radioactive carbon in a rock or fossil to work out its age.
carbon dioxide	A gas produced in aerobic respiration.
cast iron	A brittle impure form of iron obtained from the blast furnace.
catalysis	A chemical reaction that is speeded up by the use of a catalyst.
catalyst	A substance which speeds up a chemical reaction but is not used up.
catalytic decomposition	The breakdown of a compound by the action of a catalyst.
cell	A source of electrical power.
cement	A substance used in mortar and concrete made from heating powdered limestone and clay together.
ceramics	Hard solids made by heating clay, sand and other minerals such as china, bricks, concrete.
CFC gas	Gas used in aerosols and refrigerators which destroys the ozone layer.
chain reaction	When a neutron causes nuclear fission which produces another neutron which causes fission and so on.
characteristics	The features of a living thing controlled by genes.
chemical change	A change in which one or more new substances are formed and which is not easily reversed.
chemical energy	The energy stored in substances and released during chemical reactions.
chlorophyll	The green pigment in plants which absorbs sunlight energy in photosynthesis.
chloroplast	Structure inside a plant cell which contains chlorophyll.
chromatography	The separation of different solutes in a solution based on the different rates at which they move through filter paper.
chromosome	A strand of DNA which can be seen when a cell divides.
cilia	Small hair-like structures on the cells lining the windpipe.
circuit breaker	An electrical component which switches off the current when it is too large.
circuit diagram	A diagram using symbols to show how the components in a circuit are connected together.
cirrhosis	A disease of the liver which can be caused by too much alcohol.
clone	An individual produced by asexual reproduction.
cochlea	A structure in the ear containing sound sensing cells.
colloid	A colloid contains tiny gas, liquid or solid particles spread out in a liquid, solid or gas. They do not settle when the colloid is left to stand.
combustion	A chemical reaction in which a substance burns and joins with oxygen to form an oxide and gives out heat.
comet	A mass of frozen gas and dust which orbits the Sun.
community	A group of different animal and plant species which rely on each other and their surroundings.
composite materials	Materials made from two or more materials such as fibre glass.
compound	A pure substance containing molecules made up of atoms of two or more elements chemically joined together.
concentrated solution	A solution containing a large amount of solute dissolved in a small amount of solvent.
concrete	A cheap, strong building material made from mixing sand, cement, gravel and water together.
condensation or liquefication	The process in which a gas changes to a liquid as it cools.
conduction	The transfer of thermal energy without the substance moving: main method of heat transfer in a solid.
conductor (electrical)	A substance which allows an electric current to pass easily through it; for example, metals, graphite.
conductor (thermal)	A substance which allows heat to easily pass through it.
constellation	A pattern of stars seen in the sky at night.
continuous	When a variation shows a range.
contraction	The process in which a substance gets smaller, usually as it is cooled.
convection	Transfer of heat energy in gases and liquids by convection currents.
corrosion	A chemical reaction in which a metal reacts with air and or water to form a compound.
corrosive	Chemicals that react with other materials and destroy them.
covalent bond	The bond formed between atoms when they share one or more pairs of electrons.
covalent compound	The type of compound formed when atoms of non-metals join together by sharing electrons.
cracking	A chemical reaction in which larger molecules from the heavier fractions from crude oil are broken down into smaller molecules.

cracking	A chemical reaction in which larger molecules from the heavier fractions from crude oil are broken down into smaller molecules.	dissolving	The process in which a substance (the solute) disappears into a liquid (the solvent) to make a solution.
crude oil	A mixture of liquid hydrocarbons with different boiling points formed from the decay of dead plants and animals.	distance/time graph	A graph used to represent the distance something has travelled over a period of time.
crust	The outer surface of the Earth.	distillate	The liquid obtained when the vapour given off during distillation is cooled and condenses.
crystallisation	The process in which crystals of solute form from a solution as the solvent evaporates.	distillation	The separation of miscible liquids with different boiling points or the removal of a solvent from a solution by boiling the mixture and cooling the vapour formed.
crystals	A solid with a regular shape and plane faces which intersect at definite angles, such as salt, quartz, diamonds.		
current	A flow of electric charge around a circuit.	DNA	Deoxyribose Nucleic Acid, from which chromosomes and genes are made.
cystic fibrosis	An inherited disease in which the tubes in the lungs and digestive system become clogged up with mucus.	dominant allele	We always see the effect of the dominant allele of a pair of alleles.
		Down's Syndrome	The symptoms produced when a person inherits an extra chromosome (number 21).
cytoplasm	Part of the cell where chemical reactions happen.	drag	A force caused by the resistance due to air or a liquid.
		ductile	The ease with which a solid can be drawn into wires.

D

decibel (db)	The unit for measuring how loud a sound is.	dynamo	A device which transfers kinetic energy into electrical energy. A current is produced in a coil of wire as a magnet spins inside it.
decomposition	The process in which a chemical compound is broken down.		
degrees Celsius (°C)	The scale for measuring temperature. Water boils at 100°C and ice melts at 0°C.		

E

deviated	Bent.	earthquake	A shock wave in the Earth's crust often caused when plates collide together.
diabetes	A disease caused by lack of insulin. If not treated, the sufferer will have high blood sugar which can affect the brain and cause a coma or death.	echo	What we hear when waves (usually sound) reflect off a hard surface.
		echo location	When echoes are used to find the position of an object.
dialysis	A process by which blood is filtered through a machine to remove waste.	efficiency	How well something transfers energy. The fraction of energy which ends up where it is wanted.
diaphragm	A large dome-shaped sheet of muscle that forms the bottom of the chest cavity.	elastic	When an object returns to its original shape after a force is applied.
diffusion	The movement of particles from a region of high concentration to a region of low concentration.	electric bell	A bell which rings when an electric current flows through it.
digestion	Breaking down insoluble food molecules into soluble ones so they can be absorbed.	electric motor	A device which transfers electrical energy into kinetic energy. It has a coil of wire in a magnetic field which turns when a current flows through it.
dilute solution	A solution containing a small amount of solute dissolved in a large volume of solvent.		
diode	An electrical component which allows the flow of current in one direction only.	electrical energy	Energy carried by an electric current.
direct current (d.c.)	An electric current which flows in one direction from the positive terminal to the negative terminal of a cell. The electrons flow in the opposite direction.	electrode	The conductor (a metal or graphite) which passes electricity into an electrolyte.
		electrolysis	A chemical reaction caused by the passage of an electric current through an electrolyte (a molten ionic compound or solution of an ionic compound). During electrolysis, the electrolyte is decomposed or an electrode dissolves.
discontinuous	When a variation is either one thing or the other.		
displacement reaction	A chemical reaction in which one element pushes out another substance from its compound.		

electromagnetic induction	The process in which a current is produced in a wire when the magnetic field around the wire changes.
electromagnetic spectrum	The order of electromagnetic waves, from the shortest wavelengths to the longest.
electron	The smallest particle in the atom. It has a negligible mass and a negative charge. Electrons are found in particular energy levels or shells around the nucleus.
electronic structure (electronic configuration)	The way the electrons are arranged around the nucleus of the atom.
electrostatic force	The force between two charged objects.
element	Pure substances which cannot be split up into simpler substances. They contain atoms of only one type.
ecliptic	The plane on which the planets orbit the Sun.
ellipse	The path of planets around the Sun.
embryo	The name of a developing baby up until the ninth week.
emphysema	A disease of the lungs.
emulsification	The process whereby large drops of fat are broken into smaller particles.
emulsifying agent	A substance such as a detergent which is used in making an emulsion.
emulsion	The mixture of two immiscible liquids in which one liquid is present in the other as small droplets. The liquids do not separate into layers on standing.
endoscope	A device containing a very small camera and optical fibre which can be used to see inside things, such as pipes and the human body.
endothermic reaction	A reaction during which energy, usually heat energy, is taken in.
energy	Something that allows work to be done.
energy transferred	(j) = power (w) × time (s)
environment	The surroundings of animals and plants.
enzyme	A substance which speeds up a reaction in living things.
epidermis	The outer layer of the skin.
erosion	The wearing away of rocks and soil caused by things rubbing against them.
ethanol	The alcohol produced by fermentation.
eutrophication	The loss of dissolved oxygen in rivers and lakes. This is caused by the rapid growth and decay of algae due to excess fertilisers dissolved in the water.
evaporation	The process in which a liquid changes to a gas at a temperature below its boiling point.
evolution	When living things change as time goes by.
excretion	Getting rid of waste.
exothermic reaction	A reaction during which energy, usually heat energy, is given out.
expansion	The process in which a substance gets bigger, usually as it is heated.
extraction	The process of getting a pure substance from its raw material.

F

fallout	Radiation released into the atmosphere from using nuclear weapons.
fat	A substance found in the bodies of animals and plants containing carbon, hydrogen and oxygen which does not dissolve in water and is energy rich.
fermentation	A chemical reaction in which yeast acts on sugar solution to form ethanol and carbon dioxide.
fertiliser	Chemicals containing essential nutrients (including nitrogen, potassium and phosphorus) added to the soil to help plants grow well.
filtration	The separation of an insoluble solid from a liquid using a filter funnel and filter paper.
flammable	Substances which burn very easily.
flexibility	The degree to which a substance can be bent or twisted without breaking.
folding	The formation of mountains when layers of rocks are squeezed together.
force	A push or pull that changes the movement or the shape of things. Force is measured in newtons.
fossil	Found in sedimentary rocks from the hard parts of plants and animal remains which gradually turn into rock.
fossil fuel	A fuel formed from the decay of plant and animal remains which died millions of years ago, such as coal, oil, gas.
fractional distillation	The separation of mixtures of liquids such as the liquids in crude oil into different boiling point fractions. The process involves boiling the mixture and condensing the vapour given off at different parts of the fractionating column.
freezing or solidification	The process in which a liquid changes to a solid as it cools.
frequency	The number of waves produced in one second.
friction	A force caused by two substances rubbing together.
FSH	Follicle Stimulating Hormone.

fuse	A safety device in an electric circuit which 'blows' and breaks the circuit if the current is too large.

G

galaxy	Places in space where stars are attracted together. A galaxy is a group of stars.
gamete	A sex cell.
gamma rays	A type of electromagnetic radiation which can pass through metals such as aluminium.
gas	A substance which fills the space it is in. Its particles are far apart and move quickly from place to place.
Geiger–Müller tube	A device used to detect radioactivity.
gene	Part of a chromosome which controls a characteristic.
generator	A device which transfers kinetic energy into electrical energy. A current is produced in a coil of wire as it spins in a magnetic field.
genome	All the genes a particular living thing has.
geostationary satellite	A satellite orbiting the Earth above the equator which makes one complete orbit every 24 hours.
geothermal energy	Energy from hot underground rocks.
geotropism	The response of plants to gravity.
glass	Transparent materials made by heating a mixture of sand, limestone and other minerals.
global warming	The increased temperature of the Earth caused by the greenhouse effect.
glucose	Simple sugar.
glugagon	A hormone produced by the pancreas which helps the liver release glucose into the blood.
gravitational potential energy	The energy stored by something which is above ground level.
gravity	The force between any two objects due to their mass.
greenhouse effect	The effect on the Earth of a thick layer of atmospheric carbon dioxide.
group	A vertical column of elements in the Periodic Table. The elements in the same group have similar chemical properties.
guard cells	Cells which control the opening and closing of the stomatal pore.

H

habitat	The place where animals or plants live.
haemoglobin	The red substance inside red blood cells which carries oxygen.
halogens	The reactive non-metals found in group 7 of the Periodic Table.
heat energy or thermal energy	The energy transferred from something which is hot to something which is cooler.
hertz (Hz)	The unit for measuring frequency. One hertz is one cycle per second.
homeostasis	Keeping a constant internal environment.
hormone	A chemical produced by a gland which as an effect on parts of the body.
Huntington's chorea	An inherited disorder of the brain.
hydraulics	Liquid machines which send a force to where it is needed.
hydrocarbon	A compound containing hydrogen and carbon only, such as methane, petrol, paraffin wax.
hydroelectric power station	A power station where electricity is generated by moving water turning the turbines.

I

igneous rock	Rock formed when hot liquid rock cools and crystallises.
immiscible liquids	Liquids which do not mix.
immune response	When the body makes antibodies to fight off infection.
impulse	An electrical message carried by a nerve cell.
In vitro fertilisation	A technique used to treat infertility when sperm and eggs are fertilised outside the body in glass dishes.
incident ray	A ray of light striking a mirror.
indicator	A substance which changes colour when added to an acidic, alkaline or neutral solution.
inelastic	When an object does not return to its original shape after a force is applied then removed.
insoluble	Does not dissolve.
insoluble substance	A substance which will not dissolve in a particular solvent.
insulator (electrical)	A substance which does not let an electric current pass easily through it, such as plastics.
insulator (thermal)	A substance which does not let heat energy pass easily through it, such as plastics.
insulin	A hormone produced by the pancreas which helps the liver to remove glucose from the blood for storage.
ion	An atom or group of atoms with either one or more positive or negative charges.
ionic bond	Forces between the oppositely-charged ions in ionic compounds.
ionic compound	The type of compound formed when a metal combines with a non-metal. The metal donates one or more electrons to the non-metal. The metal forms a positive ion and the non-metal a negative ion.
isotope	A form of an element which has the same number of protons but a different number of neutrons.

J
joule (j) — Energy is measured in joules.

K
karyotype — When the chromosomes in a cell are arranged so we can see them.

kidney — The organ which controls water and mineral salt balance and gets rid of urea.

kinetic energy — The energy of a moving object.

L
labour — The name given to the contractions of the womb as a baby is being born.

laterally inverted — When the image in a mirror is swapped around – 'right' becomes 'left' and 'left' becomes 'right'.

lava — The hot liquid rock that comes out of a volcano.

LH — Lutenising hormone.

light energy — Energy carried by light waves.

light year — How far light travels in a year.

line of force — The line along which a force acts.

lipase — A fat digesting enzyme.

liquid — A substance which is runny and can be poured from one container to another. Its particles are close together and move from place to place.

litmus — An indicator which changes blue in alkalis and red in acids.

longitudinal wave — An energy carrying wave in which the particles move parallel to the direction in which the wave travels.

loudspeaker — A device which transfers electrical energy into sound energy.

M
magma — Hot liquid rock from inside the Earth.

magnetic field — The region around a magnet where it attracts or repels another magnet.

malleability — The ease with which a solid can be hammered into thin sheets.

mantle — The part of the Earth made up of semi-liquid rocks found between the outer crust and inner core.

mass — This is how much material there is in something. Mass is measured in grams (g) or kilograms (kg).

mass number — The number of protons plus the number of neutrons in the nucleus of the atom.

meiosis — The type of cell division which results in sex cells.

melting point — The temperature at which a substance changes from a solid to a liquid.

membrane — The thin layer surrounding a cell which controls the substances entering and leaving the cell.

menstrual cycle — A woman's monthly cycle.

mesophyll cells — Photosynthetic cells in the leaf.

metamorphic rock — Formed inside the Earth by the recrystallisation of sedimentary rocks at high temperatures and pressures.

micro-organism — Small living things such as bacteria, viruses and fungi which can only be seen with a microscope.

Milky Way — The galaxy in which our Solar System is situated.

mineral — A naturally occurring material found in the Earth containing useful substances.

mineral salts — Essential elements required by living things.

miscible liquids — Liquids which mix.

mitosis — The type of cell division which results in cells with the same number of chromosomes.

mixture — Two or more elements and/or compounds not chemically joined together.

molecule — The smallest part of an element or compound containing two or more atoms joined together.

monoculture — When farmers grow just one crop in an area.

mutation — A change in a gene.

N
national grid — The system of transmission lines that carry electricity around the country.

natural selection — The theory that organisms evolve by becoming more adapted to their surroundings.

nebula — A cloud of dust and gas in space from which stars are formed.

net force — The sum of the forces acting on an object.

neurone — A nerve cell.

neutralisation — A chemical reaction in which an acid reacts with an akali to form a neutral solution.

neutron — A particle found in the nucleus of the atom. It has a relative mass of 1 unit and no charge.

newtons (N) — The unit of force.

nicotine — The drug in tobacco.

nitrogen dioxide — An oxide of nitrogen produced in car exhaust.

noble gases — The unreactive gases found in group 8 of the Periodic Table.

non-porous — A material which has no holes in it and is not able to soak up liquids.

normal — An imaginary line drawn at right angles to a mirror or glass block which is used to measure angles.

nuclear fuel — Material used in a nuclear reactor that disintegrates to produce heat.

nuclear reaction — The changing of the nucleus of one element to another.

nuclear reactor	A power station for generating electricity using the heat energy given out when radioactive atoms break down.
nucleus	(1) The centre of the atom containing neutrons and protons; (2) The part of the cell where information is stored.
nutrition	Getting food.

O

oestrogen	A female sex hormone involved in the menstrual cycle.
ohms	Resistance is measured in ohms.
optical fibre	A thin glass or plastic cable. When light enters one end, it is totally internally reflected until it comes out of the other end.
orbit	The path of a planet moving around the Sun.
ore	A mineral obtained from the Earth which contains a useful material such as a metal which can be extracted from it.
organ	Tissues working together to do a job.
organ system	Organs working together to do a certain job.
organism	A living thing.
oscillation	A movement up and down.
oscilloscope	A device which can display the variation in an electrical signal on a screen.
osmosis	The process whereby water diffuses across a semipermeable membrane from a region of low concentration of water molecules.
ovaries	Female organs producing the gametes (ova).
ovulation	When an egg is produced.
oxidation	A chemical reaction in which oxygen is gained by a substance such as combustion and rusting.
oxyhaemoglobin	A compound of oxygen and haemoglobin.
ozone layer	A chemical layer in the atmosphere which stops UV radiation reaching the surface of the Earth.

P

palisade cells	The main photosynthetic cells in the leaf: regular columnar-shaped cells.
pascal	The unit of pressure.
period	A horizontal row of elements across the Periodic Table.
Periodic Table	An arrangement of the elements in ascending order of their atomic number.
periscope	A device which uses reflection to see around corners.
permanent magnet	A magnet which keeps its magnetism.
phloem	The tissue in a plant which specialises in transporting food substances.
photosynthesis	The process when plants use carbon dioxide and water to make food and oxygen.
photosynthetic tissue	The tissue in a leaf which is specialised to make food by photosynthesis.
phototropism	The response of plants to light.
physical change	A change in which no new substances are formed and which can be easily reversed.
pitch	How 'high' or 'low' a sound is.
plant hormones	Chemicals inside plants which control their growth.
plasma	The liquid component of blood, consisting of water, dissolved substances, and blood proteins.
plastics	Materials made of ploymers (large molecules with long chains). Many plastics are made from chemicals obtained from crude oil.
plate	A part of the Earth's crust which moves very slowly.
plate boundary	The region where two plates collide, slide past each other or move apart.
pollutant	A chemical which is harmful to the environment.
polymer	A long chained molecule made from many small molecules joined together.
polymerisation	The name of the process in which many small molecules join together to form a polymer.
population	A group of animals or plants of the same species living in a certain area.
porous	A material which has holes in it and can soak up liquids.
potential difference	The difference in voltage between two points.
power	The rate at which energy is transferred.
precipitation	A chemical reaction in which two solutions are mixed to give an insoluble substance.
predator	An animal that hunts another animal.
pressure	When a force is spread over an area.
prey	An animal that is hunted by another animal.
products	The substances which are made in a chemical reaction.
progesterone	A female sex hormone involved in the menstrual cycle.
protease	A protein digesting enzyme.
protein	A substance in all animals and plants containing carbon, hydrogen, oxygen and nitrogen.
proton	A particle found in the nucleus of the atom. It has a relative mass of 1 unit and a positive charge.
Proxima Centauri	The star nearest to the Earth, 4.3 light years away.

purification	The process for obtaining a pure substance from its mixture with other substances or impurities.	respiration	The process by which glucose in cells of living things reacts with oxygen to release energy.
		retina	The layer of sense cells in the eye.
R		reversible reaction	A chemical reaction which can go in both directions i.e. the reactants form products, then products react to form the reactants again.
radiation	The transfer of heat energy by infra-red rays.		
radioactive decay	When the nucleus of an unstable atom splits releasing radiation.		
radioactive isotope	An isotope which is unstable and decays producing radiation.	root hair cell	Long cells on the surface of a root which increase the surface are for absorption.
radioactivity	Invisible radiation released by certain materials.	roots	Organs of a plant that absorb water and mineral salts from the soil, and provide anchorage.
random motion	Movement in any direction such as the movement of gas particles.		
reactants	The substances which react together during a chemical reaction.	**S**	
		salt	A substance made when acids are neutralised. The first part of a salt is a metal or the ammonium ion and the second part is the ion from an acid; for example, sodium nitrate, calcium chloride, zinc sulphate.
reactivity series	A list of the metals in order of their reactivity. The most reactive metals are at the top.		
receptor	A cell which senses a stimulus.		
recessive allele	We only see the affects of a recessive allele in a pair if a dominant allele is not present.		
		satellite	A body which orbits the Earth.
		saturated solution	A solution which contains as much solute dissolved in it as possible at that temperature.
recycling	The process in which useful materials are processed for re-use.		
reduction	A chemical reaction in which oxygen is removed from a substance.	sedimentary rock	Rock formed from layers of sediment deposited on top of each other. The particles are sedimented together as salts crystallise out of the water.
reflected ray	A ray of light reflected from a mirror.		
reflection	When waves bounce off objects. Sound and electromagnetic radiation are reflected.	semi-conductors	Substances which are electrical insulators when cold and conductors when warm.
reflex action	An automatic response.	separating funnel	A funnel used for separating immiscible liquids.
refraction	When a wave such as sound or light passes from one material (medium) to another it changes in speed and direction.	sewage	Animal and plant waste.
		sexual reproduction	Reproduction which involves fertilisation.
		solar cell	A device which produces electricity when sunlight falls on the cells.
reinforced concrete	Concrete containing steel rods to make it stronger.		
relative atomic mass (A_r)	The mass of an atom on a scale in which carbon-12 has a mass of 12 units.	solid	A substance which has a fixed shape and volume. Its particles are packed closely together in a regular pattern with strong forces between them.
relative formula mass (M_r)	The mass of a compound on a scale in which carbon-12 has a mass of 12 units. It is found by adding up the Ars of the atoms in the compound given in its formula.		
		solidification or freezing	The process in which a liquid changes to a solid as it cools.
relay	A type of switch which uses a small current to switch on a circuit with a large current.	solubility	The amount of solute which will saturate 100 grams of solvent at a certain temperature.
		soluble substance	A substance which will dissolve in a particular solvent.
renal artery	The artery taking blood to the kidney.	solute	A substance which dissolves in a liquid (the solvent) to form a solution.
renewable energy	Energy resources which can be replaced once used.		
resistance	A measure of how much a component opposes the electric current flowing through it.	solution	The mixture formed when a substance (the solute) dissolves in a liquid (the solvent).
resistor	An electrical component which makes it more difficult for a current to flow in a circuit.	solvent	The liquid which dissolves another substance (the solute) to form a solution.

sound energy	Energy carried by sound waves.
spectrum	A way of putting waves (such as light) into order, from the shortest wavelength to the longest.
speed	The distance covered in a certain time.
speedometer	A device for measuring and displaying speed.
spontaneous fission	When atoms of certain elements split, releasing energy.
stalolith	Particles of starch inside plant cells by which plants sense the affect of gravity.
star	An object in space making its own light by nuclear fusion reactions.
starch	A carbohydrate used by plants as a food store.
static electricity	The electricity produced when an insulating material is charged up by rubbing it.
steel	An alloy of iron containing small amounts of other elements such as carbon, chromium or tungsten.
stem	Organ of the plant that supports the leaves and flowers and transports water, minerals and sugar.
stimulus	A form of energy which living things sense.
stomata	Tiny holes in leaves which allow gases to diffuse in and out.
stopping distance	How far a car travels before it stops safely.
strength	The degree to which a substance resists the effects of forces on it.
sublime	Change from a gas to a solid without forming a liquid, such as iodine.
sulphur dioxide	A poisonous gas produced by burning fossil fuel.
suspension	A mixture which contains small particles of a solid which are not dissolved in a liquid. When they are left to stand the solids slowly settle.
symbol	One or two letters which stand for 1 atom of an element.
synthesis	A chemical reaction in which elements join together to form a single compound.
synthetic or manufactured materials	Substances made from raw materials by changing them chemically.

T

temperature	A measure of how hot or cold something is.
terminal velocity	When an object falling through air reaches a steady speed.
tetanus	An acute infectious disease.
thermal decomposition	The breakdown of a compound when it is heated.
thermal energy or heat energy	The energy transferred from something which is hot to something which is cooler.
thermals	Convection currents in the air formed above areas of land which are warmer than those around.
thermometer	The instrument used for measuring temperatures.
tissue	A group of similar cells working together.
total internal reflection	If a ray of light strikes a surface at an angle greater than a critical angle, the surface acts like a mirror and the light is reflected.
transducer	A device which transfers one type of energy into another.
transformer	A device for changing the voltage and current of a.c. supply of electricity.
transition elements	A group of metallic elements found in the central block in the Periodic Table.
transparent	A clear substance which can be seen through such as glass, some plastics.
transpiration	The loss of water from a plant leaf.
transverse wave	An energy carrying wave in which the particles move at right angles to the direction in which the wave travels.
trip switch	An electrical component which switches off the current when it is too large.

U

ultrasound	A sound above the limit of human hearing.
unbalanced forces	When forces acting on an object cause it to move.
units of electricity	A measure of the amount of electricity used. 1 unit of electricity is 1 kilowatt hour (kWh).
universal indicator	An indicator which gives a different colour for a different pH value.
universe	All the galaxies, stars, planets and particles that exist.
urea	The main waste from protein which is excreted in the urine.
urine	The fluid containing water and waste which is excreted from the body.
uterus	The muscular organ where a foetus grows.

V

vacuum	A place which is completely empty of air.
variable resistor	A resistor whose resistance can be changed.
variations	The differences between living things of the same type.
vascular tissue	Transporting tissue.
vein	A blood vessel carrying blood from the tissues and organs to the heart.
velocity	Speed in a certain direction.
ventricle	One of the bottom two chambers in the heart.

virtual image	An image that cannot be formed on a screen.
virus	Living things which are smaller than bacteria and need host cells in which to reproduce.
viscosity	The ease with which a liquid can flow.
volatility	The ease with which a liquid forms a vapour.
volcano	A region where hot liquid magma is forced from deep inside of the Earth to the surface as lava. Volcanoes usually occur at plate boundaries.
voltage	The push supplied by a source of electrical power.
voltmeter	The meter used to measure the voltage across a component in a circuit.
volts (V)	The unit for measuring the size of the voltage.

W

water cycle	The cycling of water throughout the planet by a process of evaporation and condensation.
watt (W)	Power is measured in watts: 1000 watts (W) = 1 kilowatt (kW)
wavelength	The distance from one point on a wave to a similar point on the next.
weathering	The wearing away of rocks by the action of wind, rain, rivers, ice and snow.
weedkiller	A chemical which kills plants.
weight	The force on an object caused by gravity.
white dwarf	Part of the life of a star formed when the outside of a red giant drifts away.
wind farm	A power station made up of many wind generators.
wind generator	Generates electricity when the wind makes the turbines spin round.

X

X and Y chromosomes	The chromosomes which determine sex in human beings.
X rays	A type of electromagnetic radiation which does not easily pass through substances and can be used to make X-ray pictures.
xylem	The tissue in a plant which specialises in transporting water.

Y

yeast	A simple microbe which contains enzymes which ferment sugar to ethanol and carbon dioxide.
yield	The amount produced of a crop or chemical.

Z

zygote	A fertilised egg.